NARRATIVE, PIETY AND POLEMIC IN MEDIEVAL SPAIN

NARRATIVE, PIETY AND POLEMIC IN MEDIEVAL SPAIN

Biblical Rhetoric in the Reconquest Chronicles of León-Castile

Alun Williams

BLOOMSBURY ACADEMIC
LONDON • NEW YORK • OXFORD • NEW DELHI • SYDNEY

BLOOMSBURY ACADEMIC
Bloomsbury Publishing Plc, 50 Bedford Square, London, WC1B 3DP, UK
Bloomsbury Publishing Inc, 1359 Broadway, New York, NY 10018, USA
Bloomsbury Publishing Ireland, 29 Earlsfort Terrace, Dublin 2, D02 AY28, Ireland

BLOOMSBURY, BLOOMSBURY ACADEMIC and the Diana logo are trademarks of
Bloomsbury Publishing Plc

First published in Great Britain 2024
This paperback edition published 2025

Copyright © Alun Williams, 2024

Alun Williams has asserted his right under the Copyright, Designs and Patents Act, 1988, to be identified as Author of this work.

For legal purposes the Acknowledgements on p. viii constitute an extension of this copyright page.

Cover image: © Privilegium Imperatoris (Imperial Privilege) of the Emperor Alfonso VII of León and Castile granting land to an Abbot William. Anonymous scribe, 1030 © The Picture Art Collection / Alamy

All rights reserved. No part of this publication may be: i) reproduced or transmitted in any form, electronic or mechanical, including photocopying, recording or by means of any information storage or retrieval system without prior permission in writing from the publishers; or ii) used or reproduced in any way for the training, development or operation of artificial intelligence (AI) technologies, including generative AI technologies. The rights holders expressly reserve this publication from the text and data mining exception as per Article 4(3) of the Digital Single Market Directive (EU) 2019/790.

Bloomsbury Publishing Plc does not have any control over, or responsibility for, any third-party websites referred to or in this book. All internet addresses given in this book were correct at the time of going to press. The author and publisher regret any inconvenience caused if addresses have changed or sites have ceased to exist, but can accept no responsibility for any such changes.

Every effort has been made to trace the copyright holders and obtain permission to reproduce the copyright material. Please do get in touch with any enquiries or any information relating to such material or the rights holder. We would be pleased to rectify any omissions in subsequent editions of this publication should they be drawn to our attention.

A catalogue record for this book is available from the British Library.

A catalog record for this book is available from the Library of Congress.

ISBN: HB: 978-1-7883-1461-9
PB: 978-1-3504-1527-0
ePDF: 978-1-3501-4370-8
eBook: 978-1-3501-4369-2

Typeset by Newgen KnowledgeWorks Pvt. Ltd., Chennai, India

For product safety related questions contact productsafety@bloomsbury.com.

To find out more about our authors and books visit www.bloomsbury.com and sign up for our newsletters.

CONTENTS

List of Illustrations	vii
Acknowledgements	viii
List of Abbreviations	ix
Abbreviations and Full Names of Books from Biblical Sources Used in This Volume	x
INTRODUCTION	1
Overview and sources	1
Purpose and methodology	5

Chapter 1
BIBLICAL TEXTS IN THE LATIN WEST: INTEGRATION AND DIVERSITY 9
  Exegesis 10
  The Bible and the writing of history 23
  Biblical texts in Spain 33

Chapter 2
THE *HISTORIA SILENSE* AND PELAYO'S CHRONICLE 51
  The *Historia Silense* 52
  The Historia Silense and the kings of Spain 54
  Chronicon Regum Legionensium 65

Chapter 3
CHRONICA ADEFONSI IMPERATORIS: A BIBLICAL EPIC 73
  Ideology and phases of conflict 73
  Authorship and provenance 75
  Dogs of war and other animals 81
  Noble bloodline and historic precedent 88
  St James of Compostela 91
  Pilgrimage, piety and reward 94

Chapter 4
THE *CHRONICA ADEFONSI IMPERATORIS* AND THE LITERATURE OF CONQUEST 101
  Conflict and ideology 101
  De expugnatione Lyxbonensi and the *CAI*: Lisbon and Almería 102
  Holy cities 106

The *CAI* and the Maccabees	112
Skilful manipulator of holy text	121
Intended audience	125

Chapter 5
THREE THIRTEENTH-CENTURY CHRONICLERS 129
Rodrigo, Lucas and Juan	131
Isidore and the Visigothic legacy	136

Chapter 6
THE THIRTEENTH CENTURY AND BIBLICAL CONQUEST 147
The veneration of victory	149
Fernando III	158
Political squabbles and geographical perspectives	160
Representations of the enemy	163
Images of biblical conflict in Castile: A comparison of *Chronica Adefonsi Imperatoris* and the *Chronica Latina Regum Castellae*	169

CONCLUSION	175
Notes	179
Bibliography	259
Index	283

ILLUSTRATIONS

1.1	Religious houses and monastic communities referred to in Chapter 1 and elsewhere	34
1.2	León Cathedral Palimpsest	36
1.3	La Cava Bible	38
2.1	Marriage of Teresa to 'pagan' king of Toledo, Pelayo's *Chronicon*	70
3.1	Author praises Alfonso VII and denounces the worshippers of Baal, *Poema*	79
3.2	'King Avenceta' goads Christians at place identified as Almodóvar de Tendas, *CAI 2*	83
3.3	Men of León compared with lions in *Poema*	88
6.1	Fernando III extols his mother and proposes war against the Moors, Pentecost, 1224, *CLRC*	157

ACKNOWLEDGEMENTS

This book is dedicated to the memory of my former supervisor, colleague and friend, Simon Barton, whose tragic early death in 2017 left many of us bereft, saddened and in disbelief. He had written extensively on the Iberian Peninsula of the High Middle Ages and we shared similar interests, including Muslim-Christian relations and conflict, kingship, mission, ideology and cultural convergence; indeed, many of my own interests emerged because of Simon's dedication, encouragement and, perhaps most strikingly, his generous scholarship. For despite his intellectual and scholastic achievements, he remained unassuming and reflective, though profoundly authoritative. A second early influence on my work was the Anglo-Saxon medievalist, Julia Crick, whose thorough feedback and recommendations relating to the style and presentation of argument were invaluable. I should also like to thank Fernando Luis Corral, my principal contact at the University of Salamanca where I was able to work, especially in gathering material for my work on biblical texts in Spain. He organized my period of study at the university's library and facilitated my access to material not available elsewhere and enabled me to meet Francisco Bautista Pérez, a philologist and Professor of Spanish Literature at the Instituto de Estudios Medievales y Renacentistas at the University of Salamanca. My period in Salamanca enormously enriched my work, especially my research into the *Chronica Adefonsi Imperatoris*, a key text within this monograph. At the inception of this project, I received considerable support from Mary Garrison at the University of York, especially in relation to the suggestions of primary sources when I was preparing my chapter on biblical texts in the Latin west. I am also indebted to the directors and staff at Biblioteca Nacional de España, Madrid, for permitting me to use images in this volume, and to the director and staff at the Biblioteca Real Academia de la Historia, Madrid, for making the *Chronica Latina Regum Castellae* available to me and for allowing me to use an image from that text.

I wish to thank those who have read and commented on sections of my book; these include Jamie Wood (Lincoln), Alex Mallett (Waseda, Tokyo) Antonella Liuzzo-Scorpo (Lincoln) and Gregory Lippiatt (Exeter). My thanks are due to my friend Harry Hine (Emeritus Professor of Classics, St Andrews) for his comments about possible inferences from Latin texts. To those who have contributed questions, technical expertise, administrative assistance, I also offer profound thanks. This includes Simon Doubleday, Aengus Ward, Ann Christys, Richard Toye, Teresa Tinsley, John Hodgson, Imogen Smith, James Hooper, David Hillyer and, for his invaluable assistance and imaginative energy in the creation of the map in Chapter 1, my friend John Kevan. My thanks are due to the anonymous reviewers at Bloomsbury, together with editorial support from Rhodri Mogford and Gabriella Cox. Finally, I must thank Lester Crook who gave me early encouragement to write this monograph and facilitated my connections with Bloomsbury.

ABBREVIATIONS

Abbreviations referred to most frequently in the main text, notes and bibliography.

AV	Authorized Version of the Bible
BRAH	*Boletin de la Real Academia de la Historia*
CAI	*Chronica Adefonsi Imperatoris*
CCCM	*Corpus Christianorum continuatio medieaevalis*
CHE	*Cuadernos de Historia de España*
Chronicon	*Chronicon Regum Legionensium*
CLRC	*Chronica Latina Regum Castellae*
CM	*Chronicon Mundi*
CSM	Corpus Scriptorum Muzarabicorum
DEL	*De expugnatione Lyxbonensi*
DRH	*Historia de rebus Hispaniae sive Historia Gothica*
Expugnatio	*Expugnatio Hibernica*
GRA	*Gesta Regum Anglorum*
HS	*Historia Silense*
LCKC	Latin Chronicle of the Kings of Castile
Najerense	*Crónica Najerense*
NEB	New English Bible
NT	New Testament
OT	Old Testament
PL	J.-P. Migne (ed.), *Patrologia Cursus Completes Series Prima [latina]* (221 vols; Paris: J.-P. Migne, 1844–65)
Poema	*Poema de Almeria/Prefatio de Almaria*/Poem of Almeria

ABBREVIATIONS AND FULL NAMES OF BOOKS FROM BIBLICAL SOURCES USED IN THIS VOLUME

Old Testament

Gen. Genesis	2 Chron. 2 Chronicles	Ezek. Ezekiel
Exod. Exodus	Ezra	Dan. Daniel
Lev. Leviticus	Neh. Nehemiah	Hos. Hosea
Num. Numbers	Est. Esther	Joel
Deut. Deuteronomy	Job	Amos
Josh. Joshua	Ps. (pl. Pss.) Psalm	Obadiah
Judg. Judges	Prov. Proverbs	Jon. Jonah
1 Sam. 1 Samuel	Eccl. Ecclesiastes	Mic. Micah
2 Sam. 2 Samuel	Song of Solomon (or Song of Songs)	Nahum
1 Kgs 1 Kings	Isa. Isaiah	Hab. Habakkuk
2 Kgs 2 Kings	Jer. Jeremiah	Zeph. Zephaniah
1 Chron. 1 Chronicles	Lam. Lamentations (of Jeremiah)	Zech. Zechariah

Apocrypha or Deutero-Canonical Books

Tob. Tobit	Ecclesiasticus
Judith	Ba. Baruch
Wis. Book of Wisdom	1 Macc. 1 Maccabees
(or Wisdom of Solomon)	
2 Macc. 2 Maccabees	

New Testament

Mt. Gospel of Matthew	Phil. Letter to the Philippians
Mk Gospel of Mark	Col. Letter to the Colossians
Lk. Gospel of Luke	1 Tim. First letter to Timothy
Jn Gospel of John	2 Tim. Second letter to Timothy
Acts	Heb. Letter to the Hebrews
Rom. Letter to the Romans	Jas Letter of James
1 Cor. First letter to the Corinthians	1 Pet. First letter of Peter
2 Cor. Second letter to the Corinthians	2 Pet. Second letter of Peter
Gal. Letter to the Galatians	1 Jn First letter of John
Eph. Letter to the Ephesians	Rev. Book of Revelation

Unreferenced books from biblical sources are not included in this list.

INTRODUCTION

Overview and sources

In October 1147, following a period of extensive and prolonged military success against the Almoravid Muslims of al-Andalus, the Christians of León-Castile, together with their Genoese, Frankish, Pisan and Aragonese allies, wrested the Iberian port city of Almería from Muslim control. This, according to the *Anales toledanos*, was preceded by a period in which Christians, and specifically those from Genoa, had been held as captives by the Almoravids.[1] Their success is celebrated in *The Poem of Almería* (*Poema*), which was written during the peak of the Christians' extensive though short-lived period of military success against the Muslims in their southern and eastern strongholds. These victories were led by the emperor-king of León-Castile, Alfonso VII (r. 1126–57). The account is anonymous, though it was possibly penned by a Castilian bishop, and alludes to often unnamed Christian heroes as well as to Charlemagne, who is seen as the ultimate precursor to Alfonso VII himself. The poem, which comprises the third book of the *Chronica Adefonsi Imperatoris* (*CAI*), is also heavy with biblical metaphor and reminiscences. This is not the only account of the successful siege, nor is it necessarily the most reliable.[2] Even so, it reflects the plausibility that the author was a man of León-Castile; his loyalty to his homeland, together with his belief in its supremacy and in the rightness of Castilian cause, is everywhere apparent.[3] The poem itself positively pulsates with invective and drama, derived from biblical narrative, and is a conspicuous example of a twelfth-century text in which Castilian triumphalism reaches its most vivid apotheosis.

Biblical texts enriched descriptions of historical events throughout the Middle Ages and their influence was by no means an exclusively Hispanic phenomenon.[4] The aim of this study is to delineate the distinctiveness of the ways in which biblical texts shaped the character of six Hispano-Latin chronicles composed in the kingdom of León-Castile in the twelfth and thirteenth centuries.[5] All were completed between *c.* 1109 and *c.* 1243 and some are likely to have been written under royal patronage. Those who composed these chronicles saw the events in al-Andalus as part of a sacred struggle, and biblical *exempla* provided meaning and illumination. The insertion of scriptural imagery would facilitate the interpretation of historical purpose.[6] Classical and biblical imagery was used less to provide naturalistic realism than dispense contemporary understanding and as such would influence human conduct and norms of behaviour. This is a significant consideration since it implies an exploration of cause and purpose.

This study considers the ways in which medieval chroniclers in León-Castile incorporated biblical narrative and the available and evolving corpus of exegesis to justify and inform their sense of engagement in the events they describe, which assisted in the creation of persuasive texts for their own readership and for posterity. Holy text was applied to stirring polemic and a righteous belief in God's purpose in history, and demonstrates how the authors understood and interpreted their world. They therefore supplied a carefully constructed version of events – both in the presentation of biblical sources and in the compilation of their own contemporary narrative – as well as eulogizing the lives and examples of Christian monarchs and demonizing their opponents. The book will focus on the twelfth- and thirteenth-century Reconquest chronicles, especially the *CAI*[7] (divided into three books and including its third section, the *Poema*)[8] and the *Chronica Latina Regum Castellae* (*CLRC*).[9] By way of comparison, reference will be made to other literary texts produced in the Latin west, and especially those emanating from twelfth- and thirteenth-century Iberia. These will include the *Historia Silense* (*HS*)[10] and the *Chronicon Regum Legionensium* (*Chronicon*)[11] from the twelfth century and *Chronicon Mundi* (*CM*)[12] and *De Rebus Hispaniae* (*DRH*)[13] from the thirteenth century. Their shared dependence on a common clerical and biblical culture as transmitted through exegesis, commentary and liturgy will be examined. This comparison will enable the argument to delineate the distinctiveness of the biblical character of the Hispano-Latin chronicles covered in this book even if the writers of these chronicles did not necessarily see their narrative as directly related to a biblical epic. A subtle yet pervasive culture of biblical exegesis informs these chronicles and this influence is particularly striking in two of the chronicles considered, that is to say the *CAI* and the *CLRC*.

The centrality of biblical texts to medieval writing is widely acknowledged,[14] though rigorous comparison with the Latin Vulgate and its impact on chronicle composition has been largely neglected in the context of the Christian struggle for military success in Iberia. It is therefore necessary to begin by reviewing the status and function of biblical texts in the medieval Latin west. Central to this overview is the corpus of exegetical material that was available and grew throughout antiquity and the early Middle Ages. Such material is evident within liturgical texts, commentaries and in the sermons that emerged and which shaped the religious and cultural climate. However, the writers' understanding from the earliest days of the church was that events in their own time were in part the fulfilment of biblical prophecy.[15] In the Latin west, biblical texts provided a colourful and textured commentary on contemporary and recorded events. Furthermore, the chroniclers' perceptions and understanding provided a historical and allegorical source for interpretation and teaching. Different versions of the Bible and of the biblical commentaries that circulated in Iberia are relevant to this unfolding process of historical narrative, mediation and authorial familiarity, as are the religious practices and sense of mission that existed in the peninsula.

An exploration of the chronicles reveals a growing awareness and a willingness to grasp the significance of biblical narrative, especially the ways in which such narrative might be applied to and provide likely parallels with peninsular history. Two chronicles from the early twelfth century, the *HS* and Bishop Pelayo of Oviedo's *Chronicon*, are scrutinized in Chapter 2. Here, we see that these chronicles of the evolving kingdom of León-Castile often have specific biblical parallels – or are at least infused with a biblically-derived typology – and comparisons often reveal a nearness in terms of the reminiscence of both language and narrative. Quite apart from reminding readers and hearers of the link between revealed scripture and events in the chroniclers' own time, biblical influence seems to have been intrinsic to the acquisition and spread of Latinity.[16] Such texts did not occur *ex nihilo* and their indebtedness to earlier chronicles, especially to the eleventh-century *Chronicle of Sampiro* (*Sampiro*) is evident.[17] *Sampiro*, together with the early-tenth-century *Chronicle of Alfonso III*, records the deeds of the kings of Asturias and León in the ninth and tenth centuries and these are contained within the full version of the *HS* which was produced after 1109. There is a much longer version of *Sampiro* within a collection of writing known as the *Corpus Pelagianum*. Pelayo's *Chronicon*, probably written between 1121 and 1132, may have been intended as a continuation of *Sampiro*.[18]

The mid-twelfth-century *CAI*, together with the *Poema*, lionizes the life and military successes of the emperor Alfonso VII and, because of its unrelentingly biblical phraseology and dependence on biblical narrative, receives considerable attention. The prose sections of the *CAI* and the *Poema* are often considered to be the product of a single author who may have been Bishop Arnaldo of Astorga (r. 1144–52). Since this chronicle receives particular emphasis, the question of authorship is considered at length. In it, biblical texts and allusions are used more frequently and with greater sophistication than in earlier chronicles, together with a greater variety of purpose. The author's ability to incorporate powerful and subtle biblical narrative with unusual frequency is one of the most remarkable aspects of this chronicle. He also demonstrates the capacity to manipulate a particular biblical passage, sometimes with embellishments, to suit the author's fearsome rhetoric or political purpose. With the penning of the *CAI*, we have the emergence of the biblical epic, and as such there will be a discussion of the kind of imagery used by the author to reinforce defamation of the emperor's enemies, both Christian and Muslim. Initially, and principally in Book 1 of the *CAI*, the author devotes much of his narrative to Alfonso's attempts to shore up his own position within Iberian Christian realms and to enhance the position of León-Castile; elsewhere more attention is given to the king's conflicts with his Muslim enemies in al-Andalus. The imagery within the text was often used to denigrate the enemies of Christendom and harked back to earlier anti-Muslim invective in Iberia.[19] The *CAI* will also be compared with another piece of contemporary conquest literature, *De expugnatione Lyxbonensi* (*De expugnatione*), probably compiled by an Anglo-Norman priest known as Raol.[20] The *CAI* and *De expugnatione* deal with contemporary military campaigns in Iberia and the writers of both texts are conscious of the importance of scripture in providing precedent and justification.

Furthermore, the campaigns in Lisbon and Almería are both represented as decisive Christian victories over the Muslims – victories which were not replicated in the simultaneous eastern crusade.[21] A consideration of the *CAI* concludes with a discussion of the author's possible or intended audience.

Evidence from three chronicles from thirteenth-century León-Castile will then be considered: the *CM* written by, or at least under the editorship of Bishop Lucas of Túy (r. 1239–49), *DRH* by Rodrigo Jiménez de Rada, archbishop of Toledo (r. 1209–47) and the much shorter *CLRC*. This latter text is likely to have been written wholly or in part by Juan of Osma, who was chancellor to Fernando III of Castile, later León-Castile (r. 1217–52),[22] from 1217 until his death in 1246, and Bishop of Osma from 1231 and of Burgos between 1240 and 1246. If Juan was indeed the author of the *CLRC*, we have three contemporaneous chronicles compiled, or at least begun, in the first four decades of the thirteenth century by prelates who would certainly have known each other. We also know that Lucas penned his history in response to a request from the mother of Fernando III, Queen Berenguela of Castile (1180–1246),[23] in or around 1236, and that Rodrigo wrote and compiled the *DRH* on behalf of King Fernando shortly after this.[24] The *DRH* was, in any event, completed by 1243 in two marginally different versions and at least twenty-nine manuscripts have been copied since the thirteenth century, each containing the entire Latin text.[25] The *CLRC* is likely to have been composed over a longer period of time and is an unusual text in that its section dealing with the reign of Fernando III is substantially a commentary on the events witnessed by its author. This presentation has contributed to what has been described as its more journalistic approach than that of Lucas or Rodrigo, whose histories are substantially derived from other sources as well as compiled from collective memory for more recent events.[26] It is clear, as will be argued, that Rodrigo, who wrote only of Hispania and her origins, drew on the *CM* and probably on the *CLRC* too. In any event, the *CLRC* is likely to have been completed by 1239.[27]

As their names suggest, the scope of the *CM* and *DRH* was broader than that of Juan's chronicle, as were the purposes and preoccupations of Lucas and Rodrigo, and this is reflected in the scholarship that has surrounded their texts (especially that of Rodrigo). Both Lucas and Rodrigo, from similar religious and cultural environments, though with different notions of the politics of the expanding Christian frontier,[28] responded to the royal requests in terms of grandness of scale and subject matter, even though the time taken to complete their histories was much shorter than that taken by the author of the *CLRC*. The chronicles by Lucas and Rodrigo were written shortly after the reunification of Castile and León in 1230, though probably not in its immediate aftermath. As suggested earlier, the *CLRC* is likely to have been started earlier.[29] The two much longer chronicles, the *CM* and the *DRH*, draw heavily on the person and works of Isidore of Seville (d. 636) and the Visigothic legacy which he appeared to represent and embrace,[30] even though their laudatory treatment of Isidore is, in part, an attempt to claim him as their own (much more will be said about this in Chapter 5). Comparison will be made with other, earlier chronicles as well as with the ways in which the three thirteenth-century chroniclers' view of history and the treatment of the Muslim enemy had evolved from the earliest experiences of conflict. A familiarity with biblical texts[31] was central to all three chronicles, and particularly to the *CLRC*, where such narrative is much more frequently alluded to. In *CM*, Lucas used the Book of Genesis as a reference point for the beginning of his history and, like Rodrigo, made use of scriptural sources for didactic purposes as well as for sustaining and embellishing a cultural myth of Reconquista that had its origins in the Asturian period. By their emphatic assertion of Gothic genealogy and (especially in the case of Rodrigo) the imitation of Isidore's historical methodology – which included the reasoned synthesizing of his sources – they both appealed to an older, more authoritative and venerable tradition.[32] Compared with the *CLRC* (and certainly with the *CAI*), biblical references in *CM* and *DRH* are used more sparingly and without the nuanced inferences that could be drawn from individual citations and allusions. In this respect, both *CM* and *DRH* could be said to have imitated Isidore's approach. The *CLRC* does not refer to Isidore or the Gothic legacy and, because of the author's more overtly biblical treatment of the lives of the Castilian kings, it will receive more extensive treatment than both *CM* and *DRH*. The author narrates the reigns of the counts and kings of Castile from 923 onwards but with considerably more emphasis on those monarchs whose reigns he witnessed, principally Alfonso VIII (r. 1158–1214) and Fernando III. There are also occasional digressions when he refers to events outside Castile and Iberia.

All the chronicles examined here arose from a common culture that was grounded in biblical text mediated through exegesis, commentary and liturgy. The authors also used classical Latin texts in their accounts. We cannot be certain of the extent to which these biblical references were deliberately incorporated or whether they tended to flow naturally from the pen of the individual writer. What is clear is that the deployment of such texts varied between authors and could be used rather passively or more assertively. We will attempt to distinguish the ways in which such texts were used, the historical context that surrounded their composition and the purposes that may be discernible within them.

Purpose and methodology

The central purpose of this study is to examine the extent to which the writers of the Hispano-Latin chronicles of the twelfth and thirteenth centuries used their knowledge and understanding of biblical texts to describe and interpret events in their own time. Integral to this aim is a consideration of how the chroniclers were able to draw on the body of exegetical material that had accumulated since patristic times and the ways in which their own texts were enriched by such material. An appreciation of the importance of individual texts contributes to our understanding of the way the biblically derived literature that emerged was central to the culture that came to dominate perceptions of conquest in Castile and beyond. Central to our awareness of how this convergent and growing body of material was disseminated and understood is the appreciation of the relationship between the life of the scribe and the way he accessed and was immersed in this biblical culture. This was doubtless reinforced through liturgy, the development of biblical commentary and the way in which passages and pericopes from scriptural books were remembered. This was done as much through hearing and reciting scriptures during the celebration of the Mass and other divine offices held each day as by accessing the written sources.

We will also seek to examine the extent to which biblical citations and allusions were used more by some chroniclers than others, how and why this was so and the teleological purposes that may be discerned from within the chronicles: literary as well as political and religious. In two of the chronicles analysed, the twelfth-century *CAI* and the thirteenth-century *CLRC*, the extent of biblical allegory and the use of narrative is much more emphatic and relentless than in the other contemporary chronicles produced under royal patronage in León-Castile. In addition to analysing the use of biblical narrative within the chronicles and the purposes that this might appear to serve, this study offers a short section at the end of the final chapter that distils the way in which scriptural references are used in these two chronicles. Of particular interest is the frequency with which scriptural references are used in the two texts and how they are woven into the fabric of historical narrative. This does not imply nor will it be suggested that the later chronicler knew of the existence of the *CAI* (we cannot know whether this was so). This study will, however, seek to discover what circumstances – though separated by almost a century – led to the composition of two chronicles that were, at least in an Iberian context, particularly rich in scriptural allusions and references. In terms of the volume of such references, they were at variance with other contemporaneous texts. This is designed to focus our consideration on the unique qualities and characteristics of these two chronicles and their authors.

In addressing these questions, an exploration of a range of biblical texts and commentaries whose presence and influence has been detected within all six chronicles will be pursued and the argument that the choice of biblical reference helped to determine the tone of the event being described will be presented – just as the event may have prompted the use of a particular text. Biblical citations and allusions also imply authorial intent. We may infer from such chronicles how and why, during the twelfth and thirteenth centuries, the engagement with biblical texts became an especially active process. It seems certain that all chroniclers writing in twelfth- and thirteenth-century León-Castile inhabited very similar intellectual and spiritual environments even if we cannot always be certain which patristic sources each author consulted.

The methodology is therefore essentially a comparative one that seeks to demonstrate the variety of ways in which biblical texts were used in these chronicles by analysis and comparison with contemporaneous texts, both from Hispanic writing and with texts from elsewhere in the Latin west. In the Hispano-Latin chronicles, allusion is frequently made to events, people and places, suggesting some of the preoccupations of the writers rather than demonstrating a settled and emphatic view of a kind of Hispanic-biblical identity.

Whether such consensus existed or was to emerge, the pivotal place of biblical material in constructing an evolving Leonese-Castilian political and religious identity seems clear. Such a culture arose from precedent and lineage but rested also on the integration of scripture into a growing awareness of a shared historical narrative. The Bible and the sources from which knowledge of this narrative are likely to have been derived, feature in all the texts to be considered, and indeed may be said to be central to each of them. The way in which biblical teaching, belief, allusion and narrative were used by the Leonese-Castilian chroniclers suggests an insight and crafting of the scriptures that went beyond mere awareness of the holy text. Such carefully selected and elaborately fashioned texts suggest deliberate authorial choices as well as what may be referred to as commonly used figures of speech. Both would feature in the compilation of historical narrative, and it is sometimes difficult to distinguish between the familiar and the reference that was deliberately chosen, even if in the study of specific texts, specific and well-known passages from the Bible are used with particular emphasis or frequency. Yet even within the uncertainty and occasional ambiguity of authorial choice, subtle and more emphatic inferences can be drawn from chronicles, just as they can from the chronicles where the use of biblical text is more sparing and oblique.

1

BIBLICAL TEXTS IN THE LATIN WEST: INTEGRATION AND DIVERSITY

This study is concerned with the way biblical texts were circulated and used in the chronicles of the twelfth- and thirteenth-century kingdoms of León and Castile. To appreciate the ways in which this process may have worked, the aim is to establish the delineation of power within biblical narrative, together with its legacy in imagery, allusion, teaching, faith and conflict in examples of historical narrative throughout the Latin west.[1] Biblical authority, together with what has been described as the naturalization of classical myth,[2] helped forge an evolving national consciousness and narrative, though this seems to have been more firmly entrenched in some early medieval societies than in others.[3]

Firstly, there are the ways in which biblical understanding and exegesis imposed themselves on the writing and wider culture of western Christendom. The biblical and cultural milieu in which medieval chroniclers worked, their intellectual culture, was defined by their debt to the early church fathers and to subsequent exegetes. It is important, therefore, to review the exegetical and liturgical material that accumulated in ecclesiastical libraries and which is likely to have been available to those who wrote historical narrative. Secondly, specific examples of historical and literary narrative that emerged in the Latin west are used to explore the idea of a shared exegetical experience; this includes an appreciation of the importance of biblical texts within the Iberian Peninsula, enabling an assessment of the range of exegetical material that is most likely to have been available to chroniclers from the kingdoms of León and Castile during the twelfth and thirteenth centuries – and earlier.

Scriptural readings, meditation and exegesis represented the pre-eminent intellectual activities in the twelfth-century Latin west. They shaped the habitat in which drama, art and artefacts flourished, having been enhanced and enriched by an understanding of the entirety of biblical text.[4] It was a culture of flexibility and variety: biblical texts, with their references to characters, places and events, were used with a considerable range of purpose and imagination, especially in the twelfth and thirteenth centuries, when Iberian Christians were involved in campaigns against the Muslims. Their dissemination had been largely dependent on a range of exegetical texts and scriptural material embedded in liturgies that had emerged in the antique and early medieval periods.

Exegesis

The interpretation of biblical narrative

That medieval chroniclers depended on the interpretation of scripture for the composition of their texts is a given. Yet access to biblical narrative and precedent was complex; the sources were frequently fragmentary and varied, and there was often not a direct link between the chronicler and written biblical sources. Complete copies of the Bible were relatively rare, even in monasteries with important libraries and scriptoria.[5] Although the numbers of complete Bibles increased from the eleventh century onwards,[6] they were exceptional until the thirteenth century, judging by the few one-volume Bibles, known as pandects, that survive.[7] The earliest complete (or almost complete) copy of the Latin Bible is probably the eighth-century Northumbrian *Codex Amiatinus*, based at least in part on the lost *Codex Grandior*.[8] Biblical texts were therefore dispersed throughout the western church in a number of different forms and often in competing versions. For medieval chroniclers, the interpretation and analysis of these texts provided the key to the way they understood their world and what made Christian statements of belief intelligible.[9] Indeed, the relationship between the exegesis practised by the early church fathers, together with their understanding of liturgy and creed, is a complex one: patristic exegesis creates doctrine, just as allegory and parable are prerequisites to belief in the Christian creeds.[10]

An appreciation of this intellectual and cultural environment is central to the understanding of the way scriptural exegesis exerted its control and mediation over the chroniclers and historians of later centuries. This awareness predicates our enquiry when reviewing the extent, nature and evolution of biblical allusion in the chronicles covered in this volume. The arbitration of scriptural precedent by generations of exegetes was centrally important to the writers of the six twelfth- and thirteenth-century chronicles from León-Castile that are discussed, as it was elsewhere. I argue that in two of the chronicles likely to have been produced under royal patronage during this period, the *CAI* and the *CLRC*, biblical allusions and references were used with originality, distinctiveness and in unusual profusion. Yet this inventiveness took place within a culture that had evolved from the early exegetical practice of the church fathers in the Latin Church, the Carolingian Renaissance from the late eighth century onwards and through its dissemination within schools and universities – particularly from the twelfth century onwards. It was communicated through sermons, canon law and liturgical familiarity; it created an ambience within which the religious worked. It represented a collective and unimpeachable wisdom and defined the ways in which scribes and chroniclers would interpret their world. It is inconceivable that medieval chroniclers and commentators could operate outside patristic certainty and power.[11]

Patristic exegesis in the early church was, nevertheless, an evolving process of interpretation that provided later chroniclers with a rich heritage within which they could work and which would inform their own narratives.[12] Here, focus is on some key exegetical works written between the fourth and the eighth centuries as well as on considering the literal understanding of holy text and the additional allegorical interpretations of biblical passages. Even if we cannot be certain that a particular twelfth- or thirteenth-century chronicler had a familiarity with a specific work of exegesis, the early patristic books will have conditioned the way that those biblical texts were read and created the convention in which they were understood, interpreted and commented upon by later generations. This implies an understanding of the legacy of patristic commentary and the body of exegesis that had accumulated since pre-medieval times in the western church. This enabled biblical texts to permeate the liturgy as well as to continue the process of exegesis itself from and during the Carolingian and later periods. Since our principal Hispanic chronicles belong to the twelfth and thirteenth centuries, the impact of the exegesis that emerged from the ninth century onwards is of particular interest.

Versions of the Bible

In exploring the exegetical tradition and its impact on later medieval writers, we should note that different versions of the Bible circulated in the Latin west and some or all of these may have been available to chroniclers during the High Middle Ages. Jerome's translation of the Bible (385–405) gradually replaced earlier translations. These, known as the *Vetus Latina*, were not a single version but existed in several regional variations.[13] Versions were already in place by the time of the earliest Latin father, Tertullian of Carthage (*c.* 160–*c.* 220). It was he who in *Adversus Praxean* was the first to write directly of Trinitarian theology[14] and who translated parts of the gospels from *koine* Greek into Latin.[15] Furthermore, parts of the Bible that Augustine of Hippo (354–430) drew upon were also from the *Vetus Latina* and his commentaries had wide circulation both during and after the appearance of Jerome's translation.[16] Bede (*c.* 672–735), whilst using Jerome's translation as the basis for his own exegesis, accessed other Latin versions of certain OT books and he did not, as he admits, hesitate to use a variety of Latin sources.[17] He was also indebted to Augustine for the composition of at least one particular commentary.[18] Nevertheless, Jerome's version seems to have been used as the basis for at least three versions of the Bible completed in Bede's time at his monastery at Wearmouth-Jarrow.[19] It is clear therefore that a range of Latin translations continued to provide an invaluable source for major exegetes into the eighth century. Although Jerome's Bible emerged and continued to be regarded as the one authoritative source for subsequent exegesis and interpretation, some of the most venerated commentary came from an earlier tradition, albeit one which was flawed and plagued with inconsistent translation.[20] In the centuries following Jerome's translation, errors were identified in the Vulgate and attempts were made to introduce one authoritative text. In 1502 the so-called *Sixto-Clementine Vulgate* was produced. This became the official Vulgate of the Catholic Church, though it too has been subjected to various revisions.[21]

The difficulties in working with a problematic translation were acknowledged by Augustine, who advocated the acquisition of other ancient languages (i.e. Hebrew and Greek) to gain a better understanding of the OT.[22] So even if Augustine had used the *Vetus Latina*, ensuring that it might be regarded as a true source on which exegetes could work, he understood its limitations. This difficulty had earlier been noted in the east by Origen of Alexandria (*c.* 184–*c.* 251) who had also recognized the problem of making translations from texts that were themselves translations from Hebrew scriptures. He addressed the issue by compiling between 230 and 240 Hebrew and Greek texts into an enormous *Hexapla*, a synoptic or parallel arrangement of the different texts.[23] Augustine and the exegetes who followed him continued to exercise a pervasive influence over the religious culture that evolved in the ensuing centuries of the Latin west and their work consistently determined the parameters of biblical understanding and interpretation.[24]

Patristic exegesis

Much of the earliest extant patristic exegesis dates from the third century AD,[25] beginning in the western church with Hippolytus of Rome (170–235) and in the east with Origen. In addition to the compilation of the *Hexapla*, Origen is important for asserting the distinctiveness of three strands of exegesis. The first, historical exegesis, is hermeneutic and seeks to ascertain the real intentions of the author. Secondly, moral exegesis, as its name suggests, stresses the primacy of tropology or moral interpretation. The third strand, spiritual exegesis, although perhaps more elusive, sought to see Christ, the church and even the NT scriptures as whole and discernible within OT narrative.[26] In contrast, the ascetic and theologian John Cassian (*c.* 360–435) proposed a fourfold explanation of scripture: the spiritual, allegorical, moral and anagogic (or mystical) senses or interpretations. Origen's early interpretation was later supported by Ambrose of Milan (*c.* 338–397), who argued that one of the purposes of OT eschatology was to provide a foretaste or hope which would be revealed in the NT.[27]

The patristic period from the fourth to the eighth centuries sets the intellectual and cultural environment for the interpretation of most scriptural books in the centuries that followed.[28] In the Latin-speaking west, the primary exegetes and doctors of the church in the fourth and fifth centuries, Jerome, Augustine and Ambrose, have already been referred to. To these we should add Pope Leo I (r. 440–61) and St Peter Chysologus, bishop of Ravenna (r. 433–50).[29] Although there were many other exegetes during this period, subsequent churchmen owed their greatest debt to these few: 'they are the authorities ... under whose aegis the full range of catholic argument and interpretation is most clearly represented to later ages.'[30]

Augustine seems to have had a notable legacy in Iberia[31] and his authority would have been recognized in other forms of artistic expression. For example, highly educated monastic orders would have accredited paintings and illustrations that appeared in complete Bibles produced much later as emanating from Augustine's *Tractatus in Evangelicum Ioannis*.[32] Many of Augustine's 224 tractates on John, written between 406 and 420, were part of a familiar pastoral theology to be delivered orally to congregations,[33] rather than being designed primarily for private study. In his citation of the opening words of John's Gospel,[34] the *Tractatus* could be used as an argument against Arianism, which would have a particular resonance in the Spanish Visigothic kingdom as its leaders reflected on its conversion to Trinitarian Catholicism in 589. There is a declaration of the historic assertion of Trinitarianism; in his homily, Augustine argues that John's Trinitarian Christology in the first five verses of the gospel is consistent with OT declarations (notably in the psalms) as well as with NT, and especially Pauline, teaching.[35]

Perhaps the most vociferous assault on Arianism was conducted by Augustine's great proponent and follower, Fulgentius, bishop of the North African city of Ruspe (c. 468–c. 533). He was involved in the debate against Arianism and composed, in the early sixth century, a rhyming psalm that explicitly condemned the heresy and seems to have been modelled on Augustine's Psalm against the Donatists [*Psalmus Contra Partem Donati*],[36] as well as on certain biblical abecedarian texts such as Psalm 119.[37] In the conscious imitation of biblical and patristic exegesis, Fulgentius's argument would have had increased intellectual and spiritual authority.

In view of the extraordinary output of the early church fathers, and especially of Jerome, it is impossible to refer to more than a fraction of their exegetical legacy. It is not their precise interpretation of specific biblical texts but the canon of early patristic literature that conditioned the way in which the parameters of debate were set for later exegetes as well as for medieval chroniclers. The church fathers also used pre-Christian thinkers such as Cicero, Plato and even Pythagoras, enabling classical ideas to influence medieval philosophy and religion.[38] Yet each exegete represented an element in the development of a tradition that mediated successive understanding. Jerome, for example, derived his allegorical method from Origen, though he was not uncritical of his predecessor's approach to the interpretation of Jesus' parables.[39] Just as the literal acceptance of events recorded in the Bible is never really challenged by the church fathers, so their own commentary and exposition would be venerated in an almost seamless fabric of theological thinking. Jesus had pointed to OT prophecies and those that prefigured his own incarnation and person, validating the allegorical and mystical interpretations of the church fathers. Yet the interpretation would not be static: 'Jerome refers to Origen's "line by line" [*commaticum*] interpretation of Matthew ... for Jerome the context should be strictly examined and function as a stringent control on all secondary exegesis.'[40] Jerome's authority on allegorical method is balanced by his meticulous explanation of biblical phrases that take the reader beyond the obvious while embedding Jerome's interpretation in the OT precedent.[41]

By the fourth century, the allegorical approach had produced early advocates and became commonplace, even if Jerome's own emphasis had been on the literal interpretation of the text. This was especially the case when he was writing for specific audiences.[42] The work of the second-century martyr Justin of Caesarea (103-65)[43] and, more expansively, the example of Ephrem the Syrian (c. 306-73), whose old age overlapped with the early years of Ambrose, Augustine and Jerome and who wrote biblical exegesis, poems, sermons and hymns which are of notable interest.[44] Jerome's own reputation as a linguist and scholar was important in settling such matters as the interpretation of text and seeing off heretical challenges.[45] Even so, his contribution was, according to his own lights, as a collaborator with those exegetes who had preceded him and with his contemporaries, even if he had the opportunity to work on the books of prophecy as no one before him had been able to do.[46] His other legacy to future scholars was to provide a reasoned assessment of possible interpretations, enabling them to judge between the spurious and the genuine.[47]

In the same section of his *Apology*, Jerome concedes his debt to Origen, Didymus and Apollinaris, though he emphasizes important differences with them.[48] He and two major contemporary exegetes, Augustine and Ambrose, came to exert a much more powerful and settled influence over future exegetes and compilers of history than those who had preceded them. That is not to say that patristic exegetes always followed each other's scholarship or interpretation of the religious life. Jerome demonstrated this in his criticism of Ambrose.[49] Yet for all their differences, their collective exegetical material would form an undisputed corpus. Also, though Ambrose's written exegetical works may have been limited and largely unoriginal,[50] such considerations would not necessarily undermine his authority or his capacity to influence doctrine. His importance lay in his ability to enlighten and influence his audiences as a preacher rather than as an exegete.[51] This specific influence over Augustine is recognized: 'in 387 Augustine heard Ambrose's sermons, catechetical addresses, and those given at special services for *competentes* [petitioners] and neophytes.'[52] Yet this is more than acknowledgement. What Augustine heard from the bishop of Milan, who baptized him at Easter 397 following his conversion to Christianity, he was able to transmit to future generations, even if the written words of Ambrose had been lost. Certainly, collections of sermons by the early church fathers – or those attributed to them – were published and would have been disseminated.[53]

This review of patristic exegesis has attempted to establish the cultural context in which the writing of historical composition could proceed as well as the ways in which clerics were able to access biblical texts from which spiritual and allegorical homilies were derived.[54] Furthermore, the Carolingians and those who were to follow them had a vision of Christian society that would encourage commentary on books from the OT that dealt with the historic struggle of God's people. The mediation of these early exegetes exercised a profound and lasting influence over the way in which subsequent clerics understood scripture and interpreted events in their own time. It is nevertheless important to consider the ways in which major ecclesiastical figures such as Isidore and Bede, whilst not undermining the patristic legacy, added considerably to the interpretation of history in their exegetical and non-exegetical works – and the relationship between these two genres would not be entirely distinct. Such intervention not only marked them out from ordinary clerics, from those who studied in monasteries and later in cathedral schools; it also delineated the purpose and work of those who were ordinary, those who had indeed espoused monasticism: 'Monks were not remembering the past. The object of their memories was the text, scriptural and patristic, which clothed timeless, eternal, universal truths.'[55]

Gregory the Great, Isidore and Bede

Pope Gregory the Great (r. 590–604) was born one hundred years after the deaths of Augustine and Jerome and is a figure of transition between the patristic period and the Middle Ages. And although Gregory puts forward a threefold order of exegesis (historical, allegorical and moral), in practice he appears to follow the Pauline pattern, that is *littera* and *spiritus*.[56] He and the principal patristic exegetes who preceded him were recognized by the ninth-century Carolingian scholars as integral to the understanding of holy text.[57] Together they may be regarded as a favoured pantheon of biblical authority and interpretation. Not that the work of subsequent clerics and exegetes was solely derived from these three. Other scholars included Cassiodorus (490–c. 585), the Roman statesman, writer and monk, who wrote a number of exegetical works, perhaps the most important being his commentary on the psalms.[58] The work done from the sixth-century onwards, and especially following the period of the Carolingian exegetes in the ninth century, paved the way for biblical commentaries to proliferate before and during the twelfth-century renaissance.[59] It has been observed that Bede's influence on ninth-century Francia was probably greater than that on the eighth-century Anglo-Saxon kingdoms[60] and that Isidore of Seville (c. 560–636) was also a major inspiration for the Carolingian revival.[61] The belief that the cohesion of a people was based on the Catholic creeds, so central to the Carolingian revival, was derived from both Isidore and Bede[62] – a complex contribution and convergence in ninth-century scholarship and biblical understanding.

The importance of these major figures to subsequent scholars was assured by their collective exegetical corpus as well as by their individual commentaries. Although derivation existed, this did not mean that there was collusion between the exegetes: Gregory himself is regarded as having had a large measure of scholarly independence and rarely cites his precursors.[63] Rather, this union was represented by a shared sense of scriptural meaning only understood by a small number of exegetes: 'The western church fathers ... shared the assumption that the spiritual sense of the Bible was its hidden yet true meaning, only perceptible to those who were initiated in the mysteries of the faith.'[64] Indeed, for Gregory, the disclosure of the Bible's true meaning enabled the contemplation of God and what may be interpreted as his salvation history.[65] This was a reflection of his attempts to create a balance between the historical and allegorical, the outward expression and the spiritual interpretation. Perhaps this finds its most eloquent expression in his teaching on the contemplation of God expressed in his 35-book *magnum opus*, *Moralium Libri sive Expositio in Librum Beati Job*, usually shortened to *Moralia in Job* (henceforward *Moralia*).[66] Here it is possible to piece together a vision of God derived from reflecting on the sufferings of the righteous man: 'The plan for the commentary on Job perfectly comprises the idea of a correct balance between the inward and the outward in exegesis, as it is said about Job, Ezekiel or other biblical figures who in all their external ordeals are an example of a balanced and even tempered mood.'[67] This equilibrium, first expressed in his earliest exegetical work, *Expositio in Canticis Canticorum*, is preparatory to the vision of God, a condition reserved for the afterlife, and is a prayerful learning process.[68] This is linked to Gregory's teaching on salvation and is made explicit in his Homily on Lk. 3.1-11 (*Homilia XX*) that sets the stage for salvation history by contrasting the division of the kingdom of Judea under its many kings and priests with the work of Christ who represented both kingship and the priesthood.[69] Although a direct link with Iberia is elusive, division and loss would be replaced with unity and consummation, themes that would have had a resonance with those historians who describe the dynastic events in twelfth- and thirteenth-century León-Castile.[70]

Isidore's moral authority and contribution to Spanish medieval literary culture and historiography are unparalleled.[71] His output suggests a wide potential audience even if the eventual recipients of his teaching might be remote from the organs of power and ecclesiastical influence. For example, Isidore's *Sententiae* argues that the power of the monarch was linked to ecclesiastical authority and that kings and princes set the moral tone so that this might be emulated by their subjects. Furthermore, his engagement with Gregory's works suggests he supported the idea that a high degree of training for the ecclesiastical elites would condition the moral climate and understanding of the less educated. Gregory makes this explicit at the beginning of the *Moralia* (written between 578 and 595), which had a major influence on the writings of Isidore and especially perhaps on his *Sententiae* (612–15).[72] José Carracedo Fraga suggests that an elite secular audience may therefore have initially been within Isidore's sights. The teaching of grammar serving to elucidate his prodigious and varied curriculum is most evident in the *Etymologiae*.[73] Furthermore, in specifically discussing the anti-Jewish theme contained in Isidore's works such as *Quaestiones*, it is probable that a key aim was to address the scholarly and pastoral deficiencies of a poorly educated clergy.[74] The chain of patristic and exegetical authority, from Augustine and Gregory through to Isidore and his successors, continued as an integrated mantle, but one that involved more than mere redaction; an analysis and comparison with other Carolingian exegetes suggests that Isidore responded to the transition between antiquity and medieval worlds with insight and creativity.[75]

The *Historia Ecclesiastica gentis Anglorum* is Bede's best-known work. Its relevance to scriptural exegesis is direct, since his interpretation of biblical text was perhaps the single most dominant force in his writing.[76] His OT exegesis was especially pertinent to his historical writing since he, like Gregory and later historians, considered the history of his own people to be comparable with that of the ancient Hebrews.[77] This comparison – which includes a meticulous study of the kings of Israel and Judah and their strength derived from military conquest – cited the particular geographical features of OT locations to indicate similarities with those of his own age.[78] Although Bede may have been reluctant to acknowledge specifically the importance of Isidore, Isidore's impact was highly influential on English churchmen during Bede's time and on the writings of Bede himself.[79] Bede, together with Isidore, developed ideas related to ascetic practice consisting of reading, meditation, prayer and intention. These ideas were posited in works such as Isidore's *Synomyna de Lamentationa*,[80] an exposition whose style was to influence the writing not just of Iberian clerics such as Ildefonsus, archbishop of Toledo (r. 657–667), but was known as far away as Ireland.[81] Bede and Isidore also showed a willingness to write about biblical passages which they admitted were beset with difficulties. An example is Bede's commentary on Ezra and Nehemiah which reveals a debt to Isidore and earlier exegetes in the Latin west.

Isidore and Bede both used classical models. In Bede's exegetical and historical writing, such models usually had a particular function. References to Virgil, Ovid, Pliny and Seneca in the *Commentary on Genesis* serve to provide examples that illuminate the grammatical content and add intellectual voltage to his work:

> Bede shows in his grammatical treatises, hagiography, exegetical works and *Historia ecclesiastica* that Vergil and other classical writers were used for latinity, models of metrical rules, figures of speech, poetic diction, rhetorical *bene dicta*, and historical corroboration of certain items of Christian learning.[82]

The influence of the Vulgate text is apparent in Bede's narrative,[83] together with his use of the *Vetus Latina*,[84] and his exegesis, although based on patristic and classical models, had a distinct character. His understanding of *vera lex historiae* arose from his belief in the importance of theological as well as literal truth, and his *historia* was based on the experiences of faithful witnesses from which moral edification might be derived.[85] This was emphasized by Bede's use of the term *simpliciter* and seems to have been used to delineate unadorned or commonly held perception from theological interpretation.[86] Although an important aim of this method was to assert the unity and orthodoxy of the church,[87] Bede's determination to distinguish between common perception and theological understanding of history linked him to his patristic predecessors and enabled him to offer two or more interpretations of the same biblical passage if they each pointed to an ultimate spiritual lesson.[88] This flexibility may be connected with the different biblical translations to which Bede had access.

An example of Bede's willingness to make use of whatever versions he had available is his commentary on Ezra and Nehemiah [*In Ezram et Neemiam*]. This is largely based on Jerome's Vulgate, yet an analysis of Bede's commentary (especially on the book devoted to Ezra) reveals at least six references that suggest an awareness of other Latin versions.[89] *In Ezram et Neemiam*, the third and final book in his innovative work on Jewish sanctuaries,[90] is a study of the journey of Ezra and the priests and Levites from Babylon to Jerusalem,[91] one that is full of mysteries [*omnia plena mysteriis*].[92] Yet the ways in which the journey may be interpreted allow insight into a true, or at least a plausible, meaning of the passage. Babylon and Jerusalem may be seen figuratively, 'Just as if, as the beginning of the first month, we were sent out from Babylon,'[93] depicting a journey of consecration and renewal. There may also be a more specific and local purpose in the commentary related to the promotion of Bede's own church in Northumbria. If this allusion can be sustained with figurative references to Solomon's temple, it suggests an approximate date of composition and an intended audience. Nevertheless, the date of the commentary remains problematic (probably between 709 and 725) and the intended audience is likely to have included not only *praedicatores* and *doctors*, but the less-educated clergy and novices too.[94] This intention provides further evidence of a link with Gregory and Isidore.

Patristic exegetes, together with their seventh- and eighth-century successors, were not always prepared to acknowledge each other's authority; neither did scriptural interpretation remain entirely static. The effects of Bede's engagement in what is referred to as *vestigia partum* [the footsteps of the fathers], and *vestigia sequimur Israhel*[95] [we follow in the footsteps of Israel], was to ensure that patristic wisdom was incorporated into medieval scholarship and understanding. Furthermore, those who followed from the ninth century onwards enriched and embellished a cherished tradition: 'All shared in one body of knowledge, one Truth, to which all had access, upon which all might draw, and consequently which any might appropriate.'[96]

Carolingian and later exegesis

Despite the way successive generations of exegetes derived inspiration from patristic and classical models, it is possible to discern shifts in emphasis which were apparent by the ninth century. There was, from the Carolingian period onwards, a greater willingness to write commentaries on some of the historical books of the OT that had been less popular during the patristic period. There is a particular fascination of Frankish kings with biblical history, and the influence of biblical texts on historical narrative is evident in a number of ways.[97] There is the example of Hrabanus, abbot of Fulda (*c.* 780–856), a favoured pupil of Alcuin of York (*c.* 740–804), who considered him to be amongst the most eminent of Carolingian scholars.[98] Hrabanus is important both for his prodigious output (he wrote over twenty biblical commentaries) and for continuing the work of Bede and Alcuin, which collectively was to contribute so powerfully to the religious culture of Carolingian exegesis. He demonstrates his debt to Isidore, not merely in his veneration of the *Etymologies*, but in his reverence for those whom Isidore particularly admired, especially Augustine.[99] Rosamund McKitterick also discusses the substantial contribution of the exegesis and commentary provided by Hrabanus,[100] who, though he wrote at the behest of kings, was driven by personal ambition.[101] Yet he was not the first Carolingian exegete to compile voluminous commentaries on the early books of the OT[102] and, like earlier exegetes such as Bede and the slightly earlier exegete at the Carolingian court, Alcuin, he quoted extensively from Origen, Augustine and a variety of other patristic sources.[103] He and his fellow Carolingian exegetes commented on the OT while continuing to acknowledge the debt to their patristic forebears.

Nevertheless, the ninth-century emphasis on OT history in the works of Hrabanus and other Frankish scholars suggests that the vision of a biblically inspired Christian society was a Carolingian one.[104] It derived its inspiration from books such as 1 and 2 Sam., 1 and 2 Chron. and 1 and 2 Kgs. This vision had its origins in the legislation of Charlemagne's father Pippin (r. 751–768), though it was after Charlemagne's coronation (800) and the emergence of empire that this was most clearly expressed.[105] The relevance of OT histories was clear and appealed to an imagination in which David and Solomon were seen as archetypes for medieval kingship. Such histories were also used by medieval kings and bishops to justify inter-religious conflict[106] and even to suggest models for monasticism.[107] Van Liere considers that the wealth of descriptive and historical information gave chroniclers an insight into little-known periods of Israelite history; for example, knowledge of the construction of Solomon's Temple seems to have inspired medieval models and also provided awareness of the circumstances surrounding the biblical account.[108] The use of OT figures as types of Christ was already widely recognized. David had been established as a type of Christ by patristic exegetes,[109] as had Adam, Moses and Jeremiah, with Eve as a type of Mary. Furthermore, the account of the Witch of Endor, who is able to call up the ghost of the deceased Samuel (1 Sam. 28.3-25), enabled Origen to identify the last of the Hebrew judges as a type of Christ.[110] It is striking that, from the ninth century onwards, these biblical figures provided historians with models for their kings and leaders: 'the annalist's judgements were full of comparisons, explicit and implicit, with the traditional benchmarks of Carolingian kingship, Frankish tradition and biblical archetypes.'[111] Such mental mythological images also formed elements in the way Christian chroniclers of the events in twelfth- and thirteenth-centuries Castile eulogized their own leaders and were able to comment on the course of events.

Between the twelfth and the fourteenth centuries, commentaries on biblical texts were often in the form of *glossae ordinariae*, which were compilations of patristic and Carolingian exegesis.[112] This was eventually superseded by a much extended form of commentary known as *magna glossatura*, which owed its origins to Peter Lombard (*c.* 1096–1154), though some scholars have preferred to emphasize the continuity between these two types of commentary.[113] In any event, the *glossae ordinariae* consisted of written commentaries, interpretations and explanations of scripture and was an assembly of glosses, from the church fathers and thereafter, printed in the margins of the Vulgate Bible. These were widely used in the education systems of Christendom in cathedral schools from the Carolingian period onwards, but fell into disuse in the fourteenth century. Although chiefly in Latin, they also appeared in vernacular editions of biblical texts such as Castilian, Anglo-Saxon and Old French. It is possible that *glossae ordinariae* were developed by the ninth-century German Benedictine monk, Walafrid Strabo (*c.* 808–849), who was employed in the Carolingian court.[114] He was a prominent Carolingian scholar and so venerated the early fathers that he has been credited with having laid the foundations for the *glossa ordinaria* by creating signs that indexed the authors of exegetical excerpts.[115] Despite this, Walafrid's overall contribution may have been comparatively modest, having probably been overstated by his biographer, Johannes Trithemius (1462–1516).[116]

The most important influence on *glossa ordinaria*, however, is attributed to Anselm of Laon (d. 1117) who developed a system of writing a commentary over the text of the Vulgate known as *glossa interlinearis*.[117] The early glosses meant that difficult parts of biblical text could be explained. Anselm's work represented a considerable advance since his glosses were to provide a definitive biblical interpretation, and he enabled his scholars and successors at Laon to work on glosses for the whole Bible, though possibly these were completed after his death.[118] Although his exegesis was considered dull by the philosopher Abelard (1079–1142),[119] Anselm's legacy played an important part in the development of *glossa ordinaria*, enabling his teaching to exercise a profound influence over later scholarship.[120]

Commentaries, including interlinear and marginal glosses[121] as well as collections of other material such as miscellaneous sentences and homilies, proliferated from the late eleventh century onwards and formed a many layered and continuously evolving scriptural interpretation.[122] This practice, which Anselm influenced, became widespread amongst twelfth-century masters as well as the mendicant orders who established themselves in Paris from the early thirteenth century.[123] International networks of such orders helped disseminate treatises by Anselm – some of which were written in Cluny from 1104 onwards – over much of the Latin west.[124]

For many generations, the *glossa ordinaria* was the standard commentary on the scriptures of Western Europe; it greatly influenced Western European Christian theology and culture and, as is evident elsewhere, was itself glossed by later commentators.[125] As professors and masters read and expounded on the books of the Bible, they would refer to these glosses or commentaries and by the end of the twelfth century such glosses would be the principal way in which the church fathers were read.[126] The use of such commentaries influenced the writing of history practised by clerics throughout the medieval world, especially in the twelfth and thirteenth centuries by which time the use of *glossae ordinariae* had become widespread.[127] These glosses are likely to have been available to historians and chroniclers in twelfth- and thirteenth-century Castile, especially since many Castilian clerics received part of their education at universities such as Paris and Bologna.[128] Such clerics would also have had access to such commentaries in the monastic libraries of Iberia which expanded faster than in other parts of the Latin west from the late tenth century.[129]

Monastic and liturgical contexts

From the twelfth century onwards, although the writing of history moved from the monastery into a more scholarly and professional discipline, chronicles were still written by senior churchmen whose training and experience would have been in religious communities, though often under royal patronage and sometimes in royal palaces. Within monasteries, historical and hagiographical narrative was steeped in patristic and subsequent exegesis and the monastic environment allowed the chronicler to practise his craft. Central to this experience would be the ways in which biblical texts were used in medieval Latin rites and permeated the daily lives of the religious in the celebration of the liturgy. They had within their own scriptoria and in the biblical readings, or pericopes, at the daily offices and at Mass, access to a bewildering variety of written material that had the potential to support the parallel processes of writing history and understanding scripture. Pericopes are collections of verses or sentences from a book that had a common theme or unity and increasingly linked with sacred scripture. Sometimes the pericope is given a title which links the verses and emphasizes the theme contained within them. The ability to remember portions of the Bible – whether this was deliberate or largely subliminal – was an inevitable result of the organization of the liturgy; and pericopes, while following the liturgical year, might also be elaborated upon and re-enacted in the liturgy itself.[130]

Most obviously, the way in which biblical readings were arranged within the liturgy implied an exegetical framework[131] and at the very least enabled scriptural and exegetical dissemination in the Middle Ages in a variety of medieval literature.[132] The daily reading and singing of scriptural texts alongside and alternating with chapters, versicles and responses, *kyries*, the *credo*, confession, absolution, preces, the collect of the day and other non-scriptural elements would place biblical lessons in a familiar and predictable context. This would apply not only to the Mass and Divine Office but to the chapter and when monks gathered in the refectory. Although the length of readings varied between religious institutions and changed over time, the liturgical season would determine the books that were used in each office. Furthermore, since the medieval church was governed by canon law and local customs, liturgical piety as expressed through the Divine Office was also mandated by church law. This served to strengthen further the familiarity of the patterns of the Vulgate contained in the lessons repeated on a regular basis.

For monks, if not for clergy involved in secular matters, this lifelong exposure to biblical texts ensured that it was central to the thought world of the medieval clerics and the monastic environment in which they lived and breathed. The Bible was everywhere and was all pervasive; it was visually present in artistic representations and was the most frequently accessed reference point that justified monasticism. Moreover, the context in which the Bible was experienced would also endow the lessons derived with the allegorical and illustrative power that had been coherently expressed by exegetes and practised by later commentators.[133] In a sung Mass on a Sunday or feast day there would be further non-scriptural content such as the *Sursum corda, Sanctus, Benedictus*, the Canon of the Mass (typically, a body of prayers said after the consecration at the Eucharist), *Pax Domini* and *Agnus Dei*.[134] The link with exegesis can be pursued further, especially with reference to the mystical content of both the liturgy and readings from the OT which may have been selected for their mystical significance. The Italian historian, Sicard of Cremona (1155–1215), makes an emphatic correlation between the liturgy of the Mass and the biblical theme of struggle which involves the people of God, Christ himself and the Christian soul.[135]

The communication and remembrance of liturgy was also enhanced by the sermon preached following the proclamation of the gospel. Intrinsic to this was the way in which the gospel reading would be expounded or elucidated during the sermon – indeed, in the early Middle Ages the pericope might dictate the structure of the sermon or homily. Those delivered by the early church fathers were often written down and disseminated throughout monastic communities. By the thirteenth century, the emphasis within a sermon might centre on a very small part of the pericope.[136] The sermon therefore reinforced the liturgy and was crucial to the way scripture was understood and communicated. The sermon was to evolve thanks to the establishment of universities and, from the thirteenth century, this process was assisted by the rise of mendicant orders. Yet the link between the liturgy and the structure of the sermon remained firm. Sermons had simply moved from being the sole repository of the monastery to the intellectual life of schools and universities. Although we cannot be certain as to the frequency with which sermons were preached in parish churches,[137] scholars would nevertheless organize their lecture notes so that they could form the basis of liturgically driven sermons. This at least suggests that such exegesis was part of the intellectual armoury of the secular orders.[138]

Biblical texts would therefore be recalled by reading (or recitation), chanting and elucidation and their narrative reinforced by visual imagery such as sculptures and stained-glass windows. They were also represented by liturgical dramas such as miracle plays[139] performed for the monks' benefit and to attempt to communicate biblical narrative to the laity. In their earliest and simplest form, they began with the question posed by the angel outside Jesus' empty tomb, *Quem queritis?* ['Whom do you seek (in the Sepulchre)?'].[140] This process, which developed into the depiction of ever more intricate and elaborate events from the NT – many of which were prefigured in the OT – is sometimes referred to as 'performative exegesis.'[141] Although the congregations who attended these liturgical dramas were originally passive observers,[142] the situation from the late-eleventh century onwards seems to have changed quite markedly. This involved a greater circulation of scriptural knowledge and was linked to the increase in literacy in parts of western Christendom and coincided with a demand for vernacular versions of the Bible.[143] This can be seen as a shift from passive to active engagement with the scriptures. Smalley discusses the increased importance of the gospels in school curricula from the twelfth century onwards, not merely in relation to the place of OT narrative, but also in rivalling the importance of Pauline epistles and the Psalter,[144] which had formerly enjoyed a more prominent place in the liturgy. The increased levels of learning amongst the more influential members of the laity,[145] together with a determination on the part of the church to improve the literacy of its secular clergy (including parish priests), were part of the change in the relationship between the monastic community, secular clergy and the laity.[146]

Yet the shift in the dynamics between these three groups seemed to strengthen more than diminish the influence of biblical exegesis. Its wider dissemination, notwithstanding changes in emphasis over time, would ensure that principles prevailed and were more firmly embedded in monastic and literate society. Even if the attempt by an exegete to communicate a particular idea was obscure, there was a shared theological vision based on Christ as the fulfilment of the law and the prophets. It is important to see the patristic employment of allegory as part of this overall vision rather than as a series of random departures from it. The process can be seen as a chain of scriptural interpretations which can be assembled from the commentaries of the fathers. Although the work of interpretation and study moved from a purely monastic setting to cathedral schools and later to universities, medieval exegesis was entirely dependent on the pattern that had been established in such monastic settings.[147] There was a plurality and evolution of interpretation encompassing tradition, faithful adherence and innovation.[148] In other words, although biblical texts had a special place in medieval schools because of their sacred character, they became, especially from the twelfth century onwards, integrated into a corpus of texts that was refined and expounded.[149]

This review of exegesis has sought to demonstrate the ways in which it influenced the subsequent practice of hermeneutics and historiography in the Middle Ages and to acknowledge and establish the remarkably dependent, durable and consistent culture of interpretation that the early fathers had established. Yet it is possible to chart variation and development over time. The practice of exegetical progress not only evolved during and after the early patristic period, there were also points when its understanding underwent particularly significant renewal as it was subjected to rejuvenated intellectual rigour. Nevertheless, while the writing of commentary and the process of dissemination remained largely within the monastery, the chain of biblical understanding and authority was linked inexorably to patristic sources. Even from the twelfth century onwards, when biblical study expanded into schools and when history was often written in courts and under royal patronage, patristic authority was more often scrutinized and refined rather than challenged and displaced.[150] During the twelfth century, allegory continued to be significant, although it became more closely aligned to literary or historical context. God's hand in history was part of a true record of events and was linked to His intervention in the affairs of men through the sacrifice of Christ and the salvation offered to the world.[151] Exegetes sought at different times to demonstrate that scripture was historical, allegorical and that it had a moral dimension. If these three facets were inextricably linked, it would be possible for medieval chroniclers to suggest that their own historical struggle could be understood through biblical allegory.

The Bible and the writing of history

An understanding of biblical texts, often made familiar through liturgy, was mediated through patristic exegesis and a growing body of commentary. This conditioned the world in which medieval writers lived and the environment in which they compiled their histories. Here, attention is given to the ways in which biblical texts and commentaries were used by chroniclers and those who described conflict and conquest. Because this is in part a comparative analysis of biblical influence on medieval texts, we look specifically at the ways in which the impact of the Normans – in England, Ireland and Sicily – was recorded by twelfth-century writers which may be analogous with descriptions of conquest describing Alfonso VII's struggles in al-Andalus. Although the pre-eminence of the Bible in a medieval cultural context is a sine qua non, its narrative, language and metaphor serve a variety of different cultural purposes as well as being a comprehensive source book. The influence of biblical texts on the writing of history in western Christendom, whilst containing a consistent thread, also revealed significant divergence over time and this is particularly the case as cultural identities evolved. In addition to scripture as a historical source for medieval chroniclers and the ways in which it might be used allegorically, there is what is described as biblical typology:

> By means of typological interpretation, the significance of the past is reaffirmed for the present; the old becomes a prophecy of the new and its predeterminant in the sense that its very existence determines the shape and the interpretation of what comes later.[152]

These distinctions are important even if there was not a rigid or self-conscious attempt within historiography to delineate the ways in which biblical texts could be used. I examine the range of uses of biblical narrative and epic in order to consider the emerging themes that were to inform and drive the specific – and at time almost parochial – interpretative process.

An important verse from 2 Pet. 1.21 which Pope Clement VI (r. 1342–52) himself invoked is cited by Mary Garrison: 'For prophecy came not in old time by the will of man: but by holy men of God as they were moved by the Holy Ghost.'[153] The holy men of old, inspired by the Holy Spirit, provided the model for those who were to inherit the mantle of guardianship and stewardship of biblical truth in Clement's own time. And Clement's significant addition, 'non potest in ea … aliquod per eum qui inferior cuiusmodi est papa,'[154] reaffirmed the truth of scripture and the pope's own lack of authority to alter it. Clement thus asserts that the imposition of perpetual and unchanging truth came not from the will of man, but only as men were moved by the Holy Spirit; defence and justification of biblical authority includes the notion of purpose and is emphatically expressed in Paul's second letter to Timothy: 'All scripture is given by inspiration of God, and is profitable for doctrine, for reproof, for correction, for instruction in righteousness.'[155] Furthermore, those who were steeped in biblical culture did much more than use scripture as a didactic tool; the scripture also justified political and religious hostility, political vigour and aspiration and the eulogy of kings and princes.

The assertions of biblical veracity within 2 Pet. and 2 Tim. may be two sides of the same coin – 2 Pet. can be seen to represent Christendom's humility before the truth revealed to its holy predecessors; 2 Tim. is much more a call to arms. If the Bible is to be used to distinguish truth from error and to correct and instruct, its use as a weapon to confront perceived error would be indispensable. Furthermore, if OT examples were to be used as models for current action, they would be for the instruction not merely of the faithful but used more assertively against those who threaten God's holy church. There is the suggestion of political expedience and Clement himself was a late example of an advocate of biblical interventionism even though he, like his predecessors, was governed by both patristic and biblical precedent.[156]

Conquest and biblical rhetoric

If NT injunctions promoted or suggested a benign or discreet biblical influence over the actions of kings, prices and prelates, OT sources provided exemplars of direct intervention. They enabled medieval writers to interpret events as if they were describing their own people with a historic and typological link to their perceived Hebrew predecessors. The 'exegetical transformation of Old Testament *milites Christi*' continued during the eleventh and twelfth centuries, during which time the kings and heroes of ancient Israel became established as models for the emerging concepts and ideals of western Christian knighthood and crusade.[157] Indeed, such exegesis not only suggested to clerics ways of understanding past conflicts, it also enabled them to come to terms with the ethical issues connected with warfare in their own time.[158] Garrison cites two writers from the late eighth century who developed an unusually rich rhetorical and historical association with the OT and personalized this link with their addressees: Tassilo of Bavaria in 772 and Charlemagne in 775. The example of a letter of a certain Clemens to Tassilo is noteworthy because the link with the Children of Israel is thoroughly and unusually explicit:

> May our Lord be with Tassilo as he was with Abraham, Abraham who pursued the kings of the five peoples and returned with the victory and their spoils; May the omnipotent Lord be a champion [*pugnator*] for you as he was with Moses and Joshua ... who triumphed over the Amalechites ... May the Lord smite your enemies in your sight just as he smote many peoples in the sight of the sons of Israel.[159]

No information exists about the identity of Clemens, though he introduces himself as *ego Clemens amicus vester peregrinus* [your friend, the pilgrim] and he may have been linked to the membership of a Bavarian religious house.[160]

Despite the devotional tone of Clemens' salutation in his letter to Tassilo, the content appeared to confirm on the addressee exceptional powers of conquest and authority.[161] Although this link between contemporary political power and the authority of ancient Israel was inconsistently applied at that time, the fact that 'Both letters (i.e. to Tassilo and Charlemagne) imply typological comparisons between their recipients, and the experience of Israel to an exceptional degree,'[162] suggests that the ancient-contemporary link was an active if intermittent element in military struggle with the enemies of Christendom. Moreover, during the succeeding centuries, OT conflict narrative would be invoked as a justification for conquest and perhaps as a sacred duty, though such an emphatically personalized connection would be, even in later documents, a rarity.[163] Indeed, OT injunctions go beyond the onus to teach doctrine [*docendumus*], for reproof [*arguendum*], correction [*corripiendum*] and instruction in righteousness [*erudiendum in justitia*], which are the more restrained messages contained in the NT epistles of St Paul. Furthermore, biblical texts were probably the simplest entry into Latin for novices as well as being an acceptable model for narrative prose. Knowledge of Latin enabled the ecclesiastic to approach the written text and its commentaries together with the ordered rule of the religious house. Understanding, despite rudimentary explanation to novices, grew only gradually and the meaning of Latin texts would be as dependent on recitation as on teaching offered by more senior clerics.[164]

The link between Christendom's journey of faith and the conquering exploits of the Children of Israel was therefore employed in a variety of medieval writing genres though comparisons were usually intricate and often lacked a consistently applied allegorical message. Yet there remains the need to recognize the ways in which medieval writers, and especially chroniclers, used biblical narrative and the writings of those who had commented on biblical texts, as sources with which their own histories could be read. The way biblical precedent was applied and adapted to suit the Latin Church therefore lacked prescribed pattern or usage. We are rarely presented with a historical account that has an uninterrupted line to a biblical source with a single provenance.

The idea of a naturally evolving diversity in the way exegetes used biblical texts should be seen as a key element, integral to an overall unity of acknowledgement and purpose. This diversity of use within medieval historiography may be illustrated with several examples, each of which addresses the matter of military conflict. Alcuin provides an eighth-century English account that can be contrasted with the letters of Clemens and Cathuulf. He left England just before the sack of Lindisfarne (793) to take up a position in Charlemagne's court, but the loss of Lindisfarne, together with the weakening of Mercia following the death of Offa in 796, was to have a profound effect on his writing.[165] These events were compounded by the fact that Æthelheard, the archbishop of Canterbury, was forced to flee his diocese. This coincided with Alcuin's own appointment as abbot of St Martin at Tours, also in 796, and he was never to return to England. As a resident of Francia, he had the opportunity to contrast the contemporary victory of Charlemagne's army over the Avars with events in his own country. Garrison offers several sources where these events are analysed in detail.[166] Certainly, Alcuin's use of the Bible as a tool to admonish, teach and correct seemed firmly based on 2 Tim. 3.16. Yet to these we would add consolation and edification which he saw as 'a duty of *caritas*.'[167]

Alcuin also tackled the painful problem of his opponents' victory directly and was unsparing in his condemnation of those he thought held the responsibility for the defeat of Christ's church. His letters relating to the devastation of Lindisfarne show that for him the loss was unimaginable and comparable to the fall of Rome. As well as his more general sense that the prophecy of Jeremiah would be fulfilled as an enemy 'out of the north' would attack the English church,[168] he wrote a series of letters identifying specific guilt. In the first, addressed to the Northumbrian king Æthelred, he delivers an uncompromising message with apocalyptic elements in a style unusually lacking in deference:

> He who reads the holy scriptures and the ancient histories and considered the outcome of the age, he shall discover that for this same kind of sin, kings have cast away their kingdoms and peoples their homelands. And while foreign powers took unjustly, the owners justly lost.[169]

Here there could be no consolation or edification. The evil actions of the king had ensured that Jeremiah's prophecy would be fulfilled in Alcuin's own time and to make his argument more compelling, used biblical citations in a direct and portentous manner; he seems to have been clear about the significance of the event, even if the inflammatory and judgemental way in which his words are couched obscured the clarity of his message. Yet Alcuin was equally clear about the ways in which the enemy might be overcome; he describes Charlemagne in terms that surpass earthly kingship,[170] and his use of the term *pontifex* seems to confer upon him a spiritual as well as a temporal authority.[171] The link between the biblical King David and the Emperor is acknowledged by Gernot Wieland;[172] David conquered his enemies and then ruled with wisdom, and Charlemagne strives to do the same as he works bravely to extend the Christian empire with arms and thus endeavours to defend, increase and reach the truth of the apostolic faith.[173] The kingdom is to be defended and expanded and this will enable the Catholic faith to be promoted and increased.[174]

A second strand in Alcuin's use of biblical typology can be seen in the way he chose to address the archbishop of Canterbury who had fled his see in 796. In his letter to Æthelheard, he reminds the archbishop of his responsibilities to his clergy and to his flock. In the wake of the loss of Lindisfarne, Alcuin's advice may have been a salutary and effective weapon and the content and tone can be contrasted with his biblically inspired rant against King Æthelred. A bishop may have been much more susceptible to biblical exhortation, especially since Alcuin chose not OT fury but the very epithets used by Jesus to describe his first disciples. The archbishop and his clergy are *lux totius Brittaniae* (a direct attempt to link the phrase *Vos estis lux mundi*/You are the light of the world[175] with their more localized vocation), *sal terrae*/the salt of the earth, *ciuitas super montem posita*/ a city set on a hill – and all are lifted directly from the Sermon on the Mount. Other NT exhortations are also quoted at length: 'But ye are a chosen generation, a royal priesthood, an holy nation, a peculiar people ... of him who hath called you out of darkness into his marvellous light.'[176] This familiar language was used as a prelude to admonish those Christians who, by implication, were militarily and politically weaker than the pagans who had settled in the island of Britain.[177]

Alcuin's words to those who had suffered for their faith and steadfastness were of a different order and it is clear when he wrote to the monks of Lindisfarne, his advocacy of edification and consolation would be important tools, though biblical imagery and language would be at the heart of his message. He quotes directly from Joel, the minor prophet who warned of the great calamity that would overrun Israel:

> Spare thy people, O Lord, and give not thine heritage to reproach, that the heathen should rule over them: wherefore should they say among the people, Where is their God?[178]

Alcuin prefaced this OT lamentation with his own rhetorical question: 'What must we say, but that our spirit must lament for you before the altar of Christ?'[179] Mournful consolation and sympathy, though would necessarily be a sufficient response. For God's ways are mysterious, and the sack of Lindisfarne, unbearably painful as it must have been for Alcuin, contained within it the seeds of chastening and to love contained within an overarching purpose: 'For whom the Lord loveth he chasteneth, and scourgeth every son whom he receiveth.'[180] The culpability of man and his responsibility is a pre-eminent theme and one to which Alcuin frequently returns in his letters and other works. In his poem *De clade Lindisfarnensis monastarii*, he sets the loss of Lindisfarne within the inevitable course of human history: 'Accordingly, God is by no means to be blamed for this punishment/ But that our lives should rapidly and visibly be improved.'[181] The monks would therefore need to mend their ways as well as to mourn the loss of their church and to bear the pain of their brethren who had been carried off into slavery.

The question as to how chroniclers should respond to attacks on and incursions into the Latin west was a matter of recurring preoccupation. Jean Dunbabin argues that the rehabilitation of the Maccabees within the canon of scripture (the inclusion of Maccabees and certain other texts was contested by some early church fathers) could have been prompted by successful Hungarian raids into Germany in the early years of the tenth century.[182] She refers to the fact that 1 and 2 Macc. are the only books in the Vulgate not to mention God,[183] yet because of their role as 'archetypes of heroic warriors,'[184] might serve as useful models to build up flagging Christian morale. Attention is also paid to the compilers of the *Annales Alamannici* and the *Annales Sangallenses maiores*, which were produced during and after Charlemagne's life and cover the period 709–926.[185] These texts refer to the Hungarian invaders as *Agareni*, making a pejorative association with the Saracens as well as with the OT enemies of the Hebrews, the Hagarenes.[186] The temptation to portray the enemies of Christendom as *barbaras gentes* and *mala gens* by linking them, sometimes randomly, with Hagarenes and Moabites would be a recurring theme in later chronicles, and especially to those writers, like the author of the *CAI*, who wrote passionately of the conflict with Islam in al-Andalus.

The Normans in England, Sicily and Ireland

Three chroniclers from the late eleventh to the thirteenth centuries who wrote about the impact of the Normans in England, Sicily and Ireland are now considered: William of Malmesbury (*c.* 1090–*c.* 1143), Gaufredus Malaterra (*fl.* 1085–94) and Gerald of Wales (*c.* 1146–*c.* 1223); they will also be set in the context of others who were writing at the same time. Like their Leonese-Castilian contemporaries, they too were concerned with the themes of conquest and settlement, although their approaches were varied, as was their use of biblical narrative and commentary.

William of Malmesbury, the Anglo-Norman cleric and historian, was a man of pre-eminent scholarly achievement in twelfth-century Europe.[187] Writing of the deeds of the Norman kings in his *Gesta Regum Anglorum* (henceforward *GRA*),[188] he was aware of the need to balance the competing claims of those who aspired to the English throne, especially when the matter of religious conflict was not an issue. He was confronted with the potentially vexed question of the Norman invasion of England. In his narrative he does not doubt the courage of William or Harold as in those qualities 'both leaders shone forth.'[189] He has, after all, Norman and English lineage,[190] yet declares in favour of William. There is, he recalls, the suggestion from Harold's younger brother Gyrth Godwinson (c. 1032–66) that Harold had been unable or unwilling to keep an oath, even if there were possible extenuating circumstances.[191] Yet Gyrth's comments are powerful because they reflect an impression of Harold's faithlessness:

> Indeed this man, though he was provided in no small quantity with courage, had insufficient care, reportedly, to acts of faithlessness and, by some trickery, sought to evade the judgement of men.[192]

The perceived breach of faith seems, according to William of Malmesbury, to have triggered the invasion of England, though some sources appear to have understood the situation differently. Other Anglo-Norman chroniclers, such as Henry of Huntingdon (c. 1084–c. 1155), Geoffrey Gaimar (fl. 1136–7) and Ailred of Rievaulx (1110–67) present a more equivocal account about the virtues of the protagonists.[193] Much less sympathetic is the view taken by the chronicler and Benedictine scholar Orderic Vitalis (1075–c. 1142) and it is clear that he considered Harold both a usurper and a perjurer (for promising the kingdom to William and then seizing it for himself). Harold was besmirched by this breach of integrity and act of defiance, and his short rule is cruel and unjust – though nothing specific is catalogued: and Harold, son of the Earl Godwin, had seized the throne of England and had held it for almost three months in a great state of loss, since he was dishonoured by perjury, barbarism and other wicked acts.[194]

William of Malmesbury seems to have considered the Saxons' descent into certain sins of the flesh[195] as the more telling in his analysis of the causes and significance of the Norman victory which he, like Orderic, proceeds to enumerate. The fate of the nation that transgresses God's laws is a familiar theme and is discussed in Chapter 2 in relation to the HS. William of Malmesbury begins with a schedule of Saxon offences that have sown the seeds of their eventual demise: 'Nevertheless, as generations proceeded, and for a number of years before the advent of the Normans, enthusiasm for literature and religion had fallen away.'[196] This has echoes of Paul's admonishments to the fledgling churches in Rome, Galatia and Colossae, where the 'sins of the flesh' are specifically enumerated.[197] Yet the term *religio* is used only in St James' epistle: 'Pure religion [*religio*] and undefiled before God'[198] and the link between religion and learning is not directly biblical. Although William of Malmesbury condemns the ignorance of the clergy and the immorality of the ruling classes, he singles out for particular attention drunkenness which had apparently been a Saxon failing from time immemorial,[199] together with its attendant debauchery; and, as if this somehow exemplified the Saxons' moral and religious disintegration, he uses their eve of battle behaviour as a portent of their imminent defeat: 'The English, as we have heard, prolonged their night without sleep in singing and drinking.' There is a contrast here between the Normans, solemnly feasting on the body of their Lord, and the Saxons who seem entirely preoccupied with physical gluttony and excess.[200] It is possible that William of Malmesbury saw more mysterious reasons to link the Saxon people with the seeds of their own destruction and implies an ancient authority. At frequent points during his history of their conflict, the Saxons are depicted as morally and spiritually inferior to their Norman counterparts. In his description of their appearance, he makes reference to Caesar's *De Bello Gallico* and appears to link the Saxons with the ancient and pre-Christian Celts.[201] There were of course many attempts to link nations and their leaders with ancient precedents and, in the process, religious and ethnic divisions were often blurred.[202] It is likely that William of Malmesbury's reading of the Bible was at least in part mediated through the commentaries and glosses of earlier exegetes,[203] more often than taken directly from biblical texts themselves. Perhaps because of William of Malmesbury's veneration of classical and biblical texts mediated through the patristic sources,[204] there is less evidence of the chronicler quoting at length from either the scriptures or the classical texts themselves. Such references are 'embedded unobtrusively' in his prose.[205] However, this is not wholly the case. In a famous description of the death of the son and grandson of William the Conqueror, he uses what Michael Evans refers to as a 'motif of death' from a biblical source.[206]

> A little later in the same wood [the New Forest], his [William I's] son William and grandson Richard, son of Duke Robert of Normandy, encountered death by the severe judgement of God; one from an arrow in his chest, the other pierced in the neck, or, it is said, pierced in the gullet by the twig of a tree.[207]

The biblical source in question is the death of Absolom, son of David, who rebels against his father, proclaiming himself as the rightful king of Israel and is killed in the forest as he runs away from the battle in Ephraim's Wood.[208] The story seems to have been a popular biblical trope in the twelfth century.[209]

Biblical texts not only provided perceived historical truth but were also a source of allegory, moral instruction and assistance in the understanding of the mysteries of Christian doctrine[210] and William of Malmesbury demonstrated this scheme of exegesis – derived from Jerome, Augustine, Isidore[211] and Bede – in his only biblical commentary, the *Commentary on Lamentations*. He believed that a single verse could convey a range of messages and appeal to different senses [*saltuatim et mixtim omnia*][212] and this is an idea which is especially important when considering the place of scriptural narrative in the twelfth-century *CAI*.

At about the same time as the Normans were imposing their rule in England, others, under Robert Guiscard and Roger de Hauteville, were extending Norman influence in Muslim-controlled Sicily. Within thirty years (1060–90), they had established suzerainty over the whole island. They have been portrayed as those in the vanguard of crusade and are also seen as protectors of the papacy.[213] In his preface to *The Normans in Sicily and Southern Italy*, C. N. L. Brooke scrupulously catalogues the biblical references in *De rebus gestis Rogerii Calabriae et Siciliae Comitis et Roberti Guiscardi Ducis fratris eius* by the eleventh-century Benedictine monk, Gaufredus Malaterra, presenting each reference within Malaterra alongside its biblical source.[214] Interestingly, the references Malaterra takes from biblical texts and which are scattered throughout his four books are usually concerned with Christian virtue and piety. He also quotes, though less extensively than from scripture, from Gregory the Great as well as from classical authors such as Sallust and Seneca.

Malaterra is much less inclined than are some of his contemporaries to use biblical narrative to justify invasion and conquest. His NT examples (constituting more than half of his references) are concerned with the quiet and godly life. His use of the Sermon on the Mount[215] recalls one of the most recognizable of the beatitudes: 'Blessed are the poor in spirit; for theirs is the kingdom of heaven.'[216] Further examples include Malaterra's use of Luke's Gospel, Paul's letters and the letter to the Hebrews. Without exception, they are concerned with Christian behaviour, the generosity of God and his unimpeachable justice. Such inferences may also be made from his use of Rom. 10.12: 'For there is no difference between the Jew and the Greek: for the same Lord over all is rich unto all that call upon him.'[217] Following, as it does, from the assertion that God's salvation is open to all, it appears to call upon the people of God to recognize their own humility in the midst of success and not to judge their enemy.

The importance of the spiritual component in Malaterra's work was, perhaps, its overwhelmingly most important comparative element,[218] and the infusion of biblical language and godly virtue, dependent on the Vulgate, was central to Malaterra, as it was to others. Malaterra used biblical narrative to promote Christian ethics (even if some citations can be unusually bizarre, uncontextualized and oblique).[219] He avoids linking OT metaphors with conquest and may be seen as temperamentally closer to William of Malmesbury than to those who advocated more strident Christian intervention to exalt its military successes. Towards the end of his fourth book there is a kind of biblical flourish in which three verses are brought together in an impassioned plea for peace: 'How beautiful are the feet of them that preach the gospel of peace'; 'Blessed are the peacemakers for they shall be called the children of God'; 'Live in peace and the God of love and peace shall be with you.'[220]

The variety of uses to which biblical texts would be put is further exemplified by another churchman, the sometime archdeacon of Brecon, Giraldus Cambrensis or Gerald of Wales (1146–1223). His *Expugnatio Hibernica* (*c.* 1189) expresses no doubts as to the justification for the Norman conquest of Ireland that began in 1171. Implicit in Gerald's text are references to Augustine's *De civitate Dei*, Jerome's *Vita Pauli*, Gregory's *Dialogum* and Isidore's *Etymologies*,[221] though he exhorts us to read these works and does not always quote directly from them. More frequently occurring are references to classical authors and those most often referred to are Ovid, Virgil, Terence and Lucan. Gerald's case for the invasion of Ireland was overwhelming and he shores up his argument by citing individual biblical references; these are most often connected with the justification for invasion but can also provide warnings and memorable imagery.[222] The *Expugnatio* makes an interesting comparison with some of the other chronicles and especially with the work of William of Malmesbury. Both William and Gerald wrote of the conquests of one Christian people by another and both invasions involved the extension of Norman suzerainty in the British Isles. Yet the tone of tentative, almost reluctant support that William of Malmesbury offers the Norman invaders at Hastings is wholly absent from Gerald's account. As is clear from the introduction to the *Expugnatio*, historical and biblical texts are ancient teaching sources that may be used to understand the present and justify the actions of Christian people.[223] Piety, imperialism and cultural progression are therefore, perhaps unsurprisingly, conflated. Biblical, patristic and classical texts would, when necessary, serve to illuminate and justify historical purpose.

Gerald does not compare the finely balanced claims of the protagonists, though he recognizes the victors as those who must behave honourably and truthfully towards their enemy. He also implies that valour is admired by the barbarous nations even if they do not practise it.[224] He saw the Norman conquest of Ireland as a potent combination of the justified ambitions of the English crown and an ecclesiastical purpose linked to lineage and classical precedent. This is coupled with a view of the conquered as morally degenerate.[225] The *Expugnatio*, notwithstanding much bombast within it,[226] can be seen as a confident, assured piece of work in which the Anglo-Norman church had a kind of assumed authority and superiority.[227] Furthermore, Gerald's certainty may have been bolstered by earlier writers who had also promoted the idea of the conquest of Ireland. William of Malmesbury, William of Newburgh and Bernard of Clairvaux (who had recorded the life of the Irish Saint, Malachy) had all supported the idea of a Norman invasion of Ireland and it is Bernard in his *Vita Sanctii Malachiae* who makes the direct religious link in his descriptions of the Irish.[228]

William of Malmesbury and Bernard of Clairvaux shared Gerald's view that Ireland needed to be conquered. The argument for conquest – first, disparage the native in his ignorance, inconstancy and brutishness and then stress the need for true Christian conquest with its imposition of peace, good order and the establishment of sound laws – was powerfully and consistently made. The assertiveness of a dominant and supposedly superior culture,[229] often crudely amounting to cultural imposition,[230] began perhaps with Henry II's claim of sovereignty over Ireland in 1171.[231] This was linked by Gerald and others to the Christian obligation to invade. In the chronicles of Norman historians, views of Ireland were interwoven with notions of religious ignorance and pastoral (and by implication, cultural) primitiveness: they were to provide the motive for invasion and the imposition of western Christianity. Yet this unanimity and sense of urgency among Gerald and his contemporaries to impose Anglo-Norman Christianity on the Irish was not an obligation that had existed since time immemorial. Donnchádh Ó Corrain[232] describes the situation in the sixth century, during which time Christian influence and Gaelic learning had 'coalesced,' that 'the Irish spliced their local genealogical superstructure to the scriptural one ... to fit into the Judaeo-Christian timescale,' and that even as late as the tenth century, the Anglo-Saxon court had not yet grown wholly to satirize or despise Celtic culture.[233] If this is so, although biblical invocations were used to justify conquest, the real imperative was twelfth-century imperialism. And so, indulging in what John Gillingham calls 'a deluge of vituperation,' twelfth-century clerics were not merely purveyors of conquest history but were themselves subjects of a changing ethnographical, religious and political climate. The narratives of Gerald and Geoffrey Gaimar were enriched by their imaginative response to the cultural climate that they witnessed and promoted. And, like their counterparts in twelfth- and thirteenth-century Spain, they were men of frontiers, shaped by their exposure to conquest, ideology and ambition.[234]

The purpose of this section has been to illustrate the complex ways in which medieval chroniclers were immersed in biblical texts often mediated and embellished through exegesis and liturgy. As is argued, such texts and experiences shaped their culture and attitude to the enemies of Christendom and rivalry within it. And Muslims too were to be depicted by later Hispanic chroniclers in ways which were often partisan, inaccurate and defamatory. Received and compounded inferences embellished and distorted biblically-derived views of the enemies of Christendom. Indeed, the fact that biblical texts were the supremely important source does not imply uniformity of purpose among our authors. Polemic as well as descriptive history is also influenced by other sources, especially those provided by classical authors and church fathers. And there is a further point that suggests possible misapplication of biblical texts which is based on a lack of scriptural knowledge, even by authors on the periphery of religious houses. Marcus Bull alludes to general ignorance of the Bible in relation to an outer circle of laymen attached to the Benedictine abbot, Gerard of Corbie (c. 1025–95)[235] who 'never read Scripture, but they exhibited great enthusiasm to obey its commands.'[236] Although they almost certainly heard biblical stories and injunctions, these are likely to have been random and anecdotal extracts. Nevertheless, such texts, from senior clerics who were immersed in biblical knowledge and exegesis, could be used to manipulate their presentation of the course of history and individual response to external events as well as retrospectively creating historical myth. It has therefore been possible to a see how a subtle and varied cultural fabric based on biblical texts moderated and, interwoven with exegetical gloss, was used by chroniclers to create a belief about their subject matter. In Iberian chronicles, the experience of biblical interpretation was equally creative and nuanced but arose from a long history of domination by an alien faith and culture and it is that subject that is now considered.

Biblical texts in Spain

The different versions of the Bible that circulated in the Latin west from the times of the early church fathers reveal how these scriptures were exposed to exegesis, commentary and liturgy. Though individual libraries may have had complete copies of the Bible, such acquisitions seem to have been relatively unusual, and few monasteries possessed more than one or two complete volumes until after the invention of the printing press in the fifteenth century.[237] Nevertheless, there is evidence that several complete Bibles had been produced in the Iberian Peninsula during Visigothic times. Because of the difficulties in generating complete copies, scribes often put together scriptural books in separate and smaller volumes.[238] The

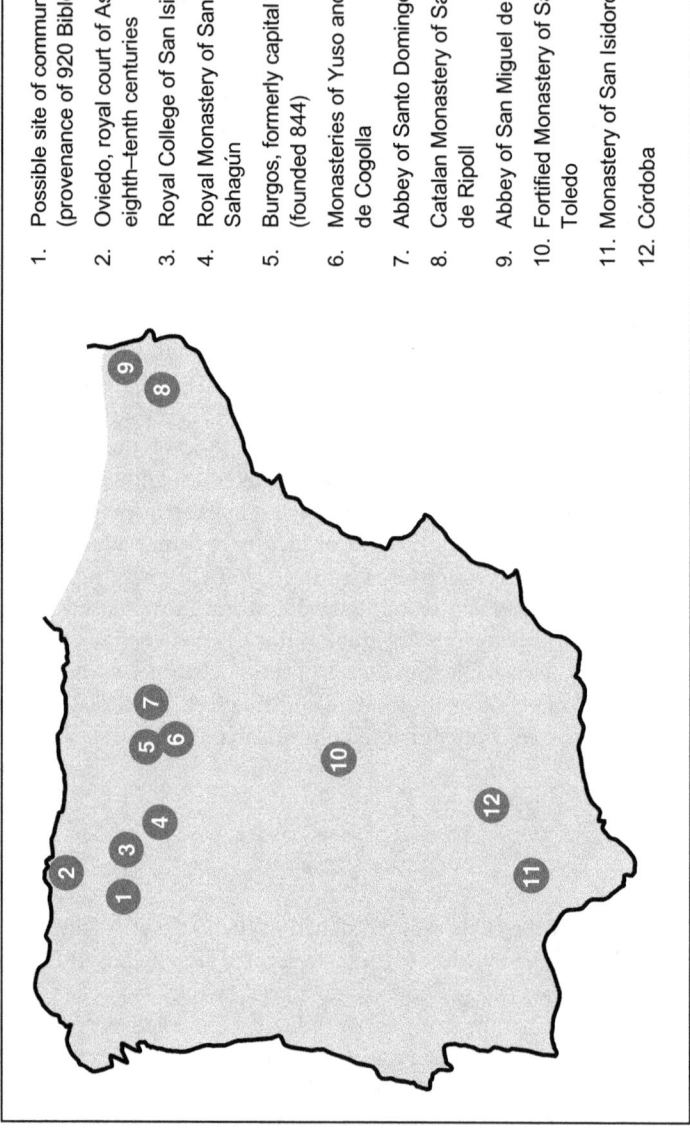

Figure 1.1 Religious houses and monastic communities referred to in Chapter 1 and elsewhere. Reproduced by permission of John Kevan.

dissemination and impact of biblical texts within chronicle writing in the Latin west was key to the production of historical narrative as well as to the presentation of Christian kings, princes as well as the enemies of Christendom.

Central to the writers of the medieval period was the tapestry of biblical texts to which they had access through copies of specific books from the Bible (or fragments of them), commentaries, sermons and liturgy. This was the case in Iberia as elsewhere. And these were not the only ways in which biblical understanding was acquired; indeed, the dissemination of texts was often complex and demonstrated variation and development over time. Here reference is made to some of the few complete copies of the Bible that are known to have existed in Iberia before and during the thirteenth century to which chroniclers may have had recourse, together with a sample of the exegetical material that is known to have circulated in the peninsula.

Early versions

Reference is now made to what is known about the versions of the Bible that circulated in the peninsula and to which Hispano-Latin chroniclers of the twelfth and thirteenth centuries may have had access. Jerome supervised Spanish scribes to copy his translation and, though no version from this early period survives, parts of what were copied were brought into Baetica in the early fifth century.[239] The activity of these scribes suggests that biblical texts were well established in Iberia from this early period.[240] Early versions within the peninsula, including the *Vetus Latina*, continued to circulate alongside Jerome's translation though their use seems to have diminished over time.[241] This transmission of material to Spain was important in establishing the peninsula as fully part of the fifth-century Mediterranean cultural milieu. Visigothic Spain became, in the second half of the sixth century, a route by which the Latin literature of north Africa, both classical and religious, could make its way to northern Europe.[242] The North African-Spanish link existed throughout the sixth century and seems to have included a strong coercive element.[243]

The Vulgate is known to have been circulated widely in the peninsula prior to the Muslim conquest, and although it did not immediately supersede earlier versions, there was a gradual imposition of the Vulgate texts. Acknowledging that a complete and systematic cataloguing of the available manuscripts is thus far incomplete, Klaus Reinhardt and Horacio Santiago-Otero refer to the existence of versions of the *Vetus Latina* in Iberia which seem in some respects to have been more faithful to the Hebrew texts than Jerome's version.[244] Moreover, late antique and early medieval theologians and exegetes supplemented their biblical understanding in a variety of ways. These included biblical paraphrase, treatises against the Jews, theological treatises on biblical themes, scriptural preaching, literature and art inspired by biblical texts.[245] These and other sources, such as sermons, breviaries and commentaries, all found their way into the ecclesiastical libraries and were part of the collective corpus conditioning later medieval Iberian culture as it did elsewhere.

Figure 1.2 León Cathedral Palimpsest, c. 650 AD.
Reproduced under licence from Alamy.

It is conceivable that Leonese-Castilian chroniclers of the twelfth and thirteenth centuries consulted earlier versions of the Bible, be they complete or fragmentary. A case in point is the version of the Bible known as the León Cathedral Palimpsest, a tenth-century compilation of two seventh-century manuscripts, a breviary and certain books from the Bible.

The presence of Visigothic symbols and motifs suggests that it was written in Spain.[246] Furthermore, although Isidore is likely to have analysed and commented upon a version of the Vulgate, no extant edition of the text can be linked with him. Two Andalusian Bibles, now lost, were bequeathed by King Alfonso III (r. 866–910) to the cathedral at Oviedo; one was referred to as the Sevillian Bible because it was rumoured to have been written down by Isidore,[247] but whether these were predominantly *Vetus Latina* versions is not known. Any speculation about how widespread any pre-Vulgate versions were in Iberia needs to be balanced by Isidore's acknowledgement that Jerome had indeed translated the scriptures, and that his translation was used throughout the church.[248] However, we do not know whether Isidore was referring only to the Bible in the Visigothic Church or to more general use of the Vulgate in western Christendom; nor can we be certain that his confidence is an entirely accurate representation of the situation in Iberia. Nevertheless, there was an awareness, acknowledged by all church fathers who followed Jerome, that his translation superseded, even if it did not entirely supplant, earlier versions, despite occasional mistranslations.[249] Loewe too refers to occasional though important examples that tended to contaminate the Spanish texts that were circulating in the fifth and sixth centuries.[250]

By the time the chroniclers of twelfth- and thirteenth-century León-Castile were penning their historical narratives, Jerome's translation had long established itself as the one authoritative version that clerics would have recognized, its long-established use conferring upon it an ancient and unimpeachable authority. This is despite discernible traces of earlier versions within the editions to be found within the peninsula. It was as central to Spanish chroniclers as it was to clerics and historians elsewhere in western Christendom, though those biblical texts copied in Spain had certain recognizable characteristics relating to etymological explanations and marginal text notations that could include extra-scriptural commentary and additions.[251] Such embellishments had the effect of conflating texts from the *Vetus Latina* with Jerome's Vulgate, especially in the NT, where differences between the versions were less marked.[252] Commentaries and other forms of exegesis available to Spanish chroniclers would have included glosses on pre-Vulgate versions likely to have been woven into literate Christian consciousness.[253] The proliferation of such glosses was the subject of research by two Spanish philologists, Ciriaca Morano Rodríguez and Antonio Moreno Hernández in their studies of 1 and 2 Sam. and 1 and 2 Kgs.[254] Their work suggests that they used a text made between the late second and late third century AD. The glosses from this text were later copied on to the Spanish Vulgate Bibles, possibly in the eighth or ninth centuries. Their scholarship is important since they were able to unearth glosses that had not been known to earlier scholars.[255]

An important example of a Bible produced in Spain is the illuminated and three-columned mid-ninth-century La Cava Bible or *Codex Cavensis* (Bibloteca de la Badia, MS. memb. I). It probably originated in Asturias, but possibly in Castile or León.[256] It was written in small round Visigothic miniscule by a scribe known as Danila, though we do not know the scriptorium in which he worked.[257] The *Codex Cavensis* has been housed at La Cava Monastery near Salerno since the twelfth century and contains the whole Bible. The codex includes elements from the *Vetus Latina*, or glosses added to it, especially in the text of the gospels and certain epistles, such as the so-called *Comma Johanneum*.[258] Although the *Codex Cavensis* languished in relative obscurity until the early decades of the nineteenth century,[259] its affinity with certain Italian manuscripts, albeit through a lost intermediary text, is recognized.[260] The ornamentation of the codex, if not the text or subsequent glosses, suggests Carolingian influence.[261] We cannot be certain of the extent of its availability or of its influence in Castile, but we shall shortly be referring to another Bible that was produced in Spain, with which there are some interesting similarities. So even if the *Codex Cavensis* did not have a direct impact on other texts and histories produced in the peninsula, its influence may have been mediated through other, though now missing, material (as suggested by Loewe).[262]

A Bible from the early tenth century and possibly produced in a monastery to the west of León, is the so-called 920 Bible (Cod. 6). The precise provenance of this is obscure since the Bible's colophon is indecipherable.[263] It is also loosely

Figure 1.3 La Cava Bible (Codex Cavensis).
Produced under licence from agefotostock.

described as 'Mozarabic';[264] its lettering is in Visigothic miniscule, but it contains illuminations that are derived from a variety of Iberian sources.[265] Only the second half of this pandect survives and it is now held in the Monastery of San Isidoro in León. It is likely, therefore, to have remained in the proximity of León for most of its existence and was conceivably available to later chroniclers such as Lucas de Túy and the author of the *CLRC*.

The *Codex Cavensis* is noted also for its symbolic representations of biblical scenes and can be compared with the late-tenth-century *Codex Toletanus* (or *Biblia Hispalense*) that came from the south of the peninsula and which is now in the Biblioteca Nacional de España in Madrid. This was written by four copyists of Servandus, the tenth-century bishop of Écija and Baza and completed before 23 December 988.[266] Thought at one time to have come from an earlier period (perhaps mid-eighth century), this codex was given to the Cathedral of St Mary in Seville by Bishop John of Córdoba shortly after its completion.[267] It contains a single finely drawn leaf, the remains of what was a set of Canon Tables; and, like the *Codex Cavensis*, it was written in Visigothic minuscule and arranged in three columns. It contains titles in Hebrew, plus Arabic notes, as well as the *Comma Johanneum*. It includes prefaces, prologues and arguments by Jerome, Isidore and others (some of whom are anonymous), as well as ancient *notae communes* derived from their works.[268] The Canon Tables in the *Toletanus* may owe something to those in the 920 Bible, though they are less stylized.[269]

The *Toletanus* and the *Codex Cavensis* are often considered to be the best examples of the so-called Hispanic tradition and classical representatives of the

Vulgate text in Spain,[270] notwithstanding the pre-Vulgate elements within the *Codex Cavensis*. For us, the important point is that the process of incorporating text from classical and patristic sources was well established by the time the codices were compiled. The overwhelming majority of theological glosses – and particularly the more expansive comments – were drawn from patristic sources and such commentaries were woven into the copying of scriptural books.[271] This process of commentary and elucidation conditioned the ways in which prelates and chroniclers understood their world.

Beatus of Liébana

Of particular interest is the work of Beatus of Liébana (*c.* 730–*c.* 800), a central figure linking the early church fathers with later exegetes from the Carolingian monasteries who gradually infiltrated the northern and north-eastern parts of the peninsula from the end of the eighth century. Beatus made a significant written contribution to the evolving exegetical tradition in northern Iberia. He was an Asturian monk, and a major opponent of Adoptionism and his opposition to this heresy was an important assertion of Christian orthodoxy,[272] though recent scholarship has linked the heresy to Augustine's Christology and Trinitarianism.[273] Adoptionism was also rejected by, among others, Pope Hadrian I (r. 772–95), Agobard of Lyon (*c.* 779–840) and most notably by Alcuin of York. Specifically, it was the theological position itself and the promotion of the teaching of the movement by Elipandus, metropolitan archbishop of Toledo (r. 783–*c.* 808) and Felix, bishop of Urgell (d. *c.* 818) that was repudiated by Beatus in his tract *Adversus Elipandum*[274] as well as by his contemporary Carolingian scholars.[275]

Although few details of the life of Beatus are known,[276] the influence of his exegetical compilation on the religious orders in Iberia was considerable.[277] This may be in part because his work was to receive praise from Alcuin, who led the Carolingian offensive against the Adoptionist heresy. Beatus's most important exegetical work, *Commentaria in Apocalypsin*, whose lavishly illustrated copies became a familiar part of monastic and artistic culture in the monastic houses north of the peninsula until well into the thirteenth century,[278] was heavily dependent on earlier church fathers, including Augustine, Jerome, Ambrose, Gregory the Great, Isidore and Fulgentius.[279] His capacity to bring to light and gather together commentaries, some of which have since been lost,[280] into a substantial work of exegesis, is a major contribution to Spanish ecclesiastical culture.[281] Although no copy from the eighth century remains, a single ninth-century illustrated fragment is still to be found in the monastery at Silos.[282] In addition, the survival of another thirty-one additional manuscripts of his work, copied between the tenth and the thirteenth centuries, speaks volumes for the popularity and influence of his work across northern Spain (primarily in the Kingdom of Asturias-León)[283] and ensured an influence that was to last into thirteenth century, parallel to the period of increased Christian expansion in the peninsula.[284]

The centrality of the Apocalypse to medieval religious thought is evident from the frequency with which apocalyptic material was the subject of exegetical commentary.[285] Such commentaries provided a specific cultural and spiritual environment for clerics and laity alike from the tenth century onwards.[286] Beatus's work became central in Iberian monastic study but could also, in Rose Walker's words, be 'defined broadly as scriptural or "patristic"',[287] enabling subsequent Iberian clerics to be part of an unbroken Western biblical tradition.[288] His work was also part of a corpus of apocalyptic literature, much of which would have been known to medieval Iberian scholars, including material from Jewish, Christian and Islamic sacred books as well as commentaries on them.[289] Beatus's work stimulated its own legacy among Castilian poets, mystics and hagiographers as well as among monks and prelates.[290] Its influence had many manifestations and included a single surviving anonymous sermon from the twelfth century, *De adventu Domini*[291] and the brief thirteenth-century poem *Signos del Juicio Final* by the Riojan priest Gonzalo de Berceo (c. 1197–1264). He studied at the Benedictine monastery of San Millán de la Cogolla,[292] and it was he who was the first named poet from the peninsula to write in the vernacular. *Signos del Juicio Final* focused on the last fourteen days in the world's history and the collective judgement on its souls. This is only part of a body of material that has survived and is an indication of the extent to which interpretations of the Apocalypse became embedded in the Spanish literary tradition.[293]

Although many aspects of Beatus's life are unknown, his legacy in medieval Spanish culture is more certain. His compilation of biblical exegesis, especially the *Commentaria in Apocalypsin*, was especially influential. His wide range of patristic sources confirmed his reputation and that of his exegesis, in spite of miscalculations in his own chronology in which he claimed that the world would end in Spanish era 838 (800 AD).[294] The copies of his commentary or fragments of it, almost all composed within Spain, and the influence of his illustrated Apocalypse cycles have been found in tenth-century manuscripts at scriptoria in Valeránica and S. Millán de la Cogolla, the latter now housed at the monastic library at Escorial.[295] Significant dissemination was evident from the tenth century onwards[296] and evidence of the influence of the commentary is suggested by a later manuscript that was copied and lavishly illustrated by monks at the Silos Monastery near Burgos between 1091 and 1109. This, the so-called Silos Apocalypse (London BL, Add MS 11695) survives in near perfect condition and is likely to have been an important exegetical source for chroniclers of the twelfth century onwards. Nevertheless, motifs illustrating different codices of the Beatus manuscripts seem to have encouraged the perception of anti-Islamic inferences by later chroniclers of the conflict in al-Andalus – whether they were intended by the author or not.[297] Beatus's influence seems to have been sporadic, though his text was lavishly illustrated across the north of Spain between the ninth and thirteenth centuries and was enduring.[298]

Influence from Francia, ninth–thirteenth centuries

From the ninth century onwards, Frankish influence in eastern Spain enriched and gradually altered the biblical and liturgical culture within Iberia.[299] Monasteries in north-eastern Iberia, especially Ripoll and Cuixá, were central to this cultural shift.[300] Carolingian influence within the biblical texts to be found in the peninsula had been tenuous or limited to decorative elements; in the early Carolingian period, Spain seems to have been resistant – or at least unreceptive – to what Loewe calls 'Carolingian biblical endeavour.'[301] Yet Carolingian scholars not only rejuvenated and transmitted patristic texts but wrote their own biblical exegesis as well as theological treatises and their work had an impact throughout the western church.[302] Reference will be made to the cross-cultural links between Francia and Spain, especially in relation to Mozarabic liturgical practices.

Carolingian influence can be found in the so-called San Isidoro or León Bible (*Codex Goticus Legionensis*) of 960, referred to earlier. This was possibly produced under the direction of the monk Florentius of Valeránica.[303] It was itself a model for future copies, including one made for the Real Colegiata de San Isidoro in 1162 and the thirteenth-century Romanesque Bible from San Millán de la Cogolla.[304] However, although the San Isidoro Bible has been linked to earlier illustrated Bibles within the peninsula, it betrays Carolingian rather than Iberian provenance in at least two important respects.[305] These relate mostly to the copying by Florentius of commentaries on liturgical readings by the Benedictine monk, Smaragdus of Saint-Mihiel (*c.* 760–843), whose work we shall shortly consider; elements in the illuminations for the 960 Bible, perhaps also by Florentius, were indebted to Carolingian examples.[306] A further fragment known as the 'Bible of 943' or Oña Bible, is held at the Archive at the Monastery of Silos, and Florentius is the likely transcriber of what remains.[307]

The 960 Bible reveals further Carolingian influence through the work of Theodulf of Orléans (*c.* 760–821), a noted poet, scholar and member of Charlemagne's court. He was of Spanish Visigothic extraction and had been born and brought up in northern Spain,[308] fleeing first to Aquitaine and afterwards being appointed to the see of Orléans in 798. He was responsible for the organization and compilation of the Bible (or, more correctly, family of Bibles, since there are six surviving manuscripts that are closely related).[309] Insertions of Baruch, Wisdom and Ecclesiasticus suggest a link with the *Codex Cavensis* and therefore indicate Spanish textual influence.[310] Theodulf's eclectic text with its several suggestions of influence seems to have been used by Carolingian monks for correcting other versions.[311] There is a clear textual link between the Psalms of the 960 Bible and the Bibles associated with Theodulf, indeed pages from the 960 Bible show verses that bear Theodulf's stamp.[312] Theodulf's reputation rests on his promotion of learning in cathedral schools, his scriptural exposition, poetry and the editing of biblical text.[313] His presence in the court of Charlemagne is testimony to the fact that the court was itself an intellectual phenomenon that included scholars from all over the Latin west, enriched by exegesis and literature from elsewhere as well as influencing biblical scholarship and liturgical practice.[314]

The so-called Touronian or Tours Bible produced between 834 and 843 by Alcuin of York seems to have been part of an unprecedented proliferation in biblical texts, described by Nees as 'unparalleled mass production.'[315] Alcuin's Bible is likely to have been the basis for other copies and some scholars have argued that it was the officially corrected text of the Carolingian Empire.[316] These were the most famous Bibles of the time, though it is likely that there were others, now lost, produced during the ninth century and which combined corrected texts from *Vetus Latina* versions and Jerome's Vulgate.[317] The extent to which these Bibles found their way into Iberia or infiltrated Spanish monastic libraries is not known but since the influence of these Carolingian texts can be detected in the 960 Bible and subsequent Iberian versions, there is likely to have been an awareness of non-peninsular texts from the tenth century onwards.[318]

Monasticism and liturgy

The liturgy that was observed from the time of Isidore until the eleventh century, the Visigothic or 'Mozarabic' rite, differed from that practised in the rest of western Christendom, though it was by no means the only alternative liturgy in the Latin west, nor was it unrelated to other liturgies which were more localized.[319] We have already noted the centrality of monasticism in promoting an understanding of biblical texts and in Visigothic Iberia this was especially so. The monastic rules combined the need for stern asceticism and bodily mortification, especially in texts identified with Fructuosus of Braga-Dumio (d. *c.* 665),[320] with the need for constant reading, reciting, listening to and reflecting on biblical passages. Such activities were pivotal to a monk's daily life.[321] Three surviving rules have been identified, all dating from the seventh century: the Rule of Isidore (early seventh century), the Rule of Fructuosus of Braga (composed sometime after the founding of the monastery of Compludo, 646) and the Common Rule,[322] also attributed to Fructuosus.[323]

However, from the ninth century onwards, the *Regula Benedicti* was gradually established in the east of the peninsula, though it seems to have been resisted in the north and west.[324] The Visigothic liturgy was officially abolished in 1080 at the Council of Burgos, seven years after Pope Gregory VII had declared a campaign against the Muslims, even though the rite could continue to be celebrated in certain parishes. Since the way in which the religious community and the laity communicated with God depended on the repetition and familiarity of a recognizable liturgy, the change to the Roman rite could be seen as undermining the essence and integrity of existing monastic institutions.[325] Gregory's implication that Spain had used the Roman liturgy at the time of its conversion to Christianity[326] meant that the ecclesiastical culture of the Visigothic period and its distinct intellectual tradition were effectively and summarily abandoned.[327] The monastery at Sahagún, under its abbot, Bernard of Sédirac (*c.* 1050–*c.* 1125, abbot between *c.* 1080–85) was an important and early centre that promoted this liturgical shift. He became archbishop of Toledo in 1086. He had originally been at Cluny and it was the Cluniacs, formed in the early tenth century, who had entered Spain in large numbers during the reign of Alfonso VI (r. 1065–1109) and were instrumental in replacing the Mozarabic liturgy with the Roman rite.[328] Nevertheless, in the ensuing centuries, sporadic resistance persisted among the Mozarabic population and certain members of the clergy.[329] Those seeking to impose the Roman rite and Catholic uniformity argued that the Mozarabic rite was contaminated with the heresy of Arianism,[330] as well as tainted by being practised by Christians under

Muslim occupation. In fact, it already contained elements of the Roman Mass, as well as liturgy derived from Orthodox, Galician and Ambrosian sources. Although it was a more ornate and joyful celebration than the Roman rite, the emphasis on the veneration of peninsular saints meant that it was seen by the papacy as a local rather than a universal celebration.[331] In any event, the imposition of the Roman rite led to a cultural chasm in Mozarabic worship in which one tradition was not enthusiastically or seamlessly subsumed into another.[332]

In some respects, distinctions between the Roman and Mozarabic liturgies may be overstated; some saints who received veneration in the Mozarabic liturgy also appear in Roman manuscripts.[333] Furthermore, surviving manuscripts suggest that the pattern of the Mozarabic liturgical year varied in different parts of Iberia since extant copies of the *officia et missae* were produced in a variety of 'non-standardised volumes,' which seem to have been a feature of the Mozarabic Church, not necessarily comprehensive or systematic but individual and idiosyncratic.[334] Nevertheless, there had been infiltration into León-Castile by earlier Frankish clerics which had influenced the Mozarab liturgy without immediately supplanting it,[335] even though there was an expressed drive towards liturgical uniformity.[336] So the liturgical picture in eleventh-century León-Castile is complex and not necessarily or wholly defined by distinctions in religious practice or observation.[337] Yet the numbers of Frankish Cluniac clergy in Iberia during the eleventh century continued to grow and there was a gradual elimination of Mozarabic texts within the homilies to be used; these were replaced with those from the Roman liturgy,[338] even if many manuscripts containing the Mozarabic liturgy were retained in monastic and cathedral libraries.[339] Several senior Cluniac prelates were elevated to major dioceses such as Braga, Toledo, Coimbra, Osma and Santiago,[340] ensuring that progress towards the adoption of the Roman rite throughout the peninsula was relentless.[341] What began with the coming of Cluniac monks to the Benedictine monasteries in Navarre and Aragón laid the foundations for the ecclesiastical revival which by the second half of the twelfth century was well established throughout northern Iberia.[342] This seems also to have enabled the further dissemination of patristic writings.

The Cluniac monks, with their strict adherence to the Rule of St Benedict, prescribed a way of life that was grounded in the reading and hearing of biblical texts – a 'lived exegesis,' as it were, in that such texts were incorporated into all aspects of daily life.[343] Although Benedict is not normally recognized as a church father, his rule has the status of a patristic document in itself;[344] it also prescribes the reading of the Divine Office by those referred to by St Benedict as the orthodox catholic fathers.[345] The rule therefore did not merely affect monasticism and exegetical understanding; in the words of Leclercq, it assumed and evoked 'an entire ancient spiritual milieu.'[346]

The rate at which Cluniac monasteries were established in Iberia decreased from the twelfth century onwards, the Cistercians having assumed the role of the next great monastic reforming movement.[347] Yet the legacy of Cluny was an enduring one and it continued to exercise an influence well beyond the monastery.[348] For at the same time as the Cistercian Order was establishing itself in Iberia, the abbot of the Benedictine abbey of Cluny, Peter the Venerable (c. 1092–1156), was visiting the Cluniac houses in León-Castile (1142–3). This seems to have been part of a polemical exercise against Islam[349] and during his visit he sent a translation of the Qur'an he had authorized, to Bernard of Clairvaux.[350] This translation became part of the *Corpus toledanum*, dedicated to Raymond, archbishop of Toledo (1125–52), a corpus of five Islamic books translated into Latin and forming what Peter referred to as his 'Christian armoury'.[351] Those charged with the writing of the history of León-Castile in the twelfth century would have been aware of the currents of reform and understanding by both Cluniacs and Cistercians. Even if we concede that the reforms of Bernard and the influence of Peter may not have been fully embedded when Pelayo and the author of the *CAI* were penning their chronicles, both men are likely to have been aware of the shifts in the religious and cultural landscape that had already taken place.

Throughout the Middle Ages, monks gained their knowledge of the Bible by hearing biblical texts more often than reading them: (the Bible) 'invaded their memories and came to constitute the furniture and texture of their minds. It was natural in that situation for one text to call forth another, which alluded to another, which led to still another.'[352] This idea of the scriptural culture being a kind of space in which the religious moved and breathed was especially important to Bernard of Clairvaux (1090–1153) whose Cistercian order established some eighty-nine abbeys in Iberia during the twelfth and thirteenth centuries,[353] and this incorporated older monasteries that accepted Cistercian reforms.[354] The twelfth-century Cistercian Revolution has been described as a 'tidal wave' that left no part of Europe, including Spain, untouched;[355] Ann Astell comments on the way in which Bernard's understanding of the bridal soul was involved in a divine quest for God [*anima sitiens Deum*]. In Bernard's commentary on *The Song of Solomon*, the erotic love of Bride and Bridegroom is superseded by a singular perception of love: The bride, according to Bernard, is a soul thirsting for God.[356] The links between the laudable aim to reorientate concupiscence with holy as well as mystical parallels were also part of the teaching of other twelfth-century exegetes from outside the Cistercian order.[357] Nevertheless, it was the 'revolutionary assault' of the so-called Gregorian Reforms of the late eleventh-century popes Alexander II and Gregory II that created the conditions for a vacuum which would be filled by the new monastic orders.[358]

We now turn to the biblical and exegetical texts that are likely to have been available to the northern Iberian chroniclers of the twelfth and thirteenth centuries as we assess the importance and variety of such material that may have been available in the monastic and cathedral libraries in the realms in which they lived and worked.

Libraries and scriptoria in León-Castile

We cannot be certain which biblical texts and commentaries were available to individual Spanish chroniclers from the twelfth and thirteenth centuries to consult; although some texts remained within specific ecclesiastical institutions, others seem to have made their way around the peninsula.[359] Yet the chroniclers of the twelfth century were immersed in a common though recently imposed liturgy and an ancient exegetical tradition. This meant that wherever they studied and wrote, the biblical and cultural environment was central to their understanding of the world and was generally uniform.[360] The culture in which they lived not only implied a shared biblical imagination, but it also extended to common metaphors derived from scripture and which permeated every aspect of life:

> Texts were … performed and lived, to become so internalised that they became rooms in their [the hearers and readers of scripture] souls, exuding energy, light and grace, constantly available to be drawn upon in guiding, reforming and renewing one's life.[361]

Even if there is often a degree of uncertainty about the specific influences that bore down on individual ecclesiastical chroniclers, there is enough material that is datable to the twelfth century and earlier in the cathedral libraries in León and Castile to infer what might have been available to these writers. Here, we can review only examples of what remains (and these in turn represent only a fragment of the original material) but are still able to gain insight into the variety of scriptural and exegetical texts that had been copied in western Iberia by the advent of the twelfth century and how these are likely to have informed the writing of chroniclers. It should be emphasized at the outset that although biblical and liturgical texts and commentaries of various kinds were to be found in ecclesiastical institutions throughout León-Castile, the distribution seems to have been very uneven. In the cathedral treasury at Zamora, for example, there was little written material apart from choir books, before 1265.[362] In order to assess the material that was available to such scholars I have looked, by way of example, at the holdings of two cathedral libraries – at Toledo and Burgos – and of the Library of the Collegiate Church of Saint Isidore in León, which began life as a monastery in the late tenth century. These ecclesiastical centres have been chosen because at least four of the chroniclers who are studied – Rodrigo Jiménez de Rada (author of *DRH*), Lucas of Túy (author of *CM*), Juan of Osma (presumed author of *CLRC*)[363] and the anonymous author of the *HS* – had links with these institutions and I have emphasized possible connections when specific ecclesiastical holdings of exegetical texts are considered. Of course, we cannot know for sure where all these clerics received their training. In the case of the author of the *CAI* (perhaps Bishop Arnaldo of Astorga), for example, it has been speculated that he may have begun his career at the Catalan abbey of Ripoll before serving as prior at the monastery of San Servando in Toledo (*c.* 1127–*c.* 1143) and then being raised to the see of Astorga in 1144.[364] Be that as it may, the surviving texts from Burgos, León and Toledo may serve as a representative 'snapshot' of the range of exegetical material then circulating in Iberia and which to a greater or lesser degree must have shaped both the intellectual horizons and 'historical vision' of our authors.

In the cathedral library at Burgos there are two codices that are particularly worthy of note. They are fragmentary manuscripts containing copies of homilies and sermons based on the gospels and epistles.[365] The one referred to as Codex 1 consists mostly of passages taken from the *Collectiones in Euangelica et Epistolas* by Smaragdus of Saint-Mihiel,[366] together with a few texts emanating from the church fathers.[367] Included in these are Augustine's Tractate 24 on John, a commentary on Matthew by Jerome, Bede's Homily 84, a sermon by Augustine on the Purification of the Virgin Mary, a homily by Ambrose on Lk. 2.58, together with sermons by John Chrysostom and the fifth-century deacon, Leo (d. 461). The *Collectiones in Euangelica et Epistolas* are derived from a collection of patristic texts, the authors of which Smaragdus enumerates in his preface.[368] The codices are very mutilated and much of the damage seems to date from the sixteenth century. The characters are in Visigothic miniscule, suggesting a date of compilation between 1050 and 1150. Although we cannot be certain where these codices originated, it is likely that they were Castilian.[369] The codices are described by Mansilla as having been 'very bulky' and even in their severely damaged and depleted state, contain 146 folios.[370]

The second codex probably comes from the early twelfth century, after the abolition of the Mozarabic rite.[371] Again many of the folios that were originally contained in the manuscript are missing, but what remains suggests a substantial original body of material.[372] There are seven further excerpts from Smaragdus's *Collectiones* in the codex, but the bulk of exegetical work is either from the church fathers and other exegetes or is of unknown origin. There are texts from familiar sources: Augustine, Gregory, Bede and Jerome as well as sermons by Leo the Deacon (d. 461) and homilies by John Chrysostom, St Maximus Confessor (*c.* 580–662), Paul the Deacon (*c.* 725–799) and Hrabanus Maurus.[373] We cannot be certain that these codices originated in Burgos, though Mansilla considers that they have an affinity with other texts that emerged from that region.[374] Furthermore, the impact of Smaragdus's writings, including his commentary on the Rule of St Benedict, influenced attempts at reform in Castile and Navarre during the tenth century.[375] Whether these codices emerged from Burgos or from another Castilian library, it is possible that in their more substantial form they were available to scholars such as Juan of Osma and perhaps other chroniclers too. In Burgos there is a particularly rich codex that includes Daniel, Judith, Esther, the Acts of the Apostles and the Maccabees, in addition to exposition, observations on parts of the Mass, genealogical tables showing the human line of Christ and books of ancient and more recent history.[376] Mansilla also catalogues slightly later material than Codices 1 and 2 in the cathedral library at Burgos, and includes numerous gospel extracts and a much deteriorated sermon of St Augustine on Fasting.[377]

Manuscripts from the cathedral library at Toledo give an indication of the breadth of biblical and exegetical material that was available to clerics and chroniclers in the twelfth and thirteenth centuries.[378] There was a Bible of unknown origin, identified as *Fragmentos de Biblia Vulgata Latina*; this is likely to have been a complete Bible dating from the late eleventh or early twelfth century and written in Caroline minuscule. Included is part of an eleventh-century Bible (containing some OT books, including Joshua and Psalms) written in Visigothic minuscule; and there is a further Bible, also from the eleventh century, in two volumes and a thirteenth-century Bible (without Psalms).[379] In addition, there are extant Bibles that were produced between the eleventh and early thirteenth centuries.[380]

Most of the glosses on biblical texts are also from the thirteenth century, though there are codices containing *glossae ordinariae* of the Pauline epistles as well as twelfth-century glosses on the whole canon of NT letters, the Apocalypse and the Lamentations of Jeremiah.[381] The compilers of the Toledo catalogue believe that the style of the gloss on Lamentations suggests that the text was not merely circulating in Castile during the twelfth and thirteenth centuries but is likely to have been composed in Iberia and possibly at Toledo.[382] Other biblical texts in Toledo with twelfth-century glosses include Daniel, Esdras and Nehemiah; they are also found on the books of two minor prophets and on the gospels of Matthew, Luke and John. There is also a *glossa ordinaria* on the book of Exodus that may date from the early thirteenth century.[383] Although we cannot be sure when the *glossa ordinaria* became widespread in Iberia or the extent to which its content was known to individual chroniclers, the growing collections of scriptural glosses would have enriched the existing biblical and cultural environment in which the scribes worked.

Commentaries, homilies and texts containing biblical exposition are also found at Toledo. Such texts include two fragments of *Moralia* (one from the tenth century, another from the eleventh) and a twelfth-century homily, also by Gregory, on the Prophet Ezekiel.[384] There is an eleventh-century copy of Augustine's commentary on the Sermon on the Mount with various marginal notes, a twelfth-century copy (of which the second half only remains) of Augustine's *Enarrationes in Psalmos 1-50*, extracts from his *Tractatus in Evangelium Johannis* and a collection of sermons (some of which appear to have been written by Augustine, others are anonymous). Jerome is the other patristic figure whose works are housed in Toledo: there is a ninth-century copy of the *Tractatus in Psalmos* and a late-twelfth-century commentary on the minor prophets (Hosea, Obadiah, Jonah, Nahum and Zechariah).[385]

A further text from the library at Toledo is an allegory by Peter of Poitiers (c. 1130–c. 1215) on the Tabernacle (Exod. 25-40)[386] as well as commentaries on Leviticus and the book of Numbers, likely to have been written in the twelfth century.[387] It was he who had accompanied Peter the Venerable to Spain in the early 1140s and, in addition to preparing and orchestrating an ideological struggle against Islam,[388] wrote a whole series of sermon-type prologues which were based on OT accounts to serve an allegorical purpose. He showed himself to be both dependent on Bede and on the Frankish theologian Peter Comestor (d. 1178).[389] Furthermore, a text used by Peter of Poitiers in *Allegoriae super tabernaculum Moysi*, though not cited *verbatim*, supplied him with a starting point for another treatise, *Distinctiones super Psalterium*.[390] The range of texts that might be accessed by clerics would at the same time be varied and complementary; Peter's own work supplied him with models he could use elsewhere in his writings and he could, like his fellow exegetes and priests, be part of an unbroken hermeneutical tradition. It is worth observing that Peter's texts would almost certainly have been available to

Rodrigo Jiménez de Rada whose long tenure as archbishop of Toledo followed the period when these treatises had been written and disseminated.

Important texts are also held at the Library of the Collegiate Church of Saint Isidore in León. In his catalogue of the codices and documents in the Real Colegiata de San Isidoro, Julio Pérez Llamazares refers to 155 manuscripts, many of them illuminated and including two of the Bibles referred to earlier (the 960 and 1162 Bibles). Other significant texts include two copies of *Moralia* (one tenth century in Visigothic minuscule, one twelfth century in Caroline minuscule).[391] The tenth-century *Moralia* is likely to have been copied, at least in part, by Florentius.[392] We know that the *Moralia* was a highly influential and substantial work[393] and dedicated to Leander of Seville.[394] It had circulated in Spain since Visigothic times and Gregory's early impact within the peninsula is demonstrated by the copies of his texts that were available in ecclesiastical libraries.[395]

A significant major holding in the Collegiate Church is a codex of the works of Saint Martín (c. 1125–1203), a canon of the Collegiate. The work, the *Sancti Martini Legionesis opera*, is now in two volumes and contains a collection of sermons together with writings by Augustine, Isidore and Bede. Augustine's many works held at León include pericopes of Mt. 18.15[396] and several from John's gospel.[397] These deal with specific points in Jesus' teaching or are preliminary to them.[398] Martín's codex also contains the first reference in any Spanish text to the writings of Peter Lombard. Martín himself is the subject of a short biography within *Liber de miraculis Sancti Isidori* (chapters 52–75), almost certainly written by Lucas de Túy.[399] Whether or not Lucas was the author of the *Liber*, it seems likely that the future bishop of Túy would have had access to Martín's writings which are likely to have been written in León and where Lucas was canon from 1221 to 1239.

Conclusion

The biblical exegetical heritage and the variety of biblical and cultural material and exposition from which it arose influenced the evolving intellectual climate in Iberia[400] as it did elsewhere. The early exegetes are seen as striving for 'one seamless exposition'[401] and even by the twelfth century the understanding of scripture had been enriched by scholastic exegesis rather than by the imposition of new orthodoxies: 'As had always been the case, so in the twelfth century, the goal of monastic commentators was to inspire unction and compunction in their monastic audience.'[402] Yet our chroniclers were also charged with the writing of history and the collection of written and visual material that derived from a study of biblical texts conditioned the cultural and religious climate. Those clerics who chronicled events within the Iberian Peninsula were part of the monastic and ecclesiastical collective that had been immersed in a biblical and liturgical setting. Biblical historical narrative, which included an intermittent focus on apocalyptic texts, formed an indispensable element in their understanding of the world. This cultural environment was enriched by reading contemplative texts such as the Psalms, which would offer additional opportunities to seek meaning and insight.

As we shall see, the twelfth- and thirteenth-century Castilian chroniclers did not seek to reinterpret the books of the Bible so much as recognize that events in their own time were part of a continuing understanding of their own history; biblical narrative provided models and examples to those who had commissioned their histories as well as dogma, instruction and solace for their cloistered audience.

2

THE *HISTORIA SILENSE* AND PELAYO'S CHRONICLE

This chapter will focus on two chronicles written in the early and mid-twelfth century. The first of these is an anonymous compilation known as the *Historia Silense*,[1] which was almost certainly written between 1109 and 1118 and dealt with a complex and somewhat uncoordinated range of events in the eleventh century, though it also included earlier narratives. The two main sources for the *HS* covering Iberia's history from the late seventh century to the accession of Fernando I, Count of Castile from 1029 to 1037 as king of León in 1037 are *The Chronicle of Alfonso III*, probably composed in c. 883, and the Chronicle of Sampiro.[2] We also analyse a second chronicle known as the *Chronicon Regum Legionensium* [Chronicle of the Kings of León], written by Pelayo, bishop of Oviedo (two terms, 1101–30 and 1142–3), probably in the third decade of the twelfth century. Both the *HS* and a far larger collection of Pelayo's work known as the *Corpus Pelagianum*,[3] which includes the *Chronicon*, incorporate the so-called chronicle of Sampiro, attributed to Sampiro, bishop of Astorga from 1034 until his death in 1041. Furthermore, the chronicle, notwithstanding its importance and uniqueness within eleventh-century historiography, does not exist as an independent historical work.[4] Yet the two versions of *Sampiro*, the one intended as a continuation of *The Chronicle of Alfonso III* and the redaction, which is within the *HS*, are not identical either in length or in authorial intention.[5]

Despite the textual problems of the *HS* and those related to brevity and opportunism within the *Chronicon*, these chronicles are a valuable commentary on what might be seen as a period of transition in Castilian chronicle writing. The narrative of the *Chronicon* is more compressed than that of the *HS* and there is a greater sense of chronological progression. Both chronicles are part of a small body of chronicle writing undertaken in León-Castile during the early twelfth century, the others being the *Historia Compostelana*, the *Chronicon Iriense*[6] and the *Crónicas anónimas de Sahagún*.[7] The *HS* and the *Chronicon* are an important link between the chronicles of the restless and sometimes resentfully conquered and those written by the emerging and ambitious conquerors, somewhere between lament, indignation, oppression and confident aspiration. There is also a recurring theme of lament linked to the suggestion that the sins of the Visigothic monarchs had been visited on the Iberian Christians' divine punishment. Such a lament is most famously present within the *Mozarabic Chronicle of 754*.[8] In his discussion of what he refers to as a 'collective ethic myth,' Luís A. García Moreno links these expressions of grief in the *Chronicle of 754* to an overriding sense of the inherent superiority of Spain over neighbouring territory. García links this sense of self-belief to ideas in Isidore's *Laus Hispaniae*[9] and this spirit of conviction and assuredness also found expression in the *HS*. As much as an aggressive assertion of purpose as a mournful reflection, this was soon to find full voice in the *CAI*, written during a period of military success and optimism in León-Castile and possibly by someone close to the emperor, Alfonso VII. Nevertheless, both the *HS* and the *Chronicon* reveal traces of biblical influence, knowledge and narrative suggesting a sense of Judaic-Christian teleology as well as a consistent and evolving view of the Muslim enemy. These chronicles are considered in the order in which they are likely to have been written, though common biblical themes and allusion also form an important textual and ideological comparison.

The *Historia Silense*

The *HS* has a likely earlier date of composition than the *Chronicon* and was probably written between 1109 and 1118.[10] It begins with a lament on the fate of Hispania; the author makes an early reference to the Roman emperor Constantine (r. 306–337) and then moves swiftly on to the reign of the Visigothic king Wittiza (d. c. 710).[11] It concludes with the death of King Fernando I in 1065, though there is an earlier oblique reference to the capture of Toledo by the Christians in 1085.[12] Perhaps because it incorporates three separate blocks of narrative (in addition to the author's own account), it is unsurprising that the *HS* lacks a clear chronological framework.[13] It contains a version of *Chronicle of Sampiro* which had been completed perhaps more than seventy years before the writer of the *HS* compiled his work. In addition to the *Chronicle of Sampiro*, a further section has been inserted within the *HS*. This is of uncertain authorship or intention[14] and in Pérez de Urbel's edition this is identified as chapters 39–47. It begins with the reign of Alfonso III and ends abruptly by breaking off part-way through a sentence with the words *Post cuius obitum*[15] which follows the account of the death of Ordoño II (924) and may have had implications that extended beyond his reign.[16] The *Chronicle of Sampiro* which follows this insertion also begins with the accession of Alfonso III and ends with the reign of Alfonso V (r. 999–1027).

The provenance of the *HS* is debated: some scholars have suggested that it may have been written at the Monastery at Silos, Sahagún or the Community of St Isidore at León. A record of the period described in the *HS*, including the author's crucially important coverage of the ascendancy of León, is confusing and inadequate and the text is described by Fletcher as 'desperately corrupt,'[17] the earliest extant manuscript being perhaps 350 years distant from any original. The text is in the form 'of a series of unreconciled notices and overlapping drafts,'[18] though this view of the *HS* has been challenged.[19] In spite of these difficulties with the text itself, it has been possible to advance a hypothesis about the place where it might have been written. The community at Léon, where the remains of Isidore were installed in 1063 (a description of their transfer from Seville to

León is contained in the *HS*, chapters 96–102), is considered by some scholars to be the most likely location for the authorship of *HS*,[20] with the monastery at Silos seeming to be the least likely provenance. This is not universally accepted; Linehan believes that Sahagún is a likely place of composition,[21] and José Canal Sánchez-Pagín sets out to make just such a link, remarking that if the document had a Leonese provenance, it is surprising that this is not referred to by the author:

> it would be surprising if, once he had announced that he had subjected his neck to the yoke of Christ [at St Isidoro], he did not refer to it at least once to its convent throughout his account.[22]

We can have no idea as to the identity of the author, though it is possible to suggest the types of monastic libraries to which he may have had access.[23] His familiarity with biblical texts, as well as with classical writers such as Ovid, Virgil and particularly Sallust, clearly indicate that he had a well-stocked classical background with access to a range of significant monastic collections.[24] He also drew extensively on Einhard's *Vita Karoli* (written, c. 817–830) as well as on Gregory the Great, Isidore and on other works which were less well known, including an early Latin hagiographical text.[25] The author's use of these authors and of quotations from biblical texts, provide literary allusions[26] and, more interestingly, help to create what Pérez de Urbel sees as an incongruous epic tone in his historical narration.[27] In addition, the author leans heavily on both Sallust and Einhard for inspiration for his account of the Leonese monarchy between 1037 and 1072 (the reign of Fernando I, Sancho II and the early years of Alfonso VI) as well as for the much wider scope of his narrative which runs from the time of Wittiza:

> He has read and reread them and he uses their phrases as if they were a methodical arrangement of ready clichés to treat a determined subject or to develop an idea: the description of a battle, the death of a notable, the conclusion of a pact, the progress of an army, etc. [28]

If this is so, that the author of the *HS* almost strains to give his narrative an ancient authority, it is probable that biblical texts too have a similar function within the chronicle. They enrich the history that the author is describing as do the texts he selects from classical authors and the church fathers. Biblical influence is evident throughout the chronicle, though references, along with those from classical sources, serve more often as literary flourishes that add texture to the narrative; they are less often used as polemic or to justify vengeance, though, as we shall see, the collective sins of an unspecified number [*irremisse diuersis flagitiis irretitos*] are central to the fall of the Visigothic kingdom.[29] Pérez de Urbel, who does not seek to exaggerate the direct use of biblical passages in the *HS*, nevertheless acknowledges the author's awareness of scriptural texts as sources for the narrative. He also draws attention to the use of specific phrases which were borrowed from Paul's letters, though texts are sometimes misremembered and incorrectly recorded, one of which is from a section on Pelayo and includes a nonsensical reference to the

Battle of Covadonga.[30] There was therefore a widespread, if not always direct or coherent, use of biblical sources, the memory of which may, on occasions, have been muddled. An essential consideration of the way biblical texts are invoked by the author as well as the way his narrative is conditioned by biblical precedent. Pérez de Urbel and his co-editor Atilano Gonzalez Ruiz-Zorrilla of the *HS* also note that even if the author's reminiscences and embellishments of biblical and patristic texts as well as his selection of familiar phrases are sometimes obscure or misremembered, it is nevertheless possible to infer likely ancient sources.[31]

The references to Alfonso VI, already noted, do not amount to a *gesta* of the emperor in spite of an intention to do so by the author.[32] This omission is clear but this does not necessarily mean that we have a text that is fundamentally undermined by errors and corrections or that Sampiro's narrative has been crudely inserted. The value of the *HS* is acknowledged 'as a literary work and as the principal narrative source for the kings of León during much of the eleventh century.'[33] This is in contrast to Linehan's view that the importance of the *HS* as a single source for the period from the late ninth century until the mid-eleventh century is diminished by its grievous weaknesses.[34] Despite its difficulties as a literary and historical compilation, the *HS* remains a repository of biblical and classical narrative and therefore is able to make a valuable contribution to the overall impact of holy text on the chronicles of León-Castile even if its clarity is frequently compromised. Although there is considerable overlapping of ideas and preoccupations within the chronicle, Fletcher believes that these nevertheless constitute a single vision that allows the author to use past events to bring comfort during a troubled period of León-Castile's history.[35]

Events in the *HS* are sometimes confusingly presented.[36] The chronology is interrupted with various insertions and resumptions, yet there are clear themes that resonate throughout the chronicle. These include the conduct, legitimate genealogy and orthodoxy of kings, and the author is therefore able to assert that the kingdom of León is the legitimate political successor to the Visigothic monarchy. This may be evident from the seemingly important incorporation of a lengthy account (chapters 97–103) on the translation of the remains of Isidore of Seville to León in 1063. The author is also preoccupied with the Christian-Muslim conflict and the ways in which this has been used to exact retribution on the Iberian people. Notably, he is hostile to the Franks and dismissive of the impact of Charlemagne in assisting the Iberian Christians in their struggle against the Muslim enemy.[37]

The Historia Silense and the kings of Spain

If we take the author of the *HS* at his word, we must assume that it was his intention to present a dispassionate record of the kings of León, 'However, my sole aim is to write down the exploits of the kings.'[38] He also writes of the miraculous manifestation of Isidore who appears as a vision before Bishop Alvito of León.[39] Sometimes he included what might be considered excessive detail. For example, following the brave and pious exploits of Fernando I in Lamego, Coimbra and

Santiago in 1057/8, the author feels it important to justify the inclusion of certain details:

> I considered that the articulation [of divine help] would be appropriate [*dignum duxi*], so that it would be plain to everyone that his most faithful prayer was answered by God.[40]

Nevertheless, this inclusion of detail is at times tangential and reflects the author's desire to comment on the deeds of the kings. And there is the further suggestion that links the piety and bravery of kings such as Fernando I with subliminal biblical references to specific Hebrew kings: 'It may be, therefore, that our author was ultimately stirred to literary activity by commentaries on the Old Testament's Books of Kings.'[41] This is not directly demonstrated and may only be inferred from the text together with the author's own stated desire to link the historical events of tenth- and eleventh-century León with biblical precedent. These links sometimes appear tenuous, but the fellowship between God, king and people constantly asserts itself.[42] He is reluctant to list the number and frequency of miracles[43] or to refer to whom such miracles might be acknowledged or even those who might benefit from miraculous intervention. Yet the author's approach to divine or godly intercession is not always consistent, especially when considering the way such involvement may be procured. This is the case even when a biblical text is suggested. Nowhere is this more complex than in chapter 88.[44] Here, following the unceasing efforts by St James to intercede on behalf of Fernando I to ensure victory at Coimbra, we are told that the king's success had been a form of heavenly concession [*celitus concessum triumfum*].[45] Yet this miracle, or piece of divine grace, is within the context of the deeds of Fernando I and is consistent with the king's direct appeal which is an invocation of Jn 15.16: 'that whatsoever ye shall ask of the Father in my name, he may give it to you.' Was the success at Coimbra related more closely to the relentless petitioning of St James as intercessor, or to the direct appeal of the king himself? The suggestion is that the intervention has been granted because of Fernando's supplications, though it was made known [*innotuit*] by the apostle of Compostella, though the recipient of this saintly transmission is not specified.[46]

Fundamental to the author's understanding of Iberian kingship is the individual king's place within a recognized and legitimate lineage. This did not mean that accession to kingship would be seamless or uncontested, even if chroniclers emphasized perceived qualities of their subjects rather than on their more violent or dubious appropriation of territory. Fernando I, whose own acquisition of León is disputed, made way for his second son, Alfonso VI, seemingly his father's favourite, to inherit the symbolic and prestigious region of León. Furthermore, Fernando's declaration, in 1063, on the distribution of his kingdom was made on the occasion when the translation of the remains of Isidore of Seville in the city of León were celebrated.[47] Actions and personal qualities, although significant enough to be meticulously reported, are not in themselves sufficient without an attempt to assert ancestral legitimacy. The idea of an ancient and impeccable lineage is powerfully and frequently asserted. Although this is not done by a direct appeal to biblical precedent, the author would certainly have been aware of the importance of lineage within the OT and to specific verses where the importance of lineage was stressed.[48] In the *HS*, the importance of such a line could hardly be more direct: 'Alfonso [i.e. Alfonso VI, r. 1065–1109] therefore, rose from the illustrious Gothic line [*prosapia ortus*], was of vast power both in capacity for judgement and arms to a point scarcely encountered among men.'[49] Although the author embellishes his claims concerning the legitimacy of kingship with literary quotations, the lineage is unambiguously expressed:[50]

> The kingdom, then, was legitimised by its past, its ancestry. So too was its ruling dynasty. Possibly unaware that the Visigothic monarchy had been elective, not hereditary, the author could allude in chapter 15 – in another of his additions to the *Chronicle of Alfonso III* – to the *stirps regalis Gotorum*, 'the royal stock of the Goths.'[51]

Whether or not the author had any awareness of the Visigothic institution of an elective monarchy, he links the royal house of León with what he perceives to be a venerable and divinely endowed authority. He seeks to assert the supremacy of the king's bloodline by linking Alfonso VI to Alfonso I, King of the Asturias (r. 739–757) who in turn was descended from Reccared, the first Visigothic Catholic king (r. 586–601 and who was revered for his decision to renounce Arianism in 589).[52] Later, the author declares his intention carefully to weave together [*texere statui*] the genealogy of Alfonso VI.[53] This involved omitting some early Asturian kings from his genealogy who were not directly related to Alfonso I.[54] Furthermore, although the author's streamlined presentation of Alfonso VI's ancestors may represent a skilful and original departure from the more familiar and prosaic genealogical tables, such tampering suggests that the author wanted to stress a more refined lineage, drawing attention to the restoration of the legitimate Asturian kingdom. He drew particular attention to Alfonso I (r. 739–757) and his successor (and brother), Fruella I (r. 757–768).[55] The idea of editing out those who might be seen as spurious, awkward or unnecessary, which would cast doubt on the attempt to demonstrate a clear line of descent, is one that is familiar in scriptural genealogical compilations. Three consecutive kings of Judah are omitted from Matthew's genealogy of Jesus (Mt. 1.1-16), Ahaziah, Jehoash and Amaziah. Nevertheless, the 'generation of Jesus Christ,' listed in Mt. 1, which proceeds from Abraham (not, be it noted, from Adam or even Noah) is presented in a truncated form: genealogy is traced through the line of David and among those who came to rule and inhabit Judah, rather than through the kings and their heirs who lived in the more populous and initially more prosperous northern kingdom, Israel. It was after all, the northern kingdom that had rebelled against Solomon's son, Rehoboam, effectively isolating itself from mainstream Judaism.[56] Furthermore, the holy city of Jerusalem remained in Judah, not Israel. Even if the author of the *HS* was unaware of a possible parallel between the three kings omitted from the biblical genealogy and those removed from his own, he would almost certainly have known of the considerable genealogical sifting that had taken place in biblical narrative (compare, for example, the list of kings in 2 Kgs with the lineage of Jesus in Mt. 1). If this was the pattern he chose to emulate, his fine-tuning and ability to master his material suggests that he was well acquainted with what he understood to be biblical practice and purpose.

It is therefore at least feasible that the author sees the conduct and response of God towards the Spanish people as being linked to the behaviour and expectations of the kings upon whom he comments. Although he says little more about Alfonso VI, he unquestionably eulogizes both the king's qualities and lineage. The descriptions of Alfonso (contained in chapters 7–10 and dealing with matters relating to his other family members as well as the author's own stated intentions) make a succinct assertion of the king's remarkable qualities, legitimacy and orthodoxy.[57]

Central to the author's argument is the endurance of the Gothic monarchy and the bloodline that legitimized the descendants of Reccared and Alfonso I. He also deals with specific kings – sometimes at length, sometimes fleetingly, despite a declared reluctance to dwell either on the behaviour of kings or the loss of his homeland: 'In truth, it grieves me to allude to the destruction of my ancestral land and the perverse conduct of its kings.'[58] However, he is explicit about what has laid the kingdom low just as he praises the qualities of individuals. In referring to the wickedness of kings, he conflates two short passages from Sallust's *Bellum Catilinae* and *Bellum Iugurthinum*, to justify his need to dwell on the subject. The conduct of kings (accompanied by a complex and lurid reference to King Wittiza, r. c. 692–710)[59] is reminiscent of Jeremiah's graphic picture of the desolation of Judah in which, in a peroration against idolatry, the prophet refers, inter alia, to 'the wickedness of the kings of Judah.'[60] As prefigured in a warning to the Children of Israel in Deuteronomy,[61] the consequences for God's people are dire: 'Behold, I will set my face against you for evil, and to cut off all Judah.'[62] Yet the author of the *HS* does not shrink from heaping praise on kings such as Vermudo II (king of Galicia and León, 984–999), describing him as 'a nobleman of substantial skills' (this contrasts with the far more critical portrait of Vermudo by Pelayo). The final peroration for Vermudo II which the author places just before the section dealing with the restoration of the resting place of St James is reminiscent of the words of the *Magnificat*.[63] Here the purposes of both the heavenly and earthly kings coincide: 'The heavenly king, remembering his mercy, caused retribution to fall on his enemies.'[64]

The presentation and assessment of kingship within the *HS* take place alongside a wider consideration of godly retribution;[65] it bears comparison with the prophecy of Baruch, subtitled in the NEB as 'A message to a conquered people.'[66] It is delivered following the Chaldeans' (or Babylonians') sack of Jerusalem in 587 BC and, although God's people are in captivity in an alien land, their plight may be compared with that of Iberian Christians living under Muslim rule in what had in effect become the land of alien occupation. At the beginning of the *HS*, the author refers to those who had tasted of the 'spring of wisdom' [*fontem sapientie*][67] and who had, in spite of their earlier reverence for learning, subsequently been overwhelmed by the power of the enemy.[68] The author is indebted to Baruch's use of the same phrase[69] and, indeed, the context of the use of *fontem sapientie* in the Book of Baruch is one in which understanding and learning have been lost and need to be rediscovered in order that God's purposes might be fulfilled, and such an observation is continued into the following verse.[70] And in the first chapter of the *HS*, the link with Ps. 25.10 ('All the paths of the Lord are mercy and truth') is noted by Pérez de Urbel and Ruiz-Zorrilla,[71] suggesting the author's deliberate use and incorporation of a familiar well-known image in his own narrative, and indeed the similarity of the Latin of Ps. 25.10 in the Vulgate and that contained in the short passage in chapter 1 of the *HS* is very striking.[72] A biblical provenance seems obvious even if we cannot be emphatic that this was mediated through a liturgical source or from memory.[73]

However restrained or understated the commentary on the lives and reigns of some of the kings may have been, the pattern of making reference to kings themselves and also to those who surrounded and advised them was recognized as a familiar element in biblical narrative and closely linked to genealogical representation. Unfavourable comment on the conduct of David (as in 2 Sam. 11.27) had been picked up in *Sampiro*[74] and the *HS* contains many echoes of the consequences of an incompetent, fickle and morally confused leadership. This perversion of kingship tore apart the kingdom of the Children of Israel and this would enable the author of the *HS* – and others – to use this biblical episode as a measure by which the exercise of power within the emerging kingdom of León might be judged and the kind of punishment that could be meted out on God's people. The author's view about the uncompromising attempts of Ramiro II of León to shore up his kingship is not entirely clear: Ramiro had blinded his half-brother – who had briefly reigned as Alfonso IV (925–31) – as well as the three sons of Fruella II in order to crush opposition and deter potential rivals. Nevertheless, the author tells us that the land will again be overrun by Muslims, though not until the reign of his son, Sancho I (r. 956–958, 960–966).[75] His warning harks back to the days of the struggle between the ancient Israelites and their neighbours:

> Just as foreign races pressed the Israelites in many ways (*or* various races scourged the Israelites), because of their many shameful acts [*diuresis flagitiis*], so by divine permission, the Moors were able to exercise control over the Spanish (people). [76]

God had allowed the Muslims to advance in tenth-century Léon, just as he had permitted the Israelites to descend into political impotence and confusion; lineage, though central in establishing the veracity of Christian kingship, did not confer unfettered divine approval.

The author was concerned about the reputation of individual kings. Sound kingship is linked to military success as well as to individual piety.[77] The author's most reverential praise is reserved for the life and especially the last days of Fernando, who is sometimes represented as 'the true hero of the *Historia Silense*'.[78] He was certainly the champion of the capture of Coimbra in 1064 and his devotions before the city's fall include the prayerful confidence probably derived from John's gospel which, as we noted, complemented the intervention of James of Compostela resulting in the perceived veracity of Christian mission and military victory. The eulogy to the king is adorned with descriptions based largely on Einhard's *Vita Karoli*, a text that the author clearly revered, even if he was hostile to Charlemagne himself.[79] The death of Fernando is set within a deeply liturgical context. Because of the likely date of composition of the *HS*, it is improbable that the author was an eyewitness to the events surrounding Fernando's death,[80] yet the details demonstrate his meticulous knowledge of the ceremonial character of the Mozarabic rite that accompanied the final moments of the king's life. In particular, the king's closing prayer of committal is based on the OT recognition of God's omnipotence and generosity: 'O Lord, Thine is the power, the kingdom; thou art over all kings … and therefore I return to thee the royal authority which I received as gift from thee.'[81] Bishko does not believe that this was part of the Christmas Day liturgy, though it was used at other times in the Mozarabic breviary.[82] Furthermore, the liturgical prayer is clearly derived from the OT prayer preceding the death of King David,[83] although it is an abbreviated and slightly altered version.

Punishment, retribution and reward

The idea of an orthodox kingship linked to ancient lineage was central to the author of the *HS*, who used classical descriptions and biblically derived ideas to create greater legitimacy. In addition, and crucially, the *HS* provides us with a reflection on the nature of God and how the behaviour of kings and rulers affected the course of divine retribution, pity and forgiveness. Furthermore, the significant references to the ruin of the author's homeland, *me patrie exitii*,[84] are indebted to biblical narrative as is the fraternal enmity and is a recurring, though intermittent, theme.

It is clearly painful [*pigeret*] for the author to recall the circumstances surrounding the events that permitted the alien occupation of Spain – *barbaras gentes Yspaniam ocupare permisit*[85] – yet the decline and the humiliation of his people are rooted in their own sins and wilfulness. For example, he assigns some, caught in their shameful acts, to perpetual retribution.[86] He invites his readers to compare the heavenly joys accorded to the righteous[87] with the eternal damnation reserved for those enmeshed in sin. He also refers to a third group, those who will be purged in a transitory fire,[88] an idea that is both biblical and patristic.[89] He consciously invokes Ps. 109.29, and the *HS* version can be translated as follows: 'May they bury themselves in confusion, just like a cloak [wrapped around the body]'[90] to describe the confused torment of the recipients of God's wrath, yet the whole of the introduction is laced with OT-derived notions of judgement, punishment and reward.

Biblical precedent is both explicit and implied in chapter 1 to justify the punishment inflicted on the people of Iberia. The idea of God being provoked to anger is a frequent and uncompromising image, and several verses in Deut. 32 are explicit about the fire that is kindled in God's anger ('for a fire is kindled in my anger')[91] and his full wrath is meted out on his fickle and faithless people: 'They shall be burnt with hunger, and devoured with burning heat, and with bitter destruction: I will also send the teeth of beasts upon them, with the poison of serpents of the dust.'[92] This is the possible context in which the author of the *HS* viewed the fate and saw his own people and homeland. The language of the *HS* is almost apocalyptic, presaging long and unbearable punishment in which, recalling the biblical flood, few would be saved [*paucis christianorum reseruatis*].[93] Thus the prelude to the author's lament is grounded in OT history and this is further underpinned by his references we have already noted to the corrupt behaviour of kings: *prauosque mores regem*.[94]

From the outset, the author demonstrates his awareness of the ways such narrative might be played out in the events of the times he is describing: 'Thus it follows that for those who remain unchastised, the anguish of the said punishments will be the beginnings of the torture that will follow.'[95] Central to this consideration of possible parallels between the Hebrews and the Iberian Christians is the chronicler's approach to the enemies of Christendom and, the idea that, for the author of the *HS*, the Christians were indeed 'the new Israelites.'[96] Yet though it is possible to infer such an idea from the text, nowhere is this directly asserted by the author and the use of such a phrase may be to overplay the biblical comparison. The author's reference to a historical precedent implies a comparison rather than a precise identification. Possibly, the author's hatred of the Muslims was matched only by his denigration of those he calls 'Franks'[*Franci*], who are linked to the 'Arian party' in Narbonne and its attempts to manoeuvre the Hispanic throne away from King Reccared.[97] The tirade against the Franks continues in chapter 18. Here, the author refers to the claims of Frankish military successes against the Muslims in the north of the peninsula prior to Charlemagne's Spanish incursion in 778 as a deception.[98] So, the Iberian Christians are to be distinguished from the Franks and are in a separate and favoured category.[99] But his attitude to the Muslim threat is more complex. As in the OT, the enemies of the Hebrew people are used by God to punish an immoral and faithless generation as well as feckless and treacherous leadership. This would seem to be the case when the legendary and perfidious Count Julian of Ceuta[100] and the equally ambiguous 'sons of Wittiza' who sought the protection of the Muslims.[101] They collaborated with the Muslims in 711 in the overthrow of King Rodrigo (688–711), the last Visigothic king – who had deposed Wittiza in the previous year. Yet in eighth-century Spain, as in Israel during the time of the Judges and despite contemporary lamentation, the will and judgement of God, of which the Muslim advance was an integral part, would ultimately prevail.

A further example of this pattern of collaboration, treachery, betrayal and devastation is found in the description of the confrontation, probably in 984, between Ramiro III (961–985), 'still of tender years,'[102] and the *hajib* or grand vizier Almanzor (*c*. 938–1002).[103] Whatever the accuracy of the historical background to this encounter, there can be no question that the Muslim enemy is shown as having seized the opportunity presented by an apparent power struggle within the Christian kingdom. The author records this hiatus and opportunity as having been prompted by a further contest for supremacy following the death of Sancho I of León, whose hapless period as king ended with his death in 966:

> Therefore, when the barbarian (Almanzor) heard about this strife between the Christians he crossed the River Duero at a shallow place, a strip [*limite*] that marked the boundary [*vado traiecit*] between the Christians and barbarians.[104]

Yet the self-inflicted weakness of the Christians, both in 711 and in the 960s, seems only to constitute one element – though a crucial one – in determining the success of their Muslim enemies. The author of the *HS* is equally conscious of the virtues of the leaders of Islam who were to be victorious over Rodrigo (711) and in the following century over Ramiro I, king of the Asturias (846). In this respect the author is in line with a convention that routinely lauded, and even exaggerated, the bravery and strength of a victorious enemy.[105] Hulit, who is listed with Count Julian and Tariq ibn-Ziyad, and who successfully invaded Spain in 711, is described as 'the most powerful [*fortissimus*] (or courageous) barbarian king in all Africa'[106] and, although *fortissimus* literally refers to strength or power rather than courage, the praise is unreservedly fulsome. A similarly flattering portrait is painted of the conqueror of León, Almanzor, 'the most distinguished foreigner of all,' and again the epithet used on this occasion, *maximus*, could allude to might, power or distinguished military service. The picture of Almanzor in the following chapter (71) is of a man with rare leadership qualities who identifies with the humiliation as well as the triumph of his troops[107] and who is also credited with the creative ability to form alliances which enabled him to achieve military success in León but also in Pamplona and against the Franks.[108] And although he is impious and profane, he is used by the Christian God for divine retribution. The picture is therefore more mixed but suggests that the author recognizes Almanzor's qualities. Despite qualities as a leader, his end was a gruesome and ignoble one (Almanzor was stolen away near the noble city of Medinaceli by a demon who had possessed him in (his) life to be interred in the place of the damned).[109] Bravery and leadership would not sufficiently compensate for Almanzor's separation from the Christian faith. Apparently, he was punished for blasphemy and dangerous adventurism: 'he casually (or recklessly) degraded all that was consecrated.'[110] He had been used by God to implement divine retribution on the Christians between 988 and 1002 but this godly intervention was replaced by divine mercy[111] – not, it seems, because of any Christian repentance but because God was moved to pity for the Christians of Spain and wished to spare them further ordeal. So, there is the important though speculative inference that the divine denouement might take place without being entirely determined by the behaviour of his people, though the idea that their conduct was unimportant in determining the forgiveness of God is to miss the point. Punishment for His people would not last forever (as the author makes clear in his introduction) and forgiveness would be linked to divine purpose: 'yet God chastens but to save and it is he who helps the Spaniards to deliver the Holy Church from the power of Islam.'[112]

Allied to the principle of sound lineage is the idea that biblical figures could provide models for comparison and emulation. Yet such examples are rarely stated directly in the *HS*[113] and biblical precedent can only be inferred for the kings of León. Nevertheless, the early biblical examples of fratricide, as well as betrayal and enmity, would have provided a familiar backdrop, whether they were to supply subliminal messages or to be more blatantly invoked. Furthermore, there is the suggestion that the author – on at least two occasions – alludes to some kind of greater good emerging from fraternal strife, a truth which lies at the heart of the conflict between Jacob and Esau as well as with Joseph and his brothers.[114] First, in dealing with the death of Fernando I and the subsequent war that broke out because of sibling rivalry, the author hints at biblical precedent, though the author's narrative at this point appears arcane and elusive:

> So powerful was the dissent among the brothers [i.e. Fernando's two sons, Sancho and Alfonso], that who can doubt that between men this has existed from the beginning [*ab initio*] – apart from he who has yielded to other activities and cannot pay attention to the study of reading.[115]

This is a confusing sentence but key to this idea is ab initio, 'from the beginning.'[116] Fraternal strife might have a higher purpose, one that is blest by God, and the author elaborates on what this might mean by suggesting that royal authority could supersede loyalty to brothers and parents.[117] Secondly, in the rivalry between the brothers Alfonso and Sancho, in which Alfonso is exiled to Toledo (1072), the purposes of God are much more directly stated (but we also believe that this was achieved by the prudent inclination of God).[118] Alfonso's period of banishment enabled him to make allies among the Muslims within the city of Toledo and increase his personal and military prestige. Such cross-border collaboration and diplomacy was not only a feature of eleventh-century power politics and diplomacy in Iberia, it could be represented as God's opportunity and there are parallels with Joseph's banishment, period of exile and subsequent rise to power in another alien land, Egypt. Joseph's survival and growth in influence in the hands of a providential and far-seeing creator are key elements in the OT narrative. Perhaps too, Alfonso's own single-minded ruthlessness in the treatment of his younger brother García of Galicia – who was captured and imprisoned in 1072[119] – served to emphasize his personal determination and military prowess as well as introducing further complexity into the ideas of banishment and brotherhood.

There are other parallels that may be made with Alfonso VI, suggesting biblical precedent. If the author is indebted to the morality and genealogy within the Books of Kings, the link with biblical figures may be pursued a little further. King David is referred to directly[120] and may be linked to the 'most serene king,' Fernando I.[121] And the author's references to Isidore may indeed make the link more secure. Isidore is clearly a towering figure whose presence infuses much of the chronicle and whose works are integral to its content. Isidore had written about Solomon's reign and commented on his teaching in the *Sententiae* and the work contains seventeen separate references to the legacy of the OT king.[122] Furthermore, the image that emerges from the *Sententiae* contributes to the idea of Solomon as a brilliant, wise, but ultimately flawed king whose kingdom was ultimately to fall apart under his son, Rehoboam. So, one reading of the military and dynastic reversals in the reign of Alfonso VI following his capture of Toledo in 1085[123] make it possible to infer parallels between the reign of Solomon and that of the conqueror of Toledo.[124] David and Solomon could be construed as models for Fernando I and Alfonso VI. But what we have are little more than inferences; despite the implications within the texts of Isidore and his significance for the author of the *HS*, the author makes much more frequent and emphatic use of the works of classical scholars such as Virgil and Sallust as well as of Einhard's *Vita Karoli*. The author included a restated passage from Einhard in chapter 81, dealing with the way Fernando I wished to raise his sons.[125]

Increasingly successful though intermittent incursions by the Almohads from 1086 and the death of Alfonso's son Sancho at the battle of Uclés in 1108 led to a succession crisis which resulted in the accession of his only daughter, Urraca (r. 1109–26). The perception of weakness in the kingdom of León following the king's death can be compared with that of Solomon's kingdom in the immediate aftermath of his death, though the comparison may be flawed. Weakness, in the case of Alfonso's León, did not result in permanent and irreconcilable division. The parallel of the division of the biblical kingdom with that of León-Castile is therefore a far from perfect one and in any case judgements on the character of Urraca's reign are disputed, as discussed elsewhere. Nevertheless, the weakened state in which León-Castile found itself at the emperor's death and doubts about its future might imply that the author of the *HS* is delivering a subtle though belligerent verdict on the reign of King Alfonso VI, his judgement and legacy.[126] The critique may be so discreet as to be undiscernible and such an interpretation cannot be deduced from the text alone which seeks unambiguously to present the king's reign as glorious.[127] If the author of the *HS* is contrasting the merits of Fernando and Alfonso, the distinction seems to have a more limited and specific purpose and, from evidence within the text, distinctions in the reigns of father and son are related to questions of piety, humility and Fernando's clearly expressed love of the church. Alfonso is praised for the extension of his father's kingdom;[128] far from precipitating the kingdom's division, he seems, according to the author of the *HS*, to have been only too aware of the possible matters of his own infirmity [*dolose*][129] or the death of his brother that imperilled its continued vitality and survival.[130]

The complex web of familial relationships is apparent when the author retraces his steps and returns to events following the death of King Sancho III of Navarre (1035).[131] Here the combination of personal ambition, brotherly rivalry and biblical precedent are apparent, and there is the additional ingredient of illegitimate lineage of Sancho's son, Ramiro I, the first king of Aragón (r. 1035–62). The reference to Ramiro, *ex concubina ortum*[132] [born of a concubine] is reminiscent of the relationship of Abraham (or, as he then was, Abram) with Hagar and her son Ishmael. However, Hagar is not referred to as *concubina* but as *ancilla*, which might mean slave girl or maid servant and she was the property of Abraham's wife, Sarai.[133] Whether or not the parallel with Abraham was in the mind of the author of the *HS*, OT notions of lineage are likely to have seeped into his thinking. We are told that although Abraham was generous in making concubines available to his sons, the greatest prize was reserved for his legitimate heir, Isaac: 'And Abraham gave all that he had unto Isaac.'[134] In the account of the treachery [*insidias*] and outrageous crime [*facinus*] of Ramiro in allying himself with Muslim kings against his brother García, Ramiro's behaviour is linked to a lack of moral self-restraint. He is contrasted with his pious brother, who had recently returned from Rome, having fulfilled a solemn vow to God.[135] As if to contrast Ramiro even more strikingly with legitimate rulers such as Alfonso VI, the author describes Ramiro's attempts to secure the support of the Muslim kings. His warlike threats against his brother are roundly condemned as 'shameful' [*bellum fratri indigne*][136] and his defeat at García's hands is portrayed as an ignoble, humiliating and squalid reversal. It is suggested that the story of Ramiro may be a metaphor for the crown of Aragón: 'his ignominious flight from the battlefield' implies that 'the kingdom and its rulers lacked legitimacy and dignity'[137] – and this distinction between what is 'royal' (*regalis* and *regius* and their declensions and derivatives) and what is merely 'noble' [*nobilis*] seems to have been used in the *HS* to distinguish between higher and lesser claims of kingship as between different noble houses.[138] Any attempt to link this idea with biblical precedent is tenuous. Nevertheless, there seem to be specific implications for Ramiro himself: like Ishmael, conceived by Hagar, Ramiro can be seen as morally and socially vulnerable, subject to the capricious whim of those more powerful than he. The whole episode regarding Ramiro's illegitimacy, treachery and cowardice is set within a framework and context reminiscent of the OT. Sancho at his death, is described as 'full of days' [*plenus dierum*] which has a reminiscence with Jer. 6.11;[139] yet it also relates to the death of the patriarchs which may provide a more apposite comparison within the phrase as used in the *HS*. It is used to describe the death of Abraham (Gen. 25.8), of Isaac (Gen. 35.29) and of the priest, Jehoiada (2 Chron. 24.15).

Although, as we might expect, references to Christ are common, other biblical figures from whom the characters within the *HS* could be derived or who provide reminiscences are usually suggested rather than explicit. David, as we have seen, is an exception, and we know that Noah is also briefly referred to in chapter 6,[140] though he is not in any sense depicted because he is a progenitor or example: he is mentioned almost in passing to identify the period of the deluge which became a metaphor for the way in which Spain was overwhelmed by the Muslim invasion. As if to underline the irrelevance of Noah in any context other than as a historical signpost, the author immediately launches into a tirade on what he describes as the perverse character of its kings,[141] which may indicate an early expression of the author's intention, that is to record dispassionately the deeds of kings and princes. The biblical vein within the *HS* is evident because of references to punishment and reward (especially in chapter 1) and to the piety of individual kings. And we should note the epithets that follow the death at the Battle of Tamarón, of Vermudo III (r. 1028–37) He was brother to Sancha of León (1018–67). He is described as a jewel in the wall of celestial Jerusalem: 'hoc mundo abstratum, lapidem ad celestis Iherusalem.'[142] This is followed by two references derived from OT sources which seem to relate to Vermudo's death but are otherwise unconnected.[143] In addition, other biblical, especially OT, allusions are suggested but cannot be considered as specific insertions. For example, members of the familiar patriarchal family, such as that of Adam, Noah and Abraham are not named and therefore do not provide secure precedents in themselves, even if the legitimacy of the royal line of León has echoes of references to unnamed kings of Israel and Judah.

Chronicon Regum Legionensium

Much more limited in scope than either *Sampiro* or the *HS* is the Chronicle of Pelayo (or Pelagius), bishop of Oviedo (r. 1101–30 and 1142–3) and probably written between 1121 and 1132. Although details of the author's early life and origins are sketchy, Pelayo had a long association with Oviedo where he was a deacon, archdeacon and eventually, between 1096 and 1101, auxiliary bishop of the see.[144] His devotion to the city drove him to promote Oviedo as a centre for Christian pilgrimage as an alternative to Santiago de Compostela.[145] In spite of its title, which suggests ambition and a grand sweep of history, the *Chronicon Regum Legionensium* is part of a collection of historical works, supervised by Pelayo himself, known as the *Liber Chronicorum*. It appears to be one of the few original compositions within the impressively large, though substantially fraudulent, *Corpus Pelagianum*.[146] Nevertheless, although the *Chronicon* was probably written by or at the behest of Pelayo, historical narrative is often infused with fiction. It almost picks up where *Sampiro* concludes (the overlap in the two chronicles is the reign of Vermudo II, 982–999) and takes us through to 1109, the year of Alfonso VI's death and includes material not found in early Asturian-Leonese chronicles.[147] Yet not only did he fabricate and interpolate numerous parts – enough in itself to ensure his enduring reputation as a forgerer[148] – but there was also an apparent lightness in historical detail or scope.[149] Furthermore, the unusual brevity in the scope of the chronicle may be seen as contributing to Pelayo's mercurial character.[150] Nevertheless, as Sholod notes 'new points relating to the ninth century [are] not found in earlier Asturo-Leonese chronicles,'[151] so Pelayo's partial treatment of his subject matter might not in every case undermine the verity of the events described. Yet a more profound purpose may be detected. Linehan acknowledges that Pelayo's obsession to present information that promoted national myth and his blurring of the distinction between Christianity, Spanish Catholicism and political objective as well as serving the interests of the see of Oviedo was effective: 'Scratch any piece of evidence for our subject before about 1130 ... and out sheepishly will come that prince of falsifiers, bishop Pelayo of Oviedo, the ink still wet on his fingers.'[152] The man of many parts had a clear if circumscribed idea of the direction in which his account was to travel and this foresight would incorporate an unreliable presentation of events. Our exploration of his use of scriptural sources will add a further dimension to his narrative which may be as important as observations about his brevity and fabrication.

Nevertheless, it is the author's awareness of direction and his barely concealed attitudes to the events he describes that are striking. Bishop Pelayo's interpretative narrative helps to create a conspicuous belief in a fortuitous and heaven-sent awareness of history[153] and may be able to provide us with clues as to how the events he describes were part of a biblical or religious purpose. And such clues are not hard to find. The lack of a reliable historical structure may indeed provide additional scope for opportunistic use of biblical allusion and precedent, and grand and well-rehearsed themes are present. For in this short chronicle, we find forgiveness and vengeance, healing and the treatment of the enemy as well as images linked to these ideas such as drought and the work of God in nurturing the earth. If we add to this Pelayo's conspicuous and detailed interest in genealogy[154] and his willingness to integrate this genealogical and political framework into a driven religious imperative, then a biblical framework would seem to be in place and is sustained in his narrative.

Vermudo II, who ascended to the throne of León in 984, is described in *Chronicon* 61 as 'foolish', 'tyrannical' and his propensity for wickedness is enumerated: 'That most impious prince conducted a further sin' and seems to have ushered in a period of divine vengeance and this is linked directly to the author's allegation of Vermudo's tyranny. The author of the *HS*, as we noted earlier, made reference to the biblical deluge when describing the way in which Spain had been overwhelmed by the Muslim invasion of 711.[155] In his *Chronicon*, Pelayo uses the idea of the deliberate intervention of a divinely ordained drought: 'Meanwhile the Saviour of the world [*Interior Saluator mundi*] dispatched a drought of such magnitude on the earth';[156] this conflated the ideas of the visions of God's servants and false imprisonment. This has stirring echoes of Joseph's exile in Egypt: the dreams of Joseph and those of the pharaoh's servants,[157] the seven years' period of drought[158] and the imprisonment of the pharaoh's baker and butler[159] – even the contemporaneous imprisonment of Joseph himself. Just as the alleviation of drought and its corollary, famine, were affected by what may be described as the restoration of Joseph, so the liberation and reinstatement of Pelayo's predecessor, Bishop Godesteo of Oviedo, seems to have generated a period of plenty (accordingly, from that day the Lord Jesus provided rain upon the face of the earth and the earth produced its fruit, and famine was driven from his kingdom).[160] Even more pertinently, it may be that the idea of drought would have a spiritually purging effect without the need to refer this to a specific biblical event or narrative. In *HS*, drought has precisely this function and is referred to as a 'passing fire'[161] [*transitorii ignis*] and the same idea of the transient nature of punishment that has a specific corrective purpose is present in Pelayo's *Chronicon*. The author's words, 'the fact that no man was able to plough or to plant,'[162] can be seen as an abridgement of the curses for disobedience contained in Deut. 28.15-68 which is an almost unending and grisly litany of detailed punishments visited upon God's people for general moral lapse rather than the flouting of divine law. It is a tribute to Pelayo, whose horizons have been seen as geographically, historically and politically limited and whose Latin may best be described as competent rather than scholarly, that he is able in his first short paragraph to convey such a wealth of biblical implication and religious invective. So as a piece of medieval scholarship, Pelayo's chronicle may be said to lack profound intellectual content or presentation yet, because of its clear sense of purpose – notwithstanding how specifically this was directed to the see of Oviedo – it merits academic attention.[163] Where there is punishment, forgiveness is never far away; if drought is linked with the moral indolence and vindictiveness of an earthly king (i.e. Vermudo II), then the mercy of a steadfast heavenly king will be showered on his own people. The phrase *memorans misericordie sue*[164] [mindful of his mercy] is very close to biblical sources and is reminiscent of those occasions of God's fidelity to those he loves and has many biblical echoes[165] as well as being part of monastic liturgy in the evening office. In Pelayo's account, the mercy of God towards his own people is integral to the concept of vengeance to be visited upon the Muslim enemy and to the specific punishment of Vermudo himself, who was to suffer henceforth from *podagra* [gout of the foot].[166] Pelayo is here indebted to the *Chronicle of Sampiro*,[167] and the writers of both chronicles would have been familiar with the frequently employed biblical practice of linking reward and punishment, mercy and vengeance. This is succinctly expressed in God's double-edged promise to David: 'I will be his father, and he shall be my son. If he commit iniquity, I will chasten him with the rod of men, and with the stripes of the children of men: But my mercy shall not depart away from him.'[168]

While the subject of the Davidic kingship is detectable in the *HS* (in the *Sampiro* block), such comparisons are less obvious in the *Chronicon*. God's judgement on Vermudo in the *Chronicon* (who died in 999, two years after being stricken with gout) may be compared with the withdrawal of divine mercy from David's predecessor, Saul.[169] What is more certain is that Pelayo and his ecclesiastical contemporaries would have recognized general principles with regard to judgement and mercy in OT precedent.[170] This may be exemplified by Pelayo describing the prayers of Bishop Adaúlfo of Santiago-Iria when he entered the cathedral at Oviedo. These called for familiar biblical punishments (leprosy, blindness and physical disability) to be visited upon his detractors and their descendants because of what are described as 'false crimes'[171] against the bishop:

> He (Bishop Adaúlfo) prayed and declared that until the world's end some of their seed (the descendants of Cadón, Ensión and Zadón, the bishop's detractors] would be destroyed by leprosy, others made blind, crippled and maimed for the false crimes (they) attributed to him.[172]

The term translated as 'blind' – *ceci* or *caeci* – might also refer to moral confusion. Here again, punishment would be as searing and relentless as mercy would be magnanimous and unlimited, even though there is no specific biblical reference or reminiscence. Pelayo's lament for Alfonso VI, however, could indicate an awareness of biblical as well as contemporary events. Towards the end of the Chronicon, Pelayo asks, 'Why, O shepherd, have you abandoned your sheep?'[173] and this may have been a timely reminder of the death of David as the earthly shepherd of Israel.[174] Yet it could also allude to the precarious position of the see of Oviedo – a city which had become increasingly marginalized since the capital of the kingdom had been transferred to León in 914.[175] It is pointless to speculate as to which idea was predominant but it seems likely that Pelayo's history is a fusion of biblical precedent and narrative, an awareness of saintly example and fervent ecclesiastical grandstanding; references to events are sometimes awkward or at least simplistic, fanciful and opinionated and it is not always clear to what extent biblical precedent is a conscious prerequisite to Pelayo's commentary.

Yet there is one further sense in which the *Chronicon* is an important repository of biblically inspired material, even if it does not necessarily deal with the great themes of mercy, forgiveness, judgement, punishment and vengeance. The author enriches his narrative with phrases that are recognizably and famously biblical – almost as if there was a deliberate attempt to enhance the ordinary and familiar with the eternal and the divine. In his description of events following the death of Bishop Adaúlfo, the author concludes the passage with words strongly redolent of those used by the author of John's gospel: 'Thereupon everybody returned to his particular (home).'[176] The biblical phrase, 'And every man returned to his own house'[177] is not a precise template but there is such striking similarity between the two sentences, following on as they do from a piece of narrative, that it is likely that the insertion of the passage into Pelayo's *Chronicon* was intentional.

The question as to why the gospel account and Pelayo's commentary on the aftermath of Adaúlfo's death should end with a similarly passive resolution is intriguing though unresolved. It is possible to infer comparisons between the false accusations made by Vermudo II against Adaúlfo [*crimina pessimo*][178] and the mutterings of the Jewish authorities against Christ who had preached at the Feast of the Tabernacles and was accused of blasphemy.[179] In a general sense, the evocation of a familiar biblical motif would have reminded Pelayo's hearers and readers of the risks of oppression of holy men at hands of their powerful political and religious enemies. And there is also the question of place. Danger is present in both accounts, but both Jesus and the bishop were on familiar territory where danger had, so to speak, infiltrated. The opening statement from Jn 7 reads: 'After these things Jesus walked in Galilee: for he would not walk in Jewry, because the Jews sought to kill him.' In places of relative security from those who might be expected to harm God's messengers – in remote and sparsely populated Oviedo and in Galilee, away from the heartland of Judaism – they were still at risk, even if the risk was diminished. Secondly, both events took place at the time of important religious festivals and within recognized places of worship. The bishop was to celebrate Mass on the eve of Easter (Maundy Thursday) and the discourse of Jesus within the temple was during the period of the Jewish feast of Tabernacles: 'Now the Jew's feast of tabernacles was at hand.'[180] The proximity of holy festivals celebrating pivotal moments in the history of God's relations with his people may have served to heighten the drama and sense of opportunity, prescience and the confirmation of God's favour. And this hope may have been confirmed since both Jesus and the bishop seem to have experienced a measure of the Father's protection. Jesus, though in the presence of his detractors, was unharmed: 'And some of them would have taken him; but no man laid hands on him.'[181] There is here the suggestion that those who would have harmed him were prevented from so doing so, and there is therefore a hint of the miraculous. In the much more dramatic case of Bishop Adaúlfo, who died shortly after leaving Oviedo, the force that ensured his final resting place had none of the gospel subtlety ('But our heavenly king rendered him hard to move; indeed, the hands of a thousand men could move him but a very little').[182] Yet in both cases, the hand of God had intervened to restrain the actions of men.

All these elements may suggest reasons why Pelayo chose to conclude his chapter on the fate of Bishop Adaúlfo with the words of Jn 7. The most compelling reason for their inclusion comes from the implicit authority of the words themselves and Pelayo would have had an easy familiarity with the gospel account of the week-long celebrations. In both the gospel account and in Pelayo's narrative we have, after a period of turbulence and danger, the quiet assertion of the restoration of good order. Whatever the threat to God's earthly servants, they will receive ultimate protection; the sense of quiet, understated triumph is evident in both accounts and the insertion of these words, especially in the account of Pelayo – where they serve as a counterpoint to histrionic scenes that precede them – suggests the confident assurance of God's justice and power.

There is an important passage within the *Chronicon* that has an even more striking link with an incident in John's gospel. Pelayo places the words of Jesus who, following his resurrection, gently rebukes Mary Magdalene, *noli me tangere* [touch me not],[183] into the mouth of Teresa, daughter of Vermudo II (who is himself implicated in religious treachery), following her marriage to 'an unidentified pagan king of Toledo'[184] which was carried out, it seems, as some kind of Christian-Muslim peace offering.[185]

Teresa rejects her unnamed husband's approaches because he is a pagan, and warns him that sexual congress will lead to his being killed by an angel: 'Noli me tangere, quia paganus es; si uero me tetigeris, Angelus Domini interficiet te.'[186] Pelayo would have been aware of the significance of the three opening words and their resonance within familiar liturgy, words which would represent a powerful and confident assertion of sanctity modelled on Christ's example. Pelayo's fellow prelates and wider public would have known the context of these words – they were part of a familiar gospel account which immediately follows the emergence of Jesus from the tomb but in the gospel account the words are placed before the resurrection had become known and prior to Jesus being re-united with his disciples. The importance of this phrase from John's Gospel is emphasized by its inclusion in the description of the same event (i.e. the marriage of Teresa to the pagan king of Toledo) in the late-twelfth-century *Chronica Naierensis*.[187] The refrain *noli me tangere* was also a familiar trope within Gregorian chant.[188] Pelayo's purpose in using the easily recognizable biblical phrase demonstrated his ability to use the text originally and as a literary device for drawing attention to the contrasting fortunes following the decisions of the Magdalene and the Muslim king of Toledo (referred to by Pelayo as a 'pagan'). The bishop suggests a kind of ironic religious justice. For in Pelayo's account, the unbelieving king was indeed slain by God's angel because he had violated a Christian woman; in the case of the Magdalene, she witnessed angels who had been guarding the tomb of her lord: 'And seeth two angels in white sitting, the one at the head, and the other at the feet, where the body of Jesus had lain.'[189] When she finally recognizes Jesus, she

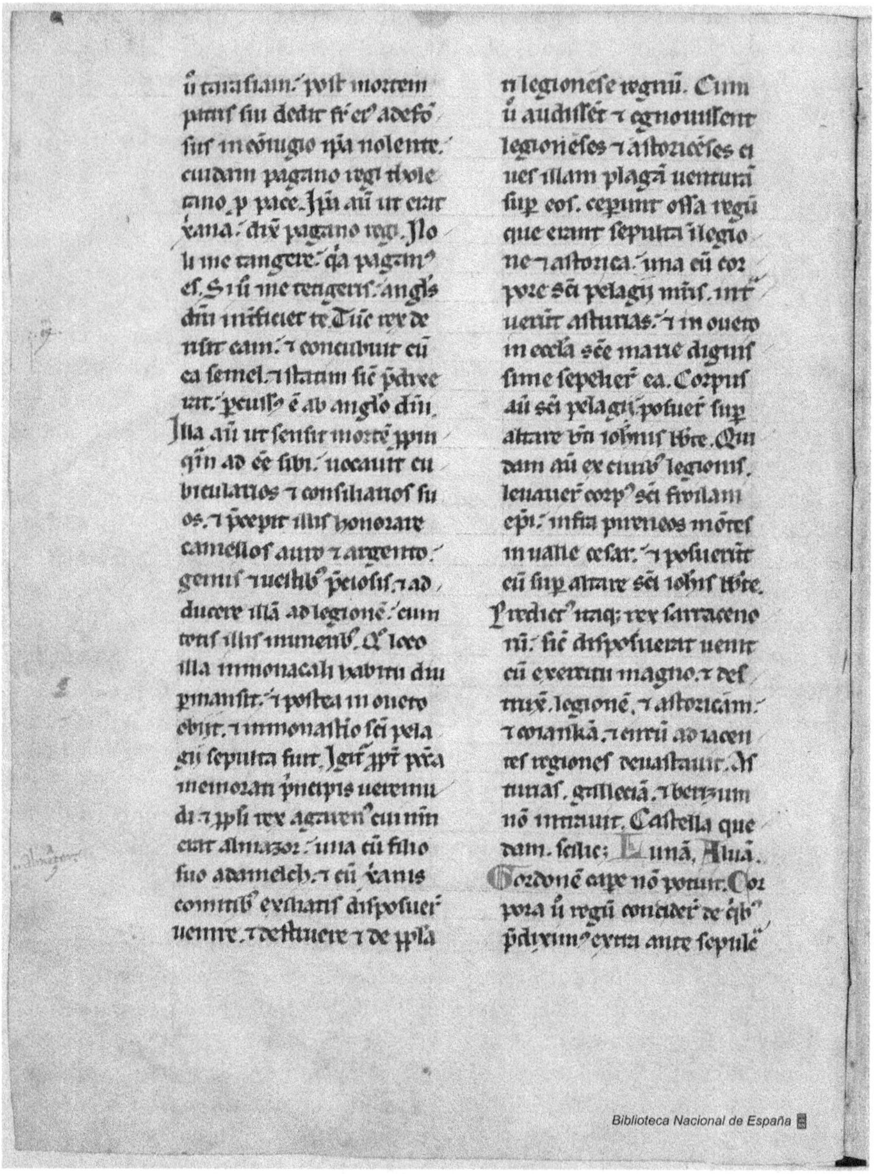

Figure 2.1 Marriage of Teresa to 'pagan' king of Toledo, Pelayo's *Chronicon*. MSS1513 136/245 folio inserted between 65/66.

Imágene procedentes de los fondos de la Biblioteca Nacional de España//Image from the collections of the National Library of Spain.

meekly and serenely accepts his request to her to keep her distance and, instead of asserting herself, happily withdraws, quietly rejoicing in her discovery. Her obedience is rewarded with joy; on the other hand, the king of Toledo's derision in the face of his wife's request heralds his own death. There is the suggestion that the deathbed orders of the Muslim king, which involved the return of Teresa and her possessions to León, represents an acknowledgement of the supremacy of the Christian God and to the extent that the biblical account also celebrates the triumph of faith over doubt, there may be a further parallel in Pelayo's account. However, in lifting the words of Jesus to the Magdalene from the biblical account into his own narrative, the bishop is again invoking the authority and tenacity of the Christian gospel to demonstrate the power of the faith in his own day and to cast light on events in the northern Christian kingdom.

The author's preoccupation with the see of Oviedo has added to the issues surrounding Pelayo's *Chronicon*. This, together with his inventiveness and the scale of his willingness to fabricate and manipulate strengthened his reputation as *el Fabulador*, though this sobriquet is based primarily on his wider body of works, including a number of forged diplomas, rather than exclusively on the *Chronicon*.[190] Perhaps too, because of the brevity of the *Chronicon* and its narrow focus, we may not properly be able to refer to it as a reconquest chronicle. Nevertheless, he deals in passing with Alfonso VI's sweeping short-term successes following the capture of Toledo:

> He ravaged and laid waste many of their [Saracen] settlements and also blockaded and took possession of many Saracen cities and castles. [191]

The author then enumerates the towns that Alfonso was able to capture in the immediate aftermath of his success at Toledo; furthermore, the roll call was impressively extensive and not limited to a consolidation of his authority in the Tagus Valley. Pelayo immediately links Alfonso's success with his position as father and champion [*defensor*] of the Spanish Church and one whose reign proved to be a period of unprecedented peace and tranquility. In *Chronicon* 82, the author lists over thirty towns and castles, including Lisbon, Alicante, Salamanca and Madrid, which he captured and settled. Pelayo's willingness to tackle great biblical themes within the context of Christian governance as well as juxtaposing mercy and punishment as a means of administering judgement on those he regards as Christian tyrants and on the pagan enemy suggest that accusations of naked regionalism are only part of the picture. The biblical imperative is central to his narrative and the fact that episodes from his *Chronicon* can be seen alongside gospel precedents indicates that the scriptural influence was wide as well as profound.

Both the *HS* and the *Chronicon* give distinct, yet complementary pictures of the complexity of the Asturian kingdom as it extended its frontiers southwards and eastwards into the relatively empty regions of León, Castile and the Upper Ebro Valley. Each chronicle deals, sometimes in withering terms, with the foibles of its kings and rulers. Both chronicles make references to the inception of conquest itself, even if the details of the slow transition and incorporation of the Asturian kingdom into what was to become León and Castile remain obscure. Each chronicle is part of a biblically infused picture by clerics who were conscious of the consequences of the past misdeeds of their people and those of their kings.

They were equally convinced of the rightness of their cause and of the need for Christian princes to resist sporadic Muslim attack. And although each chronicler makes numerous moral judgements about the powerful, the pious and the avaricious referred to in his narrative, no evidence of a collaborative ideological purpose emerges. Yet these texts could still supply the elements of a cultural construct and national myth based on biblical allusion and narrative, though one which emerged from the monastic libraries and royal courts of León, even if such sources lacked orchestration. If, as can be argued, myth may be recognized as part of the process of a personal or collective story of identity,[192] each text informs subsequent historians, contributing to the evolving cultural and spiritual identity of the northern Iberian Christian kingdoms.

3

CHRONICA ADEFONSI IMPERATORIS: A BIBLICAL EPIC

Ideology and phases of conflict

The *Chronica Adefonsi Imperatoris* is a text so central to the idea of biblical narrative in the historiographical tradition of León-Castile that it merits specific and detailed exploration.[1] This chapter is devoted to the question of authorship together with the themes with which the author deals and especially with imagery, lineage, Christian piety and loyalty to the emperor.[2] The *CAI* is, as its name suggests, an encomium composed to commemorate the life and kingship of Alfonso VII (1105–1157), of León-Castile. The chronicle is divided into two prose sections and to these is added a 385½ line poem written in rhythmic hexameters, The *Poem of Almería*.[3] The entire chronicle has been described as 'a prolonged eulogy of the king and his court'[4] and its uniqueness, with or without the *Poema*, is evident and acknowledged.[5]

It is, however, the qualities of the *CAI* as a biblically driven narrative that mark it out and which are of particular interest. It is with the notion that OT narrative provides an enduring parallel for the written accounts of the history of God's people in León-Castile that we are principally concerned. The fact that it is a text steeped in biblical narrative is readily acknowledged,[6] and further, that its setting and the tone of biblical drama within this narrative set it apart from earlier and near contemporary texts.[7] It may even have influenced subsequent Hispanic writing, though not the texts that are considered in this present study.[8] Perhaps the Hispano-Latin texts up to and including those of the early twelfth century indicate a kind of prescience of the shadowy and evolving idea of Reconquista, prefiguring chronicles such as the *CAI* and the thirteenth-century *CLRC*. Both used biblical texts more directly than the earlier chronicles to describe and deliberate on the reigns of kings and on the conflict between the Christians and Muslims (and inter-Christian rivalry). Nevertheless, it is in the mid-twelfth-century *CAI* that the language of suggestion and inference yields, quite suddenly and explosively, to crusading polemic and it is to that chronicle that we now turn.

The content of the first book, divided into 95 chapters, may be in part a narrative based on earlier, though near contemporary annals, now lost.[9] It is principally concerned with the domestic policy of Alfonso VII. The king sought to consolidate his grip on the kingdom of his mother, Urraca, in 1126. Bernard Reilly, who has made a study of the charters relating to her reign, considers that the queen's reign was prudent and led to a period that was characterized by increasing peace. Accusations of weakness that emerged later cannot easily be sustained from contemporary texts.[10] Following a short preamble, chapter 1 of the *CAI* begins with an acknowledgement of Urraca's death. In addition to shoring up the military and political power of his own kingdom which included dealing with intrigue amongst the aristocracy of León-Castile, Alfonso was also intent on subduing his Christian neighbours in Aragón, Navarre and Portugal. The marginally longer second book, consisting of 111 chapters, is concerned primarily with the campaigns of Alfonso VII against the Muslims, and with the conquest of the enemies of Christendom as an idea that could unite competing Christian ambitions within the Peninsula.[11] The second book takes as its starting point the death of Alfonso VI in 1109. Occasionally, the sequence of events in Books 1 and 2 is suspended, though this may – at least in part – have had a specific purpose and the author makes this departure clear. This nonsequential presentation of events and their locations may also be attributable to authorial confusion as well as being an artful attempt to gain political advantage. Certainly, the books are not strictly chronological but organized according to political themes.[12] It is unsurprising therefore, that the events described in the two books have separate geographical settings; in Book 1 the action takes place largely in the lands north of the Duero, though Book 2, dealing with the campaigns of Alfonso VII against the Muslims, centres much of the activity to the south of the Tagus Valley, with campaigns as far away as Córdoba, Seville and Cádiz and into Extremadura, culminating in the brief capture of Córdoba in 1146 and of Almería the following year.

Because the content of the narrative in the *CAI* is infused with biblical rhetoric and imagery to an extent that distinguishes it from the other and marginally earlier chronicles we have considered, the question of authorship and context assumes an unusual importance and this will now be considered.[13] The rest of the chapter will be devoted to the themes arising from this literary and ideological matrix on which the author draws and within which he develops his own interpretation and vision of the theatre of conflict and settlement in twelfth-century León-Castile. First, we will discuss the rich vein of animal imagery within biblical narrative on which the author is able to construct a view of the enemies of Christendom as well as a view of the Christians themselves; secondly, there will be an examination of the way the author deals with legitimacy of lineage and the way this can be linked to biblical precedent. Finally, the question of individual honour linked to zealotry and endeavour is considered in the context of a growing mood of Christian assertiveness. These three elements may be said to comprise the inspiration for conquest, legacy and duties of those charged with its execution and the rewards of the faithful. The purpose of this analysis is to prepare the ground for a comparison of a contemporary and an ancient text with the *CAI*, which is primarily the subject of Chapter 4.

Authorship and provenance

The chronicler's awareness of the changing historical landscape during the reign of Alfonso VII is everywhere apparent and all pervasive; however, it is his passion for crusading mission which scarcely wavers. Three phases in the development of such an ideology have been identified in Spain, and during the third phase (from 1130 onwards) it 'became more rooted in the Peninsula and was increasingly associated with more local traditions.'[14] Into this increasingly assertive military environment stepped the author of the *CAI*. Indeed, one could say that biblical polemic, combined with military and political invective, culminating as it does in the *Poema*, is on a relentless upward trajectory. It is the bishop of Astorga,[15] and those to whom he is sent as envoy by Alfonso VII,[16] who challenge men to take up the call to arms in the interests of their own salvation.[17] Indeed, it is Arnaldo of Astorga, introduced here in the third person, who is perhaps the most likely writer of the chronicle. The possibilities of Arnaldo's authorship are central when considering the complexities relating to the composition of the *CAI*. He makes an appearance just at the end of its prose section, as a prelude to the poem and on the eve of the struggle for Almería. Some earlier scholars have suggested other authors, though there is no settled agreement. In the seventeenth century, Francisco de Sota suggested Rodrigo Jiménez de Rada as a possible author[18] and the difficulties of authorship are further discussed by Manuel Risco.[19] In the last century, Ferrari suggested Peter of Poitiers as the possible author,[20] and this is by no means the most unlikely suggestion.[21] José María Canal Sánchez-Pagín advances the case for Don Elías, canon of the church of Roda de Isábena, Huesca (1136–43), who may have written the *Vita beati Raimundi*.[22] Although some consensus has built up around Bishop Arnaldo (r. 1144–52), his authorship is not universally accepted.[23]

The matter of the authorship of the *CAI* is further confused by uncertainty about Arnaldo himself, partly because details of his background cannot be established with confidence. Nevertheless, a persuasive case has been made for dating the work to about 1150 and attributing it to a certain Arnaldo, who was sometime prior of the monastery of San Servando, near Toledo. He may have been the very same Arnaldo who was enthroned as bishop of Astorga in 1144.[24] A still more precise date is suggested by Salvador Martínez, which places the authorship even closer to the Almería conflict:

> The author speaks ... of the Empress Berenguela as if she still lived – though she died in Palencia on 2 February 1149. We therefore conclude that, by then, the *CAI* had been completed and, therefore, that it was composed between end of August 1147 and before 1 February 1149.[25]

Some earlier scholars have suggested that Arnaldo was from the region of León, and Salvador Martínez argued that the evidence points to Arnaldo's earlier monastic experience not in San Servando but in the Cluniac monastery at Sahagún,[26] some 350 kilometres to the north of Toledo and where there was a large and famous scriptorium. All this suggests that the author was Leonese and that, in coming from the area close to León, may have had a close association with Sahagún.[27] But regarding authorship, it has been stated even more assertively that Arnaldo was the author of the chronicle and linked to possible French origins.[28] An examination of certain Hispano-Arabic lexical terms used within the *CAI* and the admiration expressed for certain Catalan noblemen suggest that the author is indeed Arnaldo, but that he was probably not French.[29] Since the identity of those who may have been involved in writing and compiling the narrative is therefore unresolved despite informed and circumstantial speculation, due weight needs to be given to the persistent controversy surrounding its authorship. More importantly, the question of authorship is of more than marginal significance to us because of the nature of the message at the heart of the chronicle and the way this was delivered. It was, at the very least, a break from the way in which Iberian history had thus far been recorded, containing a much more strident message and one steeped in biblical rhetoric.

If Arnaldo was the author of the *CAI*, his death in 1152 would explain why the concluding years of Alfonso's reign (1152–7) are not recorded. Moreover, events between 1147 and 1152 are omitted and this chronological gap adds to the difficulties and complexities of authorship and authorial intent;[30] it is also possible that the *CAI*, and particularly the *Poema*, were commissioned to celebrate the conquest of Almería. Yet the omission of the climax of this achievement is underlined by the way the poem ends so abruptly and inexplicably before the final assault on Almería itself and at the very point at which Arnaldo delivers his peroration to Alfonso's troops. H. Salvador Martínez, citing earlier authors,[31] has reiterated the belief that the sudden conclusion suggests that it had been a finished work but that at a later time the chronicle, for reasons which are not known, had been deliberately mutilated and that this is a reasonable assertion because of the way the poem is terminated.[32] But the argument that the deliberate removal of a text should begin half way through the line of a poem is not especially convincing. However, if this can be put forward as a serious explanation for the truncated text, it seems at least equally plausible to suggest that the author does not merely or inexplicably break off from his narrative, but completes his account of the Almería campaign, and that the lost or doctored work originally contained the completed poem. The suggestion that other events following Almería might have been part of the longer original is much more tenuous and speculative.[33]

Yet there are reasons why the chronicler might have taken matters further. More could have been made for papal support for the Iberian advance against the Muslims prior to the victory in Almería (which at best is muted).[34] But this interpretation is disputed. There followed a warm though short-lived afterglow of the success in Almería and Pope Eugenius III showed, at the Council of Rheims in 1148, a sudden and fulsome interest in Iberian affairs and this was not limited to the territorial ambitions of Alfonso VII.[35] Nor does it seem to have diminished following the failure of the crusade against Jaén in 1148, which suggested that the campaign against the Muslims in the south had been fleeting.[36] And this setback in Jaén was in contrast to the successes of Ramon Berenguer IV, Count of Barcelona and brother-in-law to Alfonso VII, in his own campaigns against the Muslims in Tortosa and the Ebro Valley (1148-9, culminating in the capture of Lérida), and in 1151 Alfonso and Ramon Berenguer signed the Treaty of Tudillén. This limited and defined the areas of conquest between the competing interests of the Castilians, Catalans and Aragonese in Andalucía. Yet though this may have clarified their respective ambitions, Alfonso VII's kingdom was undermined by problems relating to his own succession. Indeed, by bequeathing Castile to his son Sancho (Sancho III, r. 1157-8) and León to his other son, Fernando (Fernando II, r. 1157-88), he left a divided a kingdom[37] that would remain so until 1230 when Fernando III of Castile inherited the kingdom of León and then successfully retained it. Division suggests weakness, or at least vulnerability, and the Almohads were able to derive short-term but convincing advances against the Castilians – most notably in 1195 when Abu Yusuf Ya'qub and his Castilian rebels crushed the army of Alfonso VIII at Alarcos.

Although the author of the *CAI* would have been aware of the possible difficulties for the kingdom of León-Castile following the eventual death of Alfonso VII, he may not have foreseen it in the stark terms suggested by the chronicler of the *CLRC* who, with the benefit of hindsight, was to describe the separation as a 'wretched division' [*infelicem divisionem*].[38] Still less would he have conjectured that Almería itself would revert to Almohad control within a decade. The omission in the text of the *CAI* of other events closer to 1147, such as the failure at Jaén,[39] referred to earlier and whose inclusion might have diminished the author's peroration to Alfonso VII, invites further speculation about the authorship. Nevertheless, none of this fundamentally undermines the claim that Arnaldo was the writer of the chronicle. After all, the paucity in written commentary is by no means limited to the historical omissions in the *CAI*. The time for recording contemporary events seemed, temporarily, to have passed: 'in the ninety years after 1147, the year of Almería and Lisbon campaigns in which the author of the Chronicle of Alfonso VII laid down his pen, these moments were evidently very rare indeed.'[40] The omission of historical detail may merely reflect what Fletcher described as the 'historiographical desert' which was twelfth-century León. During the second half of the twelfth century no chronicle seems to have been produced in Castile.[41] However, this dearth of historical narrative was not limited to Iberia.[42] The situation in twelfth-century Italy records a similar dearth in the historical record,[43] though the comparison with León-Castile is not entirely straightforward since what are referred to as 'city based texts'[44] (such as the so-called *Genoese Annals*) were written by laymen rather than clerics. Equally, it is important to recognize what the *CAI* does contain, especially in its wealth of political, domestic and military detail. Although Fletcher considers the work (and that of Pelayo of Oviedo) 'bald and jejune,' this excoriating judgement is made only in comparison with the works of the author's near contemporaries, Orderic Vitalis and William of Malmesbury.[45] An early-nineteenth-century verdict recognizes a more ingeniously simple quality in the author of the *CAI* who 'exceeds all his predecessors, not only in elegance, but in the animation of his narrative.'[46] Other assessments are also comparatively generous, perhaps because the *CAI* was precisely focused and was, in providing a particularly graphic, authoritative and unique account of twelfth-century Muslim political world, a surviving Latin text of inestimable value.[47]

None of this of course points conclusively to any one hand, though the author's descriptions of events can be intense, suggesting that his own knowledge was both immediate and thorough – and this possible acquaintance is alluded to by the author himself. For just as the author of Luke's Gospel and the writer of the Acts of the Apostles (thought to be one and the same person) appealed to those 'who were from the beginning the eyewitnesses'[48] with 'many infallible proofs'[49] of Christ's passion, so the author of the *CAI* sought to set out his own highly personalized account of Alfonso VII's reign: *didici et audiui* ['I have heard and learned'].[50] Luke is the only gospel writer to refer to himself in a preface that is not integrated into the main text, and this distinctiveness seems to have provided a model for the author of the *CAI* in introducing his account. The comparison with Luke's account continues to hold good as the author proceeds to link the hope invested in the young Alfonso VII, 'like a promise happily sent from heaven,'[51] with Christ's declaration of his Father's promise to the faithful: 'I send the promise of my father upon you.'[52] The influence of the gospel promise on the simile in the *CAI* shows an explicit link[53] and the comparison of language used by the author with that of Lk. 24.49 is powerful and the similarity compelling. Yet the fact that he uses the account from Luke to begin his description of the deeds of Alfonso's reign[54] suggests that his reference to a heavenly promise [*promissum de supernis*] in the following chapter is more than a linguistic reminiscence. This passage is considered alongside references such as 'happy jubilee year.'[55]

Uncertainties about a consistent strand of authorship of the *CAI* seem more marked when comparison is made between the prose sections of the chronicle and the *Poema*, where the narrative gives way to configurations of rhythmic hexameter. Nevertheless, the author in the closing lines of Book 2 states his intention of sustaining his readers' interest by elevating the subject matter to a different genre: 'However, now we are embarking on more notable deeds in poetry, so that we may banish boredom through the variety of verse.'[56] Yet the *Poema* does not merely represent a change in genre; in his opening lines, the author seems to be making a number of related assertions, which may be oblique or explicit; and these contain a kind of mutual interdependence. For example, the courage and power of Alfonso is considered equal to that of an earlier great Christian emperor, Charlemagne ('Hic Adefonsi erat, nomen tenet imperatoris, Facta sequens Caroli, cui competit equiparari:'),[57] with whom there is also an 'admissible likeness.'[58] The Muslim enemy 'of pagan men' [*paganorum*] is compared with those who worshipped Baal – a generic title for a god worshipped in biblical Levant – they who, by implication, were destroyed by the power of Yahweh: 'They did not acknowledge the Lord and merited destruction.'[59]

This may be part of an attempt to link the Christian populations of Francia and Spain and to distance them from their common enemy by drawing attention to 'the most wicked scourge of the Moors,'[60] and this antipathy towards the Muslim foe is tenuously and tendentiously applied to those who worshipped Baal in the biblical account. Linehan does not deny that the *CAI* and the *Poema* could have shared the same author, but he remains a sceptic: 'Can the tepid observer of the

3. Biblical Epic

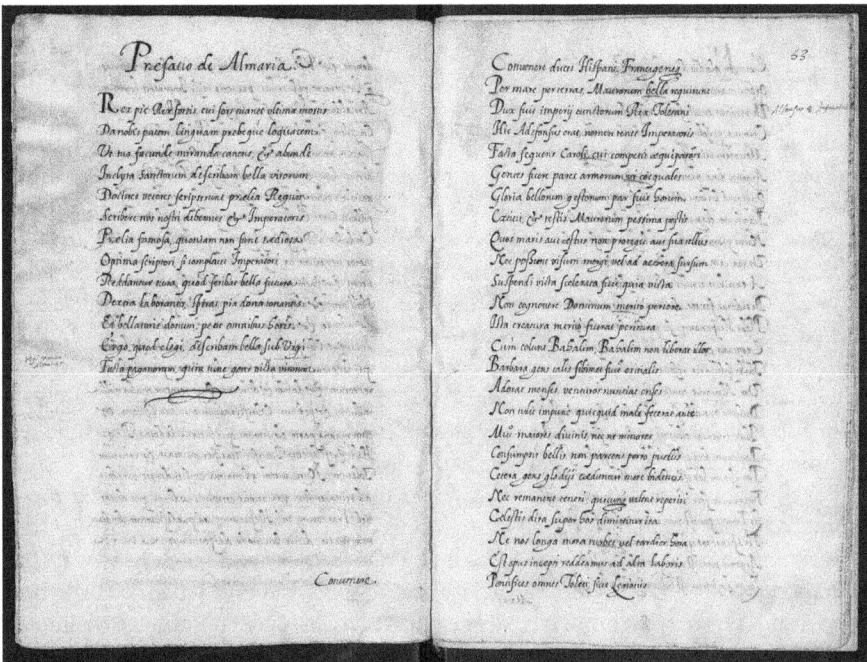

Figure 3.1 Author praises Alfonso VII and denounces the worshippers of Baal, *Poema*. MSS9237 60/72 folio 53.

Imágenes procedentes de los fondos de la Biblioteca Nacional de España//Image from the collections of the National Library of Spain.

peninsular scene and the bloodthirsty crusader really be one and the same person? ... One merely asks.'[61] Yet doubts about single authorship may have more to do with differences in genre together with the relative lack of overt biblical references in the *Poema*. There is nothing insignificant about Linehan's question; it strikes at the heart of whether we are looking at a single document within which there is a recognizable integrity or whether the chronicle and the poem have come together through historical accident and serve different purposes.

Almería could represent a literary as well as a military high-water mark in the description of Alfonso's campaigns against the Muslims. The exhortation to destroy the pirates' nest [*piratarum nidum diruendum*][62] is attributed in part to Arnaldo and is echoed within the poem itself. Here the author continues to provide us with what is perhaps the most emphatic declaration of crusading intent. Alfonso VII's Almería campaign and the intervention of Bishop Arnaldo himself seem to have been authorized by Pope Eugenius III (r. 1145–53) in his letter to the king in 1147,[63] although the purity and perhaps integrity of the Christian endeavour in Andalucía remains open to question.[64] The extent to which the pope explicitly supported Christian military mission in Iberia has already been referred to and there also appears to be a direct correlation with the reference from Book 2, 'for the redemption of their souls,'[65] to the poem itself, linking the attempt to wrest the south-eastern port city of Almería from Muslim hands in 1147 with the redemption of Christian souls 'All bishops of León and Toledo ... beseech old men and encourage young men in order that they may march together, courageously into battle.'[66] Yet the glories of the present world are never far away; glittering prizes are promised [*Argenti dona promittunt*][67] and piety will carry eternal reward: 'They pardon faults and lift their voices to the stars. They promise rewards in this life and in the life to come.'[68] The author's tendency to allow the possibility of spiritual and temporal rewards to coexist is evident, in spite of the fact that this seems to run counter to the pope's declaration in *Quantum praedecessores*.[69] This has a contemporary resonance with the Genoese chronicler and secular historian, Caffaro (c. 1080–c. 1166), author of the *Genoese Annals*.[70] In their desire for opulence, the Genoese army and that of Alfonso VII were both attempting to wrest the port city from the Muslims, even if differing military and ideological aims were also evident.[71] Nevertheless, any attempt to synthesize the accounts of the two chroniclers into a coherent ideology that is distanced from the teachings and spirit of Eugenius and Bernard of Clairvaux rather misses the point. To be sure, it seems more likely that the author of the *CAI*, in invoking the spirit of St James, may have been attempting to carve out a specifically Iberian military and religious vision. This attempt does not present a diminished crusading spirit, but one which seems to have been distinct from what is referred to as a particular Jerusalem pilgrimage tradition.[72] The different geographical settings of the first and second books of the *CAI* and the distinction in the focus of events are complementary accounts of the deeds of a single monarch. Indeed, the author asserts that this change of emphasis is both integral to his narrative and deliberate. Having provided a brief statement of the contents of Book 2 in the preamble and confirming that it will be concerned with military and other disputes,[73] the author then, in chapter 1, justifies his departure from his narrative in Book 1: 'Disregarding the natural sequence of events, we propose to discuss the fierce wars which in the past the Christians had to endure.'[74]

Because we do not specifically consider an argument that proposes a separate authorship for the *CAI* and the *Poema*, all references to the *CAI* and the poem assume the same provenance. Whether or not this laudatory discourse was written wholly or in part by, among others, Bishop Arnaldo of Astorga, it is clear that its purpose was to elevate the life and achievements of Alfonso VII of León-Castile (though the chronicle concludes in 1147, with his conquest of Almería) into a biblically-inspired epic. It is possible to argue that those prose sections of the *CAI* that deal with Alfonso's campaign against the Muslims share a greater polemical passion and urgency with the *Poema* than with the parts of the *CAI* that are devoted to Alfonso VII's attempts to consolidate his own position in León-Castile and his attempts to fight off hostility in Aragón, Navarre and Portugal. However, if there is a distinction in terms of authorial intent between the prose and poetic sections of the *CAI*, that argument is yet to be made and it is the contrast in genre that causes doubts about a single authorship to remain. The dilemma is irresolvable and the scepticism about single authorship endures. It is also worth pointing out that although specific biblical references are scarcer in the *Poema* than in the prose section, the language of the poem nevertheless makes it possible for us to detect biblical imagery that is notable for its remarkable complexity and that incorporates hyperbole discernible in medieval hymn writing.[75]

Dogs of war and other animals

Faunal imagery and biblical conquest narrative

The difficulties in assessing which sources the writer of the *CAI* had at his disposal have been discussed.[76] This is due, in part, to the continued debate over the authorship of the chronicle, compounding the difficulty in knowing what exegetical material may have been available in specific monastic libraries. Nevertheless, we have acknowledged the importance of the influence in northern Iberia of the exegetical material of Beatus and the impact that his work came to exercise on those working in monasteries throughout the later Carolingian Empire. The faunal and apocalyptic art emanating from Beatus's exegesis seems to have seeped into the monasteries of Catalonia, Navarre and northern Castile.[77] And one of the most striking features of the author's narrative is his facility to incorporate apocalyptic imagery and biblical precedent into the myth of conquest and to depictions of the infidel and Christian adversaries. His use of animal-based imagery owes a breadth and complexity to a substantial literary framework[78] – of which he was more than a mere recipient – which determines and informs his choice of subject and the way in which the original material might be applied to his description of events. Attention is given to the use of animal imagery in other parts of the medieval Latin west since there is a history of long-standing and comparable use of such imagery in the wider Mediterranean and beyond. The author was thus appealing to a well-established corpus of material made familiar to a wide public through sermons and art.[79] The Israeli theologian and archaeologist Tova Forti believes that the use of such imagery, serving a variety of purposes, is likely to have been linked to biblical narrative.[80] This complex and ancient derivation is further explored elsewhere:

> Much of the lore regarding animals in circulation around the Mediterranean during the Middle Ages is common to Arabic and Latin tradition. Also, the Arabic poetic tradition and the Biblical Hebrew poetic tradition [reflected in the Vulgate and influential in subsequent Christian literature] draw on the same imagery concerning the lion that was common in societies of the fertile crescent in antiquity.[81]

Principally, this rich vein of sources is derived from biblical accounts, even though there were also pre-biblical traditions, which served a purpose well suited to medieval ideology and culture as well as to the written narrative,[82] and this imagery was well established in Iberia and elsewhere. Some of the earlier writers used their biblical narrative to provide material with which they could verbally abuse their Muslim enemy.[83] The author of *CAI* uses this technique too, but he also shows himself to be particularly adept at deploying the imagery to enhance and illuminate other events and assertions in his chronicle.

Although his range of references is wide, the author shows a preference to select specific passages from the OT (especially those describing the struggle of the Hebrew people as well as in apocalyptic writing, much of which is to be found in the Book of Daniel as well as in the Revelation of John the Divine), all of which accentuate the warlike tone of the chronicle. The author uses other passages – where allusions can be traced from the gospels or from more reflective extracts in the Psalms or Book of Proverbs[84] – at least in part, as literary devices. They contribute stylistic confidence and biblical familiarity and can be contrasted with his use of more powerfully evocative passages. But this is by no means all; his use and embellishment of references in the Psalms is sometimes deployed to contribute to the deep-seated sense of grievance and injustice felt by those Christians whose ancestral homeland had been seized by the ancestors of those Muslims with whom they were now in conflict. This would appear to be in keeping with the power with which animal imagery is used in the Psalms: 'As it depicts rancorous enemies, Ps. 22 is more fully enriched by faunal imagery than any other individual lament.'[85] The examples indicate that the author of the *CAI* does not shrink from using benign references to provide more potent imagery than may have been intended. For example, his allusion to Ps. 42.1 ('As the hart panteth after the water brooks, so panteth my soul after thee, O God') contains the doctored (or possibly misremembered) line: 'A canibus cervus velut in sylvis agitatus'[86] ([Just] as the deer pursued by dogs in the woods). The use of the term 'by dogs' [*canibus*] does not occur in the psalm and its insertion may reflect that it was a recognizably insulting reference to the Muslim enemy. What is clear is that although Ps. 42 is in part a meditation and contains elements of a melancholy search, it has an underlying optimism which emerges in the last verse;[87] the writer of the *Poema* uses the psalmist's personal quest to provide a thinly veiled call to arms and a cry for vengeance on the part of the Christians. Effectively, the purpose and intrinsic mood of the psalm have been hijacked by the author of the *Poema* for his own purposes. Whilst there is a reference in the psalm to 'mine enemies who reproach me,'[88] the context in which this appears entirely lacks the combination of a militaristic rallying cry and there is no evidence of any intention to cast a slur on specific enemies.

In this context, it is plausible that the author's use of *canibus* reminded his hearers and readers of the distinction to be made between victorious Christians and vanquished Muslims. There is an echo of the way Jesus himself used the term to contrast children (God's chosen people) and dogs when approached by a Syrophoenician gentile woman whose daughter was possessed by an unclean spirit.[89] The routine manner in which the term turns up in the gospel account may cast doubt on whether the earliest Christians used it as a piece of intentional abuse or as a generic way to refer to those whose way of life and religious affiliation they had been taught to despise. Moreover, the woman herself seems to have partially accepted this term.[90] By the time it was being applied by Christians and Muslims to each other in the Iberian conflict, it had become a much more potent term of abuse, though it is certain that the greater offence was felt by Muslims. This link had a widespread application and deeply embedded origins and there seems to have been a widely held Christian view at the time the author of the *CAI* was penning his chronicle, of a link between Saracens and Cynocephali.[91] Although the image of dogs was only one of the terms intentionally and pejoratively applied to Muslims, it was the most enduring and persistent insult and could be traced directly to depictions of the Prophet Muhammad.[92] The link between the Muslim cry in the *CAI* 2 71. 6 and 7 (when the unidentified Muslim governor of Seville, Avenceta, mocks the Castilians as *insensati Christiani, filii canum*)[93] and the biblical image of the hart being pursued by dogs in the *Poema*[94] is likely to have been unintentional. However, the recourse to canine imagery is commonly used by the author to show how Muslims and Christians describe each other, and its recurrent feature in both the prose section and the poem strengthens the argument for a single strand of authorship between the main body of the *CAI* and the poem.

Since Muslim scholars trained in Islamic law have regarded dogs as ritually unclean, the term was a particularly potent slur and one which would offend Muslim sensibilities,[95] yet it seems to have been used only rarely and is completely absent from the eleventh-century chronicles of León-Castile as well as from the two twelfth-century chronicles we have already considered. The omission of such invective may seem curious, since its potency was well attested.[96] Perhaps Pelayo and the writer of the *HS* had other concerns and simply did not understand Muslim sensibilities

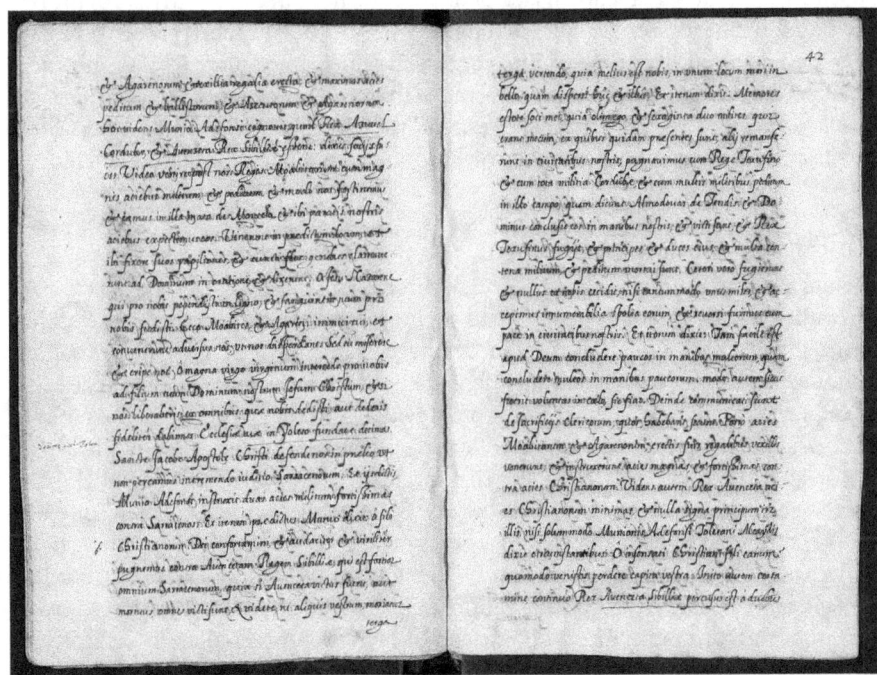

Figure 3.2 'King Avenceta' goads Christians at place identified as Almodóvar de Tendas, *CAI 2*. MSS 9237 50/72 folio 42.

Imágene procedentes de los fondos de la Biblioteca Nacional de España/Image from the collections of the National Library of Spain.

or appreciate the significance of such a slur. Ferreiro cites the *La Chanson de Roland* and the *Istoria de Mahomet*[97] as containing particularly virulent anti-Islamic invective based on canine imagery. Unsurprisingly perhaps, such imagery occurs more frequently in the ninth-century writings of Paul Alvarus, the chronicler of the Córdoban martyrs; in his *Epistulae*, Alvarus makes a gratuitous reference to the prophet's death, and although it is without accompanying commentary or embellishment, its very pithiness constitutes an effective slur: 'He [i.e. his body] was discovered and gulped down by dogs.'[98] However, Alvarus's most loquacious invective against Muhammad and the events surrounding the death of the prophet is found in *Liber Apologeticus Martyrum*: 'The dogs advanced towards his stench and gorged on his flanks ... and it was indeed fitting that so great a prophet [*talis prophetica*] should fill the stomachs of dogs.'[99] The term *talis prophetica* may simply mean 'such a prophet'; if 'great' is implied, there is the suggestion of irony.[100] In his references to dogs, we cannot be sure whether Alvarus was drawing on current or earlier traditions of anti-Muslim rhetoric and abuse, though there is a further example of the insult in the anonymous tenth-century *Vita Argenteae* to the capture and arrest of the Frank, Vulfura: 'captured by heathens as if by starved dogs, mad with fury, he [i.e. Vulfura] was dragged before a certain governor.'[101] There may be a mild verbal reminiscence between the *Liber Apologeticus Martyrum* and the *Vita Argenteae*, but there is a marked lack of direct evidence linking the writers of the two texts and, furthermore, the cult surrounding the Córdoban martyrs seems to have become neglected over time.[102] The context in which the author of *Vita Argenteae* refers to dogs is less specifically vituperative than in the references in *Epistulae* and in *Liber Apologeticus Martyrum*; suggestions, therefore, that such phrases were lifted by the anonymous author from Alvarus's works seem tenuous and even fanciful.

The place of the lion

Metaphors with animals and the way that these might be used to create the tapestry of conflict are deployed sparingly and memorably in the *Poema*, and the author varies the way they are applied, even within the same passage. Dogs, wolves, lions and sheep may be used as insulting references, and as significant and distinct images of military assault or as a means of providing detail in the backdrop of the author's historical narrative. In the account following the fulsome description of the arrival of the knights of León, 'After come the knights, the flower of the city of León,'[103] we have a scene described in which the city of León and her valiant men as well as one of conflict itself are subjected to a series of complex metaphors involving lions, wolves, sheep and the forces of nature. The author uses these examples, not in a recognizably consistent pattern to reinforce his anti-Muslim rhetoric, but to create a kind of military fable. The wolf, instead of being represented as an evil force, is used almost *en passant* to suggest the Christian harrying the Muslim 'sheep': 'Just as the wolf follows hard on the heels of the sheep and the sea overwhelms the lion's heels,'[104] in what seems an untypical reference. Lions, for example, may be feared or admired and are a metaphor for God's people as well as one who scatters them, but the reference to 'sea' [*maris*] reminds us that all creatures, even a beast with the might and nobility of a lion, is subject to enduring, eternal forces. By comparing lions with Muslim soldiers and the waves under the sea [*maris, unda*] with an all-powerful light [*lux, proterit*], the author alludes to a mighty Christian enemy, mightier even than the lion itself. He therefore paints a picture of an enemy that will ultimately be overwhelmed by more powerful and eternal forces,[105] and no physical force could crush those who fought alongside the emperor.[106] From a medieval Christian perspective, a reference to Ovid is underpinned with the more authoritative and recognizable allusion to the biblical flood.[107]

The author uses the image of the lion to include place as well as people: the city of León, which is eulogized for its integrity and scrupulous attention to aristocratic privilege,[108] provides an obvious allusion and its young men are not merely praised for their valour but are also directly compared with lions as they charge into battle.[109] The author's use of animal imagery is unique, though by the thirteenth century, the lion had become a common symbol in Castilian literature and an image that served a variety of purposes.[110]

Sheep, and particularly lambs, are often presented as docile and benign, but also with the power to propitiate, perhaps because of their innocent servility.[111] Biblical texts abound with images of fickle creatures that have gone astray or who scatter in the absence of proper guidance,[112] and this seems to be the sense in which the term is used in the *Poema*. And in this passage the weakness of the Muslims and their leadership is contrasted with the strength of the men of the city of León which, because of the sound judgement of the monarch and the courage of the men-at-arms, holds a preeminent position within Iberia ('it holds/represents the whole of the Spanish kingdom').[113] Yet the references to León and the imagery surrounding the context in which the city is described, because they are so emphatic, deserve further exploration. Furthermore, instead of relating these images immediately to the conflict, the author creates the picture of a deluge that owes its derivation to Ovid where the wolf and the lion – as well as the sheep – are passive creatures, powerless to resist the natural elements: 'the wolf swims with the sheep, the waves bear away tawny lions and tigers.'[114] In the *Poema* the creatures are energetic agents and are not merely caught up in the current of history.[115] Although the picture that emerges is of a vigorous Christian assault, the inconsistent use of images suggests that such visual references are used for whatever short-term expedient the author has in mind. It is also worth observing that the absence of graphic adjectives renders wolves and lions as fit instruments for God's purposes by neutralizing their more malevolent aspects.

The name of the city of León is derived from *Legio* (i.e. the city of the Legion); nevertheless, it is suggested that the rampant lion became a symbol of the city during the reign of Alfonso VII, though the lion motif had a much wider frequency than as the symbol of twelfth-century León.[116] It can also be found on certain coins of this period and is intimated by the author himself in his reference to 'protective ensigns.'[117] Nevertheless, the proportion of these coins that can be definitively linked to twelfth-century Leonese regal authority is not clear since they are often unnamed.[118] The text suggests that the author was well aware of this lexicographical reminiscence, even if it was based on a false etymology: the Leonese knights are compared with lions as they surge forward[119] and the image is then embellished by the author's comparisons of the quality, character or appearance [*decore*] of the lion with that of other animals and the way in which León exceeds other cities in honour [*honore*].[120] Since the two lines are sequential and part of the same verse, it is scarcely surprising that *decore* and *honore* should have been chosen in part to fit the rhyming scheme; *decore* is, nevertheless, an intriguing term to use. It could mean 'reputation,'[121] but it might equally well be translated as 'grace,' 'beauty,' 'splendour,' 'dignity,' 'virtue' or, indeed, as a synonym for 'honour' itself. This complex representation of the lion is in keeping with the biblical narrative. For example, the patriarch Jacob, in a passage that has echoes of the land of Judah being described as a 'lion's whelp' [*catulus leonis*],[122] is shown as a lion blest by God: 'He crouched, he lay down as a lion, and as a great lion: who shall stir him up? Blessed is he that blesseth thee, and cursed is he that curseth thee.'[123] The translation in the AV of *leaena* is odd; it should be emended to 'lioness' or 'lesser lion' and is so translated in other versions. The idea of employing faunal language to suggest a diminished early Hebrew kingdom (i.e. Judah) is also used by the author of the *Poema* to suggest a Hispanic kingdom (i.e. Castile), subservient to the Leonese giant, embodied by Alfonso himself ('Alone he has subdued Castile like a little she-ass [*aselam*]').[124] Small or immature animals are used to provide images of submission and dependence.

The author of the *Poema* creates in León a city and faithful community that is more than a match for the Ishmaelites who shun the light and are crushed by it,[125] so here the lion itself becomes a symbol of solitary and remote strength, a faithful and brave remnant. This is a familiar image and reflects an inspirational OT picture: 'And the remnant of Jacob shall be among the Gentiles in the midst of many people as a lion among the beasts of the forest, as a young lion among the flocks of sheep'[126] and this biblical identification with God's people would have been tempting for an author who was well acquainted with the Leonese court and who had a ready-made metaphor to hand.

Yet if the lion could be seen in a particular context as the embodiment of God's people, it could also be famously depicted as man's enemy (David is described as having killed both a lion and a bear in defence of his flock)[127] and as the representation of forces much to be feared: 'Mine heritage is unto me as a lion in the forest: it crieth out against me'[128] and this fearsome force is alluded to by the author of the *Poema* a little further on (line 113): 'Wild León seeks battles.'[129] His use of the adjective *fera* to describe the wars or battles [*bella*] compounds the implication of fierceness; it also conveys a sense of biblical terror and wildness, of untamed vengeance, and León is represented as a beast eager for the fray. And if the ferocity of a lion can be a metaphor for the power of God over his people ('The lion hath roared, who will not fear? The Lord hath spoken, who can but prophesy?'),[130] how much more powerfully will the lion serve as a weapon to be used against God's enemies? The author is not merely a man who seizes on a convenient and familiar image. He recognizes its potential creative complexity and is dexterous in using its biblical provenance and variety in the interpretation of his own history.

Nevertheless, it is in the apocalyptic writing of St John's vision that the full authority of the lion is to be demonstrated and it is with the picture created in the book of Revelation that the most spectacular interpretation of the metaphor in the *Poema* may be compared. For though the lion is a metaphor for God's people – the remnant of Judah and the flower of Leonese manhood – it is also something much more. In John's vision the lion has become Christ himself:

And one of the elders saith unto me, Weep not: behold the Lion of the tribe of Juda, the Root of David [*radix David*], hath prevailed to open the book, and loose the seven seals thereof.[131]

We deduce the link because of the reference to *radix David*.[132] And in the *Poema* the relationship between the lion and the Incarnation may also be inferred. For in his description of Count Ramiro Froilaz [*Radimirus*],[133] we have a complex conflation of salvation, lineage and a eulogy to the count and with unmistakable references to Christ himself. Count Ramiro is 'precious to Christ' [*est Christo carus*][134] and he is represented at the end of the author's description as a kind of arm of God's strength. Ramiro is the servant of Christ, of the Emperor[135] and his power base is in the city of León. The fusing of royal power, the royal city and Christ himself is a consummate but visceral attempt to confer God's blessing on the Leonese mission.[136] It is as if the author is stirred by his own rhetoric. But collaboration of image, interpretation and idealism seems to represent an idea that was to gain traction as the Christian military campaign to wrest Almería from Muslim hands gathered pace. For right at the beginning of the chronicle there is a reference to 'a promise sent down from on high,'[137] a gift to God to the newly faithful in Jerusalem in a verse at the end of Luke's gospel.[138] And here in the chronicle, the verse is used to allude to an implied link between Jerusalem and the city of León. But the metaphor of the fighting, divinely empowered, noble lions that makes such a powerful linguistic association with León emerges only in the poem.

The author has therefore used a range of faunal depictions to enrich his narrative of the struggle for supremacy between Christian and Almoravid Muslim forces within Iberia in the mid-twelfth century as well as promoting the dominance of Alfonso and the men of León within the coalition of Christian forces. Yet the poem, which in its completed form would have been a fitting apotheosis to the entire chronicle, achieves something slightly different. For it represents a denouement, a coming together, not only of the author's own thinking, but as a way of demonstrating how his use of imagery evolves into a complementary, though complex, narrative. His promotion of biblical and classical faunal imagery was used to create a myth of military assertiveness and glory, predicated, according to the author, on a kind of crafted piety and spiritual teaching.[139] If beasts from biblical and classical texts supply a range of characteristics that define protagonists (valour, cowardice, strength and weakness), so the Christian leaders are presented as exemplars of godly determination and vision.

The author largely avoids a conventional package of vituperation and the kind of crude fiction derived from early post-conquest sources (such as we saw in the writings

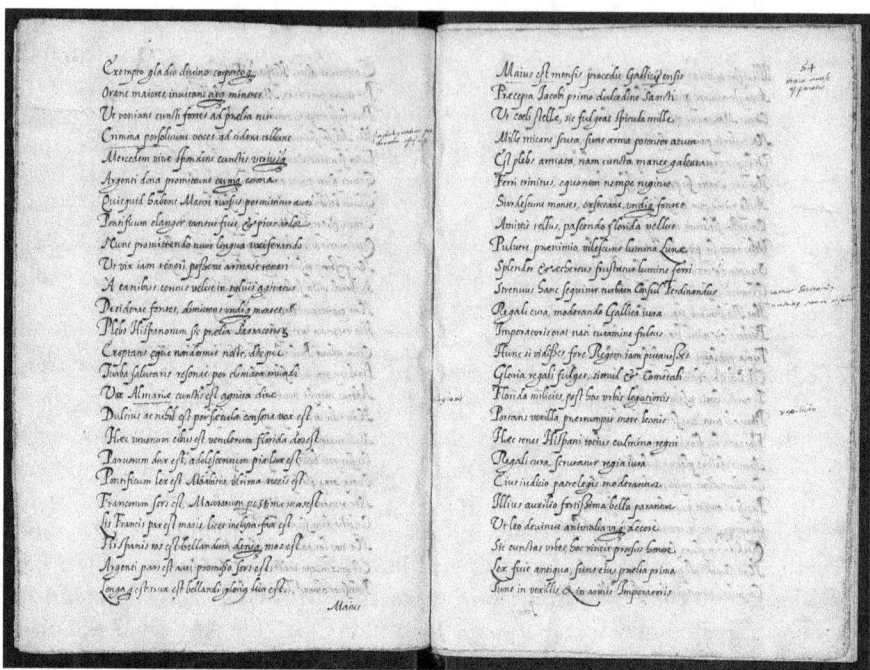

Figure 3.3 Men of León compared with lions in *Poema*. MSS 9237 61/72 folio 54.
Imágene procedentes de los fondos de la Biblioteca Nacional de España/Image from the collections of the National Library of Spain.

of Paul Alvarus and in the *Vita Argenteae*) from al-Andalus when anti-Jewish polemic was turned on the unfamiliar and more menacing threat from Umayyad North Africa. Neither was he dependent on contemporary sources such as the writings of Bishop Pelayo or the *HS*. Indeed, we cannot be sure that he was even acquainted with these works. Yet, there is an acknowledgement in his preface to his chronicle that he is aware of the importance of historical writing to inform posterity, incite memory and to make the heroes of old live again in the popular imagination.[140] But such models justify as well as inspire the language of conquest and they offer the author a penetrating discernment of divine purpose, and the imagery becomes essential in his presentation of ideology. There is admiration of the author's cultural and literary background[141] and he also has an unusual gift for recognizing the imaginative potential of the familiar and he goes directly to the sources themselves. Because he is intensely aware of how biblical precedent could be used to colour and frame his own history, the power of suggestion and allusion are his abiding and flexible tools.

Noble bloodline and historic precedent

We have thus far considered the way in which the author of the *CAI* uses biblically derived animal imagery and metaphor to infuse and enrich his historical narrative.

Attention now focuses on the qualities of the main protagonists as identified by the author and how their personal characteristics are elucidated. Especially, this will hinge on fusion of lineage, biblical and historical precedent and inherent quality. In the *CAI* there is no direct preoccupation with the ancestral legitimacy that was such a feature of the *HS* and Pelayo (and earlier chronicles), though there is the suggestion in the chronicle that Alfonso VII's own lineage was considered important by the old men of Toledo

> whom King Alfonso [VI] had left behind to watch over the city until a king should come of his own seed who might liberate it from the military threat of the Saracens.[142]

Neither does the author shy away from the idea of lineage when it suits his purposes; Count Ramiro, to whom we have just referred, is described as having royal lineage, *natus de semine regum*[143] [born of kingly stock], a reference to his descent from the Navarrese royal house – though this appellation may be part of the writer's attempt to confer greatness on the city of León. And Count Manrique, who emerges towards the end of the poem, has qualities linked with his father Count Pedro de Lara, who is referred to on six occasions in Book One of the *CAI* and once in Book Two.[144] Count Pedro was not an ally of Alfonso VII but fought on the side of the Aragonese. Yet, in references to his son Count Manrique, who is described as a friend of Christ without pretence,[145] the author seems to be praising an inherent personal quality rather than a specific Hispanic allegiance. Since there was now a common enemy against whom both Castilians and Aragonese had the strength to unite, the 'friend of Christ' could, in an echo of The Wisdom of Solomon ('thou scourgest our enemies very many ways'),[146] become the agent of the most calamitous pestilence of the Moors.[147] Although such references seem to have been employed only occasionally by the author, they are part of an evolving description and are not normally central to the themes of revenge or the consummation of God's justice in the chronicle and poem; nor are they used consistently.[148] Much more striking are the references to heroic figures of the past such as Charlemagne and also to St James of Compostela who contribute decisively to the drama of the chronicle and poem. Charlemagne, who features just once in the *Poema*[149] (and not at all in the prose books of the *CAI*), is part of a reference that is so painstakingly studded with its carefully chosen comparisons that it may be of sufficient prominence to suggest more than passing significance: 'But Alfonso is Charlemagne. Indeed, the Poem is the Song of Roland with improvements.'[150] Nevertheless this does not represent or allude to a noble bloodline, still less is it a suggestion of any kind of link with the Frankish nobility associated with Charlemagne. Yet for O'Callaghan, the implication is beyond dispute: 'A worthy rival of Charlemagne, according to the *Poem of Almería*, he was his equal in lineage, bravery, and deeds of war.'[151] Indeed, although the author acknowledges the 'illustrious' [*clara*] qualities of the Frankish messengers, their message itself and the extravagant picture they compose of their nation suggest that the author's attitude is complex and perhaps sceptical.[152]

Hagarenes and Moabites

A more direct reference to lineage relates to Sayf al-Dawla (d. 1146). Latinized to Zafadola,[153] he is described in the *CAI* as 'a certain Saracen king in Rueda,'[154] though the reason for referring to his ancestry may be more complex. He is described in the narrative Book 1 relating to Alfonso VII's campaign in 1133 and was granted estates in the land around Toledo and in Extremadura 'the King of León bequeathed to King Zafadola, castles and communities in the region of Toledo and in Extremadura and around the banks of the Duero.'[155] He is described as being of the most noble line of the Hagarene kings, and is presented fulsomely, though his fealty to Alfonso VII as well as his lineage is also recognized by the author.[156] It might seem strange that the author of such a polemical account confers such high praise on a Muslim, yet the inclusion of such a description, as we noted in a different context with Count Manrique, serves to emphasize the identity and character of the real enemy, that is Alfonso of Aragón, and Zafadola's part in his downfall.[157] And such praise is not necessarily at variance with OT models or with the mood of crusade within the poem.[158] In addition to the biblical precedent, we have an exemplary case of an infidel receiving due compensation by rank.[159] And there is a further dimension which might enable the victor to consolidate his imposition on the former enemy. With reference to the Moors of Alcoçer described in *Cartar de Mío Cid*, Israel Burshatin discusses the ways in which the manipulation of a subject may be possible through a kind of excessive and condescending paternalism: 'After colonization, the Moors of Alcoçer are turned into a projection of their master and they become the disguised (as Moorish) reflection of the Cid's ascendancy over the world of the enemy Moors.'[160]

There was a complex and confused status of those described as Hagarenes who had already been referred to by the author of the *HS*[161] and was also used, often indiscriminately, by other Spanish chroniclers.[162] The use of the term in the *CAI* is likely to have been descriptive in intention rather than specifically pejorative, or at least primarily so. For the author of the *CAI* may well have had in mind the promise of God not only to the legitimate line of Abraham via Sarai, but specifically to the descendants of Ishmael: 'And also of the son of the bondwoman will I make a nation, because he is thy seed.'[163] The author, in chapter 60, is able to elaborate on this theme.[164] In a passage dripping with biblical language and imagery, the Almoravids, with whom Zafadola's ancestors had been locked in conflict over the lordship of Zaragoza since the death of Rodrigo Díaz in 1099 and who eventually capitulated in 1110, were to be identified with the Moabites. Historically, the Moabites had been pastoral tribes living in the mountainous area east of the Dead Sea and bordering on Jordan but in the Bible were portrayed as a shadowy and sinister people, sometimes depicted as given to idolatry, arrogance and ingratitude.[165] The use of the term *Moabitae* in the *CAI* is unusually frequent and arresting, though it is unlikely that the author had any real understanding of the word.[166] This identification of current and biblical enemy is widely acknowledged and the etymological link is pursued by others.[167] But in the *CAI*, the author's distinction between Muslims does not merely separate friend and foe since the division is emphasized by both sets of protagonists having biblical names bestowed upon them: names that are flexible in their application. It is also clear that genealogy had, from the first, played an important part in Islamic culture and ideology and that this was explicit in Qur'anic teaching: 'The importance of genealogy was endorsed by the Qu'ran ... genealogies were assembled in the Middle East as early as the beginning of the ninth century.'[168]

Yet if the Hagarenes were recognized as Abraham's descendants and therefore having some affinity with – though inferior to – the Spanish Christian conquerors, the term Moabite had more ominous connotations and could mean a separate, pagan people who were widely believed to have had incestuous origins.[169] The so-called Hagarene leaders, observing the conflict around Seville, sought an alliance not with their own co-religionists but through Zafadola, Moor and faithful vassal to Alfonso VII, with the emperor himself.[170] In Chapter 4 of this volume, Zafadola's purpose and character is compared with models that the author drew from early Jewish writing known as Books 1 and 2 of the Maccabees.

It is sometimes suggested, probably misleadingly, that within the *CAI*, the terms Hagarene and Moabite might be used interchangeably, especially, but not exclusively, in Book 2.[171] This use can suggest that the Hagarenes had been coerced into fighting with the Moabites rather than because the author confused the two terms. In the description of the campaign of 1141 waged by Count Ramiro against King Afonso I of Portugal (r. 1139–85), for example, the term *Moabite et Arageni* is perhaps a kind of shorthand, though an inadequate one, to describe the perceived collective Muslim threat.[172] In other passages the author is aware of the distinctions that might be made between the two groups. For example, in emphasizing the intention of the Hagarenes to do homage to Alfonso VII and perhaps to collaborate with him, the author reminds us, in unmistakably biblical language, of the murderous nature of those described as Moabites: 'the Moabites had killed all the seed of the Hagarenes and thence stolen their kingdom.'[173] Nevertheless, in the *Poema* we have the term *Hismaelitas*/Ishmaelites (with its clear biblical connection with Hagar) introduced,[174] when the fleeing Muslim armies are vanquished by the men of León.

St James of Compostela

The other historical and religious figure in the *CAI* whose intercessions and example were crucial to Christian military success in Iberia is St James of Compostela, apostle and martyr, and his influence and authority are to be found within the prose sections and in the *Poema*. Because Book 1 is concerned primarily with Alfonso's attempts to shore up his kingdom north of the Duero, references to St James as a saviour of Iberia are indirect, being limited to settlements found on the pilgrimage route. And it may be that the presence of such settlements has no obvious implications within the text. It is reasonable, however, to assume that the reference to settlements along the *camino* which had been appropriated by Alfonso I of Aragón and Navarre, following his acrimonious estrangement from

Alfonso VII's mother (after 1114),[175] could allude to the towns being restored to their rightful status in the kingdom of León-Castile:

> Whereas the King of Aragón held Carrión, Castrojeriz and other fortified towns round about, the city of Burgos with Villafranca Montes de Oca, Nájera together with Belorado and different settlements and fortified estates and many walled towns in the vicinity which had all been snatched [*auferre*] from Queen Urraca through war and fear. [176]

The use of the pluperfect active form of the verb *auferre* seems to be used pejoratively and might mean 'had been stolen' or 'seized,' suggesting that the area was now controlled by its rightful suzerainty. Equally however, even deductions from statements in the main text can be obscure, and the reference to the 'blessed fiftieth anniversary [or jubilee year]'[177] might refer to the feast day of St James though there is no unanimity on this point. Nevertheless, the juxtaposition of the reference to this event and to the magisterial words of Luke 24.49[178] might suggest that the author is at least invoking a promise made by Jesus following the Resurrection. Therefore, the beginning of the new dispensation is suggested, however tenuously, with the power and memory of St James in the city of León, even if the primary association of the author's passage was with war.

Any reticence about a direct appeal to St James is abandoned in Book 2 and in the *Poema*, where the saint assumes an elevated status, as his intercession is sought by the knights of Ávila and Segovia on their approach to the camp of the Almoravid emir Tāshufīn on the plain of Lucena,[179] to aid their struggle: 'they cried out loudly to the God of heaven and earth, to St Mary and to St James in prayer, that they would aid and protect them.'[180] St James, traditionally regarded as the first of the twelve apostles to have been martyred, is now, together with the Virgin Mary, able to sustain, empower and inspire. Moreover, he has the power, along with the Virgin Mary, to intercede with God for the forgiveness of sins:

> The Christians moreover, cried out with all their hearts to the Lord God, the Blessed [Virgin] Mary and St James, that they should take pity on them and forget the sins of their kings, their own sins and those of their parents. [181]

This power invested in a man, however venerated, appears to have no biblical parallel, though there are suggestions within hagiography that the powers bequeathed to saints are mysterious and wide ranging.[182] But there is tension between the idea of a universal and ubiquitous accessibility of saints and the belief that their power might be more firmly rooted where their relics were held to rest.[183] The relative power of the saint is further explored elsewhere: 'the rhythm of possession and exorcism … contributed to build up a model of the working power and presence of the saints in late antique society.'[184] In terms of those saints who appear on a universal calendar (i.e. those who are celebrated with a specific feast day – of whom St James would figure prominently), there was a gradual diminution of the importance of relics from the eighth century onwards.[185] A particularly pertinent and striking example of this distinction is in the powers of major and minor saints.[186] There would, therefore, appear to have been an incremental acquisition of perceived power of universal saints even if this were further modified by what is referred to as 'the cult of Christ',[187] a term that is loaded with classical association as well as the ways in which early Christian congregations sought to distinguish themselves from the secular society and from their neighbours to whom they were bound. However, in this context the term is used to describe the growing importance of sacramental worship.

In the Bible, men are occasionally called upon to forgive the sins of their people (or to seek such forgiveness from God), even though this does not equate to the acquisition of sainthood or routinely involve absolution. The Lord's Prayer provides a possible example of forgiveness generating wider exoneration. And in Ex. 32. 30, Moses says that he can intercede [*quivero eum deprecari*]; however, this was not always the case. For example, Joseph was implored to forgive the trespasses of his brothers[188] as is clear from the verb used to denote his response to the earlier collective action of his brothers (*obliviscor*, to forget) who sold him to live as a slave in Egypt. The term is occasionally used elsewhere in the Bible as a plea to God to forget the sins of his people and individuals.[189] In *Augustine on Memory*, Grove notes that a variety of words, in addition to *oblivicor* (e.g. *delere*, *excidere*), can be used for forgetting.[190] It can also be contrasted with *dimittere*, to forgive or let go, which is the verb used by Jesus when he asks God to forgive those who have crucified him.[191]

There are examples within the *CAI* of the men of Castile calling upon the saint to give them succour in the face of the enemy. Before the Christians loyal to Muño Alfonso were taunted by Avenceta,[192] they had already implored St James to save them from the Saracen enemy. In a prayer addressed principally to Jesus and to Mary, James also plays his part: 'Saint James, apostle of Christ, defend us in battle in order that we shall not be destroyed by the terrible authority of the Saracens.'[193] And although such invocations to the saint are commonplace, accounts of apparitions are much rarer.[194] Nevertheless, such visions emerged in later narratives. One such example is that of Clavijo, now a tiny village in the centre of the Rioja district and which, according to legend, was the scene of a battle in 844 between Ramiro I of the Asturias and the Emir of Córdoba. According to this legend, St James appears as *Santiago Matamoros* to give aid to the vastly outnumbered Christian forces.[195] Although in the oration to Jesus of Nazareth, the armies of Azuel and Avenceta are referred to as *Moabites et Agareni*,[196] by the end of the prayer these terms (which, as we have noted, are not always or necessarily interchangeable) have been conflated into the recognizably more current and non-biblical appellation of *Sarracenorum*. The OT provided models of pragmatism and patristic leadership as exemplars that would suit the growing narrative of Christian conquest in Iberia. Equally, the author of the *CAI* extended this use of typology to demonstrate how enemies too, recognizable from a biblical setting or narrative, would have a resonance with the chronicler's audience.

There is in the *Poema* a short but unambiguous further reference to the influence of St James, and this time his power is specifically directed to the men of Galicia (the Galicians advance, having already received the blessing of St James).[197] It is not clear how this 'blessing' [*dulcedine*], if it may be so described,[198] was administered but there are many examples, especially in the psalms, of God's blessing being bestowed upon his people, and confirmation of this might come from a human source. David declares: 'thy blessing is upon thy people.'[199] If we consider statements such as these, the invocation of the saint's power in the *CAI* and his blessing on a Christian mission are prerequisites in a godly struggle for supremacy. Ps. 7 seems to offer a parallel between biblical conflict and the battle for Almería; here God is depicted as preparing the weapons of war as they are honed for the great conflict: 'he will brandish his sword; he hath bent his bow, and made it ready. And in it he hath prepared the instruments of death, he hath made ready his arrows for them that burn.'[200] The work of St James as the soldier of Christ seems to have had a similar impact on the Galician forces as they demonstrate their readiness for battle:

> Like the stars in the heavens, thus it is that a thousand javelins shine, a thousand shields flash and the arms have been skilfully sharpened. The citizens as a body are prepared for war and all remain in their helmets.[201]

Here the change in mood from the sublime to the commonplace is easily discernible. Nevertheless, the juxtaposition of militarism and piety is a frequently nuanced biblical image and is especially apposite for St James, the legendary slayer of Moors at Clavijo.[202] The writer of the Letter to the Ephesians urges Christians to 'Put on the whole armour of God' and in this powerful call to arms, as in the passage following St James's intervention before Almería, the purpose and significance of each weapon is elucidated. And although the struggle described in Ephesians is a metaphorical and spiritual one, the wrestle against the rulers of darkness in this world[203] is a commonly conflated theme and one which the author can use against the Muslim occupants of the city.

Pilgrimage, piety and reward

St James is a towering presence within the *CAI* and the author also makes important, though brief, references to lineage and to those whose memory he sought to 'make new' [*noua faciunt*] in the writing of his chronicle.[204] However, he makes no direct reference to Spain's Visigothic past, and the invocation of figures such as Isidore of Seville is absent. Such an omission may be deliberate or indicate the possibility of the author's non-Leonese origins. In earlier texts from within the peninsula, biblical influence has usually been apparent either as a subtle and understated guiding principle within the historical commentary and frequently offering an unmistakable historical link to the political events being described. Or it may – in an echo of the texts arising from the execution of the Córdoban Christians in the 850s – be used as part of polemical rant against Islam and a railing against injustice perpetrated on the Christians. Accordingly, Christian hegemony within twelfth-century Iberia was self-evident. The *CAI* presents us, perhaps for the first time, with an emphatic and aggressive picture of Spanish Reconquista, infused with a crusading ideology and this would override all other considerations, including the issue of individual culpability for what would otherwise be unpardonable offences. For example, the Galician nobleman, Muño Alfonso (d. 1143), who is depicted as a heroic figure in Book 2 of the *CAI*, perceives that because of his own guilt and intemperance following his sin of filicide,[205] the more noble route for him would have been to do penance in Jerusalem rather than to fight the Muslims in al-Andalus.[206] There is therefore the suggestion that Muño Alfonso regarded the campaigns in Iberia as something of a sideshow compared with the struggle for the Holy Land, but this was firmly rejected by the archbishop of Toledo. And although this response was echoed by other senior clerics, it seems to have been prompted by the emperor himself.[207] This emphasis, together with the invocation of St James on the battlefield, fusing penitence and warfare, ensures the place of pilgrimage within the author's crusading ideology in Castile. And the presence of Compostela as a penitential destination offers a further focus in the complex phenomenon of crusading mentality and especially the link between penitence and warfare.[208] Purkis concedes that the persistence of such ideas may owe more to the *Liber Sancti Jacobi* (henceforward *LSJ*), a codex compiled probably between 1160 and 1173, than to the *CAI*, though he recognizes that this development was also gaining ground elsewhere. It is perhaps also worth noting that the alternative title of the *LSJ* is *Codex Calixtinus*, which reflects the supposed influence of the former abbot of Cluny, Pope Calixtus II (r. 1119–24), on the process of enabling the work to develop and to become so influential.[209] And it may be that the archbishop who rebuked Muño Alfonso, the Benedictine and French Cluniac Raymond de Sauvetât (r. 1125–52), owed something to his near contemporary Calixtus II, both of whom succeeded in promoting the spiritual and penitential efficacy of war and within a specifically Iberian context. Indeed, it was Calixtus's encyclical in April 1123, writing to the faithful in Spain, that called upon the Iberians to defend their brothers and liberate their churches.[210] This had very specific intention: 'he [Calixtus] regarded the wars in Spain to have the same salvatory character as those in the Holy Land.'[211]

Notions of personal penitence and revenge certainly provided the chronicler with an example in Muño Alfonso of a man whose end was inevitable and personally tragic; yet he allowed Muño Alfonso's military heroism to be honoured and celebrated, though he was not uncritical of occasional lapses in military judgement.[212] A possible parallel is the OT narrative of Samson who was punished by God for the sin of fornication. Personal recognition of his wretchedness was followed by penance and his life was to end in an act of bravery that brought about the defeat of the men of Gaza.[213] The link between ruthlessness in battle and subsequent pilgrimage had already been recorded in the case of Count Rodrigo González.[214] The distinction between pilgrimage and fighting the infidel was further conflated when, in spite of the invocation of the biblical phrase 'he took his journey,'[215] which is used extensively in the parables of the synoptic gospels[216] and in Jesus' eschatological teaching;[217] it is also implicit in the story of the 'certain nobleman' who 'went into a far country.'[218] For Count Rodrigo, his far-off destination is Jerusalem and, though he sets out 'for the sake of prayer,'[219] the call to arms is integrated into his desire to serve God: (where he engaged in many battles with the Saracens).[220] This double-edged approach to pilgrimage, fusing together pilgrimage and crusade,[221] makes it almost impossible to determine individual purpose between these traditional and more modern, militaristic elements. It was not merely that the diligence of prayer and zeal for the spread of God's kingdom should converge; victory on the battlefield was the outward sign of God conferring approbation on his faithful people. This is standard OT ideology though it is explicit in the *CAI*: 'The *CAI*'s more hostile tone was … in keeping with the medieval view of history that victory in battle is heaven's reward for virtue, while defeat castigates sin.'[222]

In the *CAI*, a case that corresponds closely to this model of victory and defeat is the author's reference to 'the men of Salamanca,'[223] and alluding to events that may have taken place in 1134[224] or at least have some point of reference with the defeat of the Christians at Badajoz, close to the Portuguese border, in that year. The short account of the *Salamanticenses* contains a complex feature; clearly, God rewards the penance, self-sacrifice and prayers of his faithful soldiers with the courage and strength to wage war successfully. The men were commanded by God to give him their 'tithes and first-fruits'[225] and although these oblations are unspecific, they are preceded by acts of penitence[226] and are strongly redolent of biblical precedents. The notion of the offering of first fruits is an aggregate in the cementing of the relationship between God and his people and is commonly used in the OT (and especially in the Pentateuch) as well as in the NT. The precise phrase *decimas et primitias* is used in Deuteronomy in the Vulgate[227] in the context of teaching and specifically as to how the Israelites will govern the land promised to them by God. The link is maintained elsewhere as an example of the continuing acknowledgement and gratitude of God's people[228] and with inheritance and sacrifice.[229] *Primitia* is moreover directly linked with the idea of reward. The Children of Israel had been delivered from bondage in Egypt and into a land of milk and honey and they must now fulfil their part in the eternal covenant;[230] this organization of events suggests that the strict order of reward and punishment may not be absolute. In the NT the phrase occurs more sparingly[231] and is often used to refer to spiritual first fruits and this may not be quite the sense in which the author of the *CAI* is intending them to be understood here. Yet there are parallels that suggest even closer affinity between the *CAI* and the OT. According to the author of the book of Tobit (written in the first person), Tobit, eschewing the idolatry practised by his fellow Hebrews and their king, Jeroboam, went to Jerusalem to offer as an act of faith and adoration, his first fruits and tithes to the God of Israel: 'But I alone went often to Jerusalem at the feasts, as it was ordained unto all the people of Israel by an everlasting decree, having the firstfruits and tenths of increase.'[232] We have here the convergence of many elements: bravery, adoration, faith, first fruits and tithes: the ingredients of the rich rewards bequeathed also on the men of Salamanca.

The second feature of this passage is that it asserts the historic and biblically derived supremacy of the strength of God over that of man and that any power that might be exercised over the enemy of Christians or Hebrews is part of God's largesse; indeed the reason for the earlier failure of the men of Salamanca is their belief in their own authority rather than in that of God[233] and that this is not merely misplaced but an act of arrogant wickedness, synonymous perhaps with idolatry: 'and therefore they perished totally.'[234] The idea of God's omnipotence and ultimate authority over his people's destiny is expressed trenchantly in the OT,[235] and this may be delivered as a response to the psalmist's question, heavy with irony, 'Why boasteth thou thyself in mischief [*malitia*]?'[236] – to which the carefully crafted response is delivered six verses later: 'Lo, this is the man that made not God his strength; but trusted in the abundance of his riches, and strengthened himself in his wickedness.'[237] Other references are specifically about battle and conquest and often in circumstances that replicate the explanation given of the eventual success of the knights of Salamanca: 'For they got not the land in possession by their own sword, neither did their own arm save them; but thy right hand, and thine arm, and the light of thy countenance, because thou hadst a favour unto them.'[238] Such incidents may be recalled specifically, as when the Israelites were led across the Red Sea in their escape from Egypt; it is God, not Moses, who has triumphed and Moses himself sings of the strength and salvation that comes from the Lord.[239] Although the passage in the *CAI* rests on the glory and triumph of the ultimate authority of God as revealed in Exodus, it also has a grimness which in tone is more reflective of the warnings that are contained elsewhere in the OT where retribution and calamity are threatened on those of his people who do not acknowledge his power.[240]

These features suggest not only biblical influence but includes an increasingly precise identification with the God of the Hebrews and the writer's own growing conviction that his God was moving in the same way amongst those who were fighting the Muslims in Iberia. The third feature of the passage introduces the idea of the importance of place. For just as we noted that the status of the city of León with all its imagery and majesty was enhanced, at least in part, by the men of the city,[241] so the city of Salamanca itself would be honoured and exalted because of the piety of its knights. The practice of linking the esteem in which a city or place is held with the valour of its citizens and the events within its walls would have been familiar to the author of the *CAI* and has many biblical precedents. Most famously, Bethlehem is 'not least among the princes of Juda'[242] because of its prestige as the city of David[243] and the prophecy surrounding the birth of the Messiah. Equally, a city might be brought low because of the conduct of its people. Most notorious are the cases of Sodom and Gomorrah[244] and a further more oblique example is Nineveh, 'that great city,'[245] where the population and the city itself were threatened with a very specific and comprehensive punishment: 'and [Jonah] said, Yet forty days and Nineveh shall be overthrown.'[246] Just as the city of Nineveh was spared from divine wrath and restored to its former greatness because of its people's penitence, so it could also serve as a model for Hispanic cities. Jerusalem as a biblical model for certain Hispanic cities during the twelfth and thirteenth centuries is a recurring subject. The descriptions of Jerusalem in the book of Revelation[247] may be altogether too grandiose to make a plausible comparison with twelfth-century Salamanca; nevertheless, the link between people, place, reward and punishment was so embedded in OT perception that it offered a tempting model for the writer of the *CAI*.

The short passage about the men of Salamanca suggests a kind of awareness of biblical precedent that is a break with earlier reflections on the struggle with Islam; and it may in part be a sweeping sense of growing awareness of God's power, of conviction or confidence in the rightness of the Christian cause and in the contemporary message of biblical providence. At any rate, there is a strong sense of conviction in military destiny. And the author has a generic awareness of how God's favour might be bestowed:

> The message of the *Chronica*, common to most Christian historiography of this period, was that victory on the battlefield and its subsequent rewards – namely the acquisition of land and booty – would only be obtained if the participants were devoted to God and favoured His Church on Earth.[248]

What might tentatively be suggested is that the author of the *CAI* was more emphatic than his contemporaries and predecessors in tying his belief in God's power to firmly established biblical events and his understanding of such events as revealed through exegesis and familiarity with the daily office. This is partly perhaps because the events he was describing as well as the majesty of the emperor and his court suggested biblical parallels that enabled his narrative to assume the tone and style of an OT epic:

> Alfonso VII is God's chosen leader, sent to destroy the Almoravids and to preserve Spain for the Christians, and the use of Biblical language and incident and the implication of certain vital passages make this purpose clear.[249]

Even in a passage not obviously redolent with OT language and metaphor, belief in the power of the biblical record to allude to events in the author's own time and experience is as ubiquitous as it is pervasive.

The uniqueness of the *CAI* is in part due to its debt to biblical texts which are not only more extensively used than in previous Hispano-Latin chronicles in León-Castile, but they are also more emphatic and central to his narrative. Although there are occasional allusions to Ovid and particularly to Virgil, these are mostly clustered within the *Poema*[250] and the relative paucity of classical references has been noted;[251] nevertheless, the author's use of biblical text to weave a coherent history of Alfonso's reign suggests that he is a man of perspicacity and vision.[252] Furthermore, the clarity with which narrative and precedent are integrated into the author's account also sets the chronicle apart from earlier and contemporary Iberian accounts. This does not diminish the importance of a more understated reliance on the scriptures within other texts, where insertions from OT narrative were less deliberate and may have been more frequently linked to memory and reminiscence. The author of the *CAI* seems to have developed, quite suddenly, a pattern of polemicism and assertiveness. Put another way, the simplicity of the text – the *sermo simplex*[253] – may have made the chronicle more comprehensible to a listening audience. The *CAI* is, therefore, both a break with the past and part of a wider and evolving awareness of the character of the Iberian campaigns. In the example of Muño Alfonso and perhaps also hinted at in the passage concerning the men of Salamanca, the development of piety and crusading valour is enriched with perhaps a third and radical feature of the act of penance, suggesting what Purkis calls 'the localisation of crusading traditions'[254] and this seems to have evolved as an important idea in twelfth-century Iberia and represented a clear departure from earlier chronicles.

4

THE *CHRONICA ADEFONSI IMPERATORIS* AND THE LITERATURE OF CONQUEST

Conflict and ideology

There is a strong likelihood that both the prose books of the *CAI* and the *Poema* were penned by a single author, or substantially so. Common themes discernible throughout the chronicle were derived primarily from scripture and scripturally dependent allusions. The author used and deployed these texts as parallels with events taking place in the north of the Iberian Peninsula and in al-Andalus. The integration of biblical text to explain and enrich his historical record is central to the author's methodology. Especially important is the sense of ideological purpose that may be deduced from his chronicle as well as the character of author's intended audience.[1] We now consider the *CAI* more specifically as part of the literature of conquest that described the events in the reign of Alfonso VII by comparing its message with two other texts: one, a contemporary text describing another theatre of conflict within the Iberian Peninsula, and the other describing a biblical struggle.

A vision of history together with an ideology of mission, if that is how this may be termed, owed much to the writings of Isidore.[2] Nevertheless, the shadowy concept of conquest developed only gradually in the north and north-west of Spain and it was not until the advent of the *CAI*, that we have the arrival of unambiguous and relentless crusading parallels: 'Under the pen of the anonymous chronicler, the image of the Reconquest is built by reference to the crusade.'[3] The context and content of the *CAI* will now be compared with a contemporary historical work, the *De expugnatione Lyxbonensi* [The Conquest of Lisbon].[4] *De expugnatione* describes a more famous and fundamental confrontation that deals with a specific conflict. However, like the *CAI* (and especially the *Poema*), it celebrates an important Iberian victory against the Muslims and is a telling contrast with the fortunes of the crusaders in the eastern Mediterranean.[5] The comparison between the *CAI* and *De expugnatione* is followed by a consideration of the way biblical models were used by the author of the *CAI* to relate to the cities of twelfth-century León-Castile, considered within the context of wider medieval historiography. As well as the contemporary historiographical parallel, specific biblical sources and influences will be pursued, and reference will be made to 1 and 2 Macc. Comparisons with contemporary accounts and the author's use of scriptural sources will support the uniqueness of the *CAI*: 'The *CAI* presents a kind of Old Testament version of the emperor's divinely-countenanced wrath in the destruction of the infidel.'[6] Finally, the sheer scale of the author's achievement as a compiler of a biblically inspired narrative of conquest and revenge will be used to assert the particular qualities of his chronicle and the subtlety with which his references may be applied.

De expugnatione Lyxbonensi and the *CAI*: Lisbon and Almería

The conquests of Lisbon and Almería took place in 1147 and are almost certainly eye-witness accounts, meriting close comparison.[7] Furthermore, the author of *De expugnatione* not only asserts that crusade is a crucial element in the penitential route to salvation but also that this path may be travelled in Iberia as well as in Palestine; as such he shared some common ideology with the author of the *CAI*. This is even more intriguing, since the authorship of the two chronicles arose from distinct cultural and geographical contexts. Thus, although the authorship of *De expugnatione* may still be debated, it is not thought to have an Iberian provenance and is likely to have been written by a Norman-French priest identified as Raol who took part in the Lisbon campaign.[8] As we might expect therefore, *De expugnatione* is, in many ways, a very different kind of chronicle from the *CAI*, and such coincidental convergence may be an indication of an emerging ideology of crusade.[9] Its content is also much more varied than that of the *CAI*, it being in part a detailed description of the military campaign itself, the conduct of soldiers and the way war was to be waged, as well as a topographical description of northern and western Iberia with comments on the fauna and flora of the countryside. The chronicle also had an all-embracing character since the army it described included men of a number of nationalities and its original mission went well beyond the liberation of a particular city.[10] Nevertheless these elements are integrated into an account of the journey and its crusading purpose and are not specifically separated from the prerequisite of spiritual reward.[11] It is evident from the comparison of *De expugnatione* with the *CAI*, and especially from the description of the Lisbon and Almería campaigns, that any attempt to assert areas of commonality between the two texts serves at least in part to highlight the distinctiveness of each account – and this is without any reference to the very different theatres of war in which the conflicts took place. Nevertheless, it is worth briefly pursuing other areas of similarity, since, whatever else may be said, they are both records of simultaneous Christian military success in Iberia. These considerations would seem to represent a shift in thinking which distinguished these two mid-century chronicles from earlier Hispano-Latin chronicles in León-Castile but which, nevertheless, may have had an echo in more distant Iberian realms; additionally, the progress of the fight against al-Andalus was infiltrated by a steady flow of knights from north of the Pyrenees.[12] Like the *CAI*, *De expugnatione* demonstrates a vivid awareness of biblical ideology and this is often unambiguously expressed. The author's use of this narrative is deployed in his ongoing description of day-to-day events, though it is within certain key passages that scriptural authority is most evident. The author, in observing a familiar practice, is particularly adept at using direct references from biblical texts. He does so in three key sections of the chronicle, each of which comprises rhetoric or dialogue from senior churchmen[13] or represents the author's own summary.

Since those taking part in the conquest of Lisbon were en route to the Levant, the campaign was part of the Second Crusade (1147–9) and may be interpreted as its solitary success. This, coupled with Alfonso VII's capture of Almería, was part of a rush of victories for Christians in Iberian theatres of war where they were able to overcome the Muslims.[14] Although Alfonso's successes declined after 1148, the capture of Almería, the Spanish 'window on the Mediterranean'[15] – together with the successful Lisbon campaign – enabled a vision of the relocation of pilgrimage within Iberia to be perpetuated. In the *De expugnatione*, The bishop of Oporto appears to be justifying the participation of the many taking part in the Lisbon campaign precisely because it was possible to argue that this was a legitimate expression of piety and pilgrimage: 'It is surely evident that they have replaced all their honour and status with a fruitful pilgrimage to receive a prize from God.'[16] The transient riches of this world are readily exchanged for substantial heavenly reward. In his sermon, the bishop, recognizing that his hearers have come from distant lands to the aid of King Afonso I, delivers an address that begins with a blessing that seems to be aimed at the entire faithful of Christendom; the author points out that the bishop addresses the troops in Latin so that his words may be easily interpreted in their own language.[17] Immediately following this is his blessing: 'Happy is the nation for whom [our] God is Lord and the people whom he has elected for his own inheritance.'[18] Here there is a confident assertion of the binding historical contract between God and his people: the men gathered before the bishop are members, as it were, of a single nation. They speak with a common tongue and represent a single and indivisible faith. As the Christians joyfully enter Lisbon, Raol reports the use of liturgical extracts, notably the *Te deum laudamus* and *Asperges me* (derived from Ps. 50.9 and sung at Mass),[19] together with other devotional prayers.[20]

Nevertheless, Raol reserves his most powerful references to the Bible and his use of biblical language for specific parts of the *De expugnatione* and its invocation is for defined purposes. The will of God is central to the crusaders' activity but references to it are usually in the context of their current mission and almost any scriptural allusion is missing from the narrative of events. It is also absent from the prolonged exchanges between the king of Portugal, Hervey de Glanvill, the leader of the East Anglian contingent in the Second Crusade, and the archbishop of Braga about the crusaders' leadership.[21] In the dialogue with the alcayde, or Muslim governor of Lisbon,[22] the archbishop of Braga makes no appeal to biblical allusion, though in acknowledging what David translates as 'the common bond of humanity,'[23] he attempts first to persuade the Muslims to convert to the Christian God. What he is involved in is a dialogue with his Muslim opponent; the inherent goodness of Christians would not allow them to seize what belonged to others [*aliena non rapiat*],[24] but they will seek what was taken from them. There is a sense of injustice that characterizes this exchange, and although it lacks the relentlessly venomous invective of the *CAI*, its historic and moral purpose in restoring to the Iberian Christians their ancestral homeland is unmistakable: 'You have wrongfully and for more than three hundred and fifty years retained our cities and the country's possessions which were formerly held by Christians.'[25] The message may be less overtly vengeful than that contained in the *CAI* but its clarity and sense of the rightness of its historical claim is delivered with equal conviction.

Despite this ideological similarity with the *CAI*, the biblical theme is not picked up again until the eve of the Christians' victory in Lisbon, when an unidentified priest[26] urges his brethren to engage in a final push for the city. Here again, the message is penitential and almost sacrificial. Honour, obedience and righteousness are pitched against pride, foolishness and apostasy. The priest does not spare the Christian troops the condemnation of failing to redeem themselves, comparing them with those referred to in the synoptic gospels, who in their spitting, flagellation and with the cruel irony of the crown of thorns, mocked Christ to his face.[27] At this point there is a flurry of NT references. The prizes for the penitent faithful are again spiritual and unworldly; in an echo of Phil. 4.14,[28] the priest declares his confidence in the rewards for those who persevere for the Lord: 'Hear and grasp that [although] the prize is promised to those who begin, only those who are steadfast will be rewarded.'[29] As we noted earlier, the distinction between earthly and eternal rewards was less defined in the *CAI*, when temporal riches were promised to the Christian parties who collaborated in the campaign for Almería. Thus, although biblical texts seem to have been used more sparingly and specifically in the *De expugnatione*, this focused use seems to convey a more deep-seated sense of purpose and piety, drawing on an equal number of biblical links from the NT and OT. Of the forty-six biblical contrasts identified by David in the *De expugnatione*, twenty-three are from the NT with twenty-three from the OT. This is not an exhaustive list of possible allusions but further examples from within the text tend to support this pattern. In the *CAI*, the situation is very different and, although classical literary references are present in the chronicle, the overwhelming bulk of specific references, at least in the prose section, are biblical. In his assertion about the biblical content of the *CAI*, Maurilio Pérez González not only declares that the number of biblical references referred to by Maya Sánchez – 221 passages – to be an underestimate, since he has uncovered others,[30] but of the 221 biblical allusions and references, no fewer than 189 are from the OT and 32 are from the NT.[31] Of course, the OT provides much more striking narrative and imagery of the art and nature of conquest but, as we shall see shortly, the author of the *CAI* is able to use his sources to provide a rich ideological picture of societies in conflict. Yet even this list by no means exhausts the ways in which biblical precedent informs the author's history, even if some events relate to biblical events rather than to memorable literary allusions:

> Such biblical influences infuse everything from the stories and descriptions, to the characterization of the historical personalities, to the speeches that the chronicler puts in mouths of its main characters, to those who lament, etc.[32]

In view of the discourse between bishop and alcayde before the struggle for Lisbon began, the more modest use of OT rhetoric in *De expugnatione* is scarcely surprising. A tone more suited to reflective piety is suggested and this idea is compounded by what is said after the fall of the city when the author himself reflects on the success of the campaign. For when utter devastation is visited upon the Muslims,[33] biblical precedent informs the author's musings, recalling the prophecy of Isaiah.[34] Thanks to the Mother of God for deliverance is coupled with a sombre remembrance of past Christian sins. In an echo of Rom. 1.25,[35] the author makes a related point: 'Remembering therefore what we have been, let us give thanks to the Creator, because we have released our mental/spiritual necks [*colla mentis*] from slavery to those who procreate'.[36]

This tone and evocation of such humility is entirely absent from the *CAI*. In a description in the poem of the siege of Andújar,[37] the city is the first in the drive towards Almería to 'drink the wine of suffering,' a phrase not only reminiscent of the Last Supper,[38] but also one that has several OT precedents.[39] These links are not referred to in Maya Sánchez's edition but are powerful and arresting biblical reminiscences. Within the *CAI* there is also a key illustration of the chronicler's depiction of retribution. This is his interpretation of the protection afforded to fortresses at Guadalajara and other towns and castles[40] in the conflicts mounted by Almoravid forces in Toledo and the Tagus Valley after 1109: 'The King of Heaven, mindful of his usual piety, made retribution on the Saracens.'[41] This has clear parallels with the pleadings of the unnamed daughter of the Hebrew judge Jephthah to her father: 'Lord do unto me whatsoever thou hast promised, since the victory hath been granted to thee, and revenge of thy enemies.'[42] Although it can be argued that piety and vengeance are almost indivisible within the *CAI* – and present, though less emphatically so in *De expugnatione* – they are derived from OT notions of honour and defensive duty.[43] Nevertheless, the balance between vengeance and pity is more frequently observed in the text of *De expugnatione* than in the *CAI*.

The conclusion of the *De expugnatione* is a prayer of thanksgiving for deliverance which importantly also contains eloquent pity for the victims; in addition to the idea of compassion there is a vindication of the efficacy of pilgrimage in invoking the power of God: 'Not by means of our right actions have we struck down our enemy, but it has happened in accordance with God's great pity.'[44] A comparison with the 1132 campaign of Alfonso VII's general in Extremadura and in the land around Seville, Count Rodrigo González, shows an almost complete indifference to the suffering of his vanquished enemies: 'they came into the territory of Seville and ransacked the entire area, committed much slaughter, caused many fires and ordered the orchards to be felled.'[45] The scene of fire and the destruction of agriculture owes its uncompromising sense of the rightness in its execution to the OT campaigns in Canaan and is rooted in ancient promise: 'The Lord thy God, he will go over before thee, and he will destroy these nations from before thee, and thou shalt possess them.'[46] And, in keeping with the practice of some early Hebrew successes as revealed in the OT, the count does not eliminate his enemies: they are taken off as prisoners and slaves and their wealth is confiscated. This is much more reminiscent of the initial response of the Children of Israel to their victory over the Midianites: cattle, sheep and 'all their goods' are seized and women and children are taken into slavery.[47] *De expugnatione* and the *CAI* may represent strikingly different emphases on the spectrum of pity and vengeance, yet within each is the apparent acknowledgement of the necessity of both elements within the efficacy of the penitent nation.

On the face of it, that might seem to be the beginning and end of any comparison between the two texts. Yet, despite the divergent backgrounds and nationalities of those participating in the attempts at conquest and those describing them, parallels between the *CAI* and the *De expugnatione* continue to suggest themselves. Although Purkis considers the significance of the Mediterranean campaign to be greater than the success in Lisbon in terms of the development of a crusading ideology,[48] both chronicles seem to be reflecting an evolving common mood, distinctiveness and sense of loss. Questions arise as to why they might be seen as marking a change in emphasis and style from earlier texts. The fact that such changes should have occurred so suddenly and dramatically certainly suggests a more focused hostility within Iberia to the struggle with Islam. And, although this apparent change relates importantly to questions of authorship and provenance, we may here encounter more specific features of the ways in which the authors of the two texts portray conflict. Therefore if, as some have argued, the origins of the author of the *CAI* cannot be put to rest, questions over whether the scriptural allusions and references are part of an evolving Spanish tradition of biblically inspired historiography need to be addressed. Associated with this difficulty is the fact that the earliest surviving manuscripts of the *CAI* belong to the sixteenth century and each one contains various elements of corruption.[49] Yet the chronicle represents perhaps the first thoroughgoing and unambiguous attempt to construct a picture of a people involved in an epic and biblically inspired struggle for their ancestral homeland against the Muslim occupation. This idea is also advanced as part of the argument within the *De expugnatione*, but without the relentless presence of polemic and revenge.

Holy cities

There are occasions when cities within the *CAI* are afforded specific honour by virtue of their place in the history of the Iberian struggle; for example, the particular status and importance of Santiago, León and even Salamanca are enhanced and defined by the quality of their men, and their piety and bravery.[50] And although the author of the *CAI* does not concern himself overly with the significance of Portuguese cities, the capture of Coimbra in 1064 is miraculously announced by St James, and recorded by the author of the *HS*.[51] There is a further and perhaps more profound sense in which the cities of Spain might be said to occupy a unique place in Leonese-Castilian imagination and narrative. Biblical cities seem to have provided models and the city of Nineveh served as an example of penitence and forgiveness. Yet it is with the example of Jerusalem that more promising and enduring parallels might be made. Although within the *CAI* there are few references to Jerusalem – three in all, two of which are concerned with geographical location and the third with pilgrimage[52] – the attempt to compare biblical visions of Jerusalem with what the twelfth-century chroniclers understood to be the significance of their own historic cities suggests an understanding of the relevance of scriptural comparisons. This was in keeping with a medieval awareness and a desire to create religious spaces in their own cathedrals based on what was known about the architecture of the Holy City and the liturgy used in the temple.[53] This seems to have been a standard feature of early medieval thinking in the Latin west and the influence of other features of the biblical city was evident elsewhere.[54] For the author of the *CAI* this presented an alluring but potentially dangerous conundrum:

> For the author of the chronicle, the temptation of Jerusalem must be opposed, partly because, as we shall see, it conveys a model of confrontation between Islam and Christendom too distinct from that of the Reconquest, but also, above all, because the attraction of the crusade tends to distract the knights of León-Castile in the service of the king. [55]

The biblical parallel that would inspire the author's own sense of historical drama and ideological mission within his own country might also drain Iberian knights away from fighting the enemy on their own soil.[56]

The twelfth century was also a period when writing about cities became popular and classical and biblical comparisons abound. Catherine Clarke notes that in the *Descriptio Londonia* by the cleric and administrator William Fitzstephen (d. c. 1191), the attempt to generate comparisons with ancient models as a creative paragon often failed to 'map easily into representations of real medieval cities.'[57] Furthermore, there was sometimes a determined attempt to link a saint with a specific city – to create a patron saint.[58] The idea of deliberate association of person with place will be discussed in the thirteenth-century context in the next chapter and particularly in relation to Isidore of Seville.

We shall shortly consider how Jerusalem might have appealed to the biblically steeped medieval imagination. The idea that the city was geographically and spiritually at the world's centre is derived from a verse in Ezekiel[38] generally held to refer to Jerusalem and describing it as the world's umbilical centre.[59] We are dealing, therefore, with a tradition that was ancient even when pilgrims began to write about Jerusalem in the late seventh century. Adriaan Bredero cites two ancient descriptions in which the idea of Jerusalem as the world's navel is suggested, the earliest dating from around 680;[60] and this idea seems to have grown and embedded itself in the popular imagination: 'In the twelfth century, the idea of Jerusalem as the centre of the world became almost universal.'[61] In 1089 Pope Urban II seems to have grasped both the opportunities and pitfalls of elevating the city's earthly and religious centrality when he argued that to build the church in Tarragona was as worthy an activity as a pilgrimage to Jerusalem.[62] He seems to have recognized that Jerusalem may be more than a physical reality and by encouraging Catalan Christians to work for the church in their city, the holiness of Jerusalem was exalted rather than diminished. There was a web of ideas that constituted the medieval idea of the city: Jerusalem was 'functioning not as a single place but as a series of images, each of which explores a different strand of theological understanding and devotional practice.'[63] So Urban may have been appealing both to a physical place and a religious aspiration. This compound legacy of the ideological, theological and physical centrality bequeathed will be further explored as will the way descriptions of the cities of León-Castile were imbued with this biblical complexity.

Jerusalem is a city suffused with a combination of qualities and is represented as having human characteristics[64] (sometimes memorably described, as when the author of Lamentations compares Jerusalem with 'a menstruous woman').[65] It is a symbol of geographical isolation and power,[66] and this had particular implications for Christian witness and assertiveness as when, in using the city as a metaphor for discipleship, Jesus declares it to be 'A city that is set on a hill cannot be hid.'[67] It is a unique and pivotal religious and apocalyptic reference point and it is also addressed directly.[68] Sometimes complementary ideas, such as peace and prosperity, are to be found in the same reference.[69] Although Jerusalem will be ruined because of what its people have said and done,[70] the apocalyptic vision of Isaiah shows a glorious restoration.[71] As such it is seen as eternal, divinely endowed with mystical authority, 'thine eyes shall see Jerusalem, a rich habitation, a tabernacle that cannot be removed.'[72] This theme is embellished in the NT where the idea of the Christians' inheritance of Jerusalem is linked to the heavenly city wherein the faithful will dwell.[73] It is also a powerful poetic metaphor for the restoration of God's kingdom as the new Jerusalem pours out of heaven as a precious and engulfing gift: 'new Jerusalem which cometh down out of heaven from my God.'[74]

Such multifaceted images of a city, real and imagined, might overwhelm any comparison with Iberian cities, especially since Jerusalem itself evolved as an idea and acquired legendary and figurative status. Yet in an important sense, the model holds good. In portraying the events of Alfonso VII's campaigns as part of a biblically inspired movement, parallels between OT cities and those whose mythical and historical associations helped to forge the idea and emergence of Christian conquest – with its implicit notions of recovery and reversal. Nowhere was this more demonstrably the case than in Toledo. At the core of the taifa principality was the city captured by Alfonso VI in 1085 and despite the assault on the city by the Almoravids in 1090 and 1109 – four sieges in fact – and their successors, the Almohads, it was to remain thereafter in Christian hands. Its capture demonstrated the success of Alfonso VI in creating a frontier city facing al-Andalus, and it was Toledo, with its historic status as the capital of the old Visigothic monarchy.[75] It could boast supposed links with Isidore[76] (although he, of course, held the see of Seville) and it was the ancient seat of the Church of Spain; all this was conferred upon the conquest of Toledo, a cultural and religious as well as a strategic significance. There is a notable absence within the *CAI* of references to Spain's Visigothic past, though there is a clear recognition of the historic and spiritual significance of Toledo, undiminished and self-evident. Because of the concentration on the distant conflict being described in the *Poema*, we may not expect the emerging city of Toledo as a political and religious centre of gravity to be emphasized. Yet there is a political equivalence with León[77] and right at the beginning of the *Poema*, Alfonso VII is not only referred to as the 'overall general' [*dux*)] but, with greater prestige, as 'king of the Toledan Empire' [*imperii cunctorum rex Toletani*)].[78] Troy and Jerusalem were linked in the medieval imagination[79] so the fusing of classical and biblical precedents would not have been lost on twelfth-century readers, even if such parallels are also compared with the early loss of Visigothic Spain: 'The year 711 was worthy to be bracketed with the various calamities that had overtaken Troy, Jerusalem, Babylon and Rome.'[80]

It is within the prose sections of the *CAI*, and especially in Book 2, that there is a more emphatic and growing awareness of the particular significance of the city, importantly linking Alfonso VII with the exploits of his grandfather, Alfonso VI. Because of the curious chronology of the *CAI*, we are taken, at the beginning of Book 2, to the period following Alfonso VI's death in 1109 and there are two sections (chapters 1–8 and 12–18) that deal with the Almoravid incursions into the Tagus Valley. It is in this period of intermittent military conflict that, according to the author of the *CAI*, Toledo is described by King Alī of Córdoba[81] as *ciuitatem Christianorum*,[82] the city of the Christians. This allusion to the biblical city of Jerusalem is compounded by Toledo's lofty geographical position and its ancient ecclesiastical and political authority.

The comparison with Jerusalem is pursued by the author a little further on when Alī compels his son Tāshufīn to bring about Toledo's destruction by the sword[83] and the reference to the prophecy of Jeremiah is unmistakable: 'And I will make void the counsel of Judah and Jerusalem in this place; and I will cause them to fall by the sword before their enemies.'[84] By linking Alī with a recognizable OT parallel, the author is indulging in a piece of irony in which, unwittingly, his enemy acknowledges Christian supremacy. There may also be a further implication that Alī is guilty of a kind of blasphemy. Remembering that 'Scornful men bring a city into snare,'[85] he claims that he has been treated with contempt and turned on by the men of Toledo;[86] an analogy with those who had turned their backs on God, according to the prophecy of Jeremiah, is suggested.[87] The sword however, will not be turned upon the city of Christians because – through the intercessions of the Virgin Mary – God has heard the prayers of the faithful and has appointed the Archangel Michael, that prince and guardian of Israel,[88] to protect this holy citadel.[89] And as the walls of Jerusalem had been rebuilt and strengthened in the time of Nehemiah,[90] so the Archangel Michael would strengthen those of Toledo. The importance of Toledo as a city particularly favoured by God, and therefore reminiscent of biblical models, emerges in Book 2, since it is seen as a kind of cultural and spiritual home. Following their victory at the southern Portuguese city of Silves,[91] the soldiers of Toledo returned to their city which was, by implication, a haven of joy and celebration where they could sing praises to God: 'they went back to Toledo with confident gladness and delight, singing.'[92]

Two points have been implicit in the discussion so far. Firstly, models for Toledo can be inferred in several cities in biblical texts, though Jerusalem is probably the most important or more frequently mentioned and nuanced example. Secondly, as a corollary, the depiction of Toledo as a centre of biblically inspired Christian celebration made it unique amongst Iberian cities and some incidents appear to recur in different settings. For example, Alfonso's entry into Toledo in 1139,[93] which owes something to the coming of Jesus on Palm Sunday[94] as well as to prophecies concerning the destruction of Jerusalem,[95] is to be compared with the description of the emperor's arrival in Zaragoza five years earlier.[96] As we shall see, the allusion to the entry of Jesus into Jerusalem was also used to describe a similar triumphal entry (also into Toledo) by the author of the *CLRC*. Yet though the *benedictus* accompanies music reminiscent of that played on the instruments described in the book of Daniel,[97] the context of Alfonso's entry into Zaragoza – which serves to elevate the king and kingdom of León – is to be distinguished from the way he was received as the hero in the ancient spiritual capital of Toledo. Here he is welcomed by the entire Christian population – the powerful and the humble – as well as by Muslims and Jews.[98] Furthermore, Alfonso's link with Toledo is emphasized on other occasions as when the emperor hurried to Toledo[99] in 1143 at the behest of Empress Berengaria and Muño Alfonso to join them in celebrating their victory at the Battle of Montiel. And in the following year when they were again revelling in the destruction of Hagarene power: 'The destruction of [their kingdom] between Almería and Calatrava.'[100] The victory was also honoured in Toledo: 'Following this, the emperor and his entire army returned to Toledo carrying with them enormous riches, a great victory and peace.'[101] Toledo had developed, in spite of its remoteness from the conflicts in southern Spain, as the city where victory was to be most fully celebrated – just as the victory of the Children of Israel over the Moabites was celebrated at Jerusalem:

> Then they returned, every man of Judah and Jerusalem, and Jehoshaphat in the forefront of them, to go again to Jerusalem with joy; for the Lord hath made them to rejoice over their enemies. And they came to Jerusalem with psalteries and harps and trumpets unto the house of the Lord.[102]

The final section from the *CAI* to be considered with reference to possible parallels between Iberian cities and Jerusalem concerns the death of Muño Alfonso. As an incident, this is complex and one that involves considerable inference. When Muño Alfonso's widow and her friends lamented the nobleman's death, the city and inhabitants of the city of Toledo are represented as sharing in the collective grief: 'In the same way as a wife loves her husband, thus the city of Toledo holds you dear.'[103] This passage is redolent of the famous biblical lamentation, when David's period of mourning records the loss of Saul and Jonathan at Gilboa in 2 Sam. 1.[104] Indeed, the words of David implore the 'daughters of Israel'[105] to weep over the death of Saul, just as Toledo as a community is integral to the grieving process surrounding Muño Alfonso. So perhaps Toledo is to be identified with the nation of Israel as well as with a specific city. In the passage describing the grief at Muño Alfonso's death, the sadness of people and of place are conflated; the city of Toledo can be seen as a metaphor for Muño's widow, just as Israel collectively mourns the death of its past and present heroes. There is evidence that the Jonathan and Saul narrative was a familiar topos in medieval narrative and was referred to during similar outbursts of lamentation.[106]

Despite the resurgence of Toledo, its pre-eminence cannot really be said to diminish the author's view of León and both cities seem, certainly in the *Poema*, to march together as an indivisible symbol of Christian hegemony in Iberia. For if the author's narrative is untouched by Iberia's Visigothic past, León's long and resistant history within Iberian Christendom is pre-eminent in his account: 'It holds the highest position of all in the Hispanic kingdom ... Just as the lion exceeds other creatures in strength and beauty, so this city surpasses all others in honour.'[107] Alfonso VII's imperial coronation in León in 1135, to which the author devotes considerable attention,[108] would have further enhanced the city's status.

There are further reasons why the idea that Toledo alone should be seen in the *CAI* as a representation of Jerusalem may be facile, even though the comparison between the two cities can be inferred. Whether or not the capture of Toledo is to be presented as the symbolic beginning of Reconquista, it was certainly a turning point in terms of establishing the Muslim-Christian frontier.[109] Nevertheless, subsequent conquest was a protracted and oscillating process, so much so that there were, at the time of the capitulation of the city to Alfonso VI, no coordinated attempts at Muslim struggle[110] – or if there were, they quickly became battles of resistance and entrenchment rather than advancement. Furthermore, doubts could be raised as to whether Toledo could indeed claim to be reborn as the embodiment of the old Visigothic state (and the author of the *CAI* conspicuously fails to make any such link); church authority in Toledo was only grudgingly restored by the Cluniac Urban II in his bull *Cunctis sanctorum*, 1088,[111] though Alfonso VI's pre-emptive decision to confer primacy of Iberia on Archbishop Bernard of Sédirac[112] in 1088 – which he had no authority to do – may have contributed to the pope's irritation and lack of fulsome support. On this specific point, Linehan comments: 'whatever the politico-ecclesiastical preponderance may have amounted to in the seventh century, in the twelfth Toledo could not be expected to be more than a simulacrum of the former *urbs regia*.'[113]

Nevertheless, during the twelfth century, and perhaps earlier, it was possible to begin to characterize Toledo as a repository of Spain's past and future greatness with lessons that were not lost on military manoeuvres in far-off places. O'Callaghan describes the surrender of Toledo in 1085 as 'an event of great transcendence in the history of medieval Spain'[114] and that León was 'quickly eclipsed' as the centre of political power, yet the tension between León and Toledo was to be a persistent and evolving factor in determining ascendancy. For although Alfonso VI often styled himself as *imperator toletanus* or *Toletani imperii rex*,[115] this title was not adopted by his successors, some of whom preferred to use the somewhat older and more familiar description *imperator totius hispaniae* – a title also used by Alfonso VI himself – with its associations with the Leonese kingdom. Sancho II of Castile (r. 1065–72), who was succeeded by his brother Alfonso VI, is described by the anonymous author of the early-twelfth-century history of El Cid known as *Historia Roderici*, as *rex tocius Castelle et dominator Hyspanie*[116] (king of all Castile and lord of Spain), a phrase, notes Jesús Rodríguez-Velasco, that 'enjoys a semantic confluence with the *Imperium Totius Hispaniae*.'[117] This, and its extended title *imperator constitutes super omnes Hispaniae nationes* was perhaps used in part to assert Hispanic rather than papal hegemony over the peninsula.[118] The title was nevertheless seen as 'a pretension even more energetically affirmed by Alfonso VII.'[119] Yet it was not used explicitly to describe the power bestowed upon Alfonso VII at his coronation in 1135 but it is strongly implied in the roll call of Spanish and French kings and noblemen who proclaimed him as emperor and promised to pay homage to him.[120] In the dating clauses to his charters, in which Alfonso VII listed his realms, Toledo was placed before León: 'Adefonso imperatore / in Toleto, Legione, Sarragoza, Naiara, Castella, Galicia.'[121] In the complexity of competing claims for supremacy, it is important to recognize the distinct histories of León and Castile and the tensions that were to erupt between them. The achievement of the chronicler, whose knowledge of Toledo[122] and León[123] was intimate and affectionate, was to balance the characteristics of each kingdom.

The *CAI* and the Maccabees

Of the OT references within the *CAI*, almost a quarter are derived from the two books of the Maccabees;[124] of these the greater proportion are from the First Book. There is a marked difference in composition and style between the two books, as there is between the prose and poetic sections of the chronicle.[125] Linehan has already noted that the two prose books of the *CAI* tend to be more descriptive than the strongly polemical *PA*,[126] and the author may be aware of the value of restrained narrative – albeit with its many dramatic and belligerent insertions – as well as the more stirring and relentless apocalyptic call to arms provided by the language of the poem. The story in Maccabees involves the beginnings and successes of a Jewish rebel army led in turn by the three priestly sons of Mattathias (Judas, Jonathan and Simon) and specifically the revolt that they led against the remnant of the former Macedonian Empire of Alexander the Great (known as the Seleucid Empire);[127] the aim to reassert Jewish religious practice and dominance in Judaea was led by Judas Maccabeus and the revolt took place between 167 and 160 BC. The parallel between the Maccabees' struggle with secular authority, which was sparked by the desire of the Jews to practise their faith freely and which was to develop into an assertive zeal,[128] and comparison with the military crusades of the faithful in the Holy Land is frequently made. In addition, the details of the struggles within Iberia, including the fragmentary and intermittent campaigns involved in Christian kings shoring up their own positions as well as campaigning against the Muslims, offer some superficial historical analogies. However, as we shall see, the language of conflict was one that was dependent on an enduring biblical comparison. The accounts in Judaea do not provide a perfect template for Alfonso VII's struggles in twelfth-century Iberia, but the aims of the Maccabees and the wars that they waged against their oppressors provided the author of the *CAI* with ideological and descriptive parallels with Alfonso VII's attempts to wrest authority from the Muslims and re-impose the Catholic faith on his expanding kingdom, as well as with allusions to conflicts involving his complex relationship with his stepfather, Alfonso I of Aragón.

The books of the Maccabees had already provided frequent and eloquent source material for early descriptive comparison; Janet Nelson discusses the descriptions of the death of Emperor Charles 'the Bald' (823–877) taken from the ninth-century Annals of St Bertin and Annals of Fulda with 'the grisly death of Antiochus Epiphanes' in 2 Macc. 9.8-28.[129] A precedent for crusade literature and possibly the eleventh-century rebellion of Hereward the Wake,[130] as well as models for describing the conflict in Iberia in the twelfth- and thirteenth-centuries, had already been set.[131] We are here concerned chiefly with the influence of such accounts on the events described within the *CAI* and since the author shows a much greater awareness of the books of the Maccabees than do other Spanish chroniclers,[132] their inclusion will be especially useful in clarifying the uniqueness of the chronicle. He may have been aware of the contemporary calls of Eugene III (r. 1145–53) to link the crusading armies of the Second Crusade with the restoration of holy places in Jerusalem; there were also earlier attempts to requisition the Jewish account to serve a Christian purpose: 'a Christian context with the Maccabean army becoming the army of Christ, fighting at God's command to defend His people and seeking not gold or silver, but knowledge, heavenly conversion and martyrdom.'[133] Alfonso VII himself was presented as God's supreme agent of retribution,[134] yet – particularly amongst the coalition of forces gathered before the siege of Almería – the author's geographical, political and personal loyalties could not disguise the fact that this was more than a Castilian-Catalan mission. Indeed, if Arnaldo of Astorga was the author of the *CAI*, it is likely that he – as Alfonso's envoy to Barcelona and Montpelier – was involved in the coordination of the Christian forces on the eve of Almería.[135]

Yet it is not merely a consideration of individual texts that makes parallels between the books of the Maccabees and the *CAI* so striking and intriguing. There is also evidence that more general ideas from the *CAI* are sometimes inexplicably linked to the accounts in the Maccabees. The recurring theme of the ways in which the faithful might be rewarded for their bravery and piety is extended to include a sense of retribution and reward that would be meted out as necessary: 'Wherefore the wicked shrunk for fear of him, and all the workers of iniquity were troubled, because salvation prospered in his hand.'[136] This stark choice posed by the author between salvation and perdition contained in this single verse informs the way in which he presents divine intervention. This passage is redolent of language linked to the Resurrection – Book 1 chapter 71 begins with 'Truly on the third day'[137] – and with references to the salvation of Spain,[138] and concludes with the gruesome punishment visited upon the infidel: 'in the sight of all, some of these workers of iniquity [the *operarii iniquitatus* of Macc. 3.6 and Lk. 13.27] were caught and hanged from the gallows.'[139] The same verse had been used earlier (in Book 1, chapter 26) to describe the temporal and eternal joys experienced by the Castilians following the surrender of Herrera and Castrillo (probably located within a triangle of land between Burgos and Palencia) in 1131: 'And salvation and extensive peace were established throughout his entire kingdom.'[140] The author was adept at extracting maximum contemporary resonance from concise sacred text.

The *CAI* is nothing if not a piece of crusading polemic, and it is therefore unsurprising that the events and language of the Maccabees should be used to support an account which is intended to be both persuasive and emphatic. Nevertheless, the use of 1 and 2 Macc. within the *CAI* is complex; sometimes historical comparisons are drawn, and great themes alluded to; such themes will be addressed shortly. On other occasions however, the references are simple, terse and may suggest the blessing of God or the acquiescence of a people to God's will. For example, a reference to 1 Macc., 'After this they went home, and sang a song of thanksgiving, and praised the Lord in heaven: because he is good, because his mercy endureth forever,'[141] is alluded to at least four times in the *CAI*.[142] Of particular interest are the final three words of the verse [*saeculum misericordia eius*] and the way the phrase is appropriated – rather awkwardly, tenuously and with highly partial effect in the case of the *CAI* 1, 17 – to drive home the message of God's enduring link with his people and his mercy towards them. In the biblical account, the passage illustrates the mood of the Jews following the triumph of Judas Maccabeus over the forces of King Antiochus (led by the Syrian-Seleucid general, Gorgias), and whether the parallel triumph of Alfonso VII over Alfonso I of Aragón in 1128/9 is quite as the chronicler describes it is highly questionable; the competing claims of the two Iberian kings for political authority were, according to Reilly, much more evenly balanced:

> The king of León busied himself fortifying Morón and Medinaceli before withdrawing. The Aragonese in turn further fortified Almazán before returning to his ultimately successful siege of Molina de Aragón.[143]

The author of the *CAI* is, nevertheless, able to present the whole incident and the success of Alfonso VII over the Aragonese monarch as an adept strategic and diplomatic success.[144] Holy text could, if the 1 Macc. 4 narrative is seen as a precedent, be used shamelessly to create highly partial and misleading accounts of events which are not corroborated by other evidence. They may, however, serve a higher purpose in creating a sense of the author's belief in the rightness of his cause. This may have been especially so when authors were dealing with ideas that could be represented symbolically: 'Symbols, by their very nature, have a magnetic effect on the human psyche which mere concepts could rarely, if ever, enjoy. But symbols are often polyvalent and ambiguous.'[145] Furthermore, it will be noted that the repeated integration of holy text can almost seamlessly suggest the conflation of accounts from the Maccabees with the author's own history. This conflation becomes one of the key features of the rationale of the chronicle.

Nevertheless, because comparison of characters and the parallel language and description of events in Maccabees and the *CAI* are often inseparably imbedded in the same account, they can be seen by the author and his possible audience as part of the same connected historical narrative. And in the example cited earlier, the whole incident is prefigured when the bishop of Pamplona,[146] ensures the acquiescence of the king of Aragón by using the response of Judas to Seron, prince of Syria, when he is confronted with a much more numerous enemy:

> With God it is not a difficult matter for many men to be confined by the hands of the few. Victory in combat does not consist in the size of the army but the strength comes from heaven.[147]

Although the words quoted in the *CAI* are a summary of those spoken by Judas,[148] the reference is unmistakable and the persuasiveness of the bishop would perhaps have reminded his royal hearers of the sudden and unequivocal collapse of Seron's army;[149] the contrast between the fate of those who would not listen to Judas and those in the Aragonese court who heeded the words of the Bishop of Pamplona is telling. The expedient of using a story that depicts political and religious corruption as an example used to demonstrate that a lesson had indeed been learned by the Castilian Christians is a recurring theme and was a device favoured by the author of the *CAI*.

The comparison of the bishop and Judas is tempting, and almost certainly tendentious. If it were part of the author's overall scheme of bestowing God's blessing on the armies loyal to Alfonso VII, there are several other examples where the author of the *CAI* conflates accounts from the Maccabees with his own history. One such comparison occurs in the passage referred to earlier in which the forces loyal to Ariol Garcés at Castrojeriz[150] capitulated to Alfonso VII in 1131 and a direct comparison can be made between the siege of Castrojeriz and that of Simon Maccabeus's successful siege of Jerusalem.[151] Such a comparison may be explored a little further. For just as the struggle for Castrojeriz is compared with that of Jerusalem, it is equally plausible to suggest that Alfonso VII is a holy warrior reminiscent of Simon Maccabeus. For those from within Castrojeriz who pleaded with Alfonso[152] were dependent on his mercy just as those within the tower at Jerusalem who pleaded with Simon begged him not to consider their sin.[153] Both those in Castrojeriz and Jerusalem were perishing through hunger and the response from the two God-driven leaders is almost identically recorded; they assented to the will of the people, but in both cases those mysteriously identified as 'of foreign origin' [*alienigenus*] in the *CAI*[154] and as 'heathens' or 'Gentiles' [*gentium*] in 1 Macc. 13.41[155] were expelled from their respective cities, though the reasons for their removal would appear to be different. The Maccabees' expulsion of their enemies from the citadel is presented as part of a purging process;[156] in the *CAI* the removal of the king's enemies seems to be an essential element in the celebration of victory: ('and he [the king] drove the foreign people from them [Herrera and Castrillo] and from all Castile').[157]

There is a further example of the author using an incident as almost a mirror image of the story that explains the original revolt of the Maccabees; and it also reveals an adept and original use of his own sources. His account concerns the advice of Zafadola and the unanimity with which this advice was received by those around him. In referring to the treachery and perjury [*mentitus ... periurus*] of the king of Aragón,[158] the former ruler of the taifa of Zaragoza allied himself with the king of Castile. Simultaneously, he was placed on the side of probity and discernment. The extract is a further instance of a device already noted in which an event and the way it is described are used to demonstrate how knowledge of an ungodly response is used to promote the idea of a more discriminating and pious people in the author's own generation. In the story from the Maccabees, Antiochus is described as 'the wicked root'[159] with whom some from Israel[160] sought to form an alliance (with the heathen); the people listened and were apparently persuaded: 'so this device pleased them well.'[161] The AV translates *sermo* as 'device,' rather than 'discourse' (which seems to fit better), and 'word' is favoured by the Douay-Rheims version.[162] This may be compared to the response of the nobility who heard the words of Zafadola and praised him for his distinguished counsel and far-seeing advice.[163] and the three words at the beginning *magnum consilium tuum* [your counsel is distinguished] are perhaps inserted by way of contrast to the foolish counsel given to the Jews by those who wished to identify with their heathen overlords. The author of the *CAI* is thus drawing attention to the contrast between true counsel and the weak and feckless leadership of the Jews prior to the revolt; the slightly elaborated text in the *CAI* makes the author's case persuasive and confidently based on unchallengeable sources. The further point is the character of Zafadola himself. He is here contrasted not with Antiochus, but with those who led the Jews astray with their false counsel. The advice was similar: both groups were being advised to surrender to a more powerful enemy and the crucial difference is the character of that enemy. Yet in the speech delivered by Zafadola, there is recognition that Alfonso VII is God's chosen instrument[164] and that capitulation is therefore an act of considered wisdom. The wicked men of Israel acted purely out of perceived self-interest. Zafadola is praised by his nobility for his sound advice, not condemned for treachery to Alfonso I. One translation of the response of the men of Israel is 'And the word seemed good in their eyes'[165] and this is a plausible reading of the response of the nobility to Zafadola. It has been possible, in a pithy and memorable phrase, to contrast the moral blindness of the men of Israel with the spiritual insight of Zafadola's followers.

In pursuing individual parallels with the main players in 1 and 2 Macc., the reference to the death of Alfonso I of Aragón in 1134 can be seen as having two clear precedents relating to the death of Alexander the Great[166] and King Antiochus;[167] the allusion to Alexander may relate to the valour and prestige and fortitude of both Alexander and Alfonso I, for in the case of Alfonso, the author is scrupulous in conveying what he considers to be a suitable eulogy ('Before and after him there were no comparisons with him among past Aragonese kings: none as strong, none as judicious, none as bellicose as he').[168] Although the character of Alfonso I is modified in the author's subsequent comments, in terms of his military prowess he had no equal and therefore provided a fitting comparison with Alexander. The example of Antiochus, the old enemy, is – if anything – even more plausible. The war weary and disappointed king seems to have been laid to rest on his bed and died (the use of words *cecidit in lecto* is almost identical in the *CAI* and in the two references in 1 Macc.)[169] and in the contrasting examples of Alfonso I and Antiochus, their deaths were preceded by great trauma and sense of loss. In the case of Alfonso I, we must assume that his sorrow was caused by his failure to take the Aragonese city of Fraga in July 1134 from the Muslims who were able to resist because of a combination of forces gathered by Avengania, the *magnus princeps* of Valencia and Murcia. These forces not only included the support of the kings of Córdoba, Seville, Granada, Lérida and Valencia itself, but Almoravids and Arabs from across the sea.[170] The author also argues that Alfonso I's refusal to accept the surrender of the city at an earlier stage – which, had this taken place, may have denied Avengania[171] the opportunity to regroup – because of his desire for retribution was a major factor in his failure to take the city. And this stubbornness, though seemingly part of a complex divine strategy in which God hardened the heart of the king of Aragón and then caused him to fail because of his personal sins, meant that, in Reilly's words, 'Aragón was crippled by the disaster at Fraga.'[172]

This passage highlights the way in which the intervention of God is seen to be central to the unfolding events in the author's account and especially his use of biblical language and example to illustrate a sacred purpose. The account of the last recorded rebellion of Count Gonzalo Peláez of Asturias, probably during the autumn of 1137,[173] demonstrates how the author relies on biblical precedent for both language and content. In the first place, he reiterates a basic Christian premise, that God understands the complexity of all events 'But the Lord who seeth all things';[174] in the *CAI*, *Dominus Deus* is replaced with *Deus*, but otherwise the wording is identical. And although this phrase has echoes and perhaps more profound implications elsewhere in the Bible,[175] it is within 2 Macc. that its use is most conspicuous[176] and we may deduce that the author had these texts in mind when he was referring to the oversight of God in the territorial (and perhaps temperamental) disputes between Alfonso VII and Count Gonzalo. The fate of Count Gonzalo (and that of Count Pedro González de Lara)[177] is described as 'a timely reminder of the risks that were run by those who sought to challenge the authority of the monarch.'[178] Yet if anything, the passage underpins the power of God to order human events and it may be, in the complex world of the role of churchmen in the anointing of medieval kings, for a Christian chronicler to challenge the emperor was to undermine the influence of the church and perhaps to challenge the will and purpose of God.[179]

Secondly, the account of Count Gonzalo's demise in the *CAI* is strongly reminiscent of the story of the struggle with Antiochus and his painful and protracted death and this is reinforced with the author's use of the *Sed, Deo disponente*[180] [But, by God's ordination]. For, in what might be seen as a just punishment for Count Gonzalo's insubordination, the count dies of a fever in a foreign land. In a much more graphic and grisly account, the same fate had befallen Antiochus – this time for sustaining the sin of pride: 'But the Lord Almighty, the God of Israel, smote him with an incurable and invisible plague: or as soon as he had spoken these words, a pain of the bowels that was remediless came upon him, and sore torments of the inner parts.'[181] The intervention of God in the death of Antiochus is much more emphatic and dramatic than in the fever that carried away Count Gonzalo, and it suggests that the author is embellishing his technique of using the content of one account to shed light on, but not necessarily to replicate, another. God's active vengeance (*percussit* might also mean 'pierced') in the suffering and death of Antiochus is replaced with the justice that is tinged with regret and mercy. The source of the count's fever is not explicit and he was restored to his rightful burial place in Oviedo. Antiochus, too, dies in a 'strange country'[182] but in remote mountains and without honour. The skill of the author may be seen not merely in his willingness to use an account to influence his understanding of contemporary events, but also to demonstrate that he is sometimes dealing with the frailties of Christian princes and is able to assert that justice is an appropriate response to these failings, just as vengeance and retribution would be required to deal with a more intractable and ideological enemy. We cannot be certain, but it is plausible that the author's audience would have recognized possible biblical and contemporary parallels.

When dealing with the Muslim enemy, the tone used by the author is much more trenchant and uncompromising, and we find little evidence of the subtleties that were evident in the accounts used to inform the struggle with Alfonso VII's Christian opponents. Yet even within the campaign against the Muslims, there remains the possibility of reconciliation. In the two accounts of the terminal sufferings of Antiochus (1 Macc. 6 and 2 Macc. 9), his pleas for mercy were thwarted: 'This wicked person vowed also unto the Lord, who now no more would have mercy upon him.'[183] The battle with Antiochus is used to provide the biblical substance for the somewhat compressed history of Urraca and then Alfonso's conflicts and his struggle from 1109 onwards with the Almoravid emir, ʿAlī ibn Yūsuf. And the lively inventory of weapons and their placements, 'siege machines in advantageous places … arrows, stones, light spears, javelins and fire,'[184] employed by the enemy as they besieged Toledo (in 1110), is contrasted with a brief but effective catalogue of Christian forces which included *robustorum iuuenum*[185] [powerful young men]. And the author repeats military comparisons as he elaborates on the conflict and his debt to the Maccabees' struggle with Antiochus is clear: 'As for the sanctuary, he besieged it many days: and set there artillery with engines and instruments to cast fire and stones, and pieces to cast darts and slings.'[186]

The armoury of Antiochus is mirrored in the military hardware of the Almoravids. And the destruction of Emir ʿAlī's forces is total and vengeance and piety are, as we noted, inseparable, though the reference has a greater debt to Judg. 11.36. In view of the air of triumphalism surrounding the defeat and slaughter of the Muslims, it might seem surprising that the death of Emir ʿAlī (we now move forward to 1143) should receive such solemn and sympathetic treatment. True, he was converted, or led by God's grace, to the Christian cause[187] and the author also acknowledges that on ʿAlī's death, his heir Tāshufīn continued his father's policy of favouring the Christians.[188] This 'favour' was in the context of Tāshufīn's battles against the Almohads in the Maghreb for which purpose he imported Christian cavalry.[189] And the comparison of ʿAlī's death with that of the elderly Jewish priest Mattathias[190] with the phrase 'and was gathered to his fathers,' which remains unaltered in the transcription in the *CAI*,[191] is curiously deferential, especially since Antiochus had so conspicuously failed in his attempts to secure divine mercy. Yet the author is not a slave to his biblical sources, nor does he flinch from tailoring them to suit his specific Christian message. And 'Alī's support of the Catholic party was no death-bed conversion (though it may have been in part a response to the Almohad threat),[192] so he had a long opportunity to demonstrate his loyalty to the new-found fealty. Such considerations were absent in the attempts of Antiochus to save himself. Additionally, the author may have wished to reiterate the fact that, notwithstanding his debt to the Maccabees and other biblical sources, he was operating in a new and different dispensation in which mercy and forgiveness might intrude on retribution and what the author describes as the King of Heaven's habitual piety.[193]

The author's ability to use biblical texts to develop his version of events in the reign of Alfonso VII as a specific and flexible device is evident in the way he deals with the theme of deception; this is a central element in explaining the complexities of the *gestae* within the chronicle. As we might expect, its use does not merely involve comparison or example, but it has the power to demonstrate insight. Although Alfonso VII is not seduced by the king of Aragón's compliant words ('Allow me to slip away peacefully into my country; I will stray neither to the right nor to the left'),[194] he accedes to Alfonso I's request. This is not an exact quotation from the Bible but is strongly redolent of many OT precedents[195] and is used not so much to demonstrate Alfonso VII's gullibility or easy acquiescence but rather to indicate his ability to perceive what those around him do not. And his understanding of the nature of deception is perhaps the central point of this incident since, though it has echoes of a range of biblical sources, it is linked directly to the insight of Simon Maccabeus: 'Hereupon Simon, albeit he perceived that they spake deceitfully unto him.'[196] The similarity with the account of Alfonso's perception of the mendacity surrounding the flurry of diplomacy surrounding the king of Aragón's court is clear: 'the King of León recognized the treachery that they [the ambassadors of the king of Aragon] uttered.'[197] So Alfonso VII and his Maccabean exemplar shared a similar insight into truth and this unusual perspicacity was tempered with a willingness to appease public opinion. Despite what they knew, both leaders agreed to the deceitful requests of their enemies: the Leonese king permitted Alfonso I to return to his own country. Simon, as the fitting ancient model, had paid a ransom of a hundred talents of silver and his two nephews for hostages[198] for the release of his brother, Jonathan. And the decision of the two leaders led to the sins of the enemy being exposed: Jonathan and his sons were murdered by the ambitious tyrant, usurper and king of the Seleucid kingdom, Tryphon (r. 142–138 BC);[199] Tryphon's possible equivalent in *CAI*, Alfonso I, plundered the lands he passed through on his way home.[200] As well as demonstrating the political dilemmas facing Simon and Alfonso VII, seen in parallel, the accounts also contrast good and evil as represented by the struggle for earthly supremacy: a struggle in which evil might occasionally, though temporarily, triumph.

A second point in relation to the comparison of the two incidents is the moral chasm that might be alluded to. Both Simon and Alfonso VII knew deceit when they saw it: they recognized human frailty, but they were, so to speak, above the fray.²⁰¹ One may ask whether it is plausible to suggest that the author of 1 Macc. deliberately created a moral champion in the form of Simon Maccabeus, yet this portrayal is consistent with his having provided just such a model for the chronicler. For in the following chapter, the virtues of Alfonso VII and his wife Berengaria are meticulously recorded and bear a striking contrast with those of he who is portrayed as a liar and perjurer, Alfonso I: 'and they were [both] most God-fearing; [they were] makers of God's churches and monasteries of monks, guardians of orphans and the poor and devotees of all God-fearing men.'²⁰² Alfonso VII, who was to triumph militarily at Castrojeriz in 1131, had already emerged as the moral champion at Valle de Támara four years earlier.²⁰³ And Ariol Garcés, the knight of the king of Aragón who capitulated at Castrojeriz, recognized the moral deficit within the Aragonese leadership (however, Ariol Garcés and those who accompanied him realized that no one could have faith in the king of Aragón).²⁰⁴ Isabel Las Heras also acknowledges what seems to be a moral chasm between the kings of León-Castile and Aragón:

> Alfonso VII is compared with David, Solomon or Judas Maccabeus, according to the differing circumstances. At the beginning of his reign – when he had to face Alfonso I of Aragón and Navarre – the king of León is identified with David and *el Batallador* with Saul). ²⁰⁵

The struggle of Simon with Tryphon offered the author of the *CAI* the scope to expand on the way his subject might be seen in historic terms, that is the way in which biblical precedent would inform posterity. And it also permitted him to contrast Alfonso VII with his Hispanic contemporaries in terms of power, integrity and virtue – qualities which would not be lost on perceptive observers such as Ariol Garcés, Pedro Díaz²⁰⁶ and, most conspicuously, the nobles of Zafadola ('Which king is able to be compared with the king of León?').²⁰⁷ This key image is taken from the OT. The phrase *quis similis tui in fortibus Domine* (Exod. 15.11) is translated in the AV as 'Who is like unto thee, O Lord, among the gods?' The Douay-Rheims translates more literally, 'among the strong.' This would undoubtedly have reminded the author's contemporaries of the supreme status of Alfonso VII. Nevertheless, the author is adept at using a particular image to drive a variety of messages home. In the altercation between David and Abner, the commander-in-chief of Saul's army, we are reminded of the high expectations of God's servants and how the mighty may be brought down.²⁰⁸

This may seem to be several steps removed from the original comparison with Simon Maccabeus. Yet parallels are complex, multifaceted and contain a variety of messages. Abner, who failed to protect his king (a reminder of the feeble attempts of Jesus' disciples to keep watch in the Garden of Gethsemane)²⁰⁹ as Saul's army pitched camp at Halchilah²¹⁰ is charged with fecklessness, with lacking the true qualities of leadership and of failing to honour his obligation to the king. He, like those who found it expedient to cut their ties with the king of Aragón, the king himself as well as those in 1 Macc. with Alfonso I's possible precursor Tryphon, were all guilty of a measure of deception²¹¹ and their besmirched characters are contrasted with those of Alfonso VII and with Simon Maccabeus who provided what may be seen as an ancient and impeccable model:

> The reader is to infer that the kings and regents of the Seleucid empire are not to be trusted ... Simon's conduct was always proper. Even when he delivered Jonathan's sons into Tryphon's hands, he did so because he had no alternative.[212]

There is a third example of the way the author alludes to a duplicitous act perpetrated by Antiochus, and he uses this as a lesson in kingly probity and as a means of demonstrating that his deeds can be contrasted with those of Alfonso VII; ironical recall, it seems, can be an effective weapon. In the account in 1 Macc., Antiochus sends his chief collector of the king's tributes [*rex principem tributorum*][213] to speak warm but deceitful words to the great multitude at Jerusalem:

> And [he, i.e. the chief collector of the king's tribute] spake peaceable words unto them, but all was deceit: for when they had given him credence, he fell suddenly upon the city, and smote it very sore, and destroyed much people of Israel.[214]

The catastrophe that befell God's people at the time of the Maccabees was caused by a combination of the deceit of the enemy and the naïveté of the men of Jerusalem. The parallel incident in the *CAI* refers to events following the accession to the throne of Aragón by Ramiro II in 1134 and the meeting between Alfonso VII and García Ramírez IV, who had recently ascended to the Navarrese throne and whose legitimacy was acknowledged by the king of León. In return for honour bestowed upon him by Ramiro and his nobles, Alfonso delivers a biblical promise (and he promised with all his heart and mind to support them),[215] the key words 'heart and mind' providing a recognizable resonance.[216] Yet it is Alfonso's 'peaceable words' that provide the real contrast with 1 Macc. 1 and a demonstration of a lesson well learned.[217] Deceitful words had, under the new dispensation and when spoken by a Christian prince, been given their true and unequivocal meaning. This is compounded by the further contrast of the tyranny of Antiochus and his desecration of holy places in Jerusalem with the benevolence of Alfonso VII who shows humility before the bishop of Zaragoza and who demonstrates his respect for the sanctity of the city.

Skilful manipulator of holy text

The purpose of this chapter has been to show that the author of the *CAI* uses biblical text to an extent and with a deliberation that is unmatched by his Iberian predecessors, even by those chronologically close to him. In earlier texts, and even within the contemporaneous *De expugnatione*, we search for allusions and each one is an individual prize. In the *CAI*, such references come thick and fast and it seems as if there is no end to the possibility of discovering further echoes within these familiar biblical texts together in his narrative. Yet this is not a question of mere quantity, nor even of the author's eye for comparison between events in his own time and with biblical precedent. He also shows himself to be able to use the biblical texts with subtlety and imagination and embellishing the biblical text to suit his own historic and moral emphasis with a frequent rhetorical flourish. But perhaps a more pertinent observation is the author's creative use of biblical, and especially OT references to make a variety of contrasting comments on Alfonso VII's reign. Jean Dunbabin comments on a feature of the Maccabees that makes it intriguing as a primary inspiration and record for the author of the *CAI*: 'It is almost (in 1 and Macc.) the nation-at-arms that is the hero.'[218] In the *CAI* one man is extolled, yet the triumph – especially in the *Poema* – is of the Spanish people[219] who are triumphant and this victory is dependent on the many heroes who constitute this people. And, of course, the campaign to capture Almería was an alliance not only of León, Navarre and Barcelona, but of Pisa and Genoa too.

This attempt to suggest an underling unity of the Hispanic peoples (and, for the purposes of Almería, Frankish people too)[220] may be discernible elsewhere. The way in which the author distinguishes between Alfonso VII's humility before a Catholic bishop[221] – together with a certain generosity of spirit he shows towards his Christian contemporaries in Navarre and Aragón – and his descriptions of the unremitting and merciless push for vengeance over the Islamic enemy provides a key comparison. Linehan's rhetorical question about the contrasts in style could more pertinently apply, not between Books 1 and 2 of the *CAI* and the *Poema*, but as a distinguishing feature of the language and polemic used to invoke vengeance on the Muslims (especially on those described as Moabites) and the more restrained context and way inter-Hispanic conflict is described. There could be no clearer assertion of the author's hostility to the Muslim enemy and his sense of triumph over its defeat and subsequent suffering than in the mayhem that followed Alfonso VII's raids into areas south of the River Guadalquivir in 1138. Not only was there a concerted attempt to destroy the vestiges of the Muslim faith: 'they [i.e. Alfonso VII's raiding parties] burned the many villages that they came upon, tore down their mosques and made bonfires of the books of Mohammed's law.'[222] In a series of ensuing references, remarkable as much for their ferocity as for the clarity of their biblical precedents, the author drives home his message of retribution. All Muslim religious leaders are summarily executed,[223] along with the devastation of their land and agriculture. Following the inability of Rodrigo Fernández (the *princeps Toletanus*) and Count Rodrigo Martínez of León[224] to respond to the pleas of Alfonso's forces and their prisoners who were stranded on the wrong side of the river and vulnerable to Almoravid attack, the trapped Christians were suddenly empowered by renewed faith. They slew their hapless captives, together with their children and livestock:

> Thereupon, the Christians, very rightly prepared with faith and arms, slaughtered all the Saracen captives – the men, women, infants, all of whom they had captured, as well as the beasts they had with them. [225]

This piece of uncompromising rhetoric, as emphatic as anything with the *Poema*, seems to be directly linked to the injunction to Saul to destroy the Amalek: 'Now utterly go and smite Amalek, and utterly destroy all that they have, and spare them not; but slay both man and woman, infant and suckling, ox and sheep, camel and ass';[226] indeed Saul is rebuked by the prophet Samuel and his God for only destroying that which 'was vile and refuse'.[227] This comparison is not made in footnotes to Antonio Maya Sánchez's translation of the *CAI* – nor in Pérez González's Spanish translation – but the link seems an obvious one, especially since a pattern for such behaviour had already been set in Alfonso VII's 1138 campaign to capture Oreja and Coria. Here, the intention was to inflict death on the Moabites and Hagarenes and to overcompensate for the wrong that they perceived had been visited on them (they (i.e. the Christians) subjected greater damage on the Muslims than they endured from them).[228] The war waged against the Amalek is a formidable example of a campaign that has the language and ferocity embedded in struggle and fear and which is fuelled by uncompromising retribution and religious zealotry; in *CAI* II 20 and 39, the author turns to these militaristic recollections that had stirred the people of God in ancient times. Frequent OT precedents provide powerful suggestions and are alluded to in the *CAI*, and here they become figurative or subliminal, precise references often being absent.[229]

The chronicle and poem may be a biblical epic in a further sense. OT judges and patriarchs were often more concerned with dissent amongst their own flock as the Hebrews tried to subdue the land of Canaan and settle in it, as well as with the division of the kingdom between Israel and Judah[230] following the accession of Jeroboam. So, the author of the *CAI* must have been aware of the inherent fragility that was apparent in León-Castile before the accession of Alfonso VII in 1126,[231] a weakness which might be emphasized by the support from bishops and nobles received by the newly crowned king rather than diminished by it:

> The witness-lists that were attached to the diplomas issued by Alfonso VII provide striking evidence of the fluctuating membership of the royal entourage. Moreover, it is possible to distinguish between those magnates who may be regarded as permanent, or at any rate regular, members of the curia and those who seldom made an appearance at court.[232]

This underlines the problems Alfonso faced in the early years of his reign and these were emphasized by the revolts of Pedro Díaz del Valle and Gonzalo Peláez. Nevertheless, by the time Alfonso was proclaimed emperor in León in 1135, the description of his coronation (preceded as it was by the conquest of the Rioja and the temporary occupation of Zaragoza) demonstrates Alfonso VII's unequivocal political grip of events within León-Castile and is an assertion of his personal authority.

Yet the earlier potential weakness and threats to kingly authority would be replicated following the division of Alfonso VII's kingdom in 1157, and the military setbacks that followed in its wake would confirm this vulnerability. Furthermore, earlier precedents, as well as the competing ambitions of other Hispanic princes, would have underlined such fragility. Seared into Castilian consciousness was the figure of Alfonso I of Aragón whose death in 1134 precipitated the emergence of the newly independent kingdom of Navarre under García Ramírez IV (r. 1134–50). And, following the betrothal of the infant daughter of Ramiro II, brother of Alfonso I and successor to the throne of Aragón, to Count Ramón Berenguer IV of Barcelona (r. 1131–62),[233] came the union of the kingdom of Aragón and county of Barcelona. The fact that the relationships between other Iberian realms were also volatile undoubtedly assisted Alfonso VII's attempts to shore up his own position,[234] though underlying weaknesses remained. The way to address inter-Christian rivalry was to remain a complex problem for the author, especially since all must be demonstrable within an explicitly and overtly biblical world view. An example of the way in which the author demonstrates his perspicacity in his use of scripture to illuminate an event is found in his description of the duel between Count Pedro de Lara and Alfonso Jordan, the count of Toulouse in 1130. Count Pedro is suggested as being hostile to Alfonso VII and would fight the king's champion. The idea of a king's champion coupled with the use of the term *singulare certamen*[235] makes possible a comparison with the conflict between David and Goliath,[236] even though the lack of an inter-faith element in the Iberian clash of champions weakens this allusion. Nevertheless, it allows the author to clarify which of the Christian princes should prevail. The author invites us to make choices between competing dynastic claims and struggles within Hispanic Christendom; and the inferences and the implications of such options are clear in the author's mind. Yet his use of narrative, image and example allows our interpretation to be nuanced as well as emphatic. The author's ambivalent treatment of Count Pedro and the description of the struggle between the two counts before the siege of Bayonne tells us that the David and Goliath allusion can only take us so far: 'and they each went forth to fight, just like two powerful lions.'[237] Although only the king's champion could emerge victorious, the Christian virtues of valour, strength and integrity are applied to the two men. Yet one lion, however brave, will meet its match: 'And he that is valiant, whose heart is as the heart of a lion, shall utterly melt.'[238]

This discussion exemplifies the challenges and potential pitfalls of this chronicle when the author tries to deal with issues surrounding competing Christian claims and the struggle for supremacy in twelfth-century Iberia. A straightforward event, in which the author praises the courage of two men, unravels into a complex collection of inferences as we weave through the ways in which such qualities are explained and their limitations suggested. The writer therefore does not confine his biblical rhetoric merely to the waging of war on the Muslims; his narrative is in part revenge, but he uses biblical texts comprehensively to explain and justify all aspects of Alfonso's reign as well as the qualities of the king himself. The author has been presented as a man of original awareness and knowledge, in particular because of his unusual grasp of the nature of Muslim societies within Spain.[239] Antonio Ubieto Arteta draws attention to the author's geopolitical skills – mostly directed to the Mediterranean Basin but with a knowledge that extended eastwards towards Sicily, Bari and Constantinople.[240] Equipped as he seems to have been with this impressive interpretative ability, it is scarcely surprising that within his comprehension of conquest narrative, he should have been able to infuse his history with such a variety of skilfully applied and nuanced biblical reminiscences.

Intended audience

Discussion of a potential audience for any of our chronicles raises as many issues as it seeks to resolve and this is especially so in relation to the *CAI*. In other chronicles covered in this study, there is a level of borrowing and familiarity.[241] Texts were known about, studied, copied and reworked. The author of the *HS* incorporated earlier texts, including *Sampiro* and the *Chronicle of Alfonso III*, within his compilation. In turn, the authors of the thirteenth-century narratives made extensive use of texts such as the *HS*. The *CAI*, by contrast, is largely independent of any link with the other chronicles, though there are occasional reminiscences.[242] Also, it is not referred to in any extant chronicle from that period or later[243] and, although comparisons may be made with other chronicles (most notably with the thirteenth-century *CLRC*), there is no firm evidence that later chroniclers had read or even heard of the *CAI*. If it was not used or referred to by successive chroniclers, who would have known of its contents or message?[244] In seeking to identify the author's audience, we need to proceed with caution. The reconstruction of an original readership depends on the survival of contemporary texts. The author does not directly identify his audience, and inferences depend on suggestions from within the text and from peninsular events at the time of its composition. It will be suggested that there was an intended audience for the author's narrative even if the circle within which the text circulated was relatively restricted.

In the *prefatio*, the author establishes his noble and clear intention to recreate the exploits of Emperor Alfonso and that this encomium will reflect the words of witnesses.[245] He rarely identifies himself in the chronicle,[246] though he is clearly more than a passive observer. His description of the coronation of Alfonso in León in 1135 suggests that his information was either first-hand or gathered after the event by an eyewitness.[247] He does not say that he has been asked by the emperor to compile a history of the reign, though this is perhaps the likeliest scenario and the writing of this laudatory narrative is his most noble task [*noua faciunt, optimum*].[248] It begins quietly as befits his solemn undertaking but the narrative soon, especially in Book 2, becomes a story of high drama and intense detail. By the end of Book 2, in announcing his intention to describe the battle for Almería in verse, he suggests that he is overseeing an agreed presentation: 'we have arranged to present [the narrative] in this manner.'[249] Those in the emperor's party who survived Almería might fortify themselves with the stirring accounts, now in the manner of an epic poem, of military success in which they had participated. This could plausibly be derived from the author's phrase *ad remouendum carminis uariatione tedium*[250] ['to avoid tedium with the diversity of poetic prayer']. This certainly may have been the author's aim: 'The poem describes the build-up to the conquest ... stirring up the dust of Andalucía, making the reader sweat with the army in the heat.'[251] As is suggested later in the text, it may have been a piece of prayerful poetic drama designed to be declaimed and heard as well as read privately. Even if the prose sections of the *CAI* would normally be studied in solitary reflection (though not necessarily silently), the *Poema* is more likely to have been read aloud and this practice was not limited to any particular realm.[252]

According to the author, the text of the *CAI* was based partly, though not wholly, on the oral testimony of unnamed persons.[253] He suggests that a variety of sources supplied details for his narrative, 'I have become acquainted with and accepted, as it were, from those who have seen them,'[254] though these witnesses are not identified. It is possible to speculate which earlier material he gathered from others and who he may have consulted. If we accept that Arnaldo was the author of the *CAI* and that during the early and middle periods of Alfonso's reign (1127–44) he was prior at the community of San Servando in Toledo, access to the emperor and his court is likely to have been limited. He would have relied on sources, oral and written, now lost and unrecoverable. The author's biblical and classical references are plain to see; yet although he is likely to have consulted, inter alia, ecclesiastical sources to verify recent events, his contemporary contacts are unknown to us.[255]

A secular or ecclesiastical authority may have mandated the writer to recall the past in such a way that right would indisputably be seen to be on the Christians' side,[256] though we cannot know emphatically who the author's intended audience might be; yet there are possible clues. The first book includes the ways in which Alfonso was able to impose an authoritative political unity on and within his kingdom at the expense of other Iberian Christian realms.[257] He then provides an account for posterity and his ideological structure enabled his public to receive more than mere information. In Book 2, the outlook is more emphatic: the author reminds the reader (or hearer) of the hand of God in the battle with Islam by referring to biblical topoi – some of which would have been familiar through liturgical readings.[258] The author's style is fluent, expansive and dramatic and, in addition to being declamatory, could at times be almost conversational, revealing literary skills that incorporated versatility and, within the Hispano-Latin tradition, originality.[259] The quantity of spoken exchange that peppers the narrative might seem to be at odds with his more sombre portrayal of Alfonso's divinely inspired wrath, although it is in keeping with the author's providential sense of history.[260]

When the description of events gives way to verse, the identification of the author with the events he is describing is more emphatic and the question arises as to whether anyone or any group of people are being addressed. He begins his poem by calling on the God of glorious wars to guide his hand in his account of what is to follow. He then refers to his duty to write of the famous battles of 'our emperor.'[261] He makes his purpose clear as never before: 'I therefore address my chosen theme [i.e. the battle for Almería].'[262] His commitment to the emperor was nowhere more explicit; he has beseeched his God for fluency in his ability to record the events[263] and he may conclude that this request has been granted; he now seeks assurances that the account will please Alfonso.[264] The text not only portrays the deeds of the emperor; it is written to delight the emperor himself, which again leads us to suppose that the *CAI* may have been written under royal commission. Because subsequent extant chronicles do not betray any dependence on the *CAI*, it may be that the author's intended audience consisted primarily of Alfonso VII and his court. Despite frequent hostile rhetoric applied to the Muslim enemy within the *CAI*, Alfonso was not able to pursue the Almoravids relentlessly until after 1135, when he received his imperial title at León, having seen off his potential Iberian rivals.[265] After this, and with his full imperial might acknowledged by his contemporaries, he was able to take advantage of the withering of Almoravid power in the Guadalquivir Valley and even briefly occupying Córdoba in 1146.[266] Yet a weakened Almoravid presence was also the result of a dynastic war between them and their militant Berber rivals from the Maghreb, the Almohads.[267]

It is possible that the chronicle's influence barely outlived the military success at Almería and the loss of further territory in al-Andalus. This was compounded by the fracturing of Alfonso's existing kingdom, now divided between his two sons.[268] Were the accounts of the emperor's victory, together with those of his allies, over the Muslims at Almería and elsewhere seen subsequently as heralding a false dawn? Did the chronicle subsequently languish in a quiet corner of the cathedral library at Toledo?[269] If Alfonso's successes at Almería and elsewhere had been more enduring, the chronicle's place as a favoured source for Castilian military tales may well have survived and endured.

The dramatic style of the chronicle, and especially of the *Poema*, suggests that it was suitable for public reading. Certainly it is the kind of narrative which the author or one of his clerics could have read aloud at court; there is evidence that during the later Middle Ages, royal chronicles were recounted in the presence of kings and princes and the dedication suggests that the monarch would own his own copy.[270] Regarding the *CAI*, such an idea might be tentatively suggested rather than boldly asserted.[271] It is equally possible that extracts of the prose sections could have been copied, as they were in other realms such as England[272] and read contemplatively by members of the royal court. Even though most scholars believe that the *CAI* was written close to the time when the events in the author's narrative were taking place,[273] we do not know whether it was written as a completed text following the success at Almería or in stages.[274] The detail contained in the events from Alfonso's early period as emperor suggests that the text might have been compiled at different points during his reign, recording events more or less as they occurred. The author may not, technically, have been an eyewitness to all the events in the emperor's reign, though if we accept the argument about Arnaldo's authorship, he was present at the time of Alfonso's greatest triumph.[275]

5

THREE THIRTEENTH-CENTURY CHRONICLERS

This chapter draws on three thirteenth-century texts and focuses on the use and influence of biblical allusion and example on the writers' historical narrative, together with the ways in which their description of events was directed against the North African Almohad Caliphate that had penetrated al-Andalus. The three chronicles were written in León-Castile following the Battle of Las Navas de Tolosa (1212) and Christian successes against the Muslims in al-Andalus during the reign of Fernando III (r. 1217–52). Their depiction of events between Las Navas and the successes of Fernando, paint an evolving shift in the historical and political landscape in Castile and al-Andalus. The two largest and most comprehensive texts are *Chronicon Mundi* (*CM*), written under the direction of Lucas, bishop of Túy (from 1239 until his death in 1249), and the *Historia de Rebus Hispaniae* (*DRH*) by the archbishop of Toledo, Rodrigo Jiménez de Rada. A third and much shorter chronicle, the *Chronica Latina Regum Castellae* (*CLRC*), is likely to have been written, at least for the most part, by Bishop Juan of Osma.[1] As far as we can tell, the practice of chronicle composition in Iberia following the writing of *Chronica Adefonsi Imperatoris* and for the remainder of the twelfth century, certainly within León-Castile, withered into a state of abeyance.[2] This is not to say that up to this point we are awash with historiographical commentary as is clear from the limited number of chronicles we are able to consider.

An examination of the extent to which there was variety both in the authors' use of biblical sources and in their own purposes (or the extent to which these may be determined) is central. Each chronicle seems to have been crafted for a particular purpose and this is discernible according to its dedication.[3] The legacy of Isidore of Seville and of Iberia's Visigothic past is of particular interest, and both elements left their mark on the chronicles of Lucas and Rodrigo. Emphasis within all three chronicles on authorial use and interpretation of biblical text will be explored, and especially on the ways in which these chroniclers used such text to describe and understand events in their own time and the implications for purpose and how the favour, protection and judgement of God could be inferred. This helps to determine the extent to which the enduring Christian conquest of the thirteenth century is presented as a continuing scriptural narrative.

It might have been expected that the victory of Alfonso VIII of Castile (r. 1158–1214) over the Almohads and their Arab, Berber and Andalusian allies at the Battle of Las Navas de Tolosa in July 1212 – a victory which ended the Almohad threat to Christian Spain and was celebrated all over Western Christendom – might have propelled the Christian forces into a new era of justifiable self-confidence.[4] This certainly happened, though not immediately; the Castilian army was exhausted, war chests were depleted and the death of the Castilian king of Castile, Alfonso VIII, in 1214 and of his son Enrique three years later further postponed immediate post-1212 successes.[5] And the other Iberian forces of Portugal, Aragón and Navarre were also embroiled in difficulties that hampered collaborative Christian success against al-Andalus.[6] Yet the significance of the success at Las Navas de Tolosa was to ripple through the whole of Western Christendom,[7] and, in addition to the sense of triumph generated by the event itself, it reversed the crushing defeat at Alarcos in 1195 when Berbers, Arabs and other Africans as well as Andalusian troops, under the command of Abu Yusuf Ya'qub (c. 1160–99) overwhelmed the Spanish Christians. This was followed when Alfonso VIII and a faithful but despondent remnant was forced to beat an ignominious retreat to Toledo.[8] The defeat at Alarcos was momentous even though it was the last major Almohad victory against the Castilians; secondly, it seemed to be regarded as a collective punishment brought upon the people of Castile; furthermore, the succession of Queen Berenguela in 1217 suggested that the victory at Las Navas itself might be short-lived: 'The succession of the woman seemed like a punishment, to be compared with the defeat at Alarcos.'[9] Thus, Alarcos and Las Navas de Tolosa frame a period that Linehan calls 'conceptual readjustment' in which the lessons learned from the earlier defeat may have been rewritten with post-1212 hindsight, reflecting on the succession of traumas that plagued the royal succession following the death of Alfonso VIII.[10]

By the time of Las Navas, military and strategic lessons had been learned in a conflict that united Alfonso VIII with Pedro II of Aragón (r. 1196–1213) and Sancho VII of Navarre (r. 1194–1234) which ensured that such a coalition could destroy the power of the Almohad caliphate.[11] Not only did the Las Navas victory revive self-confidence for Iberian Catholic hegemony,[12] it also placed Castile at the centre of the struggle against Islam.[13] The fact that it seems to have provided a new enthusiasm for the role of the biblical texts and liturgy in interpretative chronicle writing in the immediate aftermath of success may be due to a combination of historical circumstances. The victory was described by O'Callaghan as 'the greatest ever achieved in the course of the reconquest.'[14] We can only speculate as to why a revival in the writing of historical narrative did not take place at that time or shortly afterwards. In fact, no Castilian chronicle was completed for a further two and a half decades – though the death of Alfonso VIII just two years after Las Navas, and the instability that followed, could feasibly have contributed to this hiatus. Perhaps the victors at Las Navas may not have appreciated the full significance of what they had achieved.[15] This may be so, but there were other contemporary events that would have kept the Castilians busy.[16] In addition, Linehan notes that the event seems to have exhausted the royal coffers to such an extent that the victory, though pivotal, was obtained at spectacular cost.[17] In any event, the importance of the event may not have been grasped immediately and it was not until the years following 1238 that the successes in al-Andalus and the momentum for conquest seems to have spawned the writing of three distinct yet complementary accounts.[18] Whether the intervention of natural disasters or political events stalled the beginnings of Iberian chronicle writing after Las Navas, Rodrigo, Lucas and Juan were much preoccupied with descriptions of the expansion of the crown of Castile in the 1220s, together with the reunification of Castile and León under Fernando III in 1230. Yet none of these conquests would be wholly secure until Córdoba was captured and under Castilian control. And the capture of Córdoba in 1236 was followed by that of Jaén in eastern Andalucía ten years later.[19] As we shall see, their accounts of the conflicts that took place were indebted to OT accounts as well as to classical references.

Rodrigo, Lucas and Juan

It was not until there were discernible shifts in the Iberian historical and political landscape that the events of Castile (and, from 1230 onwards, in reunited León-Castile) became the subject of confident and renewed attention. The pace of conquest quickened and by the time our three chroniclers were penning their histories, Fernando II's forces – by diplomacy, annexation and military strategy – had captured and repopulated a swathe of cities in the south. Quesada, to the north of Jaén, was attacked and 'totally ransacked' [*penitus desolata*][20] in 1225, Baeza fell in 1227 and a swathe of land across al-Andalus from Trujillo and Mérida to Úbeda was captured during the 1230s. The biggest prize was Córdoba, the ancient seat of the Umayyad Caliphate, that fell in 1236. Our three accounts of these conflicts were all written by senior churchmen and at least two of the chronicles came by way of royal patronage. Lucas's *Chronicon Mundi* (c.1236–8) was commissioned by Queen Berenguela, though well after she had abdicated in favour of her son and probably during the late 1230s.[21] Lucas may have been born in León and was canon at the Real Colegiata de San Isidoro de León between 1221 and 1239.[22] The work is divided into a preface and four books, though this seems to be a modern formal structure imposed on the original text.[23] The *CM* encompasses the history of the world from its creation to the conquest of Córdoba – which was not necessarily when the *CM* was completed, though it may have been the year when Lucas was charged to write his history.[24] Book 1 describes the creation of the world; the author's attempts to write a more general world history are also confined to the first book. After this, the author is chiefly concerned with peninsular events to the exclusion of almost everything else. The remaining three books (about two-thirds of the *CM*) cover the period from the Visigothic kingdom to the capture of Córdoba.[25] Among his possible sources was, according to Georges Martin, a further version of Sampiro's Chronicle (now lost);[26] in addition, Lucas used Isidore, Bishop Ildefonsus of Toledo (r. 657–667) and Julian of Toledo (642–90) as well as other sources.[27]

It was Berenguela's son Fernando III, who commissioned, possibly in 1243 or a little earlier,[28] the Navarrese-born lawyer and theologian and archbishop of Toledo,

Rodrigo Jiménez de Rada (r. 1209–47) to write the *Historia de rebus Hispanie* or *Historia Gothica* (thenceforward *DRH*). As both titles suggest, it is more limited in scope than the *CM*, though not in intellectual analysis or literary importance.[29] This is despite the assertion that 'Rodrigo's vision was actually rather parochially Toledan.'[30] Written in nine books, the chronicle is concerned solely with the history of the Iberian Peninsula from its earliest inhabitants to 1243. Rodrigo uses the *CM* but has discernible interests of his own. He traces the early history of the Goths and presents them as the direct ancestors of the royal houses of León and Castile. His history of Spain begins with the arrival of the Goths in the north of the peninsula in 414[31] and his treatment of Hispania's subsequent history at once seems more succinct and elegant compared with that of Lucas.[32] The dates of his composition suggest that the event of the conflict at Las Navas de Tolosa is likely to have been remote from the time of Rodrigo's writing, but it imposed itself in terms of its impact on his imagination and because of its continuing significance on the unfolding of the struggle for supremacy in Iberia; it was, after all, Rodrigo who had accompanied Alfonso VIII as the moral and spiritual champion of his campaign: 'What Rodrigo the warrior had helped to initiate in 1212, Rodrigo the historian completed in 1243.'[33] More will be said about the possible impact of Las Navas on *DRH* a little later. Whether or not we are disposed to compare the qualities of the two chronicles, their collective significance is considerable: not only were they used as source material for the *Primera Crónica General*, usually known as the *Estoria de España* (thenceforward *Estoria*),[34] they fill a gap between the ecclesiastical authors of Latin chronicles of the twelfth century and earlier and the vernacular tradition championed by Alfonso X.[35] More will be said about the importance and relationship of the *CM* and *DRH* to the *Estoria*.

The third chronicle is formally regarded as anonymous, but a likely author was Juan de Soria, bishop of Osma (1231–40; bishop of Burgos, 1240–6) and chancellor to Ferdinando III, king of León-Castile. This is a history of much more specific and modest intention and known as the *Chronica Latina Regum Castellae* (henceforward *CLRC*)[36] or the *Latin Chronicle of the Kings of Castile* (henceforward LCKC)[37] and completed about 1240.[38] Derek Lomax argues that although there are perhaps six potential candidates for the authorship of the chronicle, the circumstantial evidence together with the 'extraordinary precision in chronology' in *CLRC* (and here there is a clear contrast with Lucas and Rodrigo who paint a much more hazy chronological picture of the same events) points to Juan as author.[39] More recent attention to the question of authorship has been given by Inés Fernández-Ordóñez[40] and she argues that although the chronicle may have been written in three or more separate stages, there is much more that binds the authorship to the pen of one man than suggests different strands of authorship. Indeed, there is consensus around the view that the chronicle is an individual account that can be distinguished from the *CM* and *DRH* which are almost certainly textual compilations in which Lucas and Rodrigo are likely to have been editors-in-chief.[41] However, this is not unanimously accepted; Charlo Brea suggests that chapters 69–75 in the *CLRC* (covering the capture of Córdoba) may have had a second author or at least an editor of notes entrusted to him by

Juan.[42] Nevertheless, editorial delegation was inevitably difficult to attribute with certainty and, though widely practised, does not necessarily imply additional authorship. But consistency with the inclusion of detail is also a factor and Francisco Javier Hernández is puzzled by the peculiarly scant coverage of events in the early years of the reign of Fernando III, that is, in the fourth, fifth and sixth years of his reign, between July 1220 and July 1223.[43] Such omissions of course raise the possibility of lost elements within the text, an issue to which Hernández gives subsequent attention. Linehan also discusses the possibility of an uncompleted text, and he cites examples from within the text of the peremptory conclusion to Fernando III's visit to Galicia in 1230-1, recorded in chapter 62, and the extreme brevity of chapter 63 as evidence of lack of completion. He also points out that simply because there is no prologue, it cannot be assumed that none was intended, and suggests that such a preface to a narrative is often inserted after the author's text was substantially complete.[44] Whether or not this is so, the inclusion of this much shorter chronicle from an author with a different geographical provenance offers this study contrasting insight and experience that extends the scope of thirteenth-century Castilian historical composition: 'Those three write in regions of diverse political and social currents: Burgos, Toledo and León.'[45] Despite the reservations surrounding Juan's authorship of the *CLRC*, he will be referred to as the presumed writer of the chronicle; this is in keeping with most recent scholarship[46] and is supported by references within the chronicle to the see of Burgos and his familiarity with the chancery under Fernando III. An example is the reference to an unspecified but sealed charter [*quondam cartam*] issued at Carrión but, according to Juan, discovered in the sacristy at Burgos Cathedral.[47]

We do not know whether the author of *CLRC* was charged by royal authority to produce a history of such modest or precise scope[48] or at least one which is mostly concerned with events in the kingdom of Castile from the late twelfth century to the fall of Córdoba in 1236 and its immediate aftermath. But his history is not wholly concerned with Castile in the first half of the thirteenth century and the author also recognizes the relevance of parallel extra-peninsula events. Two early sections deal minimally with the genealogy of the counts of Castile from Count Fernán González (923–970) onwards, as well as incidents in the reign of Alfonso VI that bequeath information about the king's knowledge of Toledo that aided his conquest of that city. Referring to contemporary events both within and outside the peninsula which are diversions to his main narrative, he provides a view on the wider world from thirteenth-century Castile. These include references and descriptions of the campaign of King Louis VIII of France (r. 1223–6) against the Cathar Heresy in the Languedoc (the Albigensian Crusade), as well as crusade accounts and conflicts of Emperor Frederick II (r. 1220–50) with the papacy in Apulia. These are seen from a Castilian perspective, ensuring that there is an extra-peninsular dimension to what might otherwise be a more narrowly focused, though meticulously accurate, chronology.[49]

One of the themes to emerge in this chapter is the degree of convergence between the narratives of Rodrigo and Lucas, notwithstanding their separate championing of Toledo and León. Their chronicles might therefore be seen as representing competing assertions of a similar body of material. Rodrigo, Lucas and Juan were almost certainly well known to each other through attendance at the royal court (and were 'intertwined professionally').[50] Nevertheless, Juan's chronicle would appear to have a separate and independent provenance and a more specific aim which calls into question the extent to which the Latin chronicle had any profound dependence on the works of Lucas and Rodrigo.[51]

These three thirteenth-century chronicles were histories of kings and rulers who owed a debt to each other, even if the dependence was sometimes ostensible. In other words, points of familiarity should not obscure different historiographical strands within each work nor the distinct sense of purpose of each author.[52] Although the *DRH* and *CM* will not be treated as a single entity, at the outset it is important to acknowledge that the Latin chronicle, because of its size, structure and, principally because of the author's seemingly independent and precise use of sources, may have had more in common with the features of some earlier narratives. As the royal chancellor, Juan would certainly have had access to royal archives, though his awareness of earlier Hispanic chronicles is unknown and at no point is it asserted that he had access to or knew about these earlier chronicles.[53] Even if Juan had been able to consult the late-twelfth-century *Crónica Najerense* (thenceforward *Najerense*), there is no evidence that he used it as a model for his chronicle.

We have already alluded to the potential comparisons that might be made between the *DRH* and *CM*, and such similarities were not limited to the scale or scope of their canvas. Lucas and Rodrigo, according to Ruiz, 'shaped the historical discourse for the next century,'[54] and nowhere is this better illustrated than in the influence that both chronicles had on the *Estoria*. The *Estoria* was the first major history of Spain to be written in romance castellano; it was begun during the reign of Alfonso X (*el Sabio*, the 'Wise') of Castile (r. 1252–84) and completed about five years after his death, during the reign of Sancho IV (r. 1284–95). The *CM* and *DRH* were far from being the only sources for the *Estoria*,[55] but they expressed certain common linguistic conventions when describing the inhabitants of Iberia before 711, and this convergence may have commended itself to the compilers of the *Estoria*:

> As for the Visigoths, both Jiménez de Rada and Lucas de Túy always refer to them [the people of Iberia before the Muslim conquest] as *Gothi*, never as *Hispani*: '*Deploratio Hispaniae, et de causa exciddi Gothorum*' [Spain's lament and the military overthrow of the Goths] (*De rebus Hispaniae*, vol. I, iii 22). The Bishop of Túy still says that Alfonso the Catholic was elected king in 739 '*ab universe populo Gothorum*' [by the entire population of the Goths].[56]

Yet references to Isidore are entirely lacking from the *CAI* and do not feature in the *CLRC* either. Following his whistle-stop canter through the genealogy of the counts and early kings of Castile,[57] Juan begins his history proper with Alfonso's capture of Toledo in 1085 because, for him, this seems to be the beginning of a new and godly era.[58] Events of his own time would receive more detailed coverage and comment: 'The great battle of Alarcos ... is recounted in great detail, and it seems likely that the author either participated in it or – which seems more likely – heard about it from those who did.'[59] Yet throughout Juan's chronicle and within his brief description of Alfonso VI's reign, the hand of God is seen in the deeds of men,[60] even if there is in the CLRC no obvious attempt to portray the capture of the city of Toledo as a glorious restoration of the Spain of Isidore; and this omission, if that is what it is, further distinguishes Juan's history from those of his two contemporaries and aligns him more closely with the author of the CAI.[61]

Comparisons with other chronicles are plausible and we will consider the ways in which person and personality affected the writing of history and the extent to which the thirteenth-century writers saw their own people, especially their Christian kings and princes, in the light of biblical exempla. Interwoven into this consideration of the way in which victorious Christian leaders were venerated and described is the issue of place. The idea that the cities in Spain demonstrate an awareness of biblical models has already been considered in relation to the CAI. Such a biblical awareness can be extended to individual buildings and settlements within Iberia.[62] Comparisons with thirteenth-century perspectives will be explored together with the OT notion of cities being spiritually as well as historically and strategically important and how the sweep of conquest might affect the perception of the power of ancient association. Place, however, as we have noted from Linehan's observation regarding the scope of Rodrigo's account,[63] can be used to enhance the author's geographical and historical context, as well as stressing his geographical and cultural loyalties. Personality and the author's perception of the enemy also impinge on the way locations are recognized and described. The significance of places is further connected to the action of individuals, together with historical precedent and whether there is the suggestion of an ancient ecclesiastical authority.[64] This comparison will then be extended to consider how the thirteenth-century writers came to regard the religious other, represented chiefly by the Muslim enemy. In terms of the chroniclers' view of their enemy, both Lucas and Rodrigo 'continue the historiographical traditions of their Asturian and Leonese forebears, chronicling the restoration of right Gothic rule and the reclamation of churches lost to the Arab invaders,'[65] with the more substantial innovation coming with Alfonso X's *Estoria* in which there was a genuine attempt to gather together the rich legacy of the way Muslims had been portrayed in pre-*Estoria* chronicle writing. Yet the convergence of view between Lucas and Rodrigo is also acknowledged,[66] suggesting that their writing was distinct from what had preceded it and that the corpus on which Alfonso X's churchmen and jurists were to work was not a monolithic legacy. The extent to which Lucas, Rodrigo and Juan were breaking new ground in the decades before Alfonso X is also explored and there is an examination of the different individual perspectives of the writers. Before considering the importance of personal exempla, representation of the enemy and the significance of place, we will turn first to the historical figure of Isidore of Seville, whose saintly and almost mythical example as well as his unparalleled literary output, underpinned as it was by the reputation and scholarship of his *Etymologiae*, came to overshadow much of what was said and implied by Lucas and Rodrigo.[67] Since both chroniclers were writing from different ecclesiastical and geographical perspectives and traditions and would be serving the demands of particular political audiences, it is also important to consider how their interpretation of Isidore's legacy affected the question of purpose and how his presence might add weight to their differing historical narratives.

To discern the way in which biblical narrative imposed itself on the three thirteenth-century chronicles, it is necessary to set them in some sort of comparative context. Individual perspectives would, for example, include the episcopal rivalry as expressed by Rodrigo and Lucas over the relative ecclesiastical prelacy of Toledo and León over each other and over other potential rivals.[68] We therefore consider the themes and ideas which infused these chronicles and then assess the character of the authors' individual interpretation of the collective biblical legacy and how they used and developed OT rhetoric and incorporated a dexterous handling of biblical text and imagery that was so conspicuously a feature of the text of the *CAI*. A clear alternative to this possibility is that there may have been a return to the earlier and more discreet, almost subliminal, scriptural parallels, where imagery and reference might suggest a more opaque analysis, much of which was a feature of chronicle writing before the *CAI*.

Isidore and the Visigothic legacy

Rodrigo and Lucas saw themselves as keepers of the legacy of Isidore of Seville so the appeal to Spain's Visigothic past is perhaps inevitable and certainly striking.[69] Since both chroniclers were likely to have had access to the *Najerense*, they could not have helped but note the opening pre-eminence that the compiler bequeaths on Isidore: 'Here begins the chronicle of the Blessed Isidore.'[70] Rodrigo and Lucas also invoke Isidore's memory early in their narratives, so we can assume that this tribute within the *Najerense*, evoking the memory and importance of Isidore, ensures that the last Latin father of the church remains a major inspiration for their chronicles. By contrast, Juan's account contains no such preamble or acknowledgement to any distinguished predecessor. He begins, almost peremptorily, with events in Castile following the death of Fernán González [*comite Fernando Gundissalvi*] in 970. Lucas, on the other hand, conjures up the spectre of Isidore to order the arrest of Muhammad who lands on Spanish soil, at Córdoba: 'Isidore ... who at that time was returning from the papal court, immediately sent his agents to arrest him.'[71] Muhammad, narrates Lucas, being warned by the devil, was able to make his escape to Africa.[72] As O'Callaghan observes, Lucas enthusiastically records every detail and is indiscriminate in his enthusiasm to record the wildly extravagant as well as what might have contained more plausible accounts.[73] Yet this little piece of polemic from Lucas may be more than indulgent fantasy; it is interesting because it is Isidore who represents the might of the Christian church and although Muhammad makes his escape, he is successfully repelled from the Iberian mainland. The intellectual authority with which Isidore is endowed carries with it, according to his biographer, Braulios de Zaragoza, a kind of assertive and persuasive majesty.[74] Secondly, it is as if the story of the magi, who 'departed into their own country another way,'[75] is being turned on its head in Lucas's narrative. God, who warns the magi in a dream not to return to Herod,[76] and the devil, who delivers his warning to Muhammad, use similar techniques and speak, it seems, with equal eloquence to their followers.

It is also clear that despite variations that might be in style and purpose that distinguish the *CM* from the *DRH*, both chronicles represent a tradition and body of work which is of similar scope. Isidore's influence on both Lucas and Rodrigo is woven into their historical narratives and this integration of idea and language was a feature that they fashioned and which was to be carried forward by those who were to advise the future Alfonso X,[77] even if Rodrigo was to have the greater influence.[78] Nevertheless, according to Díaz y Díaz, it was to be the reworking of Isidorian principles by Rodrigo that was to have a more indelible influence on subsequent historians:

> The historical narrative at this time has enormous importance; Lucas de Túy does little more than to interpolate the corresponding sections of Isidore; it is worthy of note that Alfonso X's company of scholars did not know nor use the authentic Isidorian scripts until much later; their work is based exclusively on the work of Lucas and Rodrigo Jiménez of Rada, a highly gifted man who also takes the works of the bishop of Seville as a foundation for his history.[79]

Although Rodrigo's chronicle combines a sophisticated methodology[80] with a Toledo-based view, both he and Lucas are swift to invoke the person of Isidore and do so before their histories get under way. These early references assert and underpin the unimpeachable credentials of their narratives. In Lucas's *praefatio*, Isidore quickly emerges as a dominant figure; he is alluded to in the first sentence, as 'the man [who is] the eternal and blessed guide,'[81] and his words are summoned to embellish the warnings in Ecclus 19.2 of the fate awaiting the wise man if he should succumb to the sins of the flesh[82] and on the debilitating effects of self-indulgence on the human body and the dire warnings of death and damnation.[83] Thus although Isidore does not present Lucas with direct access to biblical sources, a link is promptly established that demonstrates the idea of biblical injunction and that of the teaching of such an eminent church leader and theologian; ideas that support each other are integrated into Lucas's narrative. Lucas gives further early consideration to Isidore who, together with his brother and predecessor as bishop of Seville, Leander (*c.* 534–*c.* 601) are considered in tandem and referred to as *ambos primates Yspanie*.[84] This reference and description has a significance since at this point in Lucas's narrative greater honour seems to be accorded to two Christian martyrs. First, St Hermenegild (*c.* 564–586), the son of King Leovigild (r. 568–586) was executed because of his conversion from Arianism to Catholicism – an offence which was compounded by his refusal to recant.[85] Secondly, there is the case of the third-century centurion, Marcellus.[86] Lucas, in a rhetorical question, 'Which blood and faith stirs the Catholic people?,'[87] asserts that it is indeed the blood of martyrs that stirs the faith of the Catholic people and gives such faith its enduring strength. This hierarchy of martyr and supreme eminence in the church seems to have been included to make a particular point about the example of valour; his other references in the *praefatio* recognize Isidore's pre-eminent role as full of glory both in scholarship and in his unchallenged position within the Spanish Church.[88] Yet from the mid-thirteenth century this emphasis was to wane and, as we have already noted, his authority had not been referred to by all Castilian authors of the Hispano-Latin texts of the twelfth century and earlier. It would not be reborn until it was taken up by Juan de Mena and others in the fifteenth century: 'the emphasis on the Gothic nature of the revived kingdom of Castile virtually disappeared, even in Castilian historians, for two centuries.'[89] This was reflected in the veneration accorded to Isidore himself. Canonization followed its usual protracted route and Isidore was not canonized until 1598 by Pope Clement VIII. Pope Innocent XIII declared him to be a Doctor of the Church in 1722, though this was partly a confirmation of a de facto recognition. He had been declared a doctor of the Spanish Church since the Eighth Council of Toledo in 653, so the title 'Doctor of the Universal Church' by Innocent represented elevation as well as recognition of Isidore's unparalleled scholarly output.[90]

The references in Lucas are in contrast with Rodrigo's more fulsome description in his *prologus*, where it is Isidore's intellectual and literary contribution and scholastic dexterity that are alluded to as much as his saintliness (*ex libris beatorum Ysidori*)[91] and this emphasis helps to set Rodrigo's history apart. Indeed, Rodrigo's range and use of sources place him in a historically pre-eminent position vis-à-vis his contemporaries and immediate predecessors: 'The number of sources used by the *Toledano* as well as his integration of Arabic chronicles has led to his being recognised as the foremost historian before Alphonse X.'[92] Nevertheless, the presence of Isidore, the venerated bishop, would appear at first sight to unite the historical perspectives of Lucas and Rodrigo and suggest an area in which their purpose and perception is very distinct from that contained in Juan's chronicle.

Lucas's further references appear to be, if not random, at least unsystematic; Book 2 of *CM* begins and ends with what seems to be a eulogy to Isidore's *Chronica maiora*, better known as the *Chronicon*, and although this is not mentioned elsewhere in the main text, there are numerous references to the work in Lucas's footnotes. The main theatres of activity in Lucas's Book 2 are Hebrew history up to the time of the Maccabees as well as the Roman Empire and the fall of Jerusalem in 70 AD. This contrasts with Isidore's methodology that divides the history of the world into six ages and takes us to about 615 AD.[93] In terms of his use of references, however, Lucas is conscious of the model set in the *Chronicon* for he, like Isidore, is sparing and discriminating in his use of the Bible as a source for his history: 'In none of the six divisions or "ages" of the *Chronicon* is the Bible the only source from which he draws, not even in his account of the very first "age." '[94] A feature of Lucas's writing is that he does not quote extensively from the Bible and his history of the world from the creation is demonstrably derived from Isidore's account, but the attempt to distinguish between biblical and non-biblical data is not always obvious. There is an imperative in the two earliest biblical citations and the purposes and declaration of God are woven into the story of Abraham. Both examples emphasize the power of God and his hand in history; the first stresses God's part in leading the patriarch from his birthplace[95] and the second is an earlier injunction in which he is instructed to leave his country: 'Now the Lord said unto Abraham: Get thee out of thy country, and from thy kindred.'[96] A further reference from Genesis in Book 1 (26.4) is also a statement of God's power which is God's promise to Abraham and is spoken by Isaac: 'In thy seed shall the nations of the earth be blessed' and it is contained within a conflated account of Isaac's life, the birth of his sons and references to the races of the earth who might be contained within his seed.[97] The sparing and emphatic use of the story in Lucas's account provides powerful recognition of the importance of genealogy and lineage. This idea would have had a particular resonance in the idea of medieval and early modern Castile even if the relative importance of noble families fluctuated and social mobility had a discernible impact on such changes of fortune.[98]

Some further examples of Lucas's inclusion of biblical passages in Book 1– into an account which clearly owes its pattern and understanding to Isidore – also centre on the power of God and his hand in history. The first example is inserted into a passage dealing with the protracted conflict between the Syrian king, Antiochus III (Anthiocus Magnus, r. 223–187 BC) and Ptolemy IV, the fourth pharaoh of Ptolemaic Egypt (r. 221–205 BC).[99] This struggle can fulfil the prophecy contained in Dan. 11.10-19. A traditional interpretation of scholars is thus stated:

> His reign [i.e. that of Antiochus III] is considered significant for the text of Daniel because he is responsible for taking Palestine out of Ptolemaic control and incorporating it into the Seleucid Kingdom, ending a century of Ptolemaic rule over Israel.[100]

Although this was a protracted conflict,[101] it is in this context that Lucas inserts a reference, not to Daniel but to a much more specific and emphatic prophecy from Isaiah: 'there shall be an altar to the Lord in Egypt and a monument within the borders thereof.'[102] Lucas's Book 1 ends with a kind of biblical profusion in the colophon that appears to usher in the new dispensation. The three biblical references that are contained in the paragraph can be seen as perpetuating the idea of the omnipotence and omniscience of God. The comparative lowliness of his creatures is implicit. In two clear references to the words of Jesus, Lucas uses a citation from Acts 1.17 translated as: 'It is not for you to know the time or moments, which the Father hath put in his own power.'[103] He links this with the short phrase *et alibi* [in another place] to an earlier verse from the gospels: 'knoweth no man, no not the angels of heaven, but my father only.'[104] Both references are concerned with Christ's second coming and therefore constitute implied eschatological and apocalyptic warnings. The final reference, from Ecclus 7.40, is therefore an elegant and apposite admonition in which Lucas, having selected scriptures that identify areas over which mortals have no control or knowledge, clarifies matters that ought to occupy human attention: 'In all thy works remember thy last end, and thou shalt never sin.'¹⁰⁵ Curiously, the inspiration for Lucas's narrative from Isidore's *Chronicon* is acknowledged in Emma Falque's footnotes, though not the reference to Ecclesiasticus; nor is it listed in the *Index Locorum Sacrae Scripturae*.¹⁰⁶

Books 2 and 3 of *CM* deal principally with the history of the Goths in Spain – which is also Rodrigo's starting point – and this part of his history is completed with the Muslim conquest in 711. Isidore's *Historia de regibus Gothorum, Vandalorum et Suevorum* is the most conspicuous source for Book 2 and this is occasionally infiltrated with biblical references. By far the most significant of these is an extended passage that elaborates on Gen. 10 and concerns the descendants of Noah (Shem, Ham and Japheth).¹⁰⁷ Lucas seeks to identify the Goths with this lineage, reiterating the link he had already made in Book 1. The other two references in Book 2 relate to the struggle of Simon and Judas Maccabeus to win control of Galilee and Galaad (1 Macc. 5.18-21);¹⁰⁸ the only occasion when the Bible is directly quoted is when an assertion of the supremacy of Christ is made: 'whether in pretence or in truth, Christ is preached'¹⁰⁹ and this is within the context of the attempt of the Visigothic king Sisebut (r. 612–621) to impose the Christian faith on the Jewish population.¹¹⁰ Much more pungent and apocalyptic biblical rhetoric is invoked in Book 3, especially when Lucas is dealing with the Muslim invasion. Here the spectre of the Nicolaitans, who seemed to occupy a place of particular loathing amongst the early Christians and who are referred to twice in the book of Revelation,¹¹¹ is introduced by Lucas;¹¹² they are linked to the cult of Balaam, though their origins are ambiguous.¹¹³ This unremittingly hostile picture is compounded in the same chapter with another apocalyptic image, that of the dragon, the consumer of children¹¹⁴ and in other parts of his book with references that stress, anger and retribution and the fall of proud princes and empires. Again, specific references are limited, but they are fulsome and create a tone which contrasts strikingly with that of Books 1 and 2.¹¹⁵ Typical is Lucas's slight reworking of Hos. 7.16: 'their princes shall topple into a trap because of the fury of God's rage; this is how he will mock them in all the land.'¹¹⁶

References to Isidore continue to influence Lucas's history – there are indeed more specific references to Isidore in Book 4 than in the rest of *CM* in total – yet because the material now covers the period following Isidore's death, there is a greater use of additional authors and later chronicles: Julian of Toledo, as well as Sampiro, Pelayo and the *Historia Silense*. Since the *HS* deals in eight chapters with plans relating to the construction of a mausoleum for Isidore and the saint's eventual translation to Lucas's own city of León, the chronicle would provide an indispensable and obvious source for Lucas. The *HS* itself incorporated text from the anonymous *Historia Translatio Sancti Isidori*, 'assumed to have been composed not long after the passage of the saint's relics from Seville to León in 1063,'¹¹⁷ and which is reworked into Lucas's account.¹¹⁸ A further thread of dependency on subsequent chroniclers is noted by Charles Fraker who comments on the sense in which the *HS* contributed to the view of Fernando I not only to Rodrigo and Lucas but also to the compilers of the *Estoria*.¹¹⁹

References to Isidore do not in themselves replace Lucas's use of the Bible, though as his chronicle proceeds, biblical sources become sparser and almost incidental even though the events at least in part describe the recovery of Iberia from God's enemies. Indeed, the single biblical reference in Book 4 occurs in the context of Pelagius's rebellion and the battle at Covadonga[120] and relates to God's protective succour, alluding to his long-term promises to his people.[121] This is a virtually intact citation of most of 1 Cor. 10.13: 'God is faithful, who will not suffer you to be tempted above that ye are able; but will with the temptation also make a way to escape, that ye may be able to bear it.' Yet the sources on which Lucas was to rely in Books 3 and 4 would enable him to indulge in a more assertive and polemical style. If, as John Tolan observes, 'For Lucas de Tuy, Muslim rule is based on violence and deceit,'[122] reconquest assertiveness could hardly be more powerfully employed.

Rodrigo's debt to Isidore is in some ways more straightforward. It has been noted that he uses Isidore's work very specifically and that it formed the heart of his chronicle.[123] If so, this seems to have important implications. For Isidore himself is described as the Visigothic kings' 'most influential propagandist' and this precise area of focus and enduring influence was seized upon by Rodrigo. He not only used Isidore but also made use of Lucas and this expanding and collective ideological and literary dependence was part of 'a growing eulogy to the Visigothic monarchy.'[124] But it does not stop there. Rodrigo seems to have had more influence over the interpretation of Iberian history through the pages of *DRH* to subsequent historians. Certainly, he seems to have used and then overshadowed the contribution of his contemporary Lucas, perhaps because of his reputation as a historian rather than as a theologian or churchman. In this respect he seems closer to the legacy of Isidore. There is a particular importance linked to Rodrigo's historical contribution to posterity: 'it is as a historian that he [i.e. Rodrigo] is still best remembered today.'[125] Certainly, as the writer considered to be the most acclaimed historian in medieval Castile,[126] Rodrigo was indebted to Isidore for both structure and content.[127] Yet it was the shared reverence for the Visigoths and their legacy that enabled both Lucas and Rodrigo, and in particular Rodrigo, to link Christians of their own time with their Christian Visigothic predecessors.[128] It was this feature that allowed Rodrigo's work to emerge centre stage as an authoritative source for the *Estoria* but significantly also for fourteenth-century chronicles such as the Aragonese *The Chronicle of San Juan de la Peña* (likely to have been commissioned by Pedro IV of Aragón, r. 1336–87, around 1370)[129] as well as for fifteenth-century writers such as Bishop Rodrigo Sánchez de Arévalo of Oviedo (1404–1470) and the diplomat and historian who was later to become bishop of Burgos, Alonso de Santa María de Cartagana (1384–1456); for all of these, the *DRH* seems to have been a specific inspiration.

Rodrigo's pre-eminence may be important in a further respect. We know that Isidore relied less on biblical narrative or allusion to describe events in his own time or as a justification for his etymological assertions than did many of his successors writing in the centuries following the Muslim invasion of Spain. If a chronicler was, so to speak, free from the legacy of Isidorian constraints – as Juan may be seen to have been – it may have been possible to pursue within his writing the idea of a more direct biblical message. Yet for Rodrigo – and, as we have seen, for Lucas too – his own scholarly aims, emboldened (or perhaps constrained) by those of royal patrons, were of a different order. Juan Fernández Valverde identifies thirty-four biblical citations in the *DRH*[130] (compared with forty-two in *CM*)[131] and the frequency of use is again patchy, there being only two references in Book 2 and none in Book 9. If the Bible is in part a campaigning tool, inclusions might be expected in Book 9 since it deals with the period from the accession of Enrique I (r. 1214–17) and subsequent campaigns of Fernando III culminating in the fall of Córdoba and the second marriage of Ferdinand III to Joan, countess of Ponthieu (before 1237). Yet although biblical rhetoric and allusion are evident in *DRH*, the narrative was not always to be used as a platform for the metaphor for conquest but also for encouragement, lamentation and reflection.[132]

With the hindsight of Muslim conquest, Rodrigo, like Lucas, was able to incorporate biblical texts into his narrative to bemoan the condition into which Iberia had fallen. Indeed, almost a third of the biblical references in *DRH* lament the judgement or punishment which had been visited upon God's people; and such reflections particularly apply to the destruction of the fall of the Visigoths. Typical are the (mostly) OT references that abound in Book 3, chapters 21 and 22 (104–8),[133] and this theme is picked up at the beginning of Book 4 (chapters 1 and 2, 114–17) when, following the rebellion of Pelagius, the tables were turned on the Muslims. Mercy and judgement are the subjects of exchanges between Pelagius and Oppa[134] and there is in the conflation of elements of Ps. 41.9, 'They determined against me an unjust word: shall he that sleepeth rise again no more?'[135] and 1 Jn 2.1, 'And if any man sin, we have an advocate with the Father, Jesus Christ the righteous,'[136] invoking the suggestion of Christian resurgence with the risen power of Christ. For Rodrigo links the two verses with the phrase 'et ego sperans in misericordia Iesu Christi'[137] (and I am confident in the mercy of Jesus Christ); resurgence, mercy and divine power, if not inseparable, are at least enriching each other. Yet the way in which God's judgement will fall on the enemies of his people, although sometimes uncompromising, is not wholly dependent on biblical precedent which is often alluded to as an element within the punishment to be meted out. For example, the fate of Pelagius's enemies is suggested in a reference to *illa Babilon* and in the ensuing passage[138] is made more starkly, though the events are not in a specifically biblical context. Thus *illa Babilon*, which seems to be a reference to Isa. 13.19, is included almost en passant and is not followed up with descriptions of the punishment awaiting the Medes and Chaldeans who are compared with those who perished in Sodom and Gomorrah.[139] And in the context of Rodrigo's description of the Christian capture of Calatrava, a fortress town on the road between Toledo and Córdoba, in 1147, there is the suggestion of ultimate triumph (but since to those who hold dear to God, all things work together for good).[140] The debt to Rom. 8.28 is striking, yet the specific choice of this verse rather than an appeal to the more colourful imagery in verse 35[141] is an indication that the consummation of God's kingdom supersedes military victory over a particular enemy. The observation that within the *DRH* there is virtually no polemic or slur directed specifically at Muslims[142] may amount to more than just apparent restraint. It reflects Isidore's more profound influence on Rodrigo's perception of history. This is also consistent with Rodrigo's commissioning of the translation of the Qur'an into Latin; the work was part of the armoury of conquest. Or, as Jerrilyn Dodds observes: 'Reconquest was the perfect cover for assimilation.'[143] Not that any of this prevented Rodrigo from referring to the sanitizing of the mosque and the application of purifying waters in the cleansing of the city of Córdoba, following its conquest. Neither did Rodrigo's more detached approach to the enemy mean that his historical allusions and sense of the Visigothic past and reborn greatness could not stir the crusading zeal within his people: 'He added to Isidore's original theme something far more national than Lucas de Tuy's pedantically theological list of great names: a sincere grief at a common loss, and a challenge to the Peninsular kingdoms.'[144]

Yet Rodrigo's history represents more than mere faith and obedience in the archbishop's interpretation of the Isidorian model. Because Isidore's history is free from biblical invective as well as being relatively, and perhaps disappointingly, terse,[145] both Lucas and Rodrigo were free to develop his primary historical legacy that the Visigoths, who had powerful biblical antecedents, were God's elect and heirs to Roman Christianity in the peninsula.[146] His impeccable authority would provide an intellectual basis for the way in which other historians might wish to present the conflict with the Muslims as a struggle dependent in part on biblical narrative – even though such polemic cannot be linked to or even derived from Isidore. Nevertheless, the historian's narrative was usually dependent on more than scriptural sources, even when these were acquired through exegesis, knowledge of the liturgy or mediated through an earlier historical source. Lucas and Rodrigo integrated a range of classical as well as earlier Iberian texts into their histories. Their debt was not purely to biblical sources, neither were scriptural allusions always used to illustrate crusading polemic. However, they often used scriptural texts to model their descriptions of armies and battles.[147] The aims of *CM* and *DRH* do not appear to be derived exclusively from such sources and the use of a range of material is in line with the pattern set by Isidore, who seems to have used the Bible, inter alia, for the purposes of teaching and assertion rather than invective. However, this did not mean that Isidore's perspectives on biblical sources and his willingness to modify understanding[148] deprived the thirteenth-century writers of León-Castile of models from scriptural antiquity on which to draw for more assertive allusions.

The conversion of the Visigothic king Reccared I (r. 560–601) and his court from Arianism to Trinitarian Catholicism in 587 signalled the beginning of the Catholic history of Spain,[149] and the rapid elimination of Arianism in Iberia was due in part to Isidore's influence and what have been called his 'historiographical interventions.'[150] This ancient precedent for reworking Iberian history in the light of a changed political or religious environment could serve as an example for Rodrigo and Lucas. They, in seeking to honour and emulate Isidore's method of using history as a means of instruction as well as interpreting the present, would have been conscious of Spain's entering a second new and confident age following Las Navas, even if Rodrigo's account was a more focused eulogy of Alfonso VIII.[151] Alfonso's triumphal procession is described by Rodrigo:

We arrived at the city of Toledo with the noble King Alfonso, and with the bishops he was received there at the church of the Blessed Virgin Mary by the clergy and the entire population in a procession, and many praised God and on musical instruments exclaimed that God had returned their king to them safe and crowned with the garland of victory.[152]

It is worth noting that this fulsome praise of Alfonso VIII lacks any direct biblical reference and makes an interesting contrast with the description offered by Juan.[153] Lucy Pick argues that Rodrigo's extended peroration eulogizing Castile following Las Navas, Alfonso VIII and Toledo is derived in part from the *Auto de los Reyes Magos*/Play of the Wise Kings, a play written in Castilian, probably about thirty years before Rodrigo embarked on the *DRH*. *Auto de los Reyes Magos* may have provided Rodrigo (a possible author of the play)[154] with some of his teaching on Judaism as well as referring to biblical exegesis, Christian learning, Muslims and the centrality of Toledo. In this case it is likely to have been a valuable source for his *DRH*;[155] but, as Alan Deyermond notes, the familiar theme of the play is in an unfamiliar setting[156] and suggests that the principal argument within the play is the nature of kingship.[157]

For Lucas and Rodrigo, parallels from Spain's Visigothic past are likely to have had a contemporary resonance. For example, the triumph of Catholicism over Arianism can be seen as prefiguring the battle against Islam in which Lucas and Rodrigo were a part.[158] Iberian historical precedent as well as biblical narrative would be seen as providing an invaluable illustrative source for understanding events in the authors' own time. There was also a relatively short time span between the withering of Arianism in the peninsula and the arrival of Islam, which might have suggested (especially to those Christians who understood little of either religion) a recurrence of the heresy.[159] Some historians have argued that Isidore's influence over the course of Christian history has been overstated or at least that some of his ideas were partly speculative.[160] An example of what might be called a paucity of evidence is his 'assumption that the successful union of *Hispania* and *Gothia* could only take place under the benevolent aegis of the Catholic Church.'[161] Yet such inferences might be built upon by those who were to venerate him in later centuries. As Hillgarth points out, both Rodrigo's history and that of Lucas depended on an Isidorian interpretation of the Visigothic legacy which was to be revived and much trumpeted.

Isidore's descriptions of Moors and Arabs in his *Etymologiae* – and there are precious few references – were written before Muslim expansion had begun, and had to be reworked by his successors in the light of Spain's subsequent history.[162] The man who would, so to speak, take up the challenge to the faith in the thirteenth century was none other than Rodrigo himself and it was he who was to expand on Isidore's somewhat detached picture of those who espoused Islam.[163] Yet although Rodrigo elaborated on Isidore's sparse descriptions by characterizing the enemy, as having blackened faces, bright eyes and being as swift as leopards, cruel as evening wolves,[164] the choice of epithets is fascinating for several reasons, as is the way they are used. Firstly, although the description of the enemy is in part derived from Isidore, it is also recognizably biblical; the characterization used by Rodrigo is strongly reminiscent of Hab. 1.8: 'Their horses also are swifter than leopards, and are more fierce than the evening wolves,' and has echoes elsewhere.[165] In spite of these clear OT parallels, these scriptural references are not suggested in Juan Fernández Valverde's footnotes or elsewhere in his edition of DRH. Secondly, it is also worth noting that depictions of the enemy are derivative and often defamatory. Nevertheless, they are part of Rodrigo's eulogy to Spain, which was itself to become part of a crusading challenge.[166] Rodrigo does not directly caricature his Muslim opponents even though their presence can be inferred from his litany of stark and memorable descriptions. Yet although it is tempting to view these as a crude or picturesque view of the enemies of Christendom in a familiar historical context, Rodrigo was fusing his sense of the promotion of unity of the Iberian kingdoms with Isidorian and biblical tradition. Isidore's *De laude Spaniae* had become the core of Rodrigo's lament and, aided and abetted by OT narrative, sought to stir Iberian national consciousness. Part of his grief was concerned with the loss of language and tradition following the Muslim invasion and that at the end of Book 2 chapter 22, the destruction of Spain is linked to the Arab invasion.[167] The cultural and linguistic imposition of Islam would have been as legitimate a target as the overthrow of a religious yoke. Lucas makes many more references to those referred to as the 'generations of Shem'[168] (though Rodrigo's are more succinct) and both authors agree that his descendants had seized and settled [parts of] Asia,[169] initially in Asia Minor or the Caucasus. Yet none of this helps us to distinguish the physical qualities of the sons of Shem, nor does it identify them directly with the Muslim enemy. Still less does it suggest how they acquired their distinctive linguistic tradition.[170]

The world for which they wrote was one of competing and often subtle rivalries and it was within this complex context that both Lucas and Rodrigo attempted to claim the mantle of Isidore from their differing perspectives, Leonese and Castilian. This situation often represented different political aims, ideals and traditions.[171] Linehan describes how Rodrigo, though dependent partly on Lucas, conspicuously chose to minimize the importance of two events, the ordination in León of Ordoño II in 914 and that of Fernando I in 1038.[172] Rodrigo, by ignoring the claim made that these kings were anointed, 'opted for something secular,'[173] and in this respect could be seen as closer to the legacy of Isidore.[174] A further example of Rodrigo's independence, as Monsalvo Antón notes, is his willingness to break with an idea embedded since the time of the Asturian Chronicles, that is, that Bishop Sampiro was born in the city of León.[175] Castile and Toledo may be said to gain in status if the city of León were marginalized.

Lucas and Rodrigo show a development of Isidore's understanding of the theme of homeland. In the case of Lucas, although he begins his *praefatio* with words that initially have the ring of Isidore's *De laude Spaniae*,[176] it quickly develops a Christian purpose (Just as the King of Kings [our] Lord Jesus Christ testifies, 'For what is a man profited, if he shall gain the whole world and lose his own soul?')[177] The reference to Mt. 16.26 is naked, direct and swift and leads inexorably through the spiritual blessings that should inevitably lead to the veneration of

Paul[178] and also, unsurprisingly St James, described by Gifford Davis as 'the ghostly leader of the reconquest.'[179] This early emphasis in Lucas's *Chronicon* suggests an attempt at convergence between Isidorian and biblical sources; biblical texts can therefore be seen to enrich the ideology of Lucas's narrative. Whether Lucas is consistent in fusing Pauline and Isidorian visions into his own account and if he is unique in doing so are also of marginal relevance. Yet there are just four specific references in *CM* to Paul's writing;[180] we might say therefore that the evidence within *CM* for a Pauline-infused view of Castilian history is discernible though not overwhelming. The inference that Isidore's teaching on the power of princes seems to be derived from Rom. 13[181] is not an indication that this idea was fully understood by Lucas nor that it was well integrated into *CM*. In the example he cites from Mt. 16, Lucas seems to be using the gospel narrative so that it might fulfil a more didactic purpose and it is weighty because it has an impeccable supreme source. In other words, we can pursue with greater confidence the question as to whether there is a difference to be identified between a biblically inspired narrative, with complex contemporary parallels and the use of the Bible, as in the passage cited earlier, to promote Christian teaching. This distinction relates to style as well as to purpose and understanding and we turn now to the ways in which such an awareness might rest on the invocation of historical precedent as revealed in the presentation of individuals and how we might interpret the intervention of a biblical model.

6

THE THIRTEENTH CENTURY AND BIBLICAL CONQUEST

For Lucas and Rodrigo, the authors of the two most influential chronicles of mid- thirteenth-century León-Castle, *Chronicon Mundi* and *De Rebus Hispaniae*, Isidore was a judicious presence and exemplar, and a vehicle for perpetuating the episcopal primacy of their own cities, León and Toledo.[1] However, it is the way in which kings and princes in their own time were modelled on biblical antecedents that is now of particular interest. The aim here is to identify historical figures from the peninsula who were evoked in the writing of the chroniclers of the period. We consider Christian aristocrats and military figures, the relative importance of Castilian kings and how comparison can be made with biblical precedents. As we have noted, biblical precedent is sometimes to be inferred,[2] but for a writer of 'solid biblical culture' we needed to await the author of the *CAI*.[3] For those writing histories that spanned several centuries, like the anonymous compilers of an unsettled text such as the *HS*,[4] the context of biblical and classical references frequently related to ways in which people and places were perceived and were made more explicit by later chroniclers. Perhaps the earliest – and certainly the most strident – example of this new and articulated clarity was the *CAI*.[5] In this, and in the three chronicles from the first half of the thirteenth century, biblical allusion was used to confer a sense of mission and blessing on Christian kings. The authors also provided historical detail and precedent for events and context for their descriptions of the interaction of Muslim and Christian worlds.[6] Such leaders were caught up in an endeavour, reminiscent of the Hebrews' struggle for their homeland, that enveloped them and their successors in a two-fold mission:

> not only as an effort to reconquer the territories and peoples lost to Christendom since the eighth century, but also an attempt to eliminate once and for all the threat to Christendom ... which sees in scripture the call to proclaim its message to all corners of the earth.[7]

The *DRH*, as we have seen, is concerned partly with the primacy of Toledo and it would therefore be surprising if the city's conquering hero, Alfonso VI, were not to be revered. Yet Rodrigo seems to have had a clear political imperative, and the legacy of Alfonso VI was primarily significant in that it enabled the city and see of

Toledo to be exalted. And Rodrigo's conception of Toledo included the recognition that it was to become once again the *urbs regia*, and the revival of its Visigothic greatness was supported by others in subsequent centuries. Nevertheless, it was not until 1284 that Alfonso X's son was crowned in Toledo as Sancho IV. Alfonso himself was approved as king in Seville in 1252, though there was no formal coronation.[8] Although Rodrigo had effectively stripped León of its spiritual primacy and prestige, the geographical centre and former city of the Goths assumed its role as the symbolic venue for the coronation of Spanish kings, in 1272, though the practice was intermittent. Fernando IV (r. 1295–1312), does not seem to have been formally crowned at all, though there was what Aurell describes as a 'general ritual of enthronement,' performed on the nine-year-old heir, at Toledo Cathedral.[9] And although it is certain Rodrigo had access to *CM* and may have used it extensively, the paths of the two churchmen would soon diverge:

> Lucas's defense of the tradition that Seville (rather than Toledo) had been in Visigothic times the primatial church of Spain brought him into collision with Rodrigo Jiménez, who was to draw very substantially – though without acknowledgement – on Lucas's work.[10]

Although the arrival of Alfonso VI and Rodrigo in Toledo are events separated by over one hundred and forty years, both king and prelate appeared to share a common vision for the city which would emerge and endure beyond the lives of both men.[11] Furthermore, it was Alfonso who created a bishopric in Toledo shortly after the occupation of the city and who was awarded primacy with the status of *Iglesia Primada de España* in October 1088 by Pope Urban II.[12] However, if the success of Christian kings (Alfonso VI and Alfonso VII) had caused Toledo to grow in power, it was Rodrigo who enabled it to prosper as a centre of learning, encouraging the translation into vernacular Castilian and Latin of Aristotle, Galen and Euclid, together with Arabic commentaries. Indeed, Rodrigo was able to attract impressive Arabic and Jewish scholars as well scholars from the Latin west.[13] Christian dominance had been consolidated by intellectual triumph and the work accomplished at Toledo, especially in mass translation, was to be felt beyond Iberia.[14]

Rodrigo and Lucas each refer to the person of Alfonso VI on over seventy occasions; in the *CLRC*, Juan makes a single reference that deals with Alfonso's knowledge of Toledo prior to its capture.[15] His senior clerical posts as a long-serving bishop were at Osma and then Burgos, both (but especially Osma) remote from the centres of rivalry that characterized Toledo and León under Rodrigo and Lucas. Yet references to Alfonso in all three chronicles are significant, as are those in earlier texts,[16] even though he remained, despite the apparent intentions of the author of the *HS* and the fulsome account in Pelayo's *Chronicon*,[17] a king without a biographer. Despite his redoubtable reputation amongst those who were to describe the events of his reign, it would not be until the time of Lucas and Rodrigo (especially Rodrigo) that there would be a further and more determined attempt to deal fully with his legacy.[18]

The veneration of victory

In the light of the considerable coverage afforded to Alfonso VI by Lucas and Rodrigo, it may seem that Juan's short chapter devoted to the fall of Toledo is not especially noteworthy. Yet in his laconic description of this event and Alfonso's part in it, the author manages to convey the idea of a man whose work is blessed by God. Juan describes Toledo as 'the most celebrated and well-protected city'[19] and Alfonso VI as a man whose power seems to be derived from that of Christ.[20] And Alfonso's attributes, whilst admired, are derived from the will and purposes of God rather than as expressions of the king's innate and independent qualities. He has been inspired by God who is the controller of events rather than a passive agent, governing the conduct of Muslims as well as Christians: 'Finally, driven by divine power, the Moors of Toledo delivered their city to King Alfonso.'[21] Even the king's subsequent attempt to extend his kingdom – abruptly brought to a halt following his humiliating defeat at Sagrajas on 23 October 1086[22] – was only possible through the power of Christ.[23] One of the areas for textual exploration will be the extent to which the *CLRC* can be seen in line with other contemporary chronicles of León-Castile in its style, purpose and use of scriptural sources. Or, perhaps it is closer in specific purpose, genre and polemic, as well as the author's use of biblical narrative to enrich and inform the narrative, to the author of Juan's twelfth-century predecessor, the author of the *CAI*. Although Fernández-Ordóñez does not refer directly to any comparisons with the *CAI*, she appears to acknowledge that as a writer of history, Juan stood apart from his thirteenth-century contemporaries. In terms of ideology, chronology and, crucially, the author's use of biblical texts, the chronicle produces an independent integrity: 'the constant resource to biblical citations reveals a creative unity.'[24] We can observe a biblically dependent narrative from an early stage. It was the advisory body [*consilium salutare*] surrounding King Alfonso VI that was divinely inspired [*Inspirauit ei Dominus* [*Deus*]][25] and in the OT the same verb is used [*inspirare*] to describe God's creative energy: 'And the Lord God formed man of the dust of the ground, and breathed [*inspiravit*] into his nostrils the breath of life; and man became a living soul.'[26] The reference has a two-pronged implication for the present study; firstly, it is possible to see the significance of this particular reference in the context of the conquest of Toledo. Secondly, it can be seen to relate to Alfonso himself. The phrase *Inspiravit ei Dominus Deus* creates and imposes a sense of divine power and intention. And there is also a more tentative but feasible link in the description of Alfonso as 'a wise and mighty man';[27] these two attributes, wisdom and might, are used in Ecclus 21, where they are linked and are part of a prolonged discourse.[28] The link may be a literary topos, though it is also possible that this was a conscious biblical reference, or both. In any event, it is not referred to by O'Callaghan, or in the *CCCM* edition; neither is it alluded to in Luis Charlo Brea's Spanish translation.

Both Rodrigo and Lucas discuss Alfonso VI at much greater length and, although the attention devoted to him is considerably more expansive in *DRH*,[29] the bulk of the information about him is derived from the *CM*. Reilly argues that it is the inclusion of two further sources (now lost), the *vita* or *gesta* of the Cluniac abbot of Sahagún and archbishop of Toledo, Bernard of Sédirac (r. 1086–1125) and the *Cantar de Alfonso VI*, that enables Rodrigo's text to display what he calls a 'much more local and "Toledan" character'.[30] Furthermore, there would seem to be a brief convergence in the veneration for Alfonso and Toledo shared by both Juan and Rodrigo, though the description of Alfonso VI and his capture of Toledo in the *CLRC* seems to have a more straightforward purpose even if the inferences may be more speculative. There was no obvious attempt in the *CLRC* to use the events of the conquest to promote one city at the expense of another. It may be that a more fulsome account of Alfonso VI might have emerged in the *CLRC* and was truncated partly because subsequent and significant defeat by the Almoravids at Sagrajas had effectively thwarted his early ambitions.[31] Yet, as Reilly notes, 'at his death in 1109 he left a kingdom permanently enlarged to almost twice its size in 1072 in geographical area and something approaching a third in population.'[32] Even if contemporary historians accorded him meagre coverage,[33] his legacy would be championed by the three thirteenth-century chroniclers.

Furthermore, Juan's record is of a different order from that of Lucas or Rodrigo and is dense with scriptural resonances.[34] There is a sense in which God, so to speak, 'breathed' his life into the minds of those who were to advise and make decisions. This had implications for the way Juan was to view Alfonso VI and Toledo and the idea of conquest itself. The notion of Christian reconquest is dependent upon divine intervention and here the point that can be derived from Juan is that conquest had been possible because of a combination of God's help and the king's own awareness of the city and his natural cunning.

Alfonso's knowledge of the city demonstrates the emperor's natural curiosity and familiarity with its geography of which he had detailed knowledge during his brief period of exile in the *taifa* and city of Toledo in 1072.[35] This seems to have enabled him to engage in the blockade of Toledo and contributed to his capacity to take the city and consolidate his position. If the Muslim population did not welcome Alfonso's occupation of the city, they appear not to have resisted it; many remained in the city, believing that they could retain their property and houses,[36] though this apparent acquiescence on the part of the enemy was also due, according to the author, to divine intervention.[37] And whether Juan's comments – made so long after the conquest itself – are entirely reliable is a moot point.[38] Here there is an important link with Rodrigo whose interpretation of Hispanic history must be considered alongside that of Juan. Rodrigo's Toledo-centred habitat and spectrum through which he mediates the history of Spain[39] facilitates his argument that the elevated status of Toledo was due in part to its having been wrested from Muslim control in 1085 – but that is only part of the argument. It had technically been occupied rather than conquered by the army of Tariq ibn Ziyad (689–720); his forces had, as it were, been able to lay claim to a largely abandoned city.[40] This emphasizes the spiritual and military mystique of Toledo in which its pre-eminence would be both eternal and evolving even if Rodrigo's own expression of this status might be variously expressed:

This same evolution of the once and future status of Toledo is outlined in a very different format in the several cartularies that were compiled under Rodrigo's aegis to detail Toledo's rights and possessions.[41]

Following Sagrajas, Alfonso's grip on power in Castile must have seemed more precarious despite the claim that he had achieved in the seizure of the city a great prize and political triumph.[42] Yet the idea that the capture of Toledo was a single feat (even allowing for prior knowledge) is challenged, since the city's capitulation to Christian forces effectively evolved in stages between 1085 and 1099.[43] The mosque was taken, defiled and reconsecrated, and the Mozarabs were finally dislodged from their stronghold in Santa María de Alficén, in the northeast of the city, in 1099, though even this indignity and betrayal did not completely extinguish their survival.[44] A faithful remnant continued to practise the Mozarabic rite even though it had officially been banned.[45] Thus with the dismantling of the Mozarabic legacy, Toledo's Visigothic past had effectively been hijacked by the king and his Cluniac archbishop, Bernard de Sédirac, and the loss of the Spanish rite was part of the papacy's drive to regularize and extend the use of Latin and this was zealously supported by senior Cluniacs. Toledo's Visigothic past had been rewritten and the faith and culture of its inhabitants rehabilitated to serve a more pressing Christian imperative which was at first to praise and then to marginalize the Mozarabs. And just such a plan for a reborn Toledo might well have been part of Rodrigo's intention:

> It is instructive to note that although there is a speech attributed to Alfonso VI by Archbishop Rodrigo Jiménez de Rada in the 1240s, in his account of the reconsecration of the Mosque for Christian worship, the passage which so ostentatiously eulogizes the Mozarabs, is glaringly absent.[46]

For the Mozarabs, it seems, approbation turned to deception;[47] by consigning them to a lowlier status than that of the king's newly acquired Muslim subjects, there is an ambiguity surrounding the city's legacy perpetuated by Rodrigo. The plurality of Toledo's Christian identity could not be sustained beyond Las Navas if conquest had become the achievable goal.[48] Yet Toledo remained, though an object of sorrow because it lacked the resonance of its perceived Visigothic past, a city that had at least come to embrace incongruous elements – it had become a 'hybrid ... that conquest alone could not have conferred upon it.'[49] Furthermore, the OT idea of place might find an echo in the ancient cities in the Christian kingdoms of León and Castile, and this notion could be linked to the fortunes of those who are associated with their historic retrieval and renewal.

The fortunes of the kings of León-Castile depended partly on genealogy and blood line and were emphasized in the success or otherwise of marriage alliances; the marriage of Urraca of León (r. 1109–26) to Alfonso I of Aragón (1096–1134) is one such example which is discussed by Theresa Earenfight,[50] and the events of Urraca's reign are briefly commented upon by Juan. According to Juan, she failed to govern competently [*quod postea pessime administravi*], though this judgement is not supported by evidence from within the chronicle. Moreover, *postea* ['afterwards' or 'later'] suggests that this crushing verdict might not have applied to her entire reign. The behaviour and probity of monarchs has parallels with those biblical kings who did evil in the sight of the Lord,[51] and the author immediately turns his attention to Urraca's estranged husband whose righteous inner anguish (which again has biblical echoes)[52] prompted him to seek revenge on the land of Castile. The comparison, noted by O'Callaghan,[53] offers the possibility that such anger is justified by the example of God's reaction to the immorality in the days before the Deluge when He subsequently sought to destroy what He had created. Furthermore, the allusion to the sexual immorality in Gen. 6.1-3 and which is subsumed into the phrase 'the wickedness of man was great in the earth,'[54] gives us an insight as to the kind of behaviour that Juan alluded to and which he seems to have found so unworthy to describe explicitly.[55] His reticence about presenting a descriptive account of the queen's foibles compounds what has been called her 'ambivalent reputation' in twelfth-century literary tradition.[56] Yet earlier chronicles and those written by those who were acquainted with the queen (Bernard de Sédirac, Bishop Pelayo of Oviedo and the author of the *CAI*) deliver more restrained and even laudatory responses to the events of her reign.[57] However, she makes a fascinating contrast with Fernando III's mother, Berenguela, about whom there is far more clarity, though she too remains mysterious.

In Juan we have an author who uses biblical narrative and language every bit as powerfully as the author of the *CAI* – and much more directly and frequently than Lucas or Rodrigo – yet with discernment that is not dependent on uncompromisingly violent imagery. Scholars have identified one hundred and thirteen biblical references in *CLRC*,[58] and this is likely to be an underestimate. Furthermore, biblical texts are much more explicit and integral to Juan's chronicle than they are in *CM* or in the *DRL*; such references are used throughout his discussion of events and are not restricted to defined clusters of relevance. There is a seamless intervention, a continuing consistent purpose and impetus in the way scripture will be made to work. There is in Juan a more comprehensive use of scripture and the author also demonstrates his scholarly awareness of books relating to the Apocalypse.[59] His ability to use familiar texts (from classical authors as well as from the Bible) in a straightforward and creative way amounts to an instinctive awareness of the importance of the cultural legacy in which he was immersed and his awareness of its relevance in setting a context for contemporary events within the peninsula.[60] The fact that he was well placed as an eyewitness to the events he described enabled Juan to offer a much more detailed description of events in the reigns of Alfonso VIII (r. 1158–1214), Enrique I (r. 1214–17) and Fernando III, and this familiarity enables him to emerge as 'a valuable witness to the large and small happenings of those three reigns'[61] This is the period of which the author had first-hand knowledge – and biblical references are subtly and meticulously applied. Descriptions of events and the accompanying commentary are direct and spare, embellishment is infrequently deployed.[62] Thus scriptural allusions are usually unmistakable and, as we shall see, such references are not often used as undiluted polemic.

The author's concluding comments on Alfonso VI remind us of his place in history as the one who infiltrated and captured Toledo[63] but we are also warned that God controls events. The Aragonese debacle at Fraga in 1134 was due not to the power of the Saracens but to the deceitful behaviour of the Aragonese.[64] The suggestion that God allows the enemies of his people to overwhelm them has powerful OT precedents;[65] nevertheless, the punishment meted out will be contained. Just as, despite the sins of King Jehoram, the Lord would not destroy the house of David,[66] so the kingdom of León-Castile, momentarily divided under Urraca, would be restored under Alfonso VII. Such a reversal of people and fortune is also attributable to the will of God or to divine favour.[67] The restoration of authority takes place with the invocation of a collect from the *Missa contra paganos*, a liturgy used in the struggle to liberate Jerusalem after 1187 in the Third Crusade.[68] Following its use in the battle for Jerusalem, the collect was used much more widely, and indeed was promoted as such by Clement V as part of a more general liturgical crusade.[69] It is part of a prayer for the emperor in the Good Friday liturgy,[70] although its probable derivation is Ecclus 10.4. The celebration itself also seems to owe much to other parts of the OT, especially to the Psalms.[71] Such evocative linguistic flourishes have other powerful contemporary parallels: in his essay on the *Poema de Fernán González*,[72] Deyermond notes that the poem portrays the Spanish in general and the Castilians in particular as God's chosen people.[73] This is a simple doctrine that is predicated on the idea of the fall of the Visigothic kingdom occurring as a result of the people's own sin [*peccatis exigentibus*].[74] The idea of *peccatis exigentibus*, probably derived from Isa. 59.2, was circulating widely in the Outremer and especially following the Second Crusade.[75] Restoration in the poem is a threefold process: ancestral calamity, afflictions of God's people and gradual recovery.[76] This idea is also important, as we noted, to the author of the *HS*.[77]

The notion that God's hand determined the struggle for supremacy in Iberia is a key element in Juan's chronicle. This assumption, once established in the reigns of the early monarchs of Alfonso VI, Urraca and Alfonso VII, provides the backdrop to the turbulent events of the twelfth century and particularly to those with which the author had direct experience. Following the death of Alfonso VII and what the author dubbed the 'wretched division'[78] of his kingdom, we are given just the bare details of the lands that were transferred to his sons, Sancho and Fernando. More importantly perhaps, is the assertion that this was as a result of the sins of men,[79] a commonly held view by the thirteenth century and a claim with a biblical resonance: 'For now they shall say, we have no king, because we feared not the Lord; what then should a king do to us?'[80]

Although Juan draws a veil over events within Alfonso's separated empire, it is tempting to suggest that the idea of the division of Solomon's kingdom into Israel and Judah[81] would have appealed, as an instructive piece of historical narrative, to the Castilian imagination, especially since the decision to divide León-Castile was, according to Juan, based on the advice of a certain Count Fernando:[82] 'in this unwise and retrograde decision, which was to split Alfonso's dominions after more than eighty years of union, the curia had no part.'[83] The division of the Jewish kingdom was in part the result of bad advice given to Solomon's son, Rehoboam; wise and experienced counsel was ignored.[84] Comparisons with the biblical division in 1 Kings may only be suggested even though there are similarities between the two events – the curia that might have been consulted with the wise and ancient counsel, the person of Count Fernando with Rehoboam's youthful advisers and, most strikingly, the division itself – all of which provide powerful reminiscences.[85] Except that Fernando was not a youthful adviser. Born in *circa* 1090, he had been *de facto* ruler of Portugal from 1121 to 1128 and fought alongside Alfonso VII at Almería.[86] Whatever individual motives those around Alfonso may have harboured, Fernando himself died in 1155. With hindsight, Juan's *infelicem divisionem* has an echo of a comment made by Jesus on the weakness of a divided kingdom: 'And if a kingdom be divided against itself, that kingdom cannot stand.'[87]

In determining how the kings of Castile in his own lifetime were to be specifically remembered, Juan was meticulous in applying honorific titles. Alfonso VI was the conqueror of Toledo and his grandson an acknowledged and widely acclaimed statesman, as 'when he gained the crown of empire, he was proclaimed Emperor by the whole world.'[88] But by far the most lavish praise is reserved for Alfonso VII's grandson, Alfonso VIII (r. 1158–1214), notwithstanding his defeat at Alarcos where he is, nevertheless, praised for a rare and persistent courage.[89] This is despite (or perhaps because of) an early demonstration of aggression, which ran counter to a treaty signed between Fernando II and Alfonso VIII in 1183: 'As soon as the young Alfonso IX took the throne of Leon upon the death of his father Fernando II in 1188, the Castilian king launched an attack, taking possession of ten castles.'[90] This adulation is replicated in *CM* and *DRH*. Rodrigo's references are peppered with accolades alluding to the king's nobility, composure, equity, serenity and temperance representing a kind of ideal Castilian monarch.

Juan, who does not spare his dramatis personae from criticism as well as praise, sees an almost pure virtue in Alfonso VIII and the king's impatience in refusing to wait for the support of the king of León before Alarcos is only obliquely drawn by referring to prudence in others (in this case by the wise advice of his closest advisers):

> Because of this [i.e. Alfonso's desire for controlling both the military timetable and an independent strategy], the glorious king of Castile was unwilling to wait for the assistance of the king of León, although certain experienced men, well-proved in military matters, advised him to do so. [91]

Juan could hardly call into question the king's faith in God,[92] but alludes to a possible recklessness.[93] Much more conspicuous is his use of the term *gloriosus* to describe the king who is variously presented as 'his [i.e. Sancho's] glorious son,' followed by a string of superlatives: *rex gloriosus, gloriosi regis Castelle* and *rex gloriosus dominus Alfonsus*[94] and although there is no overt biblical link, there are inferences that may be made. The idea of the Son of Man, in glorious majesty, is both an image derived from the gospels[95] and one that suggests an accolade that the author reserves for Fernando III enthroned in Córdoba in 1236. The author's

6. The Thirteenth Century and Biblical Conquest

reference to Córdoba as a kingdom [*Cordubensis regni*][96] is either an anachronism or a reference to the territorial jurisdiction which was applied to the city following the conquest. The *Reino de Córdoba* was, of course, part of the kingdom of Castile. Either way, it remains a potent image.

Biblical precedent is writ large in a telling passage portraying Alfonso VIII in a way which is strongly reminiscent of an important incident in the life of his grandfather, Alfonso VII – chronicled by the author of the *CAI*.[97] As his grandfather before him had been able to do in 1139, so Alfonso VIII, following his victory at Las Navas, returned to Toledo in triumph; and Juan, like the author of the *CAI*, makes a dramatic and laconic biblical intervention:

> The glorious and noble king, after subduing and striking down an arrogant foe, was taken back into Toledo with exaltation and pride by the entire population who called out, proclaiming, 'Blessed is he who cometh in the name of the Lord.'[98]

Both O'Callaghan and Charlo Brea note the relationship of this passage with Ps. 117.26, and examples of more telling and equally clear NT parallels also exist.[99] The decision of the two chroniclers to link the triumph of their subjects, Alfonso VII and Alfonso VIII, with the strategically important and historically iconic city of Toledo is salient and the distinctive style of address awarded to the kings of Castile would reflect the importance of the city.[100] For Alfonso VIII to be so identified is especially memorable; his entry into Toledo is after Las Navas and precedes his death by about two years. The celebration of victory was eventually followed, in line with the biblical reminiscences of Palm Sunday and Good Friday, by sorrow and mourning.[101] Although he appears to have died from natural causes, *ingresus est viam universe carnis*[102] [he advanced to the way of all flesh] this demise has echoes of other biblical passages, the strongest of which is within the exhortation of Joshua before his own death: 'And behold, this day I am going the way of all the earth.'[103] There are further biblical incidents that describe the frailty of human flesh that provide allusions,[104] though these do not provide obvious cross-references with incidents described by Juan.

There is a further sense in which the idea of Toledo representing a place of unique importance in the Castilian imagination, though more obliquely, is incorporated into Juan's narrative. Juan, like Rodrigo, praises Toledo as a place of victory and sacred memory, but his treatment is less parochial; his chronicle is much more concerned with the welfare and integrity of the kingdom of Castile than with asserting the unique superiority of a specific city. In an echo from 1 Macc. 10.55,[105] it is the blessings of the ancient Castilian homeland that are to be praised above all things: 'O blessed day in the kingdom of Castile, ever worthy to be loved.'[106] This eulogy may owe something to the Hebrews' affection for their homeland:

> Happy art thou, O Israel: who is like unto thee, O people saved by the Lord, the shield of thy help, and who is the sword of thy excellency! and thy enemies shall be found liars unto thee; and thou shalt tread upon their high places.[107]

As we have seen, a number of European cities, including Toledo, suggest a kind of modelling based on Jerusalem, and especially in the crusading context of a campaign against the Muslims of al-Andalus. During the twelfth and thirteenth centuries the notion of a spiritual Jerusalem being replicated in cities across Europe was widespread, though this was often at the behest of Jewish populations that had settled in cities in Europe and Africa.[108] In Spain the link is likely to have stronger biblical parallels linked to the gathering momentum of reconquest and can also be made with other Castilian cities. The idea would include, as we have seen, the idea that the land of Castile is to be compared with Israel or Judea. And it is Rodrigo, not Juan, who is recognized as the Toledan; despite the highly significant cross-references with the entry of Jesus into Jerusalem on Palm Sunday which are made by Juan and the author of the *CAI*, the attempt to shift the centre of historical and ecclesiastical gravity to an individual city is not made in either chronicle. This may be in part – and despite the attempts by Lucas and Rodrigo – because within the shifting borders of Castile there was no recognized capital.[109]

Although about a third of the *CLRC* is devoted to the reign of Alfonso VIII and his forebears, it is not until the time Berenguela emerges into the narrative, that the title 'noble' is consistently used in Juan's descriptions of the queen.[110] And this is only after her decision to bow to popular request and abdicate in favour of her son Ferdinand III.[111] However, she was still to exert considerable influence, arranging for her son's first marriage to Elisabeth (known as Beatrice or Beatriz) of Hohenstaufen (1203–1235) and helping to avert conflict between Castile and Aragón, following the death of Alfonso IX in 1230. Juan's appellation may have been an acknowledgement of Berenguela's lineage as well as a recognition of her diplomatic and political skills: and this familial power was combined with her qualities as a noble and great mother, able to operate successfully on behalf of her offspring.[112] The transfer of power from Berenguela to Ferdinand is similarly described by Rodrigo,[113] and the term *nobilis regina*[114] which is used by Juan to describe Berenguela is also found in Rodrigo's description of the way the queen prepares her son for kingship.[115] Lucas, for reasons that may relate to his Leonese allegiance, does not use the term to describe Berenguela. The term is not found in the Bible either, though there may be an inadvertent derivation[116] and it forms the opening words (used as a title) of the most famous of the four Breviary anthems of the Blessed Virgin Mary, *Salve nobilis regina fons misericordia*. The hymn of triumph and praise begin with the words, *Carissima genitrix et domina dulcissima*[117] [Most precious mother and dear lady], in which the word *genitrix* suggests progenitor as much as it does mother and is widely used in devotional prayers to the Virgin (Pray for us O Holy Mother of God) in which her eternal power is suggested. Yet these elements in Fernando's speech in praise of his mother also suggest echoes of the beauty and humility of the mother of Jesus;[118] the relationship between Berenguela and Fernando could scarcely be a more powerful assertion of lives that are modelled on NT precedent and seem to be biblically sanctioned. Berenguela is the humble maidservant who renounces the throne and while remaining a benevolent influence on Castilian politics.[119]

6. *The Thirteenth Century and Biblical Conquest*   157

The honour bestowed upon Berenguela is underlined in the account of Fernando seeking the permission of his mother, second only to God in the king's affections,[120] who responds to her son's peroration and agrees that he move against the Muslims. Even if allusions to the favour accorded to the Virgin Mary are not necessarily the focus of Juan's intentions, his implications are unmistakable. Despite Berenguela being Lucas's patron, his treatment of her, according to Miriam Shadis, is restrained and detached;[121] certainly he praises her qualities of leadership and wisdom as well

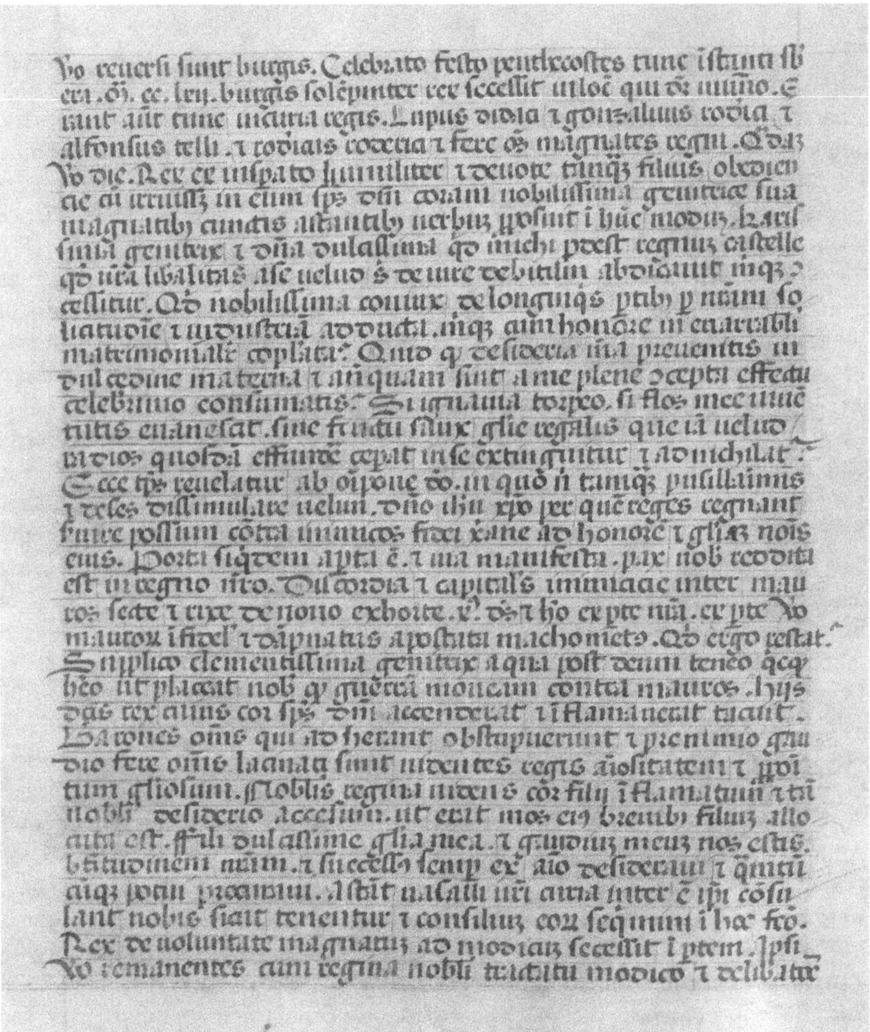

Figure 6.1 Fernando III extols his mother and proposes war against the Moors, Pentecost, 1224, *CLRC*. MSS 9/450 182-248 folio 222.

© Real Academia de la Historia. España.

as her motherly support and her determination to fight heresy: 'She inflicted such terror on heretics that they all fled from both kingdoms [Castile and León].'[122] Yet neither he nor Rodrigo makes any direct biblical allusion to the Virgin Mary, and certainly not with the soaring inferences that may be drawn from Juan's history. In the *CLRC* it is difficult to imagine Fernando's words to his mother implying a more direct affirmation of the ancient power of God resting on the royal house of Castile: 'Christ, God and man, is on our side.'[123] And it is to Fernando that we must now turn.

Fernando III

Apart from Juan's brief references to the short reign of Enrique I which includes the single eulogistic claim, *erat bone indolis*[124] [he was of noble character], the remaining Castilian monarch described by Juan, and for whom there are numerous epithets, is Fernando III. Here again, the author's Castilian loyalties and interests are in evidence even if Fernando is not always accorded the honours lavished on Alfonso VIII.[125] Yet, the epithets Juan used to describe Fernando, though less consistent, recognize a man of exceptional qualities and religious piety that suggests the highest of biblical parallels. It is also worth comparing Juan's depiction of Fernando with that of his contemporaries. For example, Fernando's ally and contemporary, Jaime I of Aragón (r. 1213–76) is only briefly referred to in the chronicle, once in respect of his divorce (or more properly, annulment of marriage on grounds of consanguinity) with Queen Leonor in 1229,[126] the conquest of Mallorca in the same year[127] and the successful siege of Burriana in 1233.[128] Nowhere is there a reference to the character or worth of the Aragonese king, though, it was precisely this alliance between the two kings that had been responsible for the collapse of the Almohads and their allies that effectively enabled their expulsion from Spain.[129] The author alludes, in his section on the Conquest of Mallorca, that he knew of correspondence between Jaime I and Fernando that suggested collaboration. Nevertheless, when they are referred to in connection with the same event, it is the Castilian who receives the acknowledgement: 'Just as we become acquainted, in fact, with the letters from our distinguished king [*illustris rex*].'[130] The title *illustris rex* is one of many such epithets heaped upon Fernando.

According to Juan, the character of Fernando, like that of his grandfather Alfonso VIII, shows signs of having evolved during his kingship. Yet unlike his grandfather who was from his earliest youth, the 'glorious son,'[131] Fernando had, so to speak, to earn his spurs, even if he began to do so at a relatively early period in his kingship. Undoubtedly his reputation was sealed by his success in forging a permanent union with León, through conquest and royal marriage alliances,[132] but also important was the way in which he was able to gain support from the *concejos* of Burgos and Ávila at the time of his succession in 1217. This support was consolidated in 1230 when he was able to acknowledge the support given to him by the *concejo* of Salamanca when he was claiming the crown of León.[133] The combination of political and diplomatic alliances, abetted by conquest and support from Castilian cities, enabled the expeditious recovery of Muslim property and land.[134] Whether or not these events prompted Juan to elevate the status of Fernando, there was a point when his greatness was recognized. Juan's description of Fernando's declaration against the Muslims in Burgos at the feast of Pentecost in 1224 has all the hallmarks of the anointing of a great OT warrior-judge: 'whereupon the Lord's spirit threw itself upon him.'[135] This translation is directly lifted from Judg. 14.6; the author's debt to this biblical blessing is footnoted by Charlo Brea,[136] but Juan's passage is redolent with the power of the Holy Spirit and is dependent on several sources. The fact that the spirit's force was to be felt at Pentecost is telling; the term *irruisset*, as in *cum irruisset in eum Spiritus Dimini*, can be translated as 'rushed,'[137] or 'invaded' and the description of the descent of the Holy Spirit in Acts 2.2, as a 'rushing mighty wind' would seem to provide an important scriptural backdrop. We have a clear picture of the sudden and overwhelming power of God. Fernando declares war on the Muslims[138] and is granted the power to do so with confidence. O'Callaghan suggests that such a move might have been inspired by a leader during the Fifth Crusade, John of Brienne, whose military success in Damietta in 1219 gave him control of the city and is implicit in Juan's account.[139] The notion of Fernando receiving inspiration from God's spirit is repeated elsewhere[140] and again there is a comparison arising from the anointing of Samuel. And the guiding power is that of the Holy Spirit, which came upon Christ at his baptism: 'and he saw the Spirit of God descending like a dove, and lighting upon him.'[141]

Despite the many accolades lavished upon Fernando, and the scriptural allusions that may abound, there are few consistently applied epithets. In addition to his humility, piety and obedience as a son, thanks to the working of the Holy Spirit,[142] he is linked with more robust qualities: 'The noble queen, understanding that the heart of her son was on fire and illuminated with a noble longing.'[143] Again, the pious king may be seen as an imitation of Christ, 'for I am meek and lowly of heart'[144] and such virtues are also to be found in Paul's teaching.[145] The references to being inflamed may owe a further debt to the power of the Holy Spirit at Pentecost when he descended on the disciples with tongues of fire.[146] And fire is a potent symbol and metaphor throughout the Bible.[147] Yet most frequently, when he is described by Juan it is as 'our king,' distributing largesse to the knights of Castile.[148] This might be used to distinguish Fernando from other kings being discussed,[149] but it also seems to affirm the author's Castilian affiliations, and the description continues to be used at the time of the unification of the two kingdoms[150] and up to the capture of Córdoba.[151] This is a title bestowed on King David[152] as well as on King Sedecias in the prophecy of Jeremiah.[153] Fernando is variously described as 'brilliant,' 'lucid' and 'illustrious,' all of which may be derived from *illustris* and its superlative *illustrissimus*.[154] By the time he has conquered Córdoba, the king is accorded appellations redolent of biblical triumph; he has transcended illustriousness and become celebrated and glorious.[155] This is an incremental affirmation of the king's supremacy and can be seen as a kind of consummation of biblical and Castilian authority; it also has echoes of the second coming: 'When the Son of Man shall come in his glory, and all the holy angels with him, then shall he sit upon the throne of his glory.'[156] Fernando was canonized in 1671 in what is described as among 'the most majestic displays that took place in Charles II's royal chapel'[157] and there is further evidence of the lavish and feverish circumstances of Fernando's canonization.[158] Fernando seems to have been an entirely suitable candidate for sainthood, having produced the structure on which the Patronato Real could develop.[159] He nevertheless questions the true saintliness of the monarch by referring, inter alia, to his misappropriation of the *tercias*, his contempt for certain senior prelates and his intermittent disdain for canon law.[160]

All three thirteenth-century chroniclers link Fernando III with piety and the qualities that are most notably emphasized in Juan's chronicle. Lucas uses the adjective *inclitus*, which can be translated as celebrated, renowned, illustrious or glorious, to describe Fernando[161] and, as we have seen, this was a term also favoured by Juan and used in the context of the king's victory in Córdoba. Lucas uses it in the same historical setting and his description of the newly established Christian court at Córdoba is not only much more expansive than that provided by Juan but contains a stronger element of vengeful cleansing: 'King Fernando entered Córdoba amid celebration and great joy and the filth of Muhammad was expunged';[162] the need to purge the city is present too in Rodrigo's account,[163] though he does not bestow upon Fernando the superlatives that were so strongly apparent in the accounts of Lucas and Juan. Juan also uses the same image to describe the cleansing of Alcaraz following its capture in 1213, *purgata maurorum spurcicia*[164] [the purging of the Moors' filth] and this seems to be directly linked through his use of *spurcicia* to what he describes as 'filthy Moorish superstition.'[165] Jerrilynn Dodds describes this as part of 'a comfortingly reductive myth that linked Christian morality with the politics of the northern kingdoms' conquest of the peninsula.'[166]

Such an uncompromising view of the enemy and pitiless attitude to conquest can be seen in the *CAI* where the author describes the vengeance exacted on those he calls *Moabitae* and *Agareni* whose city of Coria fell in 1142: 'they wrought greater destruction than they had endured from the Saracens.'[167] Yet although the notion of purging is central to biblical teaching on sacrifice, expiation and to the Hebraic conquest of Canaan, the idea of a place being ritually cleansed is relatively unusual: 'Now in the eighteenth year of his reign [i.e. that of King Josiah], when he had purged the land, and the Temple of the Lord.'[168] Furthermore, the idea of the capture of Córdoba representing a kind of consummation of the heavenly kingdom is an image to which only Juan constructs.

Political squabbles and geographical perspectives

If comment on Jaime I is restrained, Juan is more forthright about the Christian opponents of Castile. He also draws attention with little subtlety to the king of León who is tempted to betray his Castilian cousin: 'and, on the strategic advice of certain of Satan's acolytes, he became a perverse bow [*arcum pravum*] and sought reasons to withdraw help from his friend.'[169] O'Callaghan translates *arcum parvum* as 'crooked bow' and this shows a clear debt to Ps. 78.57.[170] However this phrase is to be rendered, Alfonso IX of León is portrayed as a dissembler and a man whose word is not to be relied upon. There may even be an allusion to the ultimate betrayer, Judas Iscariot, whose acts against his friend and master were prompted by the intervention of Satan.[171] Alfonso IX, who had invaded Castile following the death of Enrique, is described in witheringly biblical terms: 'but [he was] inflated with an inane ambition.'[172] Effectively, Juan associates Alfonso with the sin of pride and, by implication, with the absence of humility,[173] both of which are linked inextricably to sin in the OT,[174] as well as being the cause of Haman's downfall in the account of his overweening ambition in the Book of Esther.[175] The judgement on Alfonso is also reminiscent of a teaching epistle from Paul to Timothy: 'He is proud, knowing nothing, but doting about questions and strifes of words, whereof cometh envy, strife, railings, evil surmising.'[176] Unsurprisingly, Lucas de Túy's more frequent references to Alfonso IX in *CM* (thirty-two in all) give a much more laudatory picture of the Leonese monarch. Yet although the king and the city of León are singled out for praise, specific links with biblical texts are more tenuous. Lucas stresses Alfonso's administrative involvement and religious credentials, 'Alfonso, the Catholic king of León, had clerks with him.'[177] This clarification of the nature of Alfonso's faith, which is repeated elsewhere,[178] may have echoes of Paul's injunction to Timothy to 'fight the good fight of faith.'[179] What is portrayed as the firm faith of Alfonso may be compared to the flattering prayers [*blandis precibus*][180] of Berenguela when she came to León. However, this seems to be an aside compared with Lucas's primary purpose in this and in the subsequent paragraph, which is to remind his audience of the importance of the basilica in the city of León. It is the final resting place for St Isidore and should thus be regarded as the centre of the Catholic faith and the pre-eminent military power within Spain.[181]

We have noted the significance of Iberian cities, especially Toledo, as well as the way in which Castile might represent a new Israel or Judah. But further biblical cities, such as Nineveh – and, as we shall see, Jericho – also provide comparisons. Yet it is possible to overplay such parallels. In *CLRC*, in addition to several Castilian cities being referred to as 'noble' and 'famous,' the appellation is conferred upon Santarém (Portugal)[182] and Baghdad.[183] The idea of praising the greatness of a city, regardless of its provenance, is certainly a biblical one, so it is possible to identify an OT parallel with Juan's apparently randomly applied descriptions. A more telling avenue might be briefly to pursue the ways in which the three chroniclers sought to extol the cities with which they were most closely identified. Just as Lucas and Rodrigo sought to promote the cities of León and Toledo, so Juan – though without the same relentless passion – is identified with Burgos where he was bishop from 1240 until his death in 1246.[184] His references to Burgos imply scriptural precedent rather than stating such a link directly. Although the author avoids fulsome adjectives to describe the city, its importance is central to his narrative and its context within Juan's history is integral. It is the miraculous deliverance of Burgos in 1217 from Alfonso IX of León: 'The Lord God, as if by a miracle, had freed the city of Burgos from the hands of its enemies'[185] suggests a sacred importance. The many OT resonances are striking and Juan's reference is especially reminiscent of Isaiah's prophecy concerning his people's deliverance from the king of Assyria: 'And I will deliver thee and this city out of the hand of the king of Assyria.'[186] There is also an assertion of the ancient greatness of Burgos following the solemnization of Fernando's marriage to Beatrice: 'Not since the age of antiquity, had so great a court been witnessed in the city of Burgos.'[187] Indeed, the aim of those present at these celebratory events may have been in part to demonstrate their fealty to Beatrice as the wife of their new young king.[188] Rodrigo also describes the marriage but does not refer directly to the curia.[189] Juan seems to be suggesting an ancient pre-eminence for Burgos combined with a restoration of a time-honoured authority and there is an echo of the restoration of peoples and cities in the OT.[190] His account may not be an emphatic assertion of a biblical link but there is at least the suggestion that Burgos is a city blest by God. There is in the Bible much apocalyptic language relating to the spiritual and eschatological significance of place but its use may also be more suggestive and nuanced. A more subtle interplay between the Asturian kingdom and the Holy City is also suggested: 'the notion of Holy Jerusalem, as well as the Holy Cross was important to the Spanish rite,'[191] suggesting a time-honoured link with biblical cities that was established well before the twelfth and thirteenth centuries.

Enhancing the reputation of Toledo as the *urbs regia*, Rodrigo successfully rehabilitated (and possibly reinvented) Alfonso VI, the hero of the reconquest, partly at the expense of his sometime rival and faithful vassal, the Cid. In this, he is at variance with Lucas; by bequeathing the Reconquista in *DRH* a distinctly Castilian edge, he was almost certainly attempting to shift the centre of gravity to his own archbishopric. Yet both Rodrigo and Lucas could be seen as presenting a restricted idea of a city chosen by God wherein his people might dwell. They self-consciously asserted the worth of their chosen cities and in so doing were at variance with a biblical strand that had been advanced by Augustine; in her introduction to Henry Bettenson's translation of *De ciuitate Dei*, G. R. Evans notes:

> Augustine speaks of *civitates* not *urbes* because he has something in mind which goes far beyond living in a conurbation ... he had absorbed what the Bible had to say about it [i.e. the City of God] and related notions in scripture.[192]

Even so, Augustine's preoccupation with sophisticated arguments about the unalienable nature of citizenship and bonds of common interest were based very much on his own interpretation of the Psalms and other OT passages.[193] We are here considering the idea of the city with much more limited and specific intention. Nevertheless, to Castilianize Iberian history, Rodrigo needed to lionize the king who might be considered to have re-established the Visigothic monarchy. On the other hand, Bishop Juan as we have already noted, does not bequeath historic mysticism on Toledo, nor does he indulge in an exaggerated or prolonged peroration of Alfonso himself.

Yet three quarters of a century before *CLRC* was penned, the Anglo-Norman author of *De expugnatione Lyxbonensi* had made just such a Visigothic link with

Toledo, through Sisebut (r. 611/12–619). The reference is oblique, since there was a more direct attempt to link Isidore with Seville and Lisbon as well as with Toledo.[194] This is only a passing reference (and Toledo is only mentioned in one other context in the chronicle), but it suggests that distance in time did not necessarily determine the author's spiritual or historical perspective; intention and perhaps patronage would also play their part. Yet it is surely one thing to want to promote a city such as León or Toledo in order to assert its political or historical pre-eminence or because of the prompting of patronage (though in a treatise, *De altera vita*, Lucas also wrote about the Albigensian heresy which had entered León after 1209 and which he was charged to refute, though details are sparse).[195] The cities most memorably identified in *CLRC*, Toledo and Córdoba and especially Burgos, suggest closer scriptural parallels and, because his characters, places and events are made without a strident geographical and political agenda, allusions emerge with greater clarity.

Representations of the enemy

We now turn to consider in greater detail the ways in which the Muslim other was viewed by our thirteenth-century chroniclers. One possible counterpoint to the veneration of Christian kings and the places with which they were closely identified is the idea of the ways in which the enemy could be represented and the complexities and variations within this framework. The clarity with which Christendom was represented was a matter on which chroniclers could be unequivocal, as a further extract from the speech of Fernando extolling his mother makes clear that 'Christ [who is] God and Man is of our party; in truth, the infidel and damnable apostate Muhammad is on the side of the Moors'.[196] The frequency with which such statements are made suggests that this presentation of Christian-Muslim relationships within Hispano-Latin texts from the thirteenth century came to be a widespread cultural and religious construct.[197] Even so, Christian representation of the Muslim enemy lacked consistency within individual chronicles even if there was a recognizable attempt to stress the ideological chasm between the two faiths:

> In the Middle Ages, Latin Christian writers dedicated substantial literary energy to constructing bipolar opposites between themselves and the Muslims with whom they shared the peninsula and on whom they projected an image of cosmic alienation generated by reference to Christian dogma.[198]

Political pragmatism as much as crusading idealism – though the two are often difficult to separate – is likely to have influenced reconquest narratives and the subsequent Christian attitude to and treatment of the Muslims, even if such treatment is represented as a divinely ordained duty. As early as 1095, Pope Urban II had encouraged Iberian Christians to fight, as it were, the enemy within their own territories.[199] Yet this confusion of motive was as much a feature of the First Crusade as it was of those knights who travelled to Spain; both theatres of conflict contained confusing motivations of purpose and ideology among the individuals concerned.²⁰⁰ And it would apply equally to the complexity of struggles within contemporary Iberia itself. Despite this, as we have seen, the idea of recapturing Jerusalem or the holy sites in Palestine would come to have a powerful resonance within Spain, even if religious motives within Iberia lacked the clarity during the time of the First Crusade that they were to assume later:

> There is no trace whatsoever of any comparable fusion of acts of pious violence and pilgrimage in Iberia before 1095, and it is striking that contemporaries were more inclined to draw analogies between crusading and entry into monastic life than they were to make references to precedents created by peninsular warfare against Islam.²⁰¹

Yet the idea of religious ideology, even if overwhelmed by other motives, remains a potentially important element especially as it seems to have gathered pace and became pre-eminent after the time of the First Crusade. In terms of the Iberian conflicts in the twelfth century, diplomacy seems to have strengthened the idea and construction of the Reconquista among the Christian kings of the north. This diplomatic function, often when employed by popes and papal legates, could be coercive and demanding, though this does not seem to have totally undermined harmonious associations between Christians and Muslims.²⁰² Nevertheless, relations between the two groups of adherents were also intricate and explosive and the dynamics of an ideology can often be seen as being at odds with the skills and subtleties of diplomacy. This complexity is a key feature of the *CAI* as well as with other contemporary and later chronicles.²⁰³

The ways in which the Christian chroniclers viewed the Muslim enemy contained a clear ideological pattern during the twelfth and thirteenth centuries, though particular events and the local and regional interests of the chroniclers meant that this ideology sometimes involved considerable caricature and distortion.²⁰⁴ Where there was forcible conquest, treatment was uncompromising, and descriptions were often reminiscent of OT conflict between the Hebrews and their enemies in Canaan. According to Juan, one such place was Jaén, where, in 1225, a besieging Castilian army under Fernando III successfully, though only temporarily, captured the city. Fernando formed an alliance with al-Bayyasi, the ruler of Baeza, described as *Rex Biacie*/ King of Baeza by Juan. The city was one of many taken by the Christian forces by assault and all goods and persons were considered booty:

> Therefore drawing near to the aristocratic and celebrated city of Jaén, they attacked it for many days and took possession of it, confining its population within the city. They laid waste all the orchards, vineyards, trees and fields of grain. The appearance of that celebrated, flourishing and vibrant city became darker than charcoal; the land withered; the arable land was polluted; its former glory destroyed. ²⁰⁵

Juan's description may be compared with Lucas's account of the capture of cities in the area of Jaén, describing similar scenes of devastation.²⁰⁶ Although the idea of

God's people requisitioning their enemies as slaves is referred to as an element in the Hebrews' occupation of Canaan and even if conflict is not specifically referred to,[207] retribution on a biblical scale was more likely to be rooted in a deep-seated sense of grievance and an attitude to conquest that was to be much less conciliatory:

> And that day Joshua took Makkedah, and smote it with the edge of the sword, and the king thereof he utterly destroyed them, and all the souls that were therein; he let none remain: and he did to the king of Makkedah as he did unto the king of Jericho.[208]

The accounts of Juan and Lucas used the familiar idea of biblical conquest and, although descriptive accounts of the Christians' treatment of their enemies varied, they had not followed the example of some earlier chroniclers. For example, an early and singular example is recorded in the *HS* and describes Fernando I in vengeful strikes at Viseu and especially at Lamego as early as 1057.[209] In spite of the examples given earlier from *CLRC* and *CM*, forcible conquests were relatively unusual and many of the towns conquered by Fernando III in Andalucía, including Córdoba itself, surrendered on specific terms known as *pleitesía* [homage] and the Moors were permitted to retain their freedom and property and were often guaranteed a safe escape route.[210] This accords with the actions of Josiah, son of David who, although wishing to destroy the priests of Baal, was more concerned with righteous cleansing of centres of religious practice than with the slaughter of the enemy.[211] As we have seen, the OT idea of vengeance was not the only way of determining a view of the enemy nor was it the only yardstick by which biblical influence could be measured and the Christian view would often reflect contemporary societal conventions.

In the *CAI* and elsewhere, an indication of the chronicler's view of his enemy was to be found in the words used to depict them; there is a link made in some chronicles, between the Almoravids and their leaders and the OT Moabites.[212] The term 'Moabites' does not appear in *DRH* or *CM* but is used six times in a short passage by Juan in which he describes the coming of the Almoravids,[213] and the author is at pains to apply the term very precisely: 'the kingdom of Morocco, which was possessed by the Moors, who were referred to by the special name of Moabites and were commonly called Almoravids.'[214] It seems likely that, since Juan does not use the term elsewhere in his chronicle, the biblical invocation – although a familiar trope – is likely to be descriptive rather than pejorative, at least primarily so. Much more frequent is Juan's use of the term *Mauri* (and widely used in the *HS*) which has no biblical associations and gradually replaced biblical rhetoric in later chronicles: it was a neutral term denoting ethnic origins.[215] Juan occasionally uses the term *sarraceni*,[216] though this is not a biblical term and is again without obvious implications. He is more inclined to follow Rodrigo's example in reserving his ire for the superstitious error into which Muslims had fallen, rather than condemning them as a race eschewed by God. Yet he also refers to 'that reviled people,' without specifically naming the enemy. There is a sense in which disapprobation of his enemies is implied by the way in which the author draws attention to Fernando's own integrity: 'In truth the king, as he had promised to do, led the Moors, their wives, children and movable property to a place of safety.'[217] The efficacy of retribution was well attested; but mercy was also a tool of conquest and an element in the way in which behaviour towards the defeated and compliant enemy might be conducted. Chroniclers also portrayed Muslim leadership as merciful and honourable, though such presentations were unusual and indirect.[218]

The only one of our three thirteenth-century chroniclers to use the term *Ysmaelitas* is Lucas de Túy, and although this is not restricted to one part of the chronicle, it features on only eight occasions. It is not usually directly pejorative, though Lucas initially introduces the Ishmaelites as the offspring of Hagar[219] and then compares them, in the context of the birth of Muhammad, with wild beasts [*extimplo Hismahelite sicut bruta animalia*].[220] Neither the biblical link nor the brutish associations of the term need to be repeated; whenever Muslims are referred to as Ishmaelites, established links are suggested. As well as Rodrigo's occasional use of the terms *mauri* and *barabari* to identify Berber Muslims,[221] he also makes some general references that have more descriptive and less inflammatory implications, notably in the generic terms *Arabus* and *Sarracenus*; nevertheless, the distinction between these two terms, although noted by Isidore, was frequently misapplied.[222]

There are occasions nevertheless, and especially in *CLRC*, when the enemy is defined within a Christian, or at least within a familiar, perspective. Following the success of Alfonso IX of León at Alange in 1230, came the rout of Ibn Hûd: 'and many of them [i.e. the Muslim forces of Ibn Hûd] were killed and Ibn Hûd ran away and escaped in humiliated disorder.'[223] Yet within the story of Ibn Hûd and the rebellion in Murcia, Juan identifies an anonymous Muslim of virtue.[224] There is earlier evidence of Juan's complex attitude to individual Muslims in a further example involving Ibn Harach [*Auenharach*], 'a noble Moor of Córdoba'[225] who, in addition to his nobility, is praised for his having acted prudently in the surrender of the castle of Salvatierra. Ibn Harach is singled out because he worked in a way that favoured the Christians. His qualities are contrasted with the lack of respect for God and man shown by most of the Moors of Córdoba, who have no fear of God or respect for men,[226] just as the point of reference for the virtues of the anonymous Moor is Ibn Hûd. Noble sentiments are invoked but Muslims are compared with other Muslims and not with their Christian adversaries.

It is in Juan's chronicle that the names of biblical tribes have been replaced with creatures depicting specific OT imagery and this might suggest accusations of necromancy and original sin, though such an intention is not restricted to Fernando III's Muslim opponents. Those whose advice the king ignored are described as 'just as wizards,'[227] which has an association through Ps. 58.4 and 5 to 'the poison of a serpent.'[228] These ignoble and pusillanimous advisers are represented as potentially thwarting the king's noble mission which was to help the Christians in Córdoba: they sought with convincing words to impede such a noble act.[229] Real opponents might well exist within the king's own ranks and their inclusion in this passage may be an attempt to create a dramatic parallel with other and more easily recognizable enemies as well as with the king, who was inspired by the Lord's spirit and therefore placed his hope in Jesus Christ, dismissing those who counselled against his journeying to Córdoba to encourage the Christians who had taken the city.[230]

The language describing Christian attitudes and policy towards the Moors was therefore as much dictated by pragmatism as by biblical precedent and it was only afterwards – though sometimes quite soon afterwards – that chroniclers would interpret events from a Christian perspective. But chroniclers also had to wrestle with military confusion and even in the *CAI* there is the suggestion, though not explicitly stated, that the ferocity of destruction perpetuated against the Saracens ((The Christians) slaughtered all the Saracen captives, everyone they had seized: men, infants and women and additionally the beasts that they owned)[231] when Christians from Extremadura crossed the River Guadalquiver in 1138 without the emperor's knowledge and may have used excessive force.[232] And the Christian knights, in spite of their superiority in arms and strength of faith,[233] were rapidly and expeditiously despatched by the wave of Saracens that fell upon them. It might seem more responsible – or even honourable – to crush an alien power that had for so long deprived Spain of her ancient Visigothic capital in Toledo. Toledo had been captured, but it was not yet restored as the *urbs regia*. If, on the other hand, Alfonso VI had felt the need to tread carefully among his Muslim subjects following his capture of Toledo, his military reversal at Sagrajas eighteen months later not only humiliated the Castilian king but, according to Richard Fletcher, 'highlighted the vulnerability of Toledo.'[234] Certainly it could have confused prevailing attitudes to religious minorities within Alfonso's kingdom. None of this of itself diminishes the significance of the capture of Toledo as a key military and strategic advance and for Rodrigo, the supremacy of the city is unassailable:

> D. Rodrigo had his attention focussed on the Kingdom of Castile but concentrated on the city of Toledo, which for him was both the kingdom's kernel and quintessence and claimant to a more ecclesiastical primacy.[235]

One hundred and fifty-one years separate the psychologically important capture of Toledo in 1085 from the conquest of Córdoba in 1236[236] – and the latter conquest was ninety-seven years after Alfonso VII's triumphant return to Toledo in 1139. The two cities provide a useful contrast and details reveal clear areas of divergence and significant development during which time views of the enemy had evolved. We have noted how it was the Mozarabs rather than the Mudéjars who had been most humiliated by Toledo's fall and the treatment of conquered Muslims had few precedents before Toledo. But for the those in Córdoba in 1236, their loss was absolute and inconsolable and nowhere is this better illustrated than in a comparison of the way the mosques in the two cities were treated. In Toledo there seems to have been some confusion over the future status of the mosque and it was the king who was outraged by its desecration; in Córdoba the mosque seems, at early stage, to have been requisitioned by the invading Christians and the religious sensitivities of the Muslims disregarded. Indeed, it is seen as part of Fernando's solemn Catholic duty as well as a gesture of triumphalism to order:

> He instructed that the banner of the Cross would come before his own banner and be set on the loftiest tower of the mesquita, in order that it could flutter before his banner in the presence of all.[237]

This key phrase *palam cunctis*[238] stresses the presence of the many who witnessed the flaunting of the banner as a visible sign of domination, though not merely of Christendom over Islam but – and this is especially significant in the *CLRC* – of spiritual over temporal powers. This mirrors a passage in the *Hystoria Albigensis*, written slightly earlier (1212–18) than the *CLRC*, by the Cistercian monk, Peter of les Vaux-de-Cernay (d. *c.* 1218). This relates to the capture of Minerve (1210) and describes the placing of the Holy Cross on the top of the tower of St Stephen's Church, with the banner of the victor, Simon de Montfort, occupying a subservient position.[239] Furthermore, if the last part of the sentence *posset intremere subsequente uexillo suo* – what might be translated into an adverbial clause of reason or purpose renders the imperfect subjunctive *posset* into 'might' rather than 'could,' the writer makes the king's Christian and political intentions clear.

In Córdoba we have a description of a clandestine entry into the city and the storming of its ramparts, and this evokes a familiar biblical image. If Toledo could be described as an Iberian city modelled on the idea of Jerusalem, taken without bloodshed or devastation but with much celebration and pomp, then Córdoba might be thought of as a latter-day equivalent of Jericho, which fell spectacularly and militarily to Joshua. The secrecy surrounding the Israelite spies hidden by Rahab[240] has echoes in the description of those who were, without apparent imperial direction, mysteriously to enter as a prelude to Fernando's invasion: 'Those Christians who, by night, had furtively occupied a particular section of Córdoba.'[241] This is a striking comparison, made all the more telling by the response of those who were to emerge as victors especially with regard to those they had overcome and a comparison between chronicle and OT precedent is instructive. The weakness of those overcome in Córdoba: 'stunned, she [i.e. Córdoba] was not able to strengthen weakened hands and easily-swayed knees against the enemy.'[242] This seems to demonstrate more than a passing reminiscence with the reaction of those in the city of Jericho: 'for even all the inhabitants of the country do faint because of us.'[243] In his translation and commentary, a comparison can be made between a previous sentence in the chronicle: 'Córdoba gazed at a people of a different religion and language'[244] with a passage from Baruch 4:15,[245] and although there may be a more obvious linguistic connection, the reference from Baruch takes the form of a poetic lament and does not make reference to a specific location. Analogies are imperfect, however, and the 1236 conquest of Córdoba had been – unlike Jericho in the description of the events surrounding the battle for the city – a protracted process. According to Juan, Fernando was far from Córdoba during the time when the successful nocturnal incursion had taken place[246] and would not have been able to benefit quickly from the initial seizure.

It might have been expected that when biblical allusions were expressed by Rodrigo, Lucas and Juan, greater convergence and pattern would feature, especially since all three writers knew each other and were coming to terms with changing events within the kingdom of Castile. Yet even between Lucas and Rodrigo, both equally determined to interpret events in the light of the history of the Goths[247] and the intellectual legacy of Isidore, a collision was to occur as to appropriate geographical models for the emerging and evolving kingdom. However, in terms of their use of scriptural sources, the chasm does not exist between Rodrigo and Lucas, but between them and Juan. Imagery, language and allusions are more frequent and direct. Although Hebrew scriptures were, to use Reilly's word 'utilised'[248] by Rodrigo and Lucas, the Bible was not in general used to provide the relentless quantity of material for sustained polemic (as in the *CAI*); nor did they produce protracted, problematic and complex biblical metaphor, with which Juan's chronicle is so liberally dispersed.

Although Juan does not seek to enhance the influence of his own city Burgos, he offers fulsome praise for a surprising range of towns of varying size and importance, and such places are not only on the Iberian Peninsula or necessarily within Christendom.[249] Although he makes a brief reference to the rulers of Castile before the accession of Alfonso VI, his history is framed by the capture of Toledo in 1085 and the fall of Córdoba in 1236.[250] This, it may be said, was Juan's period of reconquest and for him the Visigoths and Isidore would appear to have played no part or at least have been peripheral to the process.[251] Neither does he even allude to the idea that the process of retrieval of territory had begun shortly after the Muslim conquest in the eighth century. Yet his invective against Muslims is every bit as strident as that of other chroniclers (especially in relation to the cleansing of the Mosque in Córdoba), even if his references are neither prolonged nor especially gratuitous.

The way in which all three thirteenth-century chroniclers integrated biblical texts into their histories demonstrates the mediation of such texts in the cultural milieu in which they lived and worked. Yet the frequency and directness with which such texts were used in the *CLRC* suggest that the chronicle may have had more in common with its twelfth-century predecessor, the *CAI*, than with those histories compiled by the author's contemporaries. Points of convergence between the *CAI* and the *CLRC* have been alluded to throughout the last two chapters. The purpose in this short concluding section is to offer a distillation of the argument regarding the character of the two narratives which seeks to stress their distinctiveness from other Hispano-Latin chronicles from the twelfth and thirteenth centuries.

Images of biblical conflict in Castile: A comparison of *Chronica Adefonsi Imperatoris* and the *Chronica Latina Regum Castellae*

Despite striking contrasts in the tone of the two chronicles and a period of perhaps ninety years in their dates of composition, there is a remarkable convergence in the way in which the authors presented Christian conquest as a kind of biblical mission or epic. The strong and frequently noted biblical parallels in both the *CAI* and the *CLRC* distinguish these narratives from other contemporary and earlier Iberian histories. In this section I argue that resemblances in theme and allusion in the two texts make them worthy of comparison. But to what end? Do similarities of connotation and subject matter suggest subliminal notions of retribution, crusade and the righteousness of religious and cultural dominance? Furthermore, one may ask whether these underlying perceptions hold good across the two centuries. If so, is it not simply the triumph of the Catholic cause that is narrated and celebrated? The roll call of events and the chroniclers' commentaries depicted Christian and Muslim leaders alike as biblically inspired figures, equally at the mercy of cosmic forces. The authors' immersion in this scriptural and Latin culture conditioned their world view since it can be distinguished from any peninsula-wide notions that they undoubtedly harboured. In this respect their interpretation of events resembled that of the other chroniclers: their view was not necessarily more deliberately parochial than that expressed in any other Hispano-Latin text. However, the way in which biblical allusion and narrative were relentlessly applied by the two chroniclers with an apparent similarity in terms of perception and purpose, together with considerations of the two chronicles in terms of length, focus and subject matter, distinguishes their works from other extant Hispanic contemporary texts.[252]

Within reconquest narratives, the *CAI* is unique as a piece of biblical polemic, even without the *Poema*.[253] This assertiveness, which is everywhere apparent, is evident from its dependence on the Old Testament Vulgate for descriptions of biblical conflict. An unusually large number of phrases and verses are incorporated verbatim into the text. The use of biblical sources in the Latin Chronicle is, by contrast, more discriminating and embraces different aspects of God's relationship with his people. This is not to say that the tone of hostility towards the Muslims, constantly reiterated in the *CAI*, is absent from the *CLRC*.[254] Yet though Juan is as capable as the author of the *CAI* of using biblical texts with passion and assertiveness as an integral part of his narrative, he does not do so unremittingly to illustrate and justify a story of righteous revenge. Biblical narrative in the *CLRC* is used as a constant reminder of God's enduring presence and omnipotence. Whether the lack of emphatic assertion suggests that the *CAI* was a literary and theological aberration or whether the biblical message had evolved to suit the events of the thirteenth century are matters that may require further exploration.

First, both chronicles are relatively short and deal with a limited range of events rather than being concerned with the general scope of Iberian or world history. They were both written to eulogize the lives of specific monarchs (possibly being written at the behest of specific monarchs), each of whom had demonstrated qualities of valour and statesmanship in keeping with biblical models. It is worth remembering that, unlike the authors of other twelfth- and thirteenth-century chronicles, neither of our chroniclers harks back to the Visigothic monarchy, nor does either make any attempt to venerate Isidore of Seville, to rehabilitate him into the contemporary Spanish Church or stress any claims about his importance. These omissions are particularly striking in the case of the *CAI*, in which the author refers fleetingly to what he has learned from witnesses to the reigns of other kings and rulers.[255] He makes it clear that he will only describe the deeds of Alfonso VII.[256] Alfonso VII's grandfather and conqueror of Toledo is mentioned just seven times in the *CAI* but the author does not comment on his reign or character and Alfonso VI is only used as a point of chronological or familial reference.

In the *CLRC*, Juan records a brief genealogy from the counts of Castile in the early tenth century but the initial emphasis within the chronicle was to record the achievements of a single king, Alfonso VIII. Following the panegyric in praise of his character, wisdom and early military achievements, the author recalls that much was achieved while the king was still in his young manhood,[257] and his history seems to grow into a more ambitious project.[258] Whatever Juan's original intention, his chronicle evolves into a tribute to two monarchs, Alfonso VIII and Fernando III, whose reigns as kings of Castile stretched, with a three-year hiatus during the minority of Enrique I and the regency of his sister Berenguela (r. 1214–17), from 1158 to 1248. Nevertheless, the author of the chronicle is likely to have died two years before Fernando's death, though he may have lived just long enough to witness the final capture of Jaén in February 1246. In the end, although the epithets applied by Juan to Alfonso VIII and Fernando III reflect different aspects of kingship, they are equally fulsome. Glory, humility and obedience are seen as complementary qualities.[259]

Secondly, both chronicles were written at a time when Christian victories over the Muslims in Castile and al-Andalus were recently celebrated events and gave grounds for optimism. Although Lucas and Rodrigo were also writing after the conquest of Córdoba, they were not specifically charged to describe recent victories over the Muslims; the chronicles are major histories of Hispania.[260] In the *CAI*, the author's eulogy of Alfonso VII and descriptions of his conquests were justified at the time of writing, even if triumph was to be followed by division and loss.[261] Its note of triumphalism and sense of righteous vindication might be more significant than the apparently well-justified enthusiasms of an author who wished to demonstrate the hand of God in Castilian history. The Christian victory at Almería in 1147 is memorably described by Linehan as 'the toast of Europe';[262] even if it had, as events turned out, been a premature and short-lived victory.

Thirdly, both chroniclers were eyewitnesses to many of the happenings they describe. In the case of the *CLRC*, the author is likely to have been a witness to most of Alfonso VIII's reign and to Fernando III's reign up to and beyond the conquest and settlement of Córdoba in 1236.[263] He would also have witnessed the brief reigns of Enrique and Berenguela. Like the author of the *CAI*, Juan deals much more expansively and with a greater profusion of comments with the royal families he knew and with those events that he witnessed.

If the authors of the *CAI* and the *CLRC* were indeed Arnaldo and Juan, there is a further point of similarity. Bishop Arnaldo is referred to twice in the *CAI*: first, as an envoy of Alfonso VII to Barcelona (Book 2, chapter 108) and secondly in the poem, as being one of the prelates whose stirring spiritual peroration spurred the troops to victory at Almería on the eve of battle, in 1147. And, following the author's description of the capture of Córdoba, Juan, who in addition to his role as bishop, was the king's chancellor, makes an appearance as the one who will transform the mosque of Córdoba into a church. Both men appear momentarily in their own histories – briefly but at pivotal moments when Christian victories over the Muslims were either enthusiastically anticipated or joyously celebrated. Nevertheless, we can have no certainty, nor are we even able to produce the flimsiest evidence, that the author (or possibly, authors) of the *CLRC* had seen or had any knowledge of the *CAI*. Reilly comments that although Juan may have depended partly on *DRH* but he is emphatic that there is no trace of the *CAI*, nor of any of the other surviving chronicles from the twelfth century, in Juan's chronicle; there is indeed an absence of any evidence of borrowed text.[264]

When dealing with the use of biblical citation and allusion within the two chronicles, it is important to note both the frequency with which such references are made and the way they are applied to the phenomenon of conflict. In the *CAI*, although the author makes particular use of Books 1 and 2 Macc. – especially when describing the details of conflict – as well as books depicting the struggle of the Hebrews against their enemies in Canaan, the whole of the prose section (Books 1 and 2) is infused with scriptural allusion and invective. Furthermore, such allusions are derived from a range of biblical texts rather than from a single discernible source. It might be said that the author of the *CAI* was almost alone in applying his consistent tone of biblical retribution, though even he demonstrates that negotiated surrender is a satisfactory outcome, notably in the Muslim surrender of Oreja in 1139.[265] Here, purging the land seemed to mean cleansing a territory of its former religious associations: desecration rather than annihilation. Furthermore, the emperor was able to use his negotiating ability to make demands of his own; his truce with the Almohad Muslims of Oreja was very much on Alfonso's terms and enabled him to take the city in October 1139.

Finally, there is the matter of the qualities of kings and other major players in the chroniclers' unfolding dramas. In both the *CAI* and in Juan's chronicle, the principal Christian subjects are linked to biblical precedent, though the way in which this is achieved shows divergence. The author of the *CAI* uses biblical phrases and verses to describe his emperor. Thus, Alfonso is the earthly agent through whom the will of the omnipotent God is fulfilled; this is intertwined with a reference from Ps. 74.12 declaring that God's will is that Christian 'in the midst of the earth' people might receive salvation.[266] He is compared with the happy fulfilment of the promise of God with His people following his accession to the throne.[267] Even his enemies acknowledged that the Lord was with him,[268] and as such was granted unusual insight: 'the king of León perceived that they [i.e. his Aragonese enemies] spoke deceitfully unto him.'[269] This is a reminiscence of Simon Maccabeus's understanding of a message sent to him by the traitor Tryphon.[270] Having established Alfonso's spiritual as well as temporal credentials, the author does not continually remind us of the emperor's godly qualities. However, at the beginning of the *Poema*, the king's holiness and valour are explicit and contained within an address of holy reverence: *Rex pie, rex fortis*.[271] There is a link to the sovereign power of God Himself and the titles are reminiscent of the way a deity is honoured.

As we have noted, in the *CLRC* Juan demonstrates similar discernment in the way he describes the qualities of Alfonso VIII and Fernando III. The term *gloriosus rex Castelle* is relentlessly applied to Alfonso and is used more than a dozen times in the chronicle. It is also clear that the heart of Fernando III, to whose many qualities we have just referred, was to be inspired by the Lord: 'the king, whose heart had been illuminated and kindled by the Lord's Spirit, fell silent'[272] and that his inspiration was infused with a desire to conduct himself in a manner, witnessed by his mother and the royal court, that combines passion with an inner nobility: 'The heart of [Berenguela's] son is inflamed with a noble longing.'[273]

Although it has only been possible to review a fraction of examples that show parallels in the way the authors of the *CAI* and the *CLRC* relied on biblical imagery and reminiscence to inform their narratives, the convergence of theme and the depiction of events and persons was not absolute. Perhaps the historical focus and the nature of the events the authors were describing facilitated the application of biblical analogy. Clearly, both chroniclers proved to be adept at understanding the many ways to which holy text could be applied. This was done to a degree that distinguishes their chronicles from those of their predecessors and contemporaries. In both chronicles, biblical references come thick and fast and it seems as if there is no end to the possibility of the ways in which echoes of such texts will inform and illuminate their narratives. This is not a matter of mere quantity, nor even of the authors' eyes for comparison between events in their own time and with biblical precedent. They also show themselves able to use the scriptures with subtlety and imagination and the skill of embellishing biblical text to suit their own purposes and to venerate their kings. But perhaps a more pertinent observation is their creative use of biblical, and especially OT, references to comment on the great and small events in the reigns of the sovereigns they chronicle.

CONCLUSION

This study has examined the way in which biblical texts were used in six chronicles written in the kingdom of León-Castile in the twelfth and thirteenth centuries. It has addressed the ways in which the integration of biblical narrative into these chronicles reflected an existing scriptural and classical cultural ambience. The chroniclers' world was one in which biblical sources were mediated through exegesis and liturgy and their milieu had depended on their understanding of patristic and later texts. Such an awareness conditioned, even if it did not determine, the chroniclers' authorial intent. I have argued that in the history writing in León-Castile, biblical narrative and allusion in the *CAI* and the *CLRC* reached their most overt and potent expression. The study of comparative texts, both within Iberia and elsewhere, has been essential in this study, although the emphasis has been to show how biblical texts were used within a specifically Hispanic dimension and how they did so to illuminate peninsular history. It has been possible, despite the modest range of primary texts available, to illustrate the features of the texts from León-Castile that most conspicuously demonstrate the use and flexibility of biblical allusion and the frequency with which such references from biblical narrative are deployed.

The chronicles considered are notable for the differing extent to which their authors used biblical texts as well as for the varying sense of purpose behind the incorporation and interpretation of such texts. This consideration of striking and more restrained use of the biblical record and allusion, reminiscence and deduction has been important in recognizing variety in the approach of chroniclers even though their culture was a common one. The use of biblical texts in the Western historiographical tradition introduced themes such as conquest, punishment and kingship as well as an attempt to demonstrate a sense of shared Christian identity. All these became recurring though intermittent themes in the Iberian chronicles where there was a permanently identifiable enemy as well as a roll call of kings and rulers on which judgement could be passed.

The reconquest chronicles considered in this study have been treated chronologically even though they derive much of their historical information, material and ideology from earlier chronicles and annals written in the peninsula as well as from a wider range of classical and patristic texts. In the two early-twelfth-century chronicles, the *HS* and the *Chronicon*, biblical references and narrative were often used to illuminate events in the peninsula. They might be used to indulge in a polemic against their enemies or to comment on the deeds of the kings of the Christian kingdoms of the Asturias and León-Castile between the eighth and eleventh centuries. These texts therefore provide an important link between the histories that emerged from the Asturias (especially since the *HS* contains versions of two earlier chronicles) with those that covered the reigns of Alfonso VII and the subsequent kings of León-Castile. The sense of continuity is also sustained in the *HS* in its reverential portrayal of the transfer of Isidore's relics from Seville to León in 1063. The use of biblical references in the *HS* and the *Chronicon* had not, even by the early twelfth century, indicated or generated that sense of unassailable mission that was soon to appear and dominate the narrative in the *CAI*. Yet there is within the *HS* and the *Chronicon* a growing awareness of the importance of the duties of kingship, and these are frequently paralleled with OT models; when used in the *CAI*, they invariably present a fiercely negative and hostile view of the Muslim enemy. Considerable attention has been devoted to the *CAI*. Though the author makes no direct reference to Iberia's Visigothic past or to Isidore, he incorporates the biblical themes that had been identified in earlier chronicles and shows himself to be adept at using scriptural references to provide a range of subtly applied messages that inform his narrative. Clearly, the author is imbued with a deep sense of the rightness of the Leonese-Castilians' cause and uses OT narrative to construct a pattern of anger and hostility towards the Almoravid Muslims. Yet the *CAI* is far more than a chronicle of revenge. Biblical texts are used to provide justification for conquest; they also supply the chronicler with the imagery of conflict. Examples of bravery, piety and leadership used by the author are rooted in biblical models. The notion of place is also important to the author and parallels between Hispanic cities and those in the Bible are evident throughout his chronicle. This study also reflects on a detailed comparison with the *De expugnatione*, which compares the treatment of two Iberian conquests – in Lisbon and Almería – by a writer from northern European and one from Hispania. This comparison considers the extent to which the inclusion of biblical texts into these chronicles was important in the explanation and understanding of Christian victory. The relentlessness with which the author of the *CAI* pursues biblical parallels is tested by comparing his history with that of the Jewish struggle against the suppression of their faith by the Greek ruler Antiochus IV Epiphanes in the second century BC as told in the deuterocanonical Books of 1 and 2 Maccabees. These constitute the most widely used and possibly significant single biblical source used by the author, and the extent to which his text is infused with material from this important source is a key comparative element in the author's historical narrative.

The study of three thirteenth-century chronicles, Lucas de Túy's *Chronicon Mundi*, Rodrigo Jiménez de Rada's *De Rebus Hispaniae* and the Bishop Juan of Osma's *Chronica Latina Regum Castellae*, concludes the study. Of these, the *CLRC* may be the closest to *CAI* in terms of the scope of its history and its wealth of biblical references. It also makes no mention of Isidore of Seville or to Spain's past, though there is a clear sense of Castilian kings being imbued with a kind of biblical authority; many descriptions are derived directly from the Bible, and Fernando III's conquest of Córdoba is represented as a kind of religious and political consummation in the battle for al-Andalus. Interestingly, although both Lucas and Rodrigo make extensive use of the Bible to frame their historical accounts (Lucas, like Isidore, used the record of events in the book of Genesis as the beginning of his own history), it is employed much less as a source for interpreting events of their own time or as crusading polemic. In contrast to Juan's narrative, the Visigothic tradition and the influence of Isidore of Seville is particularly pertinent to the way in which Lucas and Rodrigo were to interpret the history of the world and of Iberia. The three clerics were almost certainly known to each other and it is conceivable that each was aware of the narratives under construction. It is possible to regard two distinct features within Hispanic chronicles as being represented: the Visigothic and Isidorian legacy and biblical narrative mediated through patristic exegesis. Both parallel strands contributed to the chroniclers' beliefs about their own past and destiny and the extent to which each strand is linked to the purpose of the text.

More remains to be done in analysing the way biblical texts were used in other chronicles from León-Castile. In this neglected and potentially rewarding world of historical analysis, parallel comparisons between historical narrative and biblical text could profitably be pursued to include further texts such as the *Historia Compostelana*, *Historia Roderici* and the *Anonymous Chronicle of Sahagún*. This research could in part consider the way in which these texts complement those we have considered that are likely to have been produced under royal patronage. Such a study could also provide the basis for a more comprehensive awareness of the use of biblical narrative in twelfth-century Hispanic chronicle writing. This study has sought to demonstrate that within these chronicles there is considerable variety in the way biblical narrative was used and that there are distinctions in authorial purpose even though the texts emerged from a common culture based on classical texts and biblical exegesis. Further research offers the opportunity to expand this interpretative approach while recognizing the overriding dependence on a familiar and unchallenged biblical corpus.

NOTES

Introduction

1. Enrique Flórez (ed.), 'Anales toledanos I,' in *España Sagrada Theatro Geographico-Historico de la Eglesia de España*, Tomo xxiii (Madrid, 1767), 389.
2. See also the account of the siege and capture of Almería by the Geonese historian, scholar and diplomat, Caffaro di Rustico da Caschifellone (*c.* 1080–*c.* 1164) in A. Ubieto Arteta (ed.), *Caffaro, De captione Almerie et Tortuose* (Valencia. 1973). Caffaro presents a contrasting portrayal of Alfonso to that in the *Poem of Almería*; his account suggests an altogether more restrained account of the emperor's part in the siege, and stresses the role of his home city in persuading Alfonso to participate in the collaborative attempt to capture the city. These diplomatic and strategic overtures are discussed by Jonathan Phillips in *The Second Crusade: Extending the Frontiers of Christendom* (London, 2007), 252–3.
3. Gregory B. Kaplan, 'Friend "of" Foe: The Divided Loyalty of Álvar Fáñez in the *Poema de Mio Cid*,' in Cynthia Robinson and Leyla Rouhi (eds), *Under the Influence: Questioning the Comparative in Medieval Castile* (Leiden, 2005), 153–72 at 166.
4. Jaan Undusk, 'Sacred History, Profane History: Uses of the Bible in the Chronicle of Henry of Livonia,' in Marek Tamm, Linda Kaljundi and Carsten Selch Jensen (eds), *Crusading and Chronicle Writing on the Medieval Baltic Frontier: A Companion to the Chronicle of Henry of Livonia* (London, 2016), 45–77, at 47. The use of biblical texts in English chronicle writing, especially in the *Historia Rerum Anglicarum* of William of Newburgh (1136–98) is considered by C. S. Watkins, *History and the Supernatural in Medieval England* (Cambridge, 2007), 34–7. Unsurprisingly, William had a different focus from that of the twelfth-century writers of medieval Iberia and was more concerned with the miraculous and mystical than with military conquest, but, like his Castilian contemporaries, he also drew on biblical texts, often mediated through the exegesis and teaching of the Church Fathers. See also Helen Pagan, 'Trevet's Les Chronicles: Manuscript Owners and Readers', in Jaclyn Rajsic, Erik Kooper and Dominique Hoche (eds), *The Prose Brut and Other Late Medieval Chronicles: Books Have Their Histories. Essays in Honour of Lister M. Matheson* (Woodbridge, 2016), 149–64, at 151–3.
5. For the purposes of clarity, the six chronicles that will be the principal focus of this study will be *Historia Silense, Chronicon Regum Legionensium, Chronica Adefonsi Imperatoris, Chronica Latina Regum Castellae, Chronicon Mundi* and *De Rebus Hispaniae*.
6. Gabrielle M. Spiegel, *The Past as Text: The Theory and Practice of Medieval Historiography* (Baltimore, MD, 1997), 92.
7. A. Maya Sánchez (ed.), *Chronica Adefonsi Imperatoris*, in *Chronica Hispana saeculi XII*, Part I, CCCM 71 (Turnhout, 1990).
8. Ibid.

9 Luis Charlo Brea, Juan A. Estévez Sola and Rocío Carande Herrero (eds), *Chronica Latina Regum Castellae*, in *Chronica Hispana saeculi XIII* (Turnhout, 1997).
10 Justo Pérez de Urbel and Atilano González Ruiz-Zorilla (eds), *Historia Silense, Edición crítica e introducción* (Madrid, 1959).
11 Benito Sánchez Alonso (ed.), *Crónica del Obispo Don Pelayo* (Madrid, 1924).
12 Emma Falque Rey (ed.), *Lucae Tudensis, Chronicon Mundi*, CCCM 74 (Turnhout, 2003).
13 J. Fernández Valverde (ed.), *Rodrigo Jiménez de Rada, Historia de rebus Hispaniaesive Historia Gothica*, CCCM LXII (Turnhout, 1987).
14 Janet Nelson and Damian Kempf (eds), *Reading the Bible in the Middle Ages* (London, 2015). Of particular relevance are the introduction (1–6), Cornelia Linde, 'Twelfth-Century Notions of the Canon of the Bible' (7–19) and Mayke de Jong, 'Jeremiah, Job, Terence and Paschasius Radbertus: Political Rhetoric and Biblical Authority in the *Epitaphium Arsenii*' (57–77). See also Jennifer A. Harris, 'The Bible and the Meaning of History in the Middle Ages', Susan Boynton and Diane J. Reilly (eds), *The Practice of the Bible in the Middle Ages: Production, Reception and Performance in Western Christianity* (New York, 2011), 84–104.
15 Spiegel, *The Past as Text*, 92.
16 This, according to David Townsend and Andrew Taylor (eds) in their introduction to *The Tongue of the Fathers: Gender and Ideology in Twelfth-Century Latin* (Philadelphia, PA, 1998), was well under way by the twelfth century: 'the acquisition of Latinity moved increasingly from the monastic to other milieu' (10, 11).
17 The *Chronicle of Sampiro* was probably penned in the early years of the eleventh century as a continuation of the *Chronicle of Alfonso III* and well before the *HS* and the *CRL*; Justo Pérez de Urbel, *Sampiro, su crónica y la monarquía leonesa en siglo X* (Madrid, 1952), 130.
18 Simon Barton, 'Bishop Pelayo of Oviedo, *Chronicon Regum Legionensium*', Simon Barton and Richard Fletcher (eds), *The World of El Cid: Chronicles of the Spanish Reconquest* (Manchester, 2000), 65–89, at 71, 72.
19 For example, that used at the time of the Córdoban martyrs (860s). This movement is briefly considered in Chapter 3.
20 John France, 'Logistics and the Second Crusade', in John H. Pryor (ed.), *Logistics of Warfare in the Age of Crusades: Proceedings of a Workshop Held at the Centre for Medieval Studies, University of Sydney, 30 September to 4 October 2002* (Aldershot, 2006), 77–95, at 90.
21 Both campaigns, though entirely separately waged, depended on foreign military support and can be described as a Western crusading adventure. Virginia Berry notes this, together with the extraordinary coincidence of the two successes: Virginia Berry, 'The Second Crusade', in Marshall W. Baldwin and Kenneth M. Setton (eds), *A History of the Crusades, Volume I, The First Hundred Years* (London, 2nd edition, 1969), 463–512, at 482. See also Giles Constable, 'The Second Crusade Seen by Contemporaries', *Traditio* 9 (1953), 213–79. The importance of the Iberian campaign as a collaborative venture within the Second Crusade is also made more recently by Phillips, *The Second Crusade,* especially 255–68.
22 Fernando ruled as king of Castile from 1217, León from 1230 and Galicia from 1231.
23 Richard L. Kagan, *Clio and the Crown: The Politics of History in Medieval and Early Modern Spain* (Baltimore, MD, 2009), 21, n. 17.
24 Royal patronage is made clear in Lucas's *praefatio* and in Rodrigo's dedication.

25 For a comprehensive list of editions and translations, see David Thomas and Alex Mallett (eds), *Christian-Muslim Relations. A Bibliographical History, Volume 4 (1200–1350)* (Leiden, 2009), 348–9.
26 Janna Bianchini, *The Queen's Hand: Power and Authority in the Reign of Berenguela of Castile* (Philadelphia, PA, 2012), 16.
27 Inés Fernández-Ordóñez 'La técnica historiográfica del Toledano. Procedimientos de organización del relato,' *Cahiers de linguistique et de civilisation hispaniques médiévales*, No. 26 (2003), 187–221, at 191.
28 Lucy K. Pick, *Conflict and Coexistence, Archbishop Rodrigo de Toledo and the Muslims and Jews of Medieval Spain* (Kalamazoo, MI, 2004), 21–70.
29 Derek Lomax argues for a starting date as early as the accession of Afonso II of Portugal in 1211; Derek Lomax, 'The Authorship of the *Chronique Latine des Rois de Castile*,' *Bulletin of Hispanic Studies*, Vol. 40 (Liverpool, 1963), 205–11. In any event, the author seems to have been a witness to the many events he described.
30 As Jamie Wood demonstrates, Isidore had an attachment to the history of the Visigoths in pre-Trinitarian times as well as to Catholic Visigothic Spain: Jamie Wood, *The Politics of Identity in Visigothic Spain: Religion and Power in the Histories of Isidore of Seville* (Leiden, 2012), 149–51.
31 The term 'biblical texts' is preferred rather than 'The Bible' to describe the material likely to have been most readily available to medieval chroniclers who were more likely to have relied upon extracts that could be accessed through the liturgy, lectionaries to the daily offices, sermons and exegesis. Clerics would have had an easy familiarity with this material that would have permeated their patterns of language, thinking and writing. Werner Kelber, 'The History of the Closure of Biblical Texts', Annette Weissenrieder and Robert B. Coote (eds), *The Interface of Orality and Writing: Speaking, Seeing, Writing in the Shaping of New Genres* (Eugene, OR, 2015), 71–103, at 89.
32 Ernst Robert Curtius describes what is perhaps Isidore's most acclaimed work, the *Etymologiae*, as 'a book which is all of a piece and of binding authority': Ernst Robert Curtius, *European Literature and the Latin Middle Ages* (Princeton, NJ, 1990), 455. It would also serve as a model for Lucas and Rodrigo. Furthermore, Isidore's works provided them with a springboard to develop their own beliefs about Leonese and Castilian hegemony.

Chapter 1

1 Anne F. Harris, 'The Iconography of Narrative,' in Colum Hourihane (ed.), *The Routledge Guide to Medieval Iconography* (Abingdon, 2017), 282–94.
2 Kathleen Glenister Roberts, *Alterity and Narrative: Stories and the Negotiation of Western Identities* (New York, 2007), 81.
3 Claus Michael Kauffman, *Biblical Imagery in Medieval England, 700–1500* (Turnhout, 2003), 36.
4 Dom Jean Leclercq, 'The Exposition and Exegesis of Scripture: From Gregory the Great to St. Bernard,' in G. W. H. Lampe (ed.), *The Cambridge History of the Bible, Volume 2: The West from the Fathers to the Reformation* (Cambridge, 1969), 183–97, at 197.
5 An example is the extant though mutilated seventh-century version of the Latin Bible known as the *León Cathedral Palimpsest*; see John Williams, 'The Bible in Spain,' in

John Williams (ed.), *Imaging the Early Medieval Bible* (University Park, PA, 1999), 179–218, at 181–2.
6 Francis Wormald, 'Bible Illustration in Medieval Manuscripts,' in Lampe (ed.), *Cambridge Bible, Volume 2*, 309–37, at 312.
7 See Richard Gyug, 'Early Medieval Bibles, Biblical Books, and the Monastic Liturgy in the Beneventan Region,' in Susan Boynton and Diane J. Reilly (eds), *The Practice of the Bible in the Middle Ages: Production, Reception & Performance in Western Christianity* (New York, 2011), 34–60. The single-volume Bibles that did exist included what was perhaps the most meticulous copy of Jerome's translation, the *Codex Amiatinus*, commissioned in 692 at Wearmouth-Jarrow.
8 Nees discusses its independence from the *Codex Grandior* and possible Italian origins; Lawrence Nees, 'Problems of Form and Function in Early Medieval Bibles from Northwest Europe,' in Williams, *Imaging the Early Medieval Bible*, 121–78, at 156–7. The *Codex Grandior* was made either by or for Cassiodorus (*c*. 490–*c*. 580) at Vivarium in Calabria and was written in *Vetus Latina*; Benedicta Ward S. L. G., 'Bede, the Bible and the North,' in Philip McCosher (ed.), *What Is It That the Scripture Says? Essays in Biblical Interpretation, Translation and Reception in Honour of Henry Wansbrough O. S. B.* (London, 2006), 156–65, at 161.
9 The link between the skills practised by early medieval chroniclers can be related to the term *interpretatio* which meant both exegesis and translation; see Henry Fulton, 'Troy Story: The Medieval Welsh *Ystorya Dared* and *Brut* Tradition of British History,' in Juliana Dresvina and Nicholas Sparks (eds), *The Medieval Chronicle VII* (Amsterdam, 2011), 137–50, at 138, 139.
10 Jason Byassee, *Praise Seeking Understanding: Reading the Psalms with Augustine* (Grand Rapids, MI, 2007), 16.
11 I. C. Levy, *The Bible in Medieval Tradition: The Letter to the Galatians* (Cambridge, 2011), 33.
12 The methods used by scholars and theologians during the second and third centuries exercised a central influence over later patristic exegesis. For a discussion of the influence of Origen of Alexandria, see Michael Graves, 'The "Pagan" Background of Patristic Exegetical Methods,' in Mark Husband and Jeffrey P. Greenman (eds), *Ancient Faith for the Church's Future* (Downers Grove, IL, 2008), 93–109, especially 95–6. And Origen's impact on Augustine and subsequent exegesis is discussed later in the text.
13 The *Vetus Latina* was itself the result of many earlier editions carried out between the second and fourth centuries, a version of which was used in the Vulgate itself; see Christophe Rico, 'New Testament Greek,' in David E. Aune (ed.), *The Blackwell Companion to the New Testament* (Malden, MA, 2010), 61–77, at 63. And to date there is no completed full-text criticism of the *Vetus Latina*: Marvin A. Sweeney, *I and II Kings: A Commentary* (Louisville, KT, 2007), 39.
14 This countered the arguments of Monarchianism, which stressed the indivisible nature of God and was advocated by Praxius, a priest from Asia Minor who lived in the second and third centuries. For a discussion of the complex legacy of Tertullian's Trinitarian notion on subsequent Christian tradition, see Andrew B. McGowan, 'God in Early Latin Theology: Tertullian and the Trinity,' in Andrew B. McGowan, Brian E. Daley S. J. and Timothy J. Gaden (eds), *God in Early Christian Thought: Essays in Memory of Lloyd G Patterson* (Leiden, 2009), 61–82.

15 See J. N. Birdshall, 'The New Testament Text,' in P. R. Ackroyd and C. F. Evans (eds), *The Cambridge History of the Bible Volume 1: From the Beginnings to Jerome* (Cambridge, 1970), 308–77, at 345.
16 Augustine's influence was felt as far apart as Spain (where Isidore of Seville used Augustine's *De Doctrina Christiana* as the basis for his own exegesis) and England where Bede (673–735) acknowledges his own debt in his exegesis on the book of Genesis. And it may have been the first abbot of Jarrow, Benedict Biscop (c. 628–90), who enabled the monks to access Augustine's letters, sermons and especially his exegetical works. See Joseph F. Kelly, 'Carolingian Era, Late,' in Allan Fitzgerald and John Cavadini (eds), *Augustine through the Age: An Encyclopedia* (Cambridge, 1999), 129–32, at 132 and Patricia H. Coulstock, *The Collegiate Church of Wimborne Minster* (Woodbridge, 1993), 88.
17 In his exegesis on Ezra 3 as well as in his exposition on the Song of Solomon, Bede refers to *nostri codices habent* (we have our sources); *PL* Vol. 91, 887D and *PL* Vol. 91, 1090D.
18 Joseph F. Kelly, 'Bede's Use of Augustine for His *Commentarium in principium Genesis*,' in Frederick van Fleteren and Joseph C. Schnaubelt OSM (eds), *Augustine: Biblical Exegete* (New York, 2001), 189–96.
19 Scott DeGregorio (trans. and ed.), *Bede: On Ezra and Nehemiah* (Liverpool, 2006), xviii.
20 That the *Vetus Latina* was a translation not from the original Hebrew of the OT but from its Greek translation, *The Septuagint*, is a substantial weakness addressed by Jerome, though some of Augustine's biblical quotations as well as, for example, the numbering of the psalms, are other areas of divergence. See William Harmless S. J., *Augustine in His Own Words* (Washington, DC, 2010), xxi.
21 Such variations are discussed by Maurice J. Gilbert in relation to the book of Ecclesiasticus; Maurice J. Gilbert, 'Introduction to Kearns' Dissertation,' in Pancratius C. Beentjes (ed.), *Conleth Kearns, The Expanded Text of Ecclesiasticus: Its Teaching on the Future Life as a Clue to Its Origin* (Berlin, 2011), 9–21, at 16.
22 Augustine, *De Doctrina Christiana*, 2. 16, *PL* Vol. 34, 47–9.
23 The *Hexapla*, or Sixfold, was an arrangement of the OT in different versions of Hebrew and Greek for ease of comparison of which there are no extant remains; it is discussed by A. Hilhorst, 'Biblical Scholarship in the Early Church,' in J. den Boeft and M. L. van Pollvan de Lisdonk (eds), *The Impact of Scripture on Early Christianity* (Leiden, 1999), 1–19, at 5. See also Bleddyn J. Roberts, 'The Old Testament: Manuscripts, Text and Versions,' in Lampe (ed.), *Cambridge Bible, Volume 2*, 1–26, at 18–19.
24 For example, the question of allegory was to exercise a curiously ambivalent hold over Augustine's exegesis. Genesis, to be properly understood, needed to be interpreted allegorically but the NT, while aiding the allegorical interpretation of the OT, was to be seen as a literal record. See John S. Pendergast, *Religion, Allegory and Literacy in Early Modern England, 1560–1640: The Control of the Word* (Aldershot, 2006), 22.
25 Examples of exegesis from the second century were based on Jewish examples and allegory and exegetes whose importance was acknowledged by Eusebius and Jerome included Melito of Sardis (d. c. 180 AD) and Justin Martyr (103–165). Melito is the probable author of the homily *On the Pasch*, a discursive rhythmical prose drawing on analogy between the events in Christ's death and resurrection and OT models and Justin, an early apologist whose two *Apologies* and *Dialogue with Trypho* survive. See Lucien Deiss, *Springtime of the Liturgy* (St Paul, MN, 1967), 99 and R. P. C. Hanson,

'Biblical Exegesis in the Early Church,' in Ackroyd and Evans (eds), *The Cambridge Bible Volume 1*, 412–53, at 414–15.

26 Peter W. Martens, *Origen and Scripture: The Contours of an Exegetical Life* (Oxford, 2012), 7.

27 Henri Crouzel, 'NT Exegesis,' in Karl Rahner (ed.), *Encyclopaedia of Theology: A Concise Sacramentum Mundi* (New York, 1975), 124–33, especially at 127–8.

28 Since no commentaries are available from earlier centuries, Origen and Hippolytus were the first to produce formal exegetical material and, since Hippolytus's work survives only in fragments, Origen is the more dominant theologian; Frances M. Young, *Biblical Exegesis and the Formation of Christian Culture* (Cambridge, 2002), 82, 83. Nevertheless, Hippolytus may have been the author of two earlier commentaries, one on the book of Daniel and another on the Song of Solomon; Hanson observes that these are more allegorical in content and constitute homilies rather than representing true biblical commentary. R. P. C. Hanson, *Allegory and Event: A Study of the Sources and Significance of Origen's Interpretation of Scripture* (Louisville, KT, 2002), 114–15.

29 Also acknowledged as fourth-century doctors of the church are St John Chrysostom (347–407), St Basil the Great (330–379) and St Athanasius (298–373) who were ethnic Greeks; by this time exegesis within the Latin Church was well established and they are therefore not cited in this study.

30 Joseph W. Goering, 'An Introduction to Medieval Christian Biblical Interpretation,' in Jane Dammen McAuliffe, Barry D. Walfish and Joseph W. Goering (eds), *With Reverence for the Word: Medieval Scriptural Exegesis in Judaism, Christianity and Islam* (Oxford, 2003), 197–203, at 198.

31 Charles Tieszen notes an unexpected resonance between an advocation of persecution to be visited on the enemies of Christendom and the works of Paul Alvarus; Charles Lowell Tieszen, *Christian Identity amid Islam in Medieval Spain: Studies on the Children of Abraham* (Leiden, 2013), 103, n. 16.

32 Diane J. Reilly cites the example of the twelfth-century *Floreffe* Bible, illustrated for the Premonstratensian canons of Floreffe, which, as well as containing a frontispiece representing narratives and illustrations drawn from the book of Job, also contained images that were recognizably from the *Tractates*. Diane J. Reilly, 'Lectern Bibles and Liturgical Reform,' in Boynton and Reilly (eds), *Practice of the Bible*, 105–25, at 115–16.

33 John W. Rettig makes the following observation in his translation of the first ten tractates of John's Gospel: 'In the *Tractates* there are numerous indications of audience involvement: questions, imperatives, short monologistic dialogues, the recalling of attention, mention of current events, frequent repetitions of scriptural passages, recalling of previous sermons, new explanations when the first is not grasped, mention of audience reactions, leaving questions unresolved at the end of the sermon, and so on.' St Augustine, *Tractates on the Gospel of John: 1–10*, translated by John W. Rettig (Washington, DC, 1988), 5–6, n. 12.

34 John 1.1: 'In the beginning was the word and the word was with God and the word was God.'

35 See biblical allusions and specific parallels with John 1.1-5 identified by Edmund Hill OP in his translation of *Augustine of Hippo: Homilies on the Gospel of John 1–40* (New York, 2009), 39–54.

36 Carolinne White, *Early Christian Latin Poets: The Early Church Fathers* (London, 2000), 16.

37 Ibid., 5.

38 Gillian Evans discusses this influence, as well as the way in which Greek texts might be understood in an age in which the knowledge of Greek was limited in western Christendom. See G. R. Evans, *Philosophy and Theology in the Middle Ages* (London, 1993), 22. An early exception may have been Hilary of Poitiers (*c*. 300–*c*. 368), though even his competence in Greek is disputed: see Mark Weedman, *The Trinitarian Theology of Hilary of Poitiers* (Leiden, 2007), 5.
39 For a discussion of Jerome's complex and ambiguous response to Origen, *Fathers of the Church: St Jerome, Commentary on Galatians*, translated by Andrew Cain (Washington, DC, 2010), 11, 12.
40 *Fathers of the Church: St Jerome, Commentary on Matthew*, translated by Thomas P. Scheck (Washington, DC, 2008), 27.
41 His exposition on *praesenti saeculo malo* [present wicked age] is a case in point where Jerome argued that the accumulation of events rather than the times themselves were evil. See *PL*, Vol. 16, 314A.
42 Dennis Brown, 'Jerome,' in P. F. Esler (ed.), *The Early Christian World Vols I–II* (London, 2000), 1151–74 at 1168. According to Michael Graves, Jerome's own willingness to write more literal exposition in his commentaries on Matthew (398) and Jeremiah (414) may have been in deference to the fact that they were both dedicated to his friend and fellow priest, Eusebius of Cremona (d. *c*. 423).
43 Young, *Biblical Exegesis*, 126.
44 In *Hymn XIII*: 'not only is Adam a type of David, and both are types of "us," but Adam is a type of Samson, too, who falls, is outwitted by Satan, but who is also a type of Christ whose death "returned to us our heritage." Jonah and Joseph also exemplify the pattern of being cast out and rescued. Time and person are fused into exemplars of single human narrative.' Ibid., 151.
45 Almost certainly this was aided and abetted by his considerable knowledge of languages (Hebrew, Latin, Greek and even Aramaic): see H. F. D. Sparks, 'Jerome as a Biblical Scholar,' in Ackroyd and Evans (eds), *The Cambridge Bible*, 510–41 at 517. His exposition seems directed against, inter alia, second- and third-century Gnostics such as Valentinus, Basilides and Mani; see Cain, *St Jerome*, 67 n. 57.
46 Sparks, 'Jerome as Scholar,' 539.
47 Jerome, *Apology against Rufinus* (*PL* Vol. 23, 16): 'in order that the prudent reader after he has read the various interpretations and learned which of the many can be approved or rejected, will judge which is the truest and, like a good moneychanger, will condemn the counterfeit money.'
48 Ibid.
49 Jerome's well-documented disdain for Ambrose is discussed by Andrew Cain and Joseph Lössl (eds), *Jerome of Stridon: His Life, Writings and Legacy* (Farnham, 2006), 8.
50 Noting Ambrose's most significant exegetical works, Sister Maria Therese Springer of the Cross acknowledges allegorical similarities with or derived from Basil and Philo which in their content were concerned with biblical commentary and explanation of dogma. Sister Therese Springer of the Cross, *Nature-Imagery in the Works of Saint Ambrose* (Washington, DC, 1931), 1, 2.
51 Craig Alan Satterlee cites the 'almost impressionistic' approach to Ambrose's exegetical writing, suggesting meaning and ways in which biblical passages may be interpreted; see Craig Alan Satterlee, *Ambrose of Milan's Method of Mystagogical Preaching* (Collegeville, MN, 2002), 91, 92. The secondary importance of Ambrose an as exegete is also acknowledged by Neil B. McLynn, *Ambrose of Milan* (Berkeley,

CA, 1994) 238, though this would not have diminished his influence on his contemporaries as well as on future writers.

52 David C. Alexander, *Augustine's Early Theology of the Church: Emergence and Implications, 386-391* (New York, 2008), 103. This is in the context of a discussion of Augustine's earliest Christian development as revealed in his *Confessiones* (18-21, 90-103). Alexander also examines the influence of Ambrose's writings, *De sacramentis*, *De mysteriis* and *Explanatio symboli* on Augustine's subsequent writing (109-75).

53 William A. Jurgens, *The Faith of the Early Church Fathers, Vol. 3* (Collegeville, MI, 1979), 24.

54 Frans van Liere, 'The Literal Sense of the Books of Samuel and Kings: From Andrew of St Victor to Nicholas of Lyra,' in Philip D. W. Krey and Lesley Smith (eds), *Nicholas of Lyra: The Senses of Scripture* (Leiden, 2000), 59-82, at 62.

55 Coleman, Janet, *Ancient and Medieval Memories: Studies in the Reconstruction of the Past* (Cambridge, 1992), 278.

56 Kessler discusses Gregory's debt to Augustine and to earlier exegetes such as Origen as well as the features of Gregory's own exegesis; Stephan Kessler, 'Gregory the Great: A Figure of Tradition,' and 'Transition in Church Exegesis,' in Magne Sæbø (ed.), *Hebrew Bible Old Testament: The History of Interpretation* (Göttingen, 2000), 135-47, especially 136-7 and 142-3.

57 Abigail Firey, 'The Letter of the Law: Carolingian Exegetes and the Old Testament,' in McAuliffe, Walfish and Goering, *Reverence for the Word*, 204-24, at 204. Firey notes that this pre-eminence was despite an absence of a specific exegetical work on the Book of Leviticus.

58 Apart from his *Expositio Psalmorum*, Cassidorus also composed a commentary on the Letter to the Romans and short summaries of Acts, NT Letters and Revelation. Yet it was his belief in the overarching messianic nature of the psalms in his commentary composed for the monks at Vivarium (a monastery he established in the second quarter of the sixth century) that had the most widespread impact. Bede, for example, used Cassiodorus's exegesis in his own commentary on the psalms. See Stephan C. Kessler S. J., 'Gregory the Great,' in Charles Kannengiesser (ed.), *Handbook of Patristic Exegesis Volume Two: The Bible in Ancient Christianity* (Leiden, 2006), 1327-35.

59 Frans van Liere, 'Biblical Exegesis through the Twelfth Century,' in Boynton and Reilly (eds), *Practice of the Bible*, 157-78, at 164.

60 Giles Brown, 'Introduction: The Carolingian Renaissance,' in Rosamond McKitterick (ed.), *Carolingian Culture: Emulation and Innovation* (Cambridge, 1994), 1-53, at 3.

61 *Isidore of Seville: De Ecclesiasticis Officiis*, translated and edited by Thomas L. Knoebel (Mahwah, NJ, 2008), 12.

62 Brown, 'Introduction: Carolingian Renaissance,' 3.

63 G. R. Evans, *The Thought of Gregory the Great* (Cambridge, 1986), 87.

64 Van Liere, 'Biblical Exegesis,' 159. Geoffrey Shepherd makes a similar point and identifies Gregory's approach to the Bible as 'the divinely inspired disclosure of secret wisdom' a view that had a particular resonance with Anglo-Saxon scholars with whom the legacy of Gregory was of special significance (Geoffrey Shepherd, 'English Versions of the Scriptures Before Wyclif,' in Lampe (ed.), *Cambridge Bible, Volume 2*, 362-87, at 368).

65 Innocenzo Gargano, 'San Gregorio Magno esegeta della Bibbia,' (*Liber Annus* 54: 2004), 261-94.

66 See Coleman, *Ancient and Medieval Memories*, 125. Kessler considers that the incomplete commentary on Ezekiel (*Homiliae in Ezekielem Prophetam*) was intended to equal his exegesis on the book of Job; Kessler, 'Gregory the Great,' 1345.
67 Kessler, 'Gregory the Great,' 1350.
68 This is a process in which prayer seeks to 'learn the heart of God in the words of God' and is taken from *Epistola XXXI* (*PL* Vol. 77, 0706B); it is summarized by Louis Boyer, *The Christian Mystery: From Pagan Myth to Christian Mysticism*, translated by Illtyd Trethowan (London, 2004), 234–40.
69 *PL* Vol. 76, 1561.
70 For similar patterns in Isidore see Jamie Wood, *The Politics of Identity in Visigothic Spain: Religion and Power in the Histories of Isidore of Seville* (Leiden, 2012), 138–9.
71 Thomas Glick, Steven Livesey and Faith Wallis (eds), *Medieval Science, Technology, and Medicine: An Encyclopedia* (New York, 2015), 277.
72 The ideological and pedagogical relationship between Gregory's *Moralia* and Isidore's *Sententiae* is explored by Jamie Wood: Jamie Wood, 'A Family Affair: Leander, Isidore and the Legacy of Gregory the Great in Spain,' in Andrew Fear and Jamie Wood (eds), *Isidore of Seville and His Reception in the Early Middle Ages: Transmitting and Transforming Knowledge* (Amsterdam, 2016), 33–56.
73 José Carracedo Fraga, 'Isidore of Seville as a Grammarian,' trans. Geraldine Barandiarán-Muñoz, in Andrew Fear and Jamie Wood (eds), *A Companion to Isidore of Seville* (Leiden, 2019), 222–44, at 240–1.
74 Robert Chazan, '*Adversus Iudaeos* in the Carolingian Empire,' Ora Limor and Guy G. Stroumsa (eds), Contra Iudaeos: *Ancient and Medieval Polemics Between Christians and Jews* (Tübingen, 1996), 119–42, at 127. The same argument is made in his *De fide Catholica contra Iudaeos*; see for example, Wolfram Drews, *The Unknown Neighbour. The Jew in the Thought of Isidore of Seville* (Leiden, 2006).
75 Ian Christopher Levy, 'Commentaries on the Pauline Epistles in the Carolingian Era,' Steven R. Cartwright (ed.), *A Companion to St Paul in the Middle Ages* (Leiden, 2013), 145–74.
76 Bede, *On Ezra and Nehemiah*, trans. Scott DeGregorio (Translated Texts for Historians, 47) (Liverpool, 2006), xv.
77 Judith McClure, 'Bede's Old Testament Kings,' in Patrick Wormald, Donald Bullough and Roger Collins (eds), *Ideal and Reality in Frankish and Anglo-Saxon Society: Studies Presented to J M Wallace-Hadrill* (Oxford, 1983), 76–98.
78 Ibid., 83–5.
79 The sometime abbot of Malmesbury, Aldhelm (*c.* 639–709), had knowledge of Isidore's *De Natura Rerum* and Bede himself, together with Isidore and Augustine, believed that the temporal world was divided into the Six Ages, five of which had already passed. See Peter Hunter Blair, *The World of Bede* (Cambridge, 1990), 265. Isidore also remained as a key exemplar for Bede, both of whom wrote a *De Natura Rerum*, a title that invoked a respect for classical natural science; Anne Lawrence-Mathers, *Medieval Meteorology: Forecasting the Weather from Aristotle to the Almanac* (Cambridge, 2020), 19, 20.
80 *PL* Vol. 83. For more on the transmission of this text, see Urban T. Holmes, *A History of Christian Spirituality: An Analytical Introduction* (Harrisburg, PA, 2002), 50; Claudia Di Sciacca, *Finding the Right Words: Isidore's* Synomyna *in Anglo-Saxon England* (Toronto, 2008), 19 *ff*.
81 The likely compilers of the eighth-century *Collectio Hibernensis*, Cú Chuimne of Iona and Ruben of Dairnis, favoured the chronological emphasis of Isidore rather than

the allegorical interpretation of OT narrative expounded by Bede (who in turn, is indebted to Jerome and Augustine); Samuel W. Collins, *The Carolingian Debate over Sacred* Space (New York, 2012), 39–40.

82 Martin Irvine, *The Making of Textual Culture: 'Grammatica' and Literary Theory 350–1100* (Cambridge, 1994), 277–8.
83 McClure cites the text of I Samuel as being especially influential; McClure, 'Old Testament Kings,' 85–6.
84 This applied especially to liturgical modifications evident when Bede used the *Vetus Latina*: McClure, 'Old Testament Kings,' 96–7.
85 Coleman, *Ancient and Medieval Memories*, 279.
86 Walter Goffart, 'Bede's *uera lex historiae* explained,' *Anglo-Saxon England*, Vol. 34 (2005), 111–16.
87 James Campbell, *Essays in Anglo-Saxon History* (London, 1986), 22, 23.
88 For example, variety of biblical interpretation may aid and be in harmony with the truth. Arthur Holder cites Bede's interpretation of the dedication of the Acts of the Apostles to Theophilus that, following an etymology from Greek, was expressed by Jerome, in which it may be inferred that the addressee may be a generic term applied to any 'lover of God.' See Arthur G. Holder, 'Bede and the New Testament,' in Scott DeGregorio (ed.), *The Cambridge Companion to Bede* (Cambridge, 2010), 142–55, at 148.
89 Scott DeGregorio, *Ezra and Nehemiah*, xvii–xviii.
90 The earlier books, *De tabernaculo* and *De templo*, deal with the account of the tabernacle in Exodus and the description of the temple of Solomon respectively. The influence of Bede's *De tabernaculo* on the writings of the twelfth-century Cluniac, Peter of Poitiers (who was to visit Spain with Peter the Venerable in 1142–3), will be considered shortly, especially with reference to Peter's *Allegoriae super tabernaculum Moysi*.
91 Ezra 8.31-33.
92 *PL* Vol. 91, 870C.
93 Ibid.
94 DeGregorio, *Ezra and Nehemiah*, xxxvi *ff.*
95 This phrase is found in two of Bede's *Homiliae* (XVII and XXIV): *PL* Vol. 94, 92B and 265C.
96 Brown, 'Introduction: Carolingian Renaissance,' 42.
97 An example is the *Chronicon* of Freculphus Lexoviensis, the ninth-century bishop of Lisieux: 'This biblical emphasis may be observed directly in the outpouring of commentaries on Old Testament books and indirectly in the history writing informed by the sacred narrative ... or by the theory of empire denoted in Daniel's vision'; Jennifer A. Harris, 'The Bible and the Meaning of History in the Middle Ages,' in Boynton and Reilly (eds), *Practice of the Bible*, 84–104, at 92.
98 Ibid., 40.
99 Ibid., 37. For Hrabanus and Isidore see: F. S. Paxton, 'Curing Bodies – Curing Souls: Hrabanus Maurus, Medical Education, and the Clergy in Ninth-Century Francia,' *Journal of the History of Medicine* (1995) 50: 230–52.
100 Rosamond McKitterick, *History and Memory in the Carolingian World* (Cambridge, 2004), 276.
101 Mayke de Jong, 'Exegesis for an Empress,' in E. Cohen and M. B. de Jong (eds), *Medieval Transformations: Texts, Power, and Gifts in Context* (Leiden, 2001), 69–100, at 72.

102 Claudio Leonardi notes that Hrabanus was following in the footsteps of the eighth-century theologian Wigbod whose *Quaestiones in Octateuchum* were followed in the following century by Claudius, a courtier of Louis the Pius and afterwards bishop of Turin (d. *c.* 827) who wrote on Genesis, Leviticus, Numbers, Kings and Ruth; Claudio Leonardi, 'Aspects of Old Testament Interpretation in the Church from the Seventh to the Tenth Centuries,' in Sæbø, *Hebrew Bible*, 180–92, at 189–90.
103 Brown, 'Introduction: The Carolingian Renaissance,' 40.
104 John C. Contreni, 'Carolingian Church,' in Robert Benedetto, *The New Westminster Dictionary of Church History Vol. I: The Early, Medieval, and Reformation Eras* (Louisville, KT, 2008), 124; Mayke de Jong, 'The Emperor Lothar and His *Bibliotheca Historiarum*,' R. I. A. Nip, H. van Dijk, E. M. C. van Houts, C. H. J. M. Kneepkens and G. A. A. Kortekaas (eds), *Media Latinitas, a Collection of Essays to Mark the Occasion of the Retirement of L.J. Engels* (Turnhout, 1996), 229–35; McKitterick, *History and Memory*, 276.
105 Brown, 'Introduction: Carolingian Renaissance,' 24.
106 Michael E. Moore, 'Royal and Episcopal Power in the Frankish Realms,' Unpublished PhD thesis, University of Michigan, 1993, 326.
107 J.-P. Houdret declares that two major prophets, Elijah and Elisha, who feature in II Kings and are models of piety and asceticism, represent a kind of monastic ideal. J.-P. Houdret, 'L'imitation du prophète Elie chez les Carmes du XIIIe au XVIIIe siècle,' *Carmelus* 31 (1983), 208–31 (cited by van Liere, 'Literal Sense,' 61).
108 Ibid.
109 *Love Lyrics from the Carmina Burana*, translated by P. G. Walsh (Chapel Hill, NC, 1993), xv.
110 David L. Balás and D. Jeffrey Bingham, 'Patristic Exegesis of the Books of the Bible,' in Kannengiesser, *Handbook of Patristic Exegesis*, 271–373, at 293.
111 Simon MacLean, *Kingship and Politics in the Late Ninth Century: Charles the Fat and the End of the Carolingian Empire* (Cambridge, 2003), 42, 43.
112 Van Liere, 'Biblical Exegesis,' 168–9.
113 Margaret T. Gibson, *Lanfranc of Bec* (Oxford, 1978), 54–61.
114 Susan Gillingham, *Psalms through the Centuries, Volume I* (Oxford, 2008), 88. Van Liere also comments on the influence of the glosses of Lanfranc of Pavia (d. 1089); van Liere, 'Biblical Exegesis,' 167.
115 Van Liere, 'Biblical Exegesis,' 166.
116 Lesley Smith, *The* Glossa Ordinaria: *The Making of a Medieval Bible Commentary* (Leiden, 2009), 18–19.
117 Even if Anselm did not invent *glossa interlinearis*, he compiled the material from which the gloss evolved and its link to patristic sources is evident though indirect; H. H. Glunz, *A History of the Vulgate in England from Alcuin to Roger Bacon: Being an Enquiry into the Text of Some English Manuscripts of the Vulgate Gospels* (Cambridge, 1933), 205.
118 One of the first to write commentaries on the entire Bible was Rupert, the Benedictine abbot of the monastery at Deutz (*c.* 1076–1129): 'His predecessors had been content with interpreting individual books, although many, such as Bede and Hrabanus Maurus, had treated nearly all the biblical books over time.' Henning Graf Reventlow, *History of Biblical Interpretation, Vol. 2: From Late Antiquity to the End of the Middle Ages*, translated by James O. Duke (Atlanta, GA, 1994), 153.
119 R. N. Swanson, *The Twelfth-Century Renaissance* (New York, 1999), 118.

120 Leclercq, 'Exposition and Exegesis,' 190. See also Ann Collins, *Teacher in Faith and Virtue: Lanfranc of Bec's Commentary on Saint Paul* (Leiden, 2007), 29.
121 Although there have been attempts by scholars to maintain the distinctiveness of these glosses in terms of purpose, Gilbert Dahan argues that it is the length of the commentary alone that determines where the gloss is placed; Gilbert Dahan, 'Genres, Forms and Various Methods in Christian Exegesis in the Middle Ages,' in Sæbø, *Hebrew Bible*, 196–235, at 219. This is also supported by Beryl Smalley who notes that no manuscript containing the marginal without the interlinear or vice versa has ever been found; Beryl Smalley, *The Study of the Bible in the Middle Ages* (Notre Dame, IN, 1978), 56.
122 Smalley notes that singled out for particular study were the psalms and Pauline epistles. The creation story was also a popular preference; see Beryl Smalley, 'The Bible in the Medieval Schools,' in Lampe, *Cambridge Bible Volume 2*, 197–220, at 205.
123 Bert Roest also refers to the work of Hugh and Andrew St Victor, Peter the Chanter, Peter Comestor and Stephen Langton who, whilst heavily influenced themselves by church fathers such as Augustine, from the twelfth century onwards used biblical commentaries that were added to existing glosses. These were developed into *postillae* and *lecturae* for students and theologians. And by this time Hugh and his fellow scholars were able to produce a glossed Bible in its entirety, the *Postill super Tota, Bibliam*. See Bert Roest, 'Mendicant School Exegesis,' in Boynton and Reilly, *The Practice of the Bible*, 179–204, at 180–1.
124 Ibid.
125 Nevertheless, for reasons possibly related to dissemination during the Carolingian period, significant commentaries were omitted from the exegetical anthologies such as *glossae ordinariae*. A notable example is Bede's *In primam partem Samuhelis*; Peter Darby, *Bede and the End of Time* (Farnham, 2012), 166.
126 Van Liere, 'Biblical Exegesis,' 173.
127 F. E. Peters, *The Monotheists: Jews, Christians, and Muslims in Conflict and Competition Volume II, The Words and Will of God* (Princeton, NJ, 2003), 46.
128 Peter Linehan notes that the income of such clerics was guaranteed for three years for those 'who wished to study at the *escuelas generales*, Bologna, Paris, Toulouse or, more modestly, Calahorra,' Peter Linehan, *The Spanish Church and the Papacy in the Thirteenth Century* (Cambridge, 1971), 66. Calahorra is a city and diocese in northern Spain, in the province of Logroño.
129 Eltio Buringh, *Medieval Manuscript Production in the Latin West: Exploration with a Global Database* (Leiden, 2011), 345.
130 Eyal Poleg, '"A Ladder Set Up on Earth": The Bible in Medieval Sermons,' in Boynton and Reilly, *The Practice of the Bible*, 205–27, at 207.
131 Susan Boynton considers the practice of the Mass and Divine Office to have reinforced the exegetical framework: 'Traditions of interpretation shaping the medieval Mass and office created inherently exegetical structures that were concretized through enactment of time and space through performance of text, sound, and gesture.' Susan Boynton, *Shaping a Monastic Identity: Liturgy and History at the Imperial Abbey of Farfa 1000–1125* (New York, 2006), 64.
132 R. E. Kaske, Arthur Groos and Michael W. Twowey, *Medieval Christian Literary Imagery: A Guide to Interpretation* (Toronto, 1988), 55–8.
133 Two such commentators suggested by Susan Boynton are Amalarius of Metz (c. 775–c. 850), who links liturgy and OT precedents, and Guillaume Durand, bishop of Mende (1230/31–96) who compares the hours of the office with the events leading

to the death and resurrection of Christ; Susan Boynton, 'The Bible and the Liturgy,' in Boynton and Reilly (eds), *The Practice of the Bible in the Middle Ages: Production, Reception & Performance in Western Christianity* (New York, 2011), 10–33, at 11.

134 Some of the psalms chanted at a sung Mass were derived from *Vetus Latina*; Boynton, Susan, 'The Bible and the Liturgy,' 19.

135 de Lubac, *Medieval Exegesis Vol. 2: The Four Senses of Scripture*, trans. E. M. Macierowski (Grand Rapids MI, 2000), 104.

136 Poleg, 'A Ladder,' 208.

137 Siegfried Wenzel, *Latin Sermon Collections from Later Medieval England* (Cambridge, 2005), 229–52.

138 Poleg, 'A Ladder,' 210.

139 Mystery or miracle plays seem to have emerged in the ninth and tenth centuries as tropes based on sermons and penitential literature and performed at major festivals: see Robert Potter, *The Early English Morality Play: Origins, History, and Influence of a Dramatic Tradition* (London, 1975), 6–16. One of the earliest Spanish liturgical dramas is the twelfth century *Auto de los Reyes Magos*, possibly written by the archbishop of Toledo, Rodrigo Jiménez de Rada (r. 1212–47) and which is briefly referred to towards the end of this book.

140 The origins of the so-called *Quem queritis* trope within the context of the *Visitatio Sepulchri* in the Carolingian Renaissance is discussed by Dunbar H. Ogden, *The Staging of Drama in the Medieval Church* (Cranbury NJ, 2002), 20–3.

141 The term was first coined by Boynton in 'Performative Exegesis in the Fleury *Interfectio puerorum*,' *Viator: Medieval and Renaissance Studies* 29 (1998), 39–64 (see Boynton, 'Bible and the Liturgy,' 24).

142 There were occasions when the laity were more than mere observers: for example, during the re-enactment of the washing of the disciples' feet, part of the Maundy Thursday ceremonial; Isabelle Cochelin, 'When Monks were the Book: The Bible and Monasticism (6th-11th centuries),' in Boynton and Reilly (eds), *Practice of the Bible*, 61–83, at 72.

143 Ibid., 73.

144 Beryl Smalley, *The Gospels in Schools, c. 1100–c. 1280* (London, 1985), 2–4.

145 This was especially the case in France and Flanders, though less so in Germany; see Harvey J. Graff, *The Legacy of Literacy: Continuities and Contradictions in Western Culture and Society* (Chicago, IL, 1991), 62, 63. And Michael Clanchy notes that a knowledge of Latin was becoming increasingly common amongst the English merchant classes between 1100 and 1300; Michael T. Clanchy, *From Memory to Written Record* (London, 1979), 187–8.

146 Cochelin, 'When Monks Were the Book,' 73–4.

147 Robert M. Grant and David Tracy, *A Short History of the Interpretation of the Bible* (London, 1984), 3 *ff*.

148 Smalley, *Study of the Bible*, xxix, xxx.

149 Beryl Smalley, 'The Exposition and Exegesis of Scripture: The Bible in the Medieval Schools,' in Lampe, *Cambridge Bible, Volume 2*, 197–220, especially at 209.

150 M. D.- Chenu, 'The Masters of Theological "Science",' in *Nature, Man, and Society in the Twelfth Century, Essays on New Theological Perspectives in the Latin West*, translated by Jerome Taylor and Lester K. Little (London, 1968), 270–308, at 286.

151 Van Liere, 'Biblical Exegesis,' 169–70.

152 Gabrielle M. Spiegel, *The Past as Text: The Theory and Practice of Medieval Historiography* (Baltimore, MD, 1999), 92.

153 Cited by Diana Wood, 'Clement VI and the Political Use of the Bible,' in Katharine Walsh and Diana Wood (eds), *The Bible in the Medieval World: Essays in Memory of Beryl Smalley* (Oxford, 1985), 237–49, at 240.
154 Ibid., 240.
155 2 Tim. 3.16.
156 Wood, 'Clement VI,' 241.
157 Katherine Allen Smith, *War and the Making of Medieval Monastic Culture* (Woodbridge, 2011), 15.
158 Ibid., 16.
159 *Monumentia Germaniae Historica, Epistolae* IV, 496, lines 21–7; cited by Mary Garrison, 'Letters to a King and Biblical Exempla: The Examples of Cathuulf and Clemens Peregrinus,' *Early Medieval Europe*, Vol. 7, No. 3 (1998), 305–28, at 308.
160 Ibid., 323.
161 Ibid.
162 Ibid., 307.
163 'Letters are virtually catenae or florilegia of biblical … citations' (ibid., 307), rather than merely containing biblical quotations and allusions.
164 R. D. Fulk and Christopher M. Cain, *A History of Old English Literature* (Oxford, 2003), 13.
165 The effect of the sack of Lindisfarne on Alcuin may be judged by the fact that his message following the destruction of the church and community was so emphatic: 'Behold, it is almost 350 years after our fathers occupied this beautiful place and never before has such a terror come to Britain by a nation of pagans,' from '*Epistula Albini magistri ad Aeðelredum regem*,' 2, 4, lines 22–5 in Colin Chase (ed.), *Two Alcuin Letter-Books* (Toronto, 1975).
166 Mary Garrison, 'The Bible and Alcuin's Interpretation of Current Events,' *Peritia Journal of the Medieval Academy of Ireland*, Vol. 16 (2002), 68–84, at 69, n. 4.
167 Ibid., 71. His Epistles 19, 55, lines 7–9 make this explicit: 'et in sanctarum scripturarum lectione studiosi estote, ut possitis alterutrum aedificare et consolari' ['And you are to be zealous in the perusal of Divine Scripture, so that you can support and console one another']; Latin cited by Garrison, 'The Bible,' 71, n. 10.
168 Jer. 1.14: 'Then the Lord said unto me, out of the north an evil shall break forth upon the inhabitants of the land.'
169 *Alcuin Letter-Books*, 5. Ep. 16, 43, lines 12–15. Garrison considers the term *patriam perdidisse* [applied as it is to the loss of homeland] as being particularly damning, suggesting as it does not merely loss but also the squandering and destruction of something holy and precious (Garrison, 'The Bible,' 74).
170 *Adversus Elipandum Toletanum*, Book 1 (*PL* Vol. 101, 0251C).
171 Dwight D. Allman, 'Sin and the Construction of Carolingian Kingship,' in Richard Newhauser (ed.), *The Seven Deadly Sins: From Communities to Individuals* (Leiden, 2007), 19–40.
172 Gernot R. Wieland, '*Ge mid wige ge mid wisdome*: Alfred's Double-Edged Sword,' in A. E. Christa Canitz and Gernot R. Wieland (eds), *From Arabye to Engelond: Medieval Studies in Honour of Mahmoud Manzalaoui on His 75th Birthday* (Ottawa, 1999), 217–28, at 224.
173 *Beati Alcuini ad Carolum Magnum*, Book 7 (*PL* Vol. 101, 0127B).
174 Wieland, 'Double-Edged Sword,' 224.
175 Mt. 5.14.

176 From Mt. 5.14 and 1 Pet. 2.9 and used in Alcuin's letter to Æthelheard (*Epistola X*) (*PL* Vol. 100, 0154C).
177 Ibid.
178 Joel 2.17.
179 From Ep 20, 57, lines 8*ff*, cited by Garrison, 'The Bible.'
180 Heb. 12.6. See also Zech. 13.9 referring to 'refining through fire ... as silver is refined' quoted by Alcius (Ep 16, lines 85–6, 90 and 9395), cited by Garrison, 'The Bible,' 77.
181 From *De clade Lindisfarnensis monasterii*, cited by Garrison, 'Alcuin, *Carmen ix* and Hrabanus, *Ad Bonosum*: A Teacher and His Pupil Write Consolation,' in John Marenbon (ed.), *Poetry and Philosophy in the Middle Ages: A Festschrift for Peter Dronke* (Leiden, 2000), 63–78, at 77. Commenting on the theme of the paradox of punishment and love with which Alcuin deals in his *Letter Books* and *De clade Lindisfarnensis monasterii*, Renée Trilling observes: 'human suffering is linked causally to human sin; tribulations are sent to test the faithful, and if the faithful prove worthy by amending their behaviour, then they would be rewarded,' in Renée R. Trilling, *The Aesthetics of Nostalgia: Historical Representations in Old English Verse* (Toronto, 2009), 142.
182 Jean Dunbabin, 'The Maccabees as Exemplars in the Tenth and Eleventh Centuries,' in Walsh and Wood, *Bible in the Medieval World*, 31–41, at 31.
183 Dunbabin, 'The Maccabees as Exemplars,' 35. This assertion is technically not accurate since God is not mentioned in the book of Esther either.
184 Ibid., 31.
185 For a comprehensive presentation of the thirty or so minor annals that survive from this period, see Jennifer Davis, *Charlemagne's Practice of Empire* (Cambridge, 2015), 192, n. 76.
186 Dunbabin, 'The Maccabees as Exemplars,' 35.
187 Rodney M. Thomson, *William of Malmesbury* (Woodbridge, 2003), 8–11.
188 R. A. B. Mynors, R. M. Thomson and M. Winterbottom (trans. and eds), *William of Malmesbury: Gesta Regum Anglorum, The History of the English Kings Vol. I* (Oxford, 1998).
189 Ibid., 243 (454).
190 Ibid., Preface to Book III (424).
191 Ibid., 239 (452): 'Neither can you deny that you are bound to him by an oath, whether (entered into) willingly or by force.'
192 Ibid., 238 (446).
193 Alice Sheppard cites the contributions of certain Latin Anglo-Saxon and Anglo-Norman sources, including John of Worcester (d. *c.* 1140) and Eadmer of Canterbury (*c.* 1060–*c.* 1124) who portrayed Harold as a good man, trapped by the political opportunism of his future opponent. Alice Sheppard, *Families of the King: Writing Identity in the Anglo-Saxon Chronicle* (Toronto, 2004), 125.
194 Orderic Vitalis, *The Ecclesiastical History of Orderic Vitalis Vol. II*, Books III and IV, edited and translated by Marjorie Chibnall (Oxford, 1969, reprinted 2002), 134.
195 This echo is a phrase used frequently by Paul (e.g. Rom. 8.3, Col. 2.11, etc., and variously rendered as *corporis carnis*, *carnis peccati* and *peccatum in carne*) and which William of Malmesbury considered significant in analysing the significance of the Norman victory.
196 *GRA*, 244, 458.
197 Rom. 13.13, Gal. 19–21, Col. 3.5.
198 Jas 1.27.

199 'Drinking in company was everywhere apparent, in which pursuit they passed nights and days. They consumed their whole beings in small and debased houses, unlike the French and Normans who in ample and splendid buildings, conduct themselves temperately'; *GRA*, 245, 458.
200 Ibid., 241, 452–4.
201 Caesar's description of the Celts, 'Capilloque sunt promisso, atque omni parte corporis rasa, praeter caput et labrum superius' (*De Bello Gallico*, V. 14) is appropriated by William of Malmesbury and used to contrast the appearance of Saxons and Normans. The fact that the Normans are depicted as having 'the appearance of priests' may also be significant (ibid., 239, 450).
202 As we shall see, OT-derived terms such as *Moabite*, *Ismaelite* and *Hagarene* were used, sometimes indiscriminately, by Iberian chroniclers to refer to Muslims in the texts covered in this study.
203 These would most commonly be patristic sources, though William was also well acquainted with the works of Gregory the Great and Bede. He was also familiar with Carolingian writers such as Alcuin, whose letters he knew, together with his *Commentary on Ecclesiastes*; Sigbjørn Olsen Sønnesyn, *William of Malmesbury and the Ethics of History* (Woodbridge, 2012), 128–9.
204 According to Rodney Thomson, there is sufficient evidence to suggest that Malmesbury was acquainted with almost all of Gregory's works since, quite apart from his admiration revealed in *Defloratio Gregorii*, Gregory is also quoted in *GRA*, *Gesta Pontificum*, *Abbreviatio Amalarii* and in Malmesbury's *Commentary on Lamentations*. Evidence of his acquaintance with the writings of other church fathers is substantial though far from complete; Thomson, *William of Malmesbury*, 42.
205 Ibid., 49.
206 Michael R. Evans, *The Death of Kings: Royal Deaths in Medieval England* (London, 2007), 43.
207 *GRA*, 275, 505.
208 2 Sam. 18.9.
209 The parallel with Absalom is a clear one, and certainly a popular one amongst the Anglo-Norman writers including Orderic Vitalis, John of Worcester (d. *c.* 1140) and slightly later by Robert of Torigni (*c.* 1110–86).
210 Swanson, *Twelfth-Century Renaissance*, 58.
211 Rita Copeland, 'The Curricular Classics of the Middle Ages,' in Rita Copeland (ed.), *The Oxford History of the Classical Reception of English Literature, Volume 1 (800–1558)* (Oxford, 2016), 21–34, at 26.
212 From *Commentary on Lamentations*, 187 line 43; cited by Sønnesyn, *William of Malmesbury*, 44.
213 R. Allen Brown, *The Normans and the Norman Conquest* (Woodbridge, 1969), 13.
214 Lincei Lectures, 1974, *The Normans in Sicily and Southern Italy* (Oxford University Press, 1977), 33.
215 Gaufredus Malaterra, *De rebus gestis Rogerii Calabriae et Siciliae Comitis et Roibrti Guiscardi Ducis fatris eius*, Book II, vii (*PL* Vol. 149, 1125A).
216 Mt. 5.3.
217 'Non enim est distinctio Judaei et Graeci: nam idem Dominus omnium, dives in omnes qui invocat illum.' In Malaterra's abbreviated quotation, 'Nam idem Deus omnium, dives in omnes qui invocant illum,' it will be noted that Lord (*Dominus*) has been replaced with God (*Deus*); Book II, xxxiii (*PL* Vol. 149, 1140A).
218 Lincei Lectures, 7.

219 Andrew Cowell, *The Medieval Warrior Aristocracy: Gifts, Violence, Performance and the Sacred* (Cambridge, 2007), 52. Cowell's comments are in the context of an encounter between Robert Guiscard and Peter of Tyre in which the words of Jesus, 'date et dabitur vobis'/ 'Give and it shall be given unto you' (Lk. 6.38); whether it is the gifts of Robert or Peter that are being referred to is unclear.

220 Book 4, chapter 28 (*PL* Vol. 149, 1207D). The three verses are from Rom. 10.5, Mt. 5.9 and 2 Cor. 12.11.

221 Ibid., Introduction, lines 55–60 (4).

222 Ibid., II XXVII (line 29).

223 'Inasmuch as history is an ancient authority (the evidence of the times, the light of truth, the life of memory, the teacher of life),' Gerald of Wales. *Expugnatio Hibernica*, edited and translated by A. B. Scott and F. X. Martin (Dublin, 1978), Introduction, lines 128–30, 10. This familiar trope has ancient associations. It is lifted from Cicero (*De Oratio* II, 9) but was familiar to Anglo-Saxon chroniclers as well as to the poets of Elizabethan England: see discussion of its use by Sir Philip Sydney in Jűrgen Pieters, *Speaking with the Dead: Explorations in Literature and History* (Edinburgh: Edinburgh University Press, 2005), 29.

224 Ibid., II XXXVI (lines 35–42). He cites a verse from John's Gospel to support this and the choice seems apposite: 'We speak that we do know, and testify that we have seen' (Jn 3.11).

225 Terence Dolan, 'Writing in Ireland,' in David Wallace (ed.), *The Cambridge History of Medieval English Literature* (Cambridge, 1999), 208–29, at 223.

226 Though this was an age of bravado amongst the conquerors as well as historians such as Gerald, 'What is difficult for the twentieth-century historical imagination is to capture their swaggering bravado and limitless ambition.' From R. R. Davies, *Domination and Conquest: The Experience of Ireland, Scotland and Wales 1100–1300* (Cambridge, 1990), 34.

227 The Council of Cashel in Tipperary 1172 – not mentioned in Irish sources but given prominence by Gerald – seems to have established the reformed church with its very specific requirements for believers and *iuvta quod Anglicana observat ecclesia* (Ibid., I, XXXIV).

228 From Jaques Leclercq (ed.), *Vita Sancti Malachiae* in *S. Bernardi Opera Vol. III, Tractatus et Opuscula* (Rome, 1963), 325. Translated by Robert T. Meyer as follows: 'Never had he known such men, steeped in barbarism; never had he found people so wanton in their way of life, so cruel in superstition, so heedless of faith, lawless, dead-set against discipline, so foul in their lifestyle; Christians in name yet pagans at heart.' *Bernard of Clairvaux: The Life and Death of Saint Malachy the Irishman*, translated and annotated by Robert T. Meyer (Kalamazoo, MI, 1978), VIII. 16 (33).

229 A situation, albeit with degrees of reluctance, that was often conceded by the Irish themselves; Robert Bartlett, comparing the English invasion of Ireland in 1169 with the English defeat at Hastings in 1066, notes that 'something of the fateful ring in the Irish historical imagination' was stirred by this event. Robert Bartlett, *England under the Norman and Angevin Kings, 1075–1225* (Oxford, 2000), 87 *ff.*

230 This is discussed by Laura Ashe, *Fiction and History in England, 1066–1200* (Cambridge, 2007), 190; particularly striking is the way in which the raiding and plundering on the part of the English enabled them to blur any ideological distinction between Irish society and their own.

231 Their discussion of the long-term effects of this declaration is discussed by Christy L. Burns, *Gestural Politics: Stereotype and Parody in Joyce* (New York, 2000), 124 *ff.*
232 Donnchádh Ó Corrain, 'Irish Legends and Genealogy: Recurrent Aetiologies,' in Tore Nyberg (ed.), *History and the Heroic Tale: A Symposium* (Odense, 1985), 51–96.
233 Ibid., 52, 55. Nevertheless, Alaric Hall notes that some earlier rhetoric demonstrates currents of ambiguous, and sometimes hostile commentary towards the indigenous British by Bede; Alaric Hall, 'Interlinguistic Communication in Bede's *Historia ecclesiastica gentis Anglorum*,' in Alaric Hall, Olga Timofeeva, Agnes Kiricsi and Bethany Fox (eds), *Interfaces between Language and Culture in Medieval England: A Festschrift for Matti Kilpiö* (Leiden, 2010), 37–80, at 68.
234 John Gillingham, *The English in the Twelfth Century: Imperialism, National Identity and Political Values* (Woodbridge, 2000), 43.
235 Marcus Bull, *Knightly Piety and the Lay Response to the First Crusade: The Limousin and Gascony, c. 970–c1130* (Oxford, 1993), 128–32.
236 Ibid., 131.
237 Luke Timothy Johnson and William S. Kurz S. J., *The Future of Catholic Biblical Scholarship: A Constructive Conversation* (Cambridge, 2002), 43. The first printing press in Spain appears to have operated in Valencia by Lambert Palmart between 1474 and 1494, almost two hundred and fifty years after Lucas, Rodrigo and Juan of Osma completed their histories; E. Gordon Duff, *Early Printed Books* (Cambridge, 1893), 113.
238 Fred S. Kleiner, *Gardner's Art through the Ages: The Western Perspective*, Vol. 1 (Boston, MA, 2009), 289.
239 An early Andalusian exegete, Lucinius Baeticus (*fl.* 400), sent six scribes to Bethlehem to obtain copies of Jerome's writings; Williams, *Imaging the Early Medieval Bible*, 180. Although the scribes had access to his translation of most of the OT, Jerome had yet to complete his translation of the Octateuch; we cannot be certain that the scribes were able to bring back a copy of Jerome's translation into Latin of the Septuagint.
240 Williams, *Imaging the Early Medieval Bible*, 185.
241 Klaus Reinhardt and Horacio Santiago-Otero, *Biblioteca Bíblia Ibérica Medieval* (Madrid, 1986). Rebecca Maloy notes that extant Spanish Bibles mostly consist of Vulgate texts and, in her analysis of the Mozarabic rite, finds that although some elements are derived from the *Vetus Latina*, most sources appear to be from the Vulgate; Rebecca Maloy, *Inside the Offertory: Chronology and Transmission* (Oxford, 2010), 77.
242 The African Latin book trade is referred to by Cassiodorus: see Bernard Bischoff (trans. Michael Gorman), *The Manuscripts and Libraries in the Age of Charlemagne* (Cambridge, 2007), 3 *ff*; the transmission of eastern knowledge is explored by Judith Herrin, *The Formation of Christendom* (Princeton, NJ, 1987), 84–9. See also Leighton Durham Reynolds, *Texts and Transmission: A Survey of the Latin Classics* (Oxford, 1983), xv–xvii.
243 There is evidence that during this time (*c.* 570) certain Christian monks were driven out of their monasteries in the Maghreb and settled in the Iberian Peninsula; Herrin, *The Formation of Christendom*, 107 and 154.
244 Reinhardt and Santiago-Otero, *Biblioteca Bíblia Ibérica*, 12. Reinhardt and Santiago-Otero refer to the work of two sixteenth-century theologians, Pablo Burgense and Pablo de Coronel, though the codices which they used are not identified.

245 Furthermore, although Reinhardt and Santiago-Otero focus primarily on theologians from the fifteenth century onwards, there is an important reference to Rodrigo Jiménez de Rada which, in addition to his historical works, includes his thirteenth-century *Brevarium historiae catholicae*. Ibid., 5, 6, 303–5.

246 E. A. Lowe discusses the history and features of the palimpsest and its ninth-century rewriting in a Spanish scriptorium; E. A. Lowe (ed.), *Codices Latini Antiquiores, Part XI* (Oxford, 1966) 1636, 17. See also Roger Collins, *Early Medieval Spain: Unity in Diversity, 400–1100* (London, 1995), 123. The León Cathedral Palimpsest contains several books, including Maccabees, Judith, Esther II, the Books of Chronicles and Tobias, that are in a version of the *Vetus Latina*. Maloy notes this preservation in the pre-Vulgate version long after the transition to the Vulgate for other biblical texts; Maloy, *Inside the Offertory*, 77, n. 105.

247 Williams, *Imaging the Early Medieval Bible*, 181. For a discussion about the possible texts that existed in Spain both before and after the time of Isidore, see Raphael Loewe, 'The Medieval History of the Latin Vulgate,' in Lampe (ed.), *Cambridge Bible, Vol. 2*, 102–54 at 120–5.

248 Isidore, *De Ecclesiasticus Officiis* 1.12, *PL* Vol. 83, 748C.

249 Marjorie Nicholson cites the example of Gen. 3.17 where 'maledicta humus propter te' [cursed is the ground for thy sake] is rendered as 'maledicta terra in opere tuo' [cursed is the earth in thy work], a distinction still maintained in the King James Bible and in the English translation of the Douay-Rheims Bible: Marjorie Hope Nicolson, *Mountain Gloom and Mountain Glory: The Development of Aesthetics of the Infinite* (Ithaca, NY, reprinted 1997), 84. Such errors may not have been apparent to scholars until much later.

250 Loewe gives an example from 1 Jn 1.2 where κόσμος is translated in one of the pre-Vulgate manuscripts as *saeculum* and in the Vulgate as *mundi*; Loewe, 'Latin Vulgate,' 112. He then speculates that a seventh-century conflated version of Isidore's own critical edition (text Σ) based on Jerome's Vulgate and an earlier (perhaps fifth century) text, which he refers to as the 'Peregrinus-Isidore' text, was the possible source for seven subsequent Spanish codices. Ibid., 125.

251 Loewe notes additionally that Spanish texts are distinguished by doublets, glosses and legendary accretions being inserted into the content; ibid., 112.

252 Ibid., 113.

253 Marcia L. Colish suggests that Peter Lombard may have worked on a pre-Vulgate text of the psalms with a commentary by Augustine; Marcia L. Colish, *Peter Lombard Volume One* (Leiden, 1993), 181–2. Augustus's use of the *Vetus Latina* in his commentaries on the psalms is also discussed by Mary Carruthers, *The Book of Memory: A Study of Memory in Medieval Culture* (Cambridge, 2008), 123.

254 See Ciriaca Morano Rodríguez, *Glosas marginales de Vetus Latina en las Biblias Vulgatas españoles: 1-2 Samuel* (Madrid, 1989) and Antonio Moreno Hernández, *Las glosas marginales de Vetus Latina en las Biblias Vulgatas españoles: 1–2 Reyes* (Madrid, 1992).

255 Natalio Fernández Marcos, *Scribes and Translators: Septuagint and Old Latin in the Books of Kings* (Leiden, 1994), 44.

256 Williams places the date of composition slightly earlier than mid-ninth century. See Williams, *Imaging the Early Medieval Bible*, 181, 189.

257 John Williams, *Early Spanish Manuscript Illumination* (New York, 1977), 40.

258 For example, it contains the *Comma Johanneum*, a short phrase containing the Trinitarian formula in 1 Jn 5.7-8 that appears in early ninth-century versions of the

Vulgate but which may have been based on the *Vetus Latina* or at least on a gloss on that text. The phrase completes v. 7 and begins v. 8 ('For there are three that bear record in heaven, the Father, the Word, and the Holy Ghost. And these three are one. /And there are three that bear witness in earth'); Bruce M. Metzger, *The Early Versions of the New Testament* (Oxford, 1977), 338.

259 E. A. Loewe, 'The *Codex Cavensis*: New Light on Its Later History,' in Robert P. Casey, Silva Lake and Agnes K. Lake (eds), *Quantulacumque: Studies Presented to Kirsopp Lake, 1937* (London, 1937), 325–31, at 326.

260 Certain Cassino manuscripts produced between the tenth and fifteenth centuries reflect this affinity; Loewe, 'Latin Vulgate,' 114.

261 Ibid., 122.

262 Ibid.

263 Williams argued that the colophon was legible in the eighteenth century and suggested that at one time the colophon revealed the name of the monastery of Albares, west of León; Williams, *Imaging the Early Medieval Bible*, 182. I have not been able to find further references to this location.

264 The exact derivation of the Spanish word *mozárabe* is either from the Arabic *mustaʿrab* (meaning 'arabised') or from *musta ʿrib* (meaning 'tribes not originally descended from Arabs) and was used to describe the Christian inhabitants of al-Andalus. However, the original use of the term emanates from eleventh-century Christian rather than Arabic sources; Mikel de Epalza, 'Mozarabs: An Emblematic Christian Minority in Islamic al-Andalus,' in Salma Khadra Jayyusi (ed.), *The Legacy of Muslim Spain* (Leiden, 1992), 149–70, at 149.

265 Ibid.

266 Walter Kahn, *Romanesque Bible Illumination* (New York, 1982), 62.

267 Ibid.

268 W. M. Lindsay, *Notae Latinae: An Account of Abbreviation in Latin Manuscripts of the Early Minuscule Period (c. 700–850)* (Cambridge, 1915), 29.

269 Katrin Kogman-Appel, *Jewish Book Art between Islam and Christianity: The Decoration of Hebrew Bibles in Medieval Spain* (Leiden, 2004), 2.

270 Bruce M. Metzger, *The Text of the New Testament: Its Transmission, Corruption, and Restoration* (Oxford, 1968), 77. See also M. Roy Harris, 'Translations of John XII and XIII-XVIII from a Fourteenth-Century Franciscan Codex (Assisi, Chiesa Nuova MS. 9)7,' in *Transactions of the American Philosophical Society*, Vol. 75, No. 4 (1985), 40.

271 Kevin L. Hughes, *Constructing Antichrist: Paul, Biblical Doctrine, and the Development of Doctrine in the Early Middle Ages* (Washington, DC, 2005), 184.

272 John Williams notes that there were various threats to orthodoxy circulating in the Iberian Peninsula during the eighth century including the teachings of Migetius and that these might have helped to promote Adoptionism; John Williams, 'Purpose and Imagery in the Apocalypse Commentary of Beatus of Liébana,' in Richard K. Emmerson and Bernard McGinn (eds), *The Apocalypse in the Middle Ages* (New York, 1993), 217–33, at 218, 222.

273 G. Scott Davies argues that the influence of Augustine had been a significant element in the formation of Christian thought in Visigothic Iberian times and that Isidore compiled his *Etymologiae* 'in an atmosphere dominated by Augustine and Gregory.' G. Scott Davies, 'Early Medieval Ethics,' in Lawrence C. Becker and Charlotte B. Becker (eds), *A History of Western Ethics* (Oxford, 2003), 43–52, at 47. In her article discussing Augustine's doctrine of Jesus' humanity, Joanne McWilliam suggests that Augustine influenced Spanish Adoptionism; Joanne E. McWilliam, 'The

Context of Spanish Adoptionism: A Review,' in Michael Gervers and Ramzi Gibran Bikhazi (eds), *Conversion and Continuity: Indigenous Christian Communities in Islamic Lands Eighth to Eighteenth Centuries* (Toronto, 1990), 75–88, at 77. See also Josep Perarau, *Jornades internacionals d'estudi sobre el Bisbe Feliu d'Urgel. Crònica estudis* (Barcelona, 2000), 101. This is supported by John Cavadini who argues that the doctrine of Adoptionism in Iberia was derived from Augustine but drew also on Isidore and Hilary of Poitiers. John C. Cavadini, *The Last Christology of the West: Adoptionism in Spain and Gaul 785–820* (Philadelphia, PA, 1993), 105.

274   PL, Vol. 98, 0893–1030. It is likely that the first draft of this polemic was written in 776; Kevin Poole, 'Beatus of Liébana: Medieval Spain and the Othering of Islam,' in Karolyn Kinane and Michael A. Ryan (eds), *End of Days: Essays on the Apocalypse from Antiquity to Modernity* (Jefferson, NC, 2009), 47.

275   Williams, 'Purpose and Imagery,' 217. Following the publication of Augustine's *De Civitate Dei* (possibly between 412 and 426), St Vincent of Lerins (d. c. 445) denied what he saw as Augustine's speculation on the nature of Christ's relationship with the Father as being incorporated into Christian dogma; see Joseph P. Farrell, *God, History and Dialectic: The Theological Foundations of the Two Europes and Their Cultural Consequences* (Chanute, KS, 1997), 1028.

276   Poole, 'Beatus of Liébana,' 48.

277   'As biblical exegesis, preachers would reference his commentaries in their sermons; during the meditative *lectio divina* practiced by the ordered religious, the commentaries would be used as a tool for spiritual training and preparation' (ibid., 54).

278   Williams, 'Purpose and Imagery,' 217.

279   For a more expansive list of exegetical sources, see Williams, 'Purpose and Imagery,' 218. Other significant influences on Beatus were the church father, Apringius (*fl.* sixth century) who himself wrote on the Apocalypse (though only fragments remain) and the North African Donatist, Tyconius (d. c. 390), whose own commentary on the Apocalypse may have influenced Augustine's *De Civitate Dei*. Tyconius's influence was also evident in Bede's *Explanatio Apocalypsis*; the complex web of interdependence of geographically far-flung exegetes is again asserted: Johannes Van Oort, *Jerusalem and Babylon: A Study into Augustine's City of God and the Sources of His Doctrine of the Two Cities* (Leiden, 1991), 265, n. 359.

280   Van Oort notes that Beatus provided invaluable material for the study of Tyconius's commentary, even if all the material cannot be positively ascribed to a particular author; ibid., 266.

281   Roger Collins describes Beatus's commentary as 'purely a labour of compilation'; Collins, *Early Medieval Spain*, 242. According to van Oort, this was particularly the case when Beatus was transcribing Tyconius's material on Africa, which was largely recorded verbatim (van Oort, *Jerusalem and Babylon*, 265). What were unrivalled, both in their frequency, originality and lavish design, were the illustrations found in most of the surviving manuscripts. His cycle of Apocalypse illustrations is described by Williams as 'independent of any other tradition' (Williams, 'Purpose and Imagery,' 226). These illustrations, perhaps even more than his impressive access to patristic and other sources, ensured his enduring popularity.

282   Heather M. Coffey, 'Contesting the Eschaton in Medieval Iberia: The Polemical Intersection of Beatus of Liébana's Commentary on the Apocalypse and the Prophet's Miʿrājnāma,' in Christiane Gruber and Frederick Colby (eds), *The Prophet's*

Ascension: Cross-Cultural Encounters with the Islamic Miʿrāj Tales (Bloomington, IN, 2010), 97–140, at 100.
283   Klein, 'Introduction: The Apocalypse in Medieval Art,' in Boynton and Reilly (eds), *The Practice of the Bible*, 159–99, at 188.
284   Ibid., 187.
285   E. Ann Matter traces apocalyptic exegesis from late antiquity to the twelfth century and argues that the north African bishop and primate Primasius (d *c*. 560) is the founder of medieval Latin apocalyptic exegesis; E. Ann Matter, 'The Apocalypse in Early Medieval Exegesis,' in Emmerson and McGinn (eds), *Apocalypse*, 38–50. Nevertheless, Primasius himself, in the prologue to *Primasii commentariorum super Apocalypsim B. Joannis*, acknowledges his debt to Augustine, Jerome and Tynconius (*PL* Vol. 68, 0793C).
286   Mireille Mentré, *El Estilo Mozárabe: La Pintura Cristiana Hispánica en Torno al Año Mil* (Madrid, 1994), 37–252; Poole, 'Beatus of Liébana,' 47–66.
287   Rose Walker, *Views of Transition: Liturgy and Illumination in Medieval Spain* (London, 1998), 88–9.
288   Nevertheless, the reason excerpts from Beatus's commentary on the Apocalypse, which is not linked to the Mozarabic liturgy, seeped into Roman breviaries is unresolved. Walker suggests that this may have been an audacious interpretation that allowed patristic readings. Conceivably it incorporated what were becoming familiar readings in an acceptable setting and perhaps strengthened Beatus's own reputation as the 'champion of orthodoxy against the (Visigothic) church of Toledo. Ibid., 211.
289   Colbert Nepaulsingh acknowledges that scholars do not always concur as to what constitutes apocalyptic literature 'but most (Judaic apocalyptic) lists would include those of Ezekiel and Daniel, the three Books of Enoch, the Book of Jubilees, the Testaments of the Twelve Patriarchs, the Sibylline oracles, the Psalms of Solomon, the Assumption of Moses, the Life of Adam and Eve, the Apocalypse of Ezra, the Apocalypses of Baruch, the Ascension of Isaiah, the Apocalypse of Abraham and the Testament of Abraham. To these works Christians added the Little Apocalypse of the Gospels (Mt. 24, 25; Mk 13; and Lk. 21) and the classic apocalyptic work, the book of Revelation; and Islam added the revelations to Prophet Mohammed about the Last Days of Judgment referred to frequently in the Koran. Colbert I. Nepaulsingh, *Towards a History of Literary Composition in Medieval Spain* (Toronto, 1986), 64.
290   Ibid.
291   Ibid., 66 (This is a reference to *Sermones de Adventu Domini*. Manuscript. Codex MS 157, Hanna Holborn Gray Special Collections Research Center, University of Chicago Library.)
292   Ángel Flores (ed.), *An Anthology of Medieval Lyrics* (New York, 1962), 391.
293   Nepaulsingh provides a full though not exhaustive review of literature falling within the Spanish Apocalyptic tradition, though much of this is outside the period covered by this current research; Nepaulsingh, *Literary Composition*, 66–124.
294   Beatus, *Commentaria in Apocalypsin*, Book 4.
295   Klein, 'The Apocalypse,' 188. The Escorial Beatus has 151 surviving folios and contains 52 illustrated miniatures.
296   Coffey, 'Contesting the Eschaton in Medieval Iberia,' 98.
297   Otto Werckmeister discusses one such marginal illustration from the so-called Girona Manuscript (which also contains Jerome's Commentary on the book of Daniel), in O. K. Werckmeister, 'The Islamic Rider in the Beatus of Girona,' *Gesta*,

Vol. 36, No. 2, Visual Culture of Medieval Iberia (1997), 101–6. See also Richard K. Emmerson, 'Medieval Illustrated Apocalyptic Manuscripts,' in Michael A. Ryan (ed.), *A Companion to the Premodern Apocalypse* (Leiden, 2015), 21–66, at 30–3.

298 Interest in Beatus's work was again revived with the coming of the Cistercians in the twelfth and thirteenth centuries. His apocalyptic cycles were copied during the eleventh century and influenced the content of codices in the monasteries of St Domingo de Silos, St Isidoro in León and Saint-Sever (Aquitaine); in the late twelfth and early thirteenth centuries, the Cistercians authorized further illustrated copies of his text that were held in two monasteries; Klein, 'The Apocalypse,' 187.

299 The emergence of a Frankish-orientated and semi-autonomous area in north-eastern Iberia during the late ninth century is discussed by Barton Sholod, *Charlemagne in Spain: The Cultural Legacy of Roncesvalles* (Geneva, 1966), 64.

300 Thomas F. Glick, *Islamic and Christian Spain in the Early Middle Ages* (Leiden, revised edition, 2005), 363–4. Glick notes that what he calls the 'reception of the Frankish cultural current' in the east was to be paralleled in San Juan de la Peña in Aragón and Sahagún in León-Castile. See also Williams, *Imaging the Early Medieval Bible*, 187.

301 Loewe, 'Latin Vulgate,' 125.

302 Rosamond McKitterick, 'The Carolingian Renaissance of Culture and Learning,' in Joanna Story (ed.), *Charlemagne, Empire and Society* (Manchester, 2005), 151–66, at 162.

303 It seems that most of the writing of the 960 Bible was undertaken by Florentius's pupil, Sancho; Julio Escalona, Isabel Velázquez Soriano and Paloma Juárez Benítez, 'Identification of the Sole Extant Original Charter Issued by Fernán González, Count of Castile (923–970),' in *Journal of Iberian Studies*, Vol. 4, No. 2 (September 2012), 259–88, at 278.

304 Williams, *Imaging the Early Medieval Bible*, 186–7.

305 Ibid. See also J. Camps (ed.), *Cataluña en la Época Carolingia: Arte y Cultura antes del Románico* (Barcelona, 1999), 542.

306 A description of the illumination is provided by Williams, *Imaging the Early Medieval Bible*, 187, together with a photograph of the decorated Omega initial. The Canon Tables also suggest Carolingian influence.

307 A further fragment of the Oña Bible is housed in Rome; Escalona, Veláquez Soriano and Juárez Benítez, 'Identification of the Sole Extant,' 278.

308 Donald A. Bullough, *The Age of Charlemagne* (London, 1980), 102.

309 Nees, 'Problems of Form,' 127.

310 Richard Marsden, *The Text of the Old Testament in Anglo-Saxon England* (Cambridge, 1995), 21.

311 Van Liere, 'Biblical Exegesis,' 165.

312 Williams, *Imaging the Early Medieval Bible*, 187.

313 Loewe, 'Latin Vulgate,' p. 126. See also Brenda Deen Schildgen, *Power and Prejudice: The Reception of the Gospel of Mark* (Detroit, MI, 1999), 87.

314 Mary Garrison, 'The Emergence of Carolingian Latin Literature and the Court of Charlemagne (780–814),' in McKitterick, *Carolingian Culture*, 111–40, at 119.

315 Nees, 'Problems of Form,' 132. Nees notes that forty-six Bibles survive, together with eighteen gospel books, all from the period 800–53.

316 Van Liere, 'Biblical Exegesis,' 165.

317 McKitterick, 'Carolingian Renaissance,' 155.

318 Ibid.

319 See later in the text. For a discussion of other liturgies, see Andrew Louth, *The Church in History Volume Three: Greek East and Latin West, the Church AD 681–1071* (New York, 2007), especially 199–200.
320 Collins, *Early Medieval Spain*, 84–6.
321 Neil Allies, 'The Monastic Rules of Visigothic Iberia: A Study of Their Text and Language,' Unpublished PhD thesis, University of Birmingham, 2009, 33–41.
322 A further rule was probably composed by St Leander of Seville, who wrote a rule for the instruction of his sister and her companions. However, the main legislators for Visigothic monasticism were Isidore and Fructuosus; Joseph F. O'Callaghan, *A History of Medieval Spain* (New York, 1975), 81–2.
323 The rules derived from Fructuosus were particularly influential and enduring in monastic institutions in Portugal and Galicia and were followed until the late eleventh century; Robert Taft, *The Liturgy of the Hours in the East and West: The Origins of the Divine Office and Its Meaning for Today* (Collegeville, MN, 1993), 119–20. See also C. J. Bishko, 'The Pactual Tradition in Hispanic Monasticism,' in C. J. Bishko (ed.), *Spanish and Portuguese Monastic History, 600–1300* (London, 1984), 1–43.
324 The spread of such houses in the ninth and tenth centuries and the clusters of monasteries that were established in north-eastern Iberia is discussed by Antonio Linage Conde, *Los orígenes del monacato benedictinoen la Península Ibérica Vol. 3* (León, 1973). By the tenth century at least eighteen monastic houses had been established in Catalonia (Ibid., 509). See also Adam J. Kosto, *Making Agreements in Medieval Catalonia: Power, Order, and the Written Word 1000–1200* (Cambridge, 2004), 6.
325 Walker, *Views of Transition*, 22.
326 Walker quotes from a letter written by Gregory in 1074 (Reg. i, ep. LXIV, *PL* vol. 148, col. 340), in which he implies that the Mozarabic rite (which is not referred to by name) is an aberration and that Spain needs to return to its apostolic roots; ibid., 40, n. 25.
327 Ibid.
328 Dominique Iogna-Prat, *Order and Exclusion: Cluny and Christendom Face Heresy, Judaism and Islam (1000–1150)*, translated by Graham Robert Edwards (New York, 2002), 28.
329 A twelfth-century example is Gonzalo Pérez Gudiel, archbishop of Toledo (1280–99), See Susan Boynton, 'Restoration or Invention? Archbishop Cisneros and the Mozarabic Rite in Toledo,' *Yale Journal of Music & Religion*, Vol. 1, No. 1 (2015), 5–30. Boynton's paper is largely about later efforts to revive and restore the rite and the perseverance of one man, Francisco Ximénez de Cisneros, archbishop of Toledo from 1495 to 1517 to do so.
330 Heather Ecker also refers to the liturgy being 'perceived as Adoptionist by association' (Heather Ecker, 'How to Administer a Conquered City in al-Andalus: Mosques, Parish Churches and Parishes,' in Cynthia Robinson and Leyla Rouhi (eds), *Under the Influence* (Leiden, 2005), 45–66 at 57. However, no links seem to have been made between this particular heresy and the Mozarabic liturgy by Pope Gregory himself; Ramón Gonzálvez, 'The Persistence of the Mozarabic Liturgy in Toledo after A.D. 1080,' in Bernard F. Reilly (ed.), *Santiago, Saint-Denis, and Saint Peter: The Reception of the Roman Liturgy in León-Castile in 1080* (New York, 1985), 157–86, at 160.

331 Lynette Bosch discusses the history and form of the Mozarabic liturgy in Lynette M. F. Bosch, *Art, Liturgy and Legend in Renaissance Toledo* (University Park, PA, 2000), 55–6.
332 Walker, *Views of Transition*, 222–3. The demise of the Mozarabic liturgy is discussed by Roger Collins in relation to a specific manuscript copied in 1050 and acquired by the monastery at Silos. This codex is a copy of a *Liber Ordinium* or service book of the Mozarabic liturgy and demonstrates the way that the liturgy evolved over time and may have been influential after 1080; Roger Collins, 'Continuity and Loss in Medieval Spanish Culture: The Evidence of MS Silos, Archivo Monástico 4,' in Roger Collins and Anthony Goodman (eds), *Medieval Spain: Culture, Conflict and Coexistence* (Basingstoke, 2002), 1–22.
333 The veneration of saints and their feast days in Mozarabic and Roman manuscripts are enumerated by Walker, *Views of Transition*, 74–90.
334 Ibid., 72.
335 Burman following Manuel Díaz y Díaz and Klaus Reinhardt who concluded that in the late eleventh century there was a resurgence of the Visigothic-Latin heritage cultivated by the Mozarab scholars, 'especially in the Visigothic liturgy – and adopted new exegetical methods and tools introduced to Toledo by newly-arrived French clerics.' Thomas E. Burman, *Religious Polemic and the Intellectual History of the Mozarabs, c 1050–1200* (Leiden, 1994), 196.
336 Walker examines six manuscripts containing Mozarabic and Roman folios that are held at the abbey at Silos and notes the codicological alteration (the representation of the entire liturgical year in a single volume *breviarum* and *missale*) would have signalled this determination towards conformity; Walker, *Views of Transition*, 72.
337 Walker cites the treatment of the veneration of the Virgin Mary; although the Mozarabic feast was discontinued following the imposition of Roman liturgy, re-dedication and continuity rather than introduction (for example, at the monastery at Silos) were features of 'an expanded cult of the Virgin in the number of wooden statues of the Virgin dating from the late eleventh or twelfth century found in this area of northern Spain' (ibid., 78).
338 Ibid., 211.
339 Collins, 'Continuity and Loss,' 12.
340 Reilly, *Santiago, Saint-Denis, and Saint Peter*, xi.
341 O'Callaghan, *Medieval Spain*, 311.
342 Pamela A. Patton, *Romanesque Cloister: Cloister Imagery and Religious Life in Medieval Spain* (New York, 2008), 203 *ff*.
343 Beverley Mayne Kienzle, *Cistercians, Heresy and Crusade in Occitania, 1145–1229* (Woodbridge, 2001), 58.
344 Jean Leclercq O. S. B., *The Love of Learning and the Desire for God: A Study of Monastic Culture* (New York, 1974), 89.
345 *Benedicti Regula*, Book 9 (*PL* Vol. 66, 0424A).
346 Leclercq, *Love of Learning*, 89.
347 Stanley G. Payne, *Spanish Catholicism: An Overview* (Madison, WI, 1984), 16.
348 R. A. Fletcher, *The Quest for El Cid* (Oxford, 1989), 72.
349 Kenneth Stevenson, 'The Transfiguration Sermon of Peter the Venerable, Abbot of Cluny,' in Melanie Ross and Simon Jones (eds), *The Serious Business of Worship: Essays on Honour of Bryan D. Spinks* (London, 2010), 78–67, at 78.
350 Peter's aim was to encourage Bernard to refute the heresy and error of Islam; Iogna-Prat, *Order and Exclusion*, 338.

351 The five items comprise: *Fabulae Sarracenorum* and *Lex Sarracenorum* (the Qur'an), both translated by Robert of Ketton (c. 1110–c. 1160); *Liber generationis Mahumeth* and *Doctrina Muhammad*, translated by Hermann of Dalmatia (c. 1100–c. 1160) and *Epistola Sarraceni et Rescriptum Christiani*, translated by Archbishop Raymond; Dominique Iogna-Prat, *Order and Exclusion*, 338–9.

352 Dale B. Martin, *Pedagogy of the Bible: An Analysis and Proposal* (Louisville, KY, 2008), 63.

353 According to Isidro Bango Torviso, the number of Cistercian houses at the thirteenth-century peak of the order's expansion and influence was 742, of which almost a third (241) were in Francia; Isidro Bango Torviso, 'Historia del Arte Cristiano en España,' in Ricardo Garcia-Villoslada (ed.), *Historia de la Iglesia en España* (Madrid, 1982), 497–572, at 565.

354 O'Callaghan, *Medieval Spain*, 311. Early Cistercian monasteries in Catalonia include Santa María de Poblet (1151), Santa Creus (begun in 1158) and Santa María de Vallbona (originally Benedictine, it transferred to the Cistercian order in 1163).

355 Stephen Tobin, *The Cistercians: Monks and Monasteries of Europe* (New York, 1996), 73.

356 Ann W. Astell, *The Song of Songs in the Middle Ages* (New York, 1995), 19.

357 These include the Augustinian prior and Christian thinker, Richard of St Victor (d. 1173) and his predecessor at the Parisian abbey, Hugh of St Victor (c. 1096–1141). Ibid. The factors that contributed to the success with which the Cistercian Order was able to establish itself so effectively and rapidly within the peninsula are discussed by Javier Fernández Conde and Antonio Linage; Javier Fernández Conde and Antonio Linage, 'La Renovación Religiosa,' in Garcia-Villoslada (ed.), *Historia*, 339–401, especially 352–4.

358 R. A. Fletcher, *The Episcopate of León in the Twelfth Century* (Oxford, 1978), 12.

359 Manuel Díaz y Díaz cites an early example and discusses the possible circumstances in which an important manuscript containing a fragment of the book of Samuel (León Cathedral MS 22, folio 33) may have made its way from Córdoba to León in 883; Manuel C. Díaz y Díaz, 'La circulation des manuscrits dans la Péninsule Ibérique du VIIIe au XIe siècle,' in *Cahiers de civilisation médiévale*, Vol. 12 (1969), 219–41, at 223.

360 Leclercq, 'Exposition and Exegesis,' 197; Mark Kauntze, *Authority and Imitation: A Study of the Cosmographia of Bernard Silvestris* (Leiden, 2014), 94.

361 John Sullivan, 'Reading Habits, Scripture and the University,' in David Lyle Jeffrey and C. Stephen Evans (eds), *The Bible and the University* (Milton Keynes, 2007), 216–32, at 224.

362 Peter Linehan, *The Ladies of Zamora* (Manchester, 1997), 24. During the latter part of the reign of Alfonso X (r. 1252–84), the number of books steadily increased but was still minimal and outside the scope of this study; see Antonio Matilla Tascón, *Guía-Inventario de los Archívos de Zamora y su Provincia* (Madrid, 1964).

363 For the purposes of this reference, this study assumes that Juan was the author of the *CLRC*; in Chapter 5 of this volume, there is a discussion of the authorship of this chronicle.

364 Arnaldo's dates at Toledo and Astorga suggest more than mere coincidence and point to the two prelates being one and the same person; Simon Barton and Richard Fletcher, *The World of El Cid: Chronicles of the Spanish Reconquest* (Manchester, 2000), 160.

365 Demetrio Mansilla, 'Dos Códices Visigóticos de la Catedral de Burgos' (*Hispania Sacra* 2, 1949), 381–418.
366 Smaragdus's *Collectiones* were produced during the period of Carolingian reform and rely on multiple patristic authorities; see Aaron J. Kleist, *Striving with Grace: View of Free Will in Anglo-Saxon England* (Toronto, 2008), 16. Walker notes that during the ninth and tenth centuries, many Spanish manuscripts used homilies from Smaragdus; in addition to those in the library at Burgos are two (now in the Bibliothèque Nationale in Paris) believed to have come from Silos; there is an illuminated tenth-century manuscript now held at Córdoba Cathedral. She also considers that what are found in these codices are familiar excerpts from Smaragdus's *Collectiones* and not necessarily taken from complete texts of his work; Walker, *Views of Transition*, 87.
367 Mansilla, 'Dos Códices Visigóticos,' 391–2.
368 Smaragdus, *Collectiones Epistolarum de Tempore de Sanctio, Praefatio* (*PL* Vol. 102, Col. 13C).
369 Walker, *Views of Transition*, 87.
370 'The codex, which today we refer to as Signature 1, contains evidence of having been exceptionally lengthy (and detailed) and, although heavily mutilated, contains 146 pages'; Mansilla, 'Dos Códices Visigóticos,' 382.
371 The displacement of other Western European eucharistic rites in the Latin west from the eighth century onwards is traced by Paul Bradshaw and Maxwell E. Johnson, *The Eucharistic Liturgies: Their Evolution and Interpretation* (Collegeville, MN, 2012), 196–9.
372 Mansilla, 'Dos Códices Visigóticos,' 385.
373 Those folios that can be attributed to Bede are as follows: Homilies on Lk. 1.39, Mt. 2, Jn 20.22; for Gregory: Homilies on Lk. 3.3 *ff*, Mt. 10.5 *ff*, Lk. 10.1 *ff*, Mt. 22.2 *ff*, Lk. 21.25 *ff*; for Jerome: Commentary on Mt. 16.13 *ff*; for Augustine: Tractates on Jn 6.5-13, 15.1 *ff*, Jn 1.17 and a sermon (*In Dei dedicationis ecclesie*); Ibid., 408–15.
374 Ibid., 384.
375 Walker, *Views of Transition*, 88. His commentary on the Rule of St Benedict was used in the tenth century to formulate a Spanish monastic rule followed by a community of women at Nájera. Walker notes that the adaptation to the Spanish tradition substituted Mozarabic canonical hours in place of the performance of the daily office; see especially 99, n. 67.
376 Demetrio Mansilla, *Catálogo de los Códices de la Catedral de Burgos* (Madrid, 1952), 82–3.
377 Ibid., 68.
378 Klaus Reinhardt and Ramón Gonzálvez, *Catálogo de códices bíblicos de la catedral de Toledo* (Madrid, 1990). There are also many codices that are dated from the thirteenth century and later.
379 Ibid., 240–1.
380 Ibid., 81 *ff*. A further text also from the thirteenth century is now in Toledo, though it is believed to have originated in Italy and is unlikely to have been available to our chroniclers. Perhaps the most famous Bible, the *Biblia rica de Toledo*, held in the Treasury at Toledo Cathedral, is a thirteenth-century romance text and outside the scope of this study; Emily C. Francomano, 'Castilian Vernacular Bibles in Iberia, c. 1250–1500,' in Boynton and Reilly, *Practice of the Bible*, 315–37, at 325.
381 Reinhardt and Gonzálvez, *Catálogo de códices bíblicos*, 222–3.
382 Ibid., 223.

383 Ibid.
384 Ibid., 277 f.
385 Ibid. There is also a range of other works attributed to, among others, John Chrisostum, Eucherius of Lyon and Paul of Egypt (ninth-century codex) and a ninth-century copy of a tract against Adoptionism by Etherius, bishop of Osma and Beatus of Liébana, *Contra Elipandum*.
386 This is more widely known as the *Allegoriae super tabernaculum Moysi* and represents a systematic elaboration on Bede's *De tabernaculo* (written *c.* 720); Alastair Minnis, *Medieval Theory of Authorship: Scholastic Literary Attitudes in the Later Middle Ages* (Philadelphia, PA, 1988), 64.
387 Reinhardt and Gonzálvez, *Catálogo de Toledo*, 276.
388 Iogna-Prat, *Order and Exclusion*, 338.
389 Smalley, *Gospels in Schools*, 62–3. A late-thirteenth-century copy of Peter Comestor's most famous work, *Historia Scholastica* (with appendices) written in Gothic Minuscule is to be found in the cathedral library at Burgos, though we cannot know whether Juan of Osma, Rodrigo or Lucas had access to any earlier copies; see Mansilla, *Catálogo de los codices de la Catedral de Burgos*, 79–83.
390 The example is from Exod. 26.36 which provides the opening of Peter's *Distinctiones super Psalterium*. The Vulgate reads: '*facies et tentorium in introitu tabernaculi de hyacintho et purpura coccoque bis tincto et bysso retorta opere plumarii*'/ 'Thou shalt make also a hanging in the entrance of the tabernacle of violet, and purple, and scarlet twice dyed, and fine twisted linen with embroidered work' (Douay-Rheims); Peter's *Distinctiones* begins: 'Facies michi tentorium in introitu thabernaculi quatuor pretiosis coloribus contextum'/ Create a tent (or screen) at the entrance of the tabernacle continuously woven from four colours of great value.
391 Julio Pérez Llamazares, *Catálogo de los Códices y Documentos de la Real Colegiata de San Isidoro de León* (León, 1923).
392 Other extant codices composed at the scriptorium at Valeranica by Florentius include Smaragdus, *Liber Homiliarum*, which also contains Paul the Deacon's *Homilies* and Fulgentius of Ruspe's *De incarnatione Filii Dei* currently held in the Cathedral Archive at Córdoba; Escalona, Velázquez Soriano and Juárez Benítez, 'Identification of the Sole Extant,' 277–9.
393 Collins, *Early Medieval Spain*, 59.
394 Leander of Seville (*c.* 534–*c.* 600) was a brother of Isidore and his predecessor as Bishop of Seville.
395 Karen Eva Carr, *Vandals to Visigoths: Rural Settlement Patterns in Early Medieval Spain* (Ann Arbor, MI, 2002), 132. See also Wood, 'A Family Affair.'
396 'si autem peccaverit in te frater tuus vade et corripe eum inter te et ipsum solum si te audierit lucratus es fratrem tuum'/ 'Moreover if they brother shall trespass against thee, go and tell him his fault between thee and him alone: if he shall hear thee, thou hast gained thy brother.'
397 For example Jn 4.5, 6 (Jesus at the well of Samaria), Jn 8.1, 2 (beginning: 'Jesus went unto the mount of Olives'), Jn 2.13 ('And the Jews' Passover was at hand, and Jesus went up to Jerusalem'), Jn 7.4 ('Now about the midst of the feast Jesus went up into the Temple and taught'), Jn 9.1 ('And as Jesus passed by, he saw a man which was blind from his birth'), Jn 11.1 (the sickness of Lazarus), Jn 8.12 (Jesus as the Light of the World), Jn 7.32 ('The Pharisees heard that the people murmured such things concerning him; and the Pharisees and the chief priests sent officers to take him'), Jn 7.1 (Jesus remaining in Galilee, far from the Jewish authorities), Jn 10.22 (Jesus at the

Feast of the Dedication) and Jn 12.1 (his return to Bethany following the resurrection of Lazarus).
398 Antonio Viñayo González, Vicente García Lobo and Ana Suárez González, *Patrimonio cultural de San Isidoro de León* (León, 2001), 303–6.
399 Matthew Bailey, *The Poetics of Speech in the Medieval Spanish Epic* (Toronto, 2010), 31, 32. According to the story, Isidore of Seville appeared before Martín in a vision and was able to enhance his understanding of scripture.
400 Reinhardt and Gonzálvez, *Catálogo de Toledo*, 10.
401 E. Ann Matter, *The Voice of My Beloved: The Song of Songs in Medieval Christianity* (Pennsylvania, PA, 1990), 36.
402 Marcia L. Colish, *Studies in Scholasticism* (Aldershot, 2006), 81.

Chapter 2

1 This is the most used title for the work, though it should perhaps be referred to as the *Historia Legionense* (for that is what it is). The term *Silense* is confusing since it suggests an unlikely provenance.
2 The *Chronicle of Alfonso III*, which is not analysed in this study, is anonymous and survives in two related versions, the *Rotense* and *Ad Sebastianum*. It was possibly written by or under the direction of Alfonso III, king of the Asturias (r. 866–910) and covers a period of almost two hundred years between the accession of King Wamba (672) and that of Alfonso himself (966). The date of the chronicle and the king's contribution to it are discussed by Roger Collins, 'Literacy in Early Medieval Spain', in Rosamond McKitterick (ed.), *The Uses of Literacy in Early Medieval Europe* (Cambridge, 1990), 109–33, at 128 (including n. 93 that refers to the research of earlier scholars, Antonio Ubieto Arteta, Juan Gil Fernández and José Luis Moalejo). See also Richard Fletcher, 'A Twelfth-Century View of the Spanish Past', in J. R. Maddicott and D. M. Palliser (eds), *The Medieval State: Essays Presented to James Campbell* (London, 2000), 147–62, at 154.
3 The most recent guide to the contents of this corpus is F. J. Fernández Conde, *El Libro de los Testamentos de la catedral de Oviedo* (Rome, 1971), 50–69.
4 The versions used are *Historia Silense*, ed. by Dom Justo Pérez de Urbel, O. S. B. and Atilano González Ruiz-Zorrilla (Madrid, 1959) and *Crónica del obispo Don Pelayo*, ed. by Benito Sánchez Alonso (Madrid, 1924).
5 It is possible to compare the two versions, which are shown in parallel in Pérez de Urbel's edition, *Sampiro su crónica y la monarquia leonesa en el siglo X* (Madrid, 1952), 275–346.
6 The *Historia Compostelana* was commissioned by Archbishop Diego Gelmírez (archbishop of Santiago de Compostela, 1120–49) in the 1140s and records the prelate's life and times; Fletcher, *The Quest for El Cid* London, 1989), 188. The *Chronicon Iriense* is a short twelfth-century text also from Compostela and covering a period from the origins of the see of Compostella in 561 and concludes in 982. It is often appended to the *Historia Compostelana*, though it also exists in other twelfth-century codices; Sholod, *Charlemagne in Spain*, 129. A further twelfth-century chronicle, *Historia Roderici*, is devoted to the life of Rodrigo Díaz de Vivar (1043–1099), though the date of composition is uncertain.

7 The *Crónicas anónimas de Sahagún* was composed at the Benedictine monastery of Sahagún in *c.* 1118. See Antonio Ubieto Arteta (ed.), *Crónicas anónimas de Sahagún* (Zaragoza, 1987). This was scarcely a narrative account of the history of León-Castile, dealing with the marriage between Urraca and Alfonso I of Aragón as well as providing details of a rebellious society pitched against an expedient alliance with Alfonso which involved a written defence of the monks themselves against the excesses of the local nobility; see Bernard F. Reilly, *The Kingdom of León-Castilla Under Queen Urraca 1109-1126* (Princeton, NJ, 1982), 47 and Thomas N. Bisson, *The Crisis of the Twelfth Century: Power, Lordship, and the Origins of European Government* (Princeton, 2009), 251.
8 Eduard López Pereira (ed.), *Crónica mozárabe de 754 edición citica y traducción* (Zaragoza, 1980).
9 Luís A. García Moreno, 'Spanish Gothic Consciousness among the Mozarabs in al-Andalus (VIII-X Centuries),' in Alberto Ferreiro (ed.), *The Visigoths: Studies in Culture and Society* (Leiden, 1999), 303-23, at 310.
10 Barton and Fletcher, *El Cid*, 12. The author began his work following the death of Alfonso VI in 1109 and references to Cardinal Rainerius (later Pope Paschal II) suggest that he was still alive when the chronicle was written. Since Paschal died in 1118, the date of composition is likely to have been during this nine-year period.
11 Linehan considers it a mistake for the author to have been drawn back to these early periods since it meant that he was not able to complete or properly order his history; Linehan, *History and the Historians*, 128-9.
12 *HS*, 120.
13 Simon Barton, 'Islam and the West: A View from Twelfth-Century León', in Simon Barton and Peter Linehan (eds), *Cross, Crescent and Conversion, Studies in Medieval Spain and Christendom in Memory of Richard Fletcher* (Leiden, 2008), 153-74, at 153.
14 Barton and Fletcher, *El Cid*, 11.
15 *HS*, 159.
16 Linehan, *History and the Historians*, 158, n. 9.
17 Ibid., 128-9; Barton and Fletcher, *El Cid*, 9.
18 Linehan, *History and the Historians*, 129.
19 John Wreglesworth, 'The Chronicle of Alfonso III and Its Significance for the Historiography of the Asturian Kingdom, 718-910 AD' (Unpublished DPhil thesis, University of Leeds, 1995), argues that we have in the *HS* a finished piece of work which is obliquely critical of Alfonso VI. This is summarized by Richard Fletcher, though he distances himself from it; Barton and Fletcher, *El Cid*, 22-3.
20 A palaeographical argument posited by Manuel Díaz y Díaz in 1961 is cited by Fletcher to support three arguments relating to the text in *HS* – firstly, the honour with which León is accorded, secondly the suggestion that the church of San Isidoro in León is linked with the author and thirdly because of his observations of Alfonso's elder sister Urraca who was linked to the community at San Isidoro. Elsewhere, he is even more emphatic about a Leonese provenance: 'the so-called *Historia Silense* ... was composed not at the monastery at Silos, but in León about 1120.' R. A. Fletcher, 'Reconquest and Crusade in Spain, c. 1050-1150,' *Transactions of the Royal Historical Society*, 5th series, 37 (1987), 31-47, at 40.
21 Linehan, *History and the Historians*, 128.
22 J. M. Canal Sánchez-Pagín, '¿Crónica Silense o Crónica Domnis Sanctis?', *Cuadernos de Historia de España*, 63-4 (1980), 94-103 at 99-100. Canal is given qualified support by Raymond McCluskey, 'Malleable Accounts: Views of the Past in Twelfth-Century

Iberia,' in Paul Magdalino(ed.), *The Perception of the Past in Twelfth-Century Europe* (London, 1992), 211–25 at 214, n. 13. Intriguingly, John W. Williams also finds the Sahagún provenance compelling, precisely because it was so favoured by Fernando I and Alfonso VI: 'With the *Silense* we are close to the Leonese court,' from John W. Williams, 'León: The Iconography of a Capital,' Thomas N. Bisson (ed.), *Cultures of Power: Lordship, Status and Process in Twelfth-Century Europe* (Philadelphia, PA, 1995), 231–58 at 234. Yet Williams appears to conflate the competing claims of León and Sahagún (also dismissing the Silos connection completely). The implication is that although the author is likely to have come from Sahagún, the *HS* may have been written at the community of Isidoro.

23 He wrote and compiled his work at a Castilian or Leonese monastery and possibly at León itself, or Sahagún; Raymond McCluskey, 'Malleable Accounts: Views of the Past in Twelfth- Century Iberia,' in Paul Magdalino (ed.), *The Perception of the Past in Twelfth-Century Europe* (London, 1992), 214.

24 Barton and Fletcher, *El Cid*, 16, 17.

25 Notably the seventh-century (or possibly ninth-century) hagiographical work, the *Vitas Sanctorum Patrum Emeritensium*, a copy of which is likely to have been housed at Alfonso III's royal library; ibid.

26 A summary of comparisons with a more exhaustive list is made by Pérez de Urbel and Ruiz-Zorrilla (eds), *HS*, 55, 56.

27 Ibid., 55.

28 Ibid., 56.

29 Ibid., 8.

30 Ibid., 55. Pérez de Urbel draws attention to two NT sources: Gal. 4 and 1 Cor. 10.13, citing a version of 1 Cor. 10.13 which the author of *HS* has tried unsuccessfully to trawl from his memory. The misremembered text from Corinthians occurs in the author's narrative, 131–6.

31 Ibid., 54–60.

32 Ibid., 118–19.

33 John Wreglesworth, 'Sallust, Solomon and the *Historia Silense*,' in David Hook (ed.), *From Orosius to the Historia Silense, Four Essays on Late Antique and Early Medieval Historiography* (Bristol, 2005), 97–129, at 104.

34 Linehan, *History and the Historians*, 128.

35 Fletcher, 'A Twelfth-Century View', 154–5.

36 Aengus Ward, *History and Chronicles in Late Medieval Iberia: Representations of Wamba in Late Medieval Narrative Histories* (Leiden, 2011), 80.

37 *HS*, 129–30.

38 Ibid., 204.

39 Ibid., 199–200.

40 Ibid., 191.

41 Wreglesworth, 'Sallust, Solomon and the *Historia Silense*,' 110.

42 The author identifies, by way of contrasting idleness with industry, arrogance with fairness and lust and avarice with restraint, some general principles about the conduct of kings (*HS*, 114). In chapter 30, he argues that although the reign of Vermudo II had been distinguished by the king's confirmation of canon law as well as his qualities of mercy and judgement, the sins of his people meant that they would be overwhelmed by the Saracens (*HS*, 172). The conduct of God's people, as well as that of kings, is important in the establishment of a peaceful Christian kingdom.

43 *HS*, 204.

44 Ibid.
45 Ibid., 191.
46 *HS*, 191. See also Björn Weiler, *Paths to Medieval Kingship in Medieval Latin Europe, c. 950–1200* (Cambridge, 2021), 172.
47 Ibid., 204.
48 2 Chron. 7.18: 'I will raise up the throne of thy kingdom, as I promised to David thy father, saying: There shall not fail thee a man of thy stock to be ruler in Israel' (Douay-Rheims).
49 *HS*, 119. The author of the *HS* uses the singularity of leaders of Christians and Moors to elevate their current status and legacy, his description of Almanzor for whom we have already noted the author's admiration being a case in point: 'and their king who assigned a false name for himself [that is] Almanzor, was like no-one in the past nor anyone who is to come' (*HS*, 172).
50 For example, chapter 75 where the author writes of the marriage of Fernando I to the Infanta Sancha which enhance his claims about the legitimacy of their son, Alfonso VI. The description is embellished by a brief quotation from Sallust *Bellum Iugurthinum, 11, 3* ('because he was unequal to his maternal stock'), but the account is otherwise straightforward (*HS*, 179).
51 Barton and Fletcher, *El Cid*, 19.
52 *HS*, 136.
53 Ibid., 141.
54 The kings were Favila I (r. 737–739, Alfonso's brother-in-law); Aurelius (r. 768–774), his nephew; and Silo (r. 774–783), his son-in-law.
55 Wreglesworth, 'Sallust, Solomon and the *Historia Silense*,' 106–7.
56 1 Kgs 11.9-13, 29-37.
57 Fletcher, 'A Twelfth-Century View,' 156.
58 *HS*, 118.
59 Ibid. The term *vuluptabro* (translated by Fletcher as 'swinish wallowing') is derived from 2 Pet. 2.22: 'the sow that was washed to her wallowing in the mire [*volutabro*].'
60 Jer. 44.9.
61 Deut. 4.24, 26: 'For the Lord thy God is a consuming fire, even a jealous God ... I call heaven and earth to witness against you this day, that ye shall soon utterly perish from off the land.'
62 Jer. 44.11.
63 Barton and Fletcher, *El Cid*, 36, n. 76.
64 *HS*, 172.
65 Wreglesworth, 'Sallust, Solomon and the *Historia Silense*,' 104.
66 At the beginning of the book of Baruch, immediately before Bar. 1.1.
67 *HS*, 113. Here there is an echo of Prov. 18.4, 'The words of a man's mouth are as deep waters, and the wellspring of wisdom as a flowing brook.' However, this link is not noted in Pérez de Urbel's edition.
68 Ibid.
69 Bar. 3.12.
70 Bar. 3.14.
71 *HS*, 113, n. 3.
72 'vniuerse vie Domini misericordia et veritas sunt' *(HS)* and 'omnes senitae Domini misericordia et veritas' (Vulgate).
73 Barton and Fletcher, *El Cid,* 24.
74 Pérez de Urbel, *Sampiro*, 313.

75 Roger Collins describes Ramiro II as 'probably the most outstanding, at least in military terms, of the Leonese kings' (Collins, *Early Medieval Spain*, 237, 238). Indeed, the author of *HS* does not directly refer to Ramiro in blinding his half-brother and cousins, only to the corruption of some in high places; there is also the suggestion that the king's actions were justified in the light of past events. The increased Muslim presence in León followed Sancho I's refusal to sign a treaty with the Muslims negotiated by his brother Ordoño III (r. 951–956) and the Caliph of Córdoba, Abd-al-Rahman III; Sancho was deposed but even after his restoration in 960, his kingdom was in a weakened position; Norman Roth, *Jews, Visigoths and Muslims in Medieval Spain, Cooperation and Conflict* (Leiden, 1994), 84, 85.
76 *HS*, 173.
77 Patrick Henriet notes 'good kings [are] invariably ... good warriors'; Patrick Henriet, '*Historia Silense*: "The History of Silos,"' in David Thomas and Alex Mallett (eds), *Works on Christian-Muslim Relations: A Bibliographical History, Vol. 3 (1050–1200)* (Leiden, 2009), 370–4, at 371.
78 This is part of Fletcher's summary of Wreglesworth's position, which he does not find totally compelling. Since the declared aim of the chronicle was to exalt Alfonso VI, it may be wiser to describe Fernando as '*a* true hero' (along with Alfonso VI and Reccared); Barton and Fletcher, *El Cid*, 23. Alfonso VI is described in the *HS* as the most distinguished of all the kings who guided the church in a Catholic manner; *HS*, 119.
79 Robert Plötz, '*Pregrinato ad Lumina Sancti Jacobi*,' in John Williams and Alison Stones (eds), *The Codex Calixtus and the Shrine of St James* (Tübingen, 1992), 37–50, at 48.
80 C. J. Bishko, 'The Liturgical Context of Fernando I's Last Days according to the So-called «Historia Silense»,' in *H.S.*, XVII–XVIII (1964–5), reprinted in C. J. Bishko (ed.), *Spanish and Portuguese Monastic History 600–1300* (London, 1984), 47–59, at 48.
81 *HS*, 208.
82 Bishko, 'Fernando I's Last Days', 50.
83 1 Chron. 29.11-16.
84 *HS*, 118. There is an echo here of Ps. 79.7: 'For they have devoured Jacob and laid waste his dwelling place.'
85 Ibid.
86 Ibid., 113.
87 Ibid.
88 Ibid.
89 Most cited verses are: 2 Macc. 12.41-46, 2 Tim. 1.18, Mt. 12.31, Lk 16.19-26 and 23.43, 1 Cor. 3.11-15 and Heb. 12.29. The idea had an ancient provenance but perhaps its most eloquent advocate was Gregory the Great: 'Regarding certain less grievous faults, we must believe that prior to the Judgement there is a purging fire'; Gregory the Great, *Dialogorum Libri* IV (*PL* Vol. 77, 0396).
90 'Operiantur sicut deployde [may be emended to *deploide*] confusione sua'; *HS*, 114. This is not a precise rendering of the Vulgate and may be taken from another version or from memory, the verse from Ps. 109.29 is clearly the one the author intended to cite ('induantur adversarii mei confusione et operiantur quasi indumento confusione sua'/ 'Let mine adversaries be clothed with shame, and let them cover themselves with their own confusion, as with a mantle').
91 Deut. 32.22.
92 Deut. 32.24.

93 *HS*, 118. In one of his sermons, Augustine, also recalling the deluge, confirms that few will be saved: 'Without doubt, there are only a few who will be saved'; Sermo CXI (*PL* 38, 0641). See also Jer. 44.11.
94 Ibid.
95 *HS*, 113–14 (Introducción).
96 Wreglesworth, 'Salust, Solomon and the *Historia Silense*', 101.
97 *HS*, 116–17.
98 Ibid., 129–30.
99 Henriet, '*Historia Silense*', 370–4.
100 Henriet notes that this is the first historiographical reference to Julian, the Visigothic refugee in Tingitana whose daughter had been raped by King Rodrigo; ibid., 371.
101 *HS*, 128.
102 Ibid., 173. Treachery as a key element in the foundation myth of medieval Iberia is much discussed by Geraldine Hazbun, *Narratives of the Islamic Conquest of Medieval Spain* (New York, 2015). An example is her discussion, especially on 87–95 of the late-thirteenth-century historiographical text, *Crónica de Veinte Reyes*,
103 The historicity is very uncertain here. The *HS* dates the invasion of Almanzor as 966 (*defuncto Sancio rege*/on the death of King Sancho) even though he did not fully consolidate his position in al-Andalus until 981. Ramiro is likely to have been about twenty-two years of age when Almanzor invaded so the charge that he was 'adhuc teneris annis' at the time needs clarification. Almanzor sacked León in 988, four years after Ramiro had been deposed in favour of Vermudo II.
104 *HS*, 174.
105 Perhaps the most celebrated enemy is Saladin (Ṣalāḥ ad-Dīn Yūsuf ibn Ayyūbi, c. 1138–1193) himself: 'throughout the Middle Ages, the name "Saladin" was a byword for chivalry … The contemporary chronicles – by Muslims and Christians alike – that describe his campaigns and his constant fidelity to the noblest principles of dignified warfare speak volumes' (Reza Shah-Kazemi, 'From the Spirituality of *Jihād* to the Ideology of Jihadism,' in Joseph E. B. Lumbard, *Islam, Fundamentalism and the Betrayal of a Tradition, Revised and Expanded: Essays by Western Muslim Scholars* (Bloomington, IN, 2009), 119–48 at 121). Nevertheless, ulterior motives in the adulation of a brave enemy could also be at work and Marianne Ailes alludes to the possibility of the praise of Saladin deliberately aimed at undermining the French King, Philip II Augustus (r. 1180–1223); Marianne J. Ailes, 'The Admirable Enemy? Saladin and Saphadin in Ambroise's *Estoire de la guerre sainte*,' in Norman Housley (ed.), *Knighthoods of Christ, Essays on the History of the Crusades and the Knights Templar, Presented to Malcom Barber* (Aldershot, 2007), 51–64 at 63.
106 *HS*, 127, 128.
107 Ibid., 173 and 174–5.
108 Ibid., 172.
109 Ibid., 176.
110 Ibid., 175.
111 Ibid.
112 Ramón Menéndez Pidal, *The Cid and His Spain*, trans. Harold Sunderland (Ann Arbor, MI, 1934), 458.
113 Noah is an exception who is referred to in chapter 6 of the *HS* and is discussed later in the text.
114 Gen. 37.
115 *HS*, 120.

116 Fletcher argues that this piece of narrative only makes sense if placed at the beginning of the following sentence, 'Structare etenim regum gesta' (which may be translated as 'carefully to examine the governance of kings') is added to the previous sentence; Barton and Fletcher, *El Cid*, 30.
117 Ibid.
118 Ibid.
119 Ibid., 124.
120 'Thus said David: Various are the effects of war'; *HS*, 163.
121 *HS*, 207.
122 Book I, IX:10, XII:7, XXVII:5; Book II, III:4, VII:13, XXI:2,3, XLI:3 XLI:10, XLIII:3a: Book III: VI:7, IXX:5, XXIV:8, XXXII:10, XXXII:11, XLI:6, XLIV:3 and LX:17; Isidore, *Sententiae*, Pierre Cazier (ed.), CCSL, CXI (Turnhout, 1998).
123 Including the military struggle with the Almoravids and the loss of Sagrajas (1086). In the battle of Uclés (1108), he lost considerable territory in the Cuenca region and his hapless heir, Sancho Alfonso, died on the battlefield. This was followed by the troubled reign of his daughter Urraca (r. 1109–27).
124 Wreglesworth, 'Sallust, Solomon and the *HS*', 122–3.
125 Simon Barton, *The Aristocracy in Twelfth-Century León and Castile* (Cambridge, 1997), 47, n. 107.
126 Ibid., 104.
127 William Purkis, 'Eleventh- and Twelfth-Century Perspectives on State Building in the Iberian Peninsula,' *Reading Medieval Studies* 36 (2010), 57–75, at 62.
128 *HS*, 125.
129 Fletcher emends to *dolore* (Barton and Fletcher, *El Cid*, 34, n. 61).
130 Ibid., 123.
131 Ibid., 180.
132 Ibid. We are reminded of Ramiro's illegitimacy later in the same paragraph: 'Ramirus aldulterinus ille.'
133 Gen. 16.3. According to Gen. 16.2, Sarai urged Abraham to 'go in unto my maid.'
134 Gen. 25.5.
135 *HS*, 180.
136 Ibid.
137 Barton and Fletcher, *El Cid*, 20.
138 Ibid., 19.
139 Ibid., 41, n. 106.
140 *HS*, 118.
141 Ibid.
142 *HS*, 182.
143 Jer. 50.26 (the injunction in the *HS cumulandum struem fuisse* is not very close to the Vulgate 'redigite in acervos' and may have been mediated by another text) and Isa. 57.1 (here the text is slightly closer: 'Ecce quomodo periit iustus et nemo considerat'; the Vulgate reads: 'iustus perit et nemo est qui recogitet in corde').
144 Details of Pelayo's early life are unknown and even elements of his career are uncertain. Fernández-Conde speculates that Pelayo's family may have been related to the patrons of what are described as the great monasteries in the western Asturias ('la familia de Pelayo, que en tal caso estaría relacionada con los "patronos" de los grandes monasterios de las Asturias occidentales: San Juan de Corias y Santa María de Lapedo'). Fernández-Conde, *El Libro de los Testamentos de la catedral de Oviedo*, 37. An earlier paper by Marcos Martínez supplies further information: Marcos G.

Martínez, 'Regesta de Don Pelayo, Obispo de Oviedo,' *Boletín del Instituto de Estudios Asturianos* 18 (1964), 211-48. Evidence in his account of the final days of Alfonso VI in the *Chronicon* that he knew and admired the city of León: Barton and Fletcher, *El Cid*, 66.
145 See Soledad Suárez Beltrán, 'Los origenes y la expansión del culto a las reliquias de San Salvador de Oviedo,' in J. I. Ruíz de la Peña (ed.), *Las peregrinaciones a Santiago de Compostela y San Salvador de Oviedo en la Edad Media* (Oviedo, 1993), 37-55.
146 Barton and Fletcher, *El Cid*, 65.
147 This is discussed by Sholod, *Charlemagne in Spain*, who believes that Pelayo's references to certain events in the ninth century that are not referred to elsewhere have contributed his reputation as a falsifier (130).
148 In addition to Fernández Conde's frequent references to Pelayo's forgeries in *Libro de los Testamentos*, other studies include Luis Vásquez de Parga, *La División de Wamba* (Madrid, 1943) and Demetrio Mansilla, 'La supuesta metrópoli de Oviedo,' *Hispania Sacra* 8 (1955), 259-74.
149 Simon Barton, *Conquerors, Brides, and Concubines: Interfaith Relations and Social Power in Medieval Iberia* (Philadelphia, PA, 2015), 76-7.
150 Ibid., 123.
151 Sholod, *Charlemagne in Spain*, 130. See also Roger Collins's comments on Pelayo's tampering with Sampiro's Chronicle: Roger Collins, *Caliphs and Kings: Spain, 796–1031* (Chichester, 2012), 58.
152 Peter Linehan, 'Religion, Nationalism and National Identity in Medieval Spain and Portugal', Stuart Mews, *Studies in Church History* 18 (Oxford, 1982), 161-99, at 162.
153 Barton and Fletcher, *El Cid*, 73. See especially *Cronicon*, 67, 68.
154 This is evidenced by his copious information on the family of Vermudo II, where genealogical detail mingles with the misdeeds of Vermudo himself (Ibid., 76, 77).
155 *HS*, 118.
156 *Chronicon*, 58.
157 Gen. 37.5-10 (for Joseph's dreams) and Gen. 40 (for the dreams of pharaoh's servants).
158 Gen. 41–43.
159 Gen. 40.
160 *Chronicon*, 58. The term 'super faciem terre'/ 'upon the face of the earth' is resonant of the Vulgate and may be compared with a phrase in Job 37.12, 'super faciem orbis terrarium.' This is rendered rather awkwardly in the AV as 'upon the face of the world in the earth,' though 'habitable world' (RV and NEB) seems a more natural translation, especially as *orbis* can allude to mankind and might explain the use of *terrarum* (genitive plural).
161 *HS*, 113.
162 *Chronicon*, 58.
163 Richard Fletcher, *The Episcopate*, 73.
164 *Chronicon*, 68. Certainly, the idea of Oviedo's pre-eminence as a result of the sin of the people of Spain is argued in the *Chronicle of Samiro* (Redacción Pelagiana): Pérez de Urbel, *Sampiro*, 289-302.
165 The most obvious being from the *Magnificat*: 'He hath holpen his servant Israel, in remembrance of his mercy' (Lk. 1.54).
166 *Chronicon*, 68.
167 Barton and Fletcher, *El Cid*, 79.
168 2 Sam. 7.14, 15.

169 2 Sam. 7.15: 'I took it from Saul.'
170 An important principle of mercy and vengeance is stated in Deut. 7.9, 10.
171 Variously suggested as sodomy in *Historia Compostelana* and collaborating with Muslims by Rodrigo Jiménez de Rada, the issue of the testing of the bishop is discussed by Barton, *El Cid*, 76, n. 8 and Linehan, *History and the Historians*, 118, 119.
172 *Chronicon*, 60.
173 Ibid., 87.
174 Ezek. 34.23.
175 This may also refer to the unstable period following the marriage of Queen Urraca to Alfonso I of Aragón in 1109, described in 'Vida y obra del obispo Pelayo,' Fernández Conde, *El Libro de los Testamentos de la cathedral de Oviedo*, 48, in which Pelayo resolutely took the queen's part. As Raquel Alonso Álvarez points out, it was a passage also inspired by the biography of Martin of Tours; in Raquel Alonso Álvarez, 'El obispo Pelayo de Oviedo (1101–1153): historiador y promotor de códices illuminados,' in Roberto J. López and Miguel Taín Guzmán (eds), *El legado de las catedrales* (Universidad de Santiago de Compostela, 2010), 331–50, at 340.
176 Ibid.
177 Jn 7.53.
178 *Chronicon*, 60. The most heinous of crimes is usually interpreted as homosexuality. This allegation is made more explicit in the *Historia Compostelana*, although the historical context is at odds with Pelayo's account; E. Falque Rey (ed.), *Historia Compostelana*, CCCM 70 (Turnhout, 1988), 9–10. See also Linehan, *History and the Historians*, 118–19.
179 Jn 7, especially verses 32–52.
180 Jn 7.2.
181 Jn 7.44.
182 *Chronicon*, 80–1.
183 Jn 20.17.
184 *Chronicon*, 63.
185 The verification of this union, and the circumstances surrounding it, are disputed; Simon Barton, 'Marriage across Frontiers: Sexual Mixing, Power and Identity in Medieval Iberia,' *Journal of Medieval Iberian Studies*, Vol. 3, no. 1 (March 2011), 1–25, at 12.
186 *Chronicon*, 64.
187 The chasm between Christian and Muslim is emphatically expressed: 'Noli me tangere, quia ego Christiana et tu paganus es,' Juan A. Estévez Sola (ed.), *Chronica Naierensis* CCCM 71A (Turnholt, 1995), 147.
188 Julia Bolton Holloway, Joan Bechtold and Constance S. Wright, *Equally in God's Image: Women in the Middle Ages* (New York, 1990), 217.
189 Jn 20.12.
190 Fletcher, *The Episcopate*, 73.
191 *Chronicon*, 80–1.
192 Richard G. Walsh, *Mapping Myths of Biblical Interpretation: Playing the Texts 4* (Sheffield, 2001), 35.

Chapter 3

1. The principal edition used will be *Chronica Adefonsi Impertoris*, edited by A. Maya Sánchez, in *Chronica* Hispana saeculi XII, Part I, CCCM 71 (Turnhout, 1990), 109–248.
2. The importance of the theme of loyalty within the chronicle is acknowledged by Gregory B. Kaplan, 'Friend "of" Foe', 153–72.
3. Juan Gil Fernández (ed.), *Prefatio de Almaria*, in *Chronica Hispana saeculi XII*, Part I, CCCM 71 (Turnhout, 1990), 249–67.
4. Brian Powell, *Epic and Chronicle: the Poema de mio Cid and the Crónica de Veinte Reyes* (London, 1983), 16.
5. Antonio Maya Sánchez, in editing just the prose sections, aims to present to philologists and historians a text of the greatest value and reliability: 'My purpose, therefore ... has been ... to try to establish a text of maximum possible authority for philologists and historians.' *CAI*, 112.
6. Daniel Baloup is unequivocal: 'The author of the *Chroncia Adefonsi* is a prelate, contemporary to the events, equipped with a solid biblical and patristic culture'; Daniel Baloup, 'Reconquête et croisade dans la *Chronica Adefonsi Imperatoris* (ca. 1150)', in Georges Martin and Jean Rondil (eds), *Cahiers de linguistique et de civilisation hispaniques médiévales* 25 (2002), 453–80, at 458.
7. Randall Rogers, *Latin Siege Warfare in the Twelfth Century* (Oxford, 1992), 158.
8. An example of the way in which biblical phraseology is used by the author of the *Poema de Mio Cid* is cited by Colin Smith as an example of the influence of the *CAI*: 'For example, his lines (i.e. those of the author of the *Poema de Mio Cid*) about the Cid's siege of Valencia:
bien la çerca mio Çid, que non i avia hart,
viedales exir eviedales entrar (II.1204–5)
echo precisely the words of the *Chronica*', in Colin Smith, *The Making of the Poema de Mio Cid* (Cambridge, 1983), 199. Thus, although the siege of Valencia in 1138 by the king of Aragón is not described in the *CAI*, the influence of the event is asserted: 'No doubt, its capture is seen (by the author of the *CAI*) as an inspiration for the besiegers of Almería' (Powell, *Epic and Chronicle*, 17).
9. Antonio Ubieto Arteta, 'Sugerencias sobre la *Chronica Adefonsi Imperatoris*,' in *Cuadernos de Historia de España* (25.6.1957), 317–26, at 319–20.
10. Reilly, *Queen Urraca*, 13.
11. The siege of Almería was a notable example and the interests of those who formed the Christian alliance in the capture of the port city will be discussed shortly.
12. These are broad distinctions between the two books of the *CAI*. For a fuller discussion of how the themes of the two books relate to each other, see *El Cid*, 149–50. During the exploration of these two books, reference will be made to exceptions and variations that occur in the narratives.
13. Its closeness to the Latin Vulgate in terms of the author's organization of sentences, literary cadences and biblical vocabulary is analysed by M. Pérez González, 'Influencias clásicas y bíblicas en la *Chronica Adefonsi Imperatoris*,' in *I Congreso Nacional de Latín Medieval*, ed. M Pérez González (León, 1995), 349–55, especially at 351–4.
14. William J. Purkis, *Crusading Spirituality in the Holy Land and Iberia, c.1095–c.1187* (Woodbridge, 2008), 178. Such local traditions include the bestowing of the

patronage of St James on those who fought against the Infidel for the liberation of the peninsula and the idea that such activity was in the spirit of Charlemagne.
15 That is Bishop Arnaldo of Astorga (d. 1152).
16 Reference is also made to *Barchinonensem consulem* (the count of Barcelona, Ramon Berenguer IV) and *Guillelmum Montispesulani dominum* (Count William VI of Montpelier) to whom Arnaldo was despatched as an envoy. *CAI*, 247.
17 Ibid.
18 Francisco de Sota, *Chronica de los Príncipes de Asturias y Cantabria* (Madrid, 1681), 559.
19 Manuel Risco, *Historia de Alfonso VII el Emperador* (León, 1792; 1792 facsimile), 9–10.
20 Angel Ferrari, 'El Cluniacense Pedro de Poitiers y la *Chronica Adefonsi Imperatoris* y *Poema de Almería*', *Boletín de la Real Academia de la Historia*, CXXII (1963), 154–93.
21 Maya Sánchez refers to the entirely farcical suggestion of the author being an invention of the seventeenth-century Jesuit and Spanish pseudo-historian, Jerónimo Román de la Higuera (Maya Sánchez, *CAI*, 114).
22 J. M. Canal Sánchez-Pagín, 'Elías, canónigo rotense, posible autor de la *Chronica Adefonsi Imperatoris*', *Anuario de Estudios Medievales* 30/2 (2000), 735–55. This argument rests on the similarity of the *vita* with the *CAI*. Not only would the king have trusted the writer of the *vita* and the relative paucity of such potential writers in the area of León, he would also have been favoured by his queen, Berenguela of Barcelona (1116–1149), 742–3.
23 Peter Linehan, Review of *Chronica Hispana Saeculi XII. Part 1* in *Journal of Theological Studies*, Vol. 43 (1992), 731–7.
24 A combination of the chronicler's awareness of events described – as well as what is omitted – including that of the Almería Campaign itself, his selective geographical and historical knowledge, his use of Hispano-Arabic terms, Catalan sympathies and the convergence and piecing together of known biographical and chronological information suggests that 'the new incumbent of the Astorgan see was none other than Arnaldo of San Servando' (*El Cid*, 159–61).
25 H. Salvador Martínez, *El 'Poema de Almería' y la épica románica* (Madrid, 1975, *El PA*, 121.
26 The author refers to a cross containing fragments of the true cross having been stolen from Sahagún and there is the suggestion that he was acquainted with knowledge of the monastery: 'In the days of war he (e.g. the king of Aragón, Alfonso I) had seized it from the shrine of the martyrs Facundus and Primitivus which is in Leonese territory near the River Cea.' *CAI*, 43. The author however, makes no claim or suggestion that he had ever been a religious at the monastery.
27 Salvador Martínez, *El PA*, 110.
28 Smith, *The Making of the Poema*, 15.
29 Barton and Fletcher, *El Cid*, 158.
30 However, Antonio Ubieto Arteta notes that although the author writes as if the Empress Berenguela were alive throughout his account, he infers that the chronicle must have been completed by 1149, the year of her death. Ubieto Arteta, 'Sugerencias', 317–26 at 325.
31 Salvador Martínez, *El PA*, 122, n. 90. See also 126–8. Reasons for the abrupt interruption are also discussed by Luís Sánchez Belda (ed.), *Chronica Adefonsi Imperatoris* (Madrid, 1950), xx.
32 Sánchez Belda, *CAI*, xx.

33 Heather Bamford, *Cultures of the Fragment: Uses of the Iberian Manuscript 1100–1600* (Toronto, 2018), 38.
34 Reilly, *Kingdom of León-Castilla*, 101.
35 Richard Hitchcock, *Mozarabs in Medieval and Early Modern Spain* (London, 2008), 89–90.
36 John France, *The Crusades and the Expansion of Catholic Christendom, 1000–1714* (Abingdon, 2005), 146. See also *El Cid*, 249, n. 220.
37 Linehan, *History and the Historians*, 271. According to the author of *Chronica Latina Regvm Castellae*, this weakness seems to have been a result of the division rather than because of the character of Alfonso's two sons (his two sons weakened the emperor's kingdom and occasioned many killings and evils that befell the Spains). Although this suggests that the sons' conduct as kings caused the calamities that followed their accession, it is clear from the next sentence that the root cause of the weakness was Alfonso's decision to divide the kingdom; Luis Charlo Brea (ed.), *Chronica Latina Regvm Castellae* (CCCM 73), *Chronica Hispana saeculi XIII* (Turnhout, 1997), 41.
38 Ibid., 22.
39 This is part of the aftermath of failure that followed the victory at Almería that is discussed by Simon Barton, 'From Tyrants to Soldiers of Christ: The Nobility of Twelfth-Century León-Castile and the Struggle against Islam' (Nottingham Medieval Studies v.44, 2000), 28–48, at 39.
40 Linehan, *History and the Historians*, 246.
41 Fletcher, *The Episcopate*, 26, 27.
42 Twelfth-century Scotland is an interesting comparison: Nicholas Mayhew notes: 'historians of medieval Scotland have difficulty joining the major historical debates of the day because of the lack of data,' in Nicholas J. Mayhew, 'Scotland: Economy and Society,' in John Bintliff (ed.), *A Companion to Archaeology* (Oxford, 2003), 107–24 at 118–19. Although this deficiency of material is acknowledged by Dauvit Broun, he suggests that narrative could have been more widespread, citing the loss of Scottish administrative records when they were shipped to England during the reign of Edward I (r. 1272–1307); Dauvit Broun, 'The Absence of Regnal Years from the Dating Clause of Charters of the Kings of Scots, 1195–1222,' in John Gilligham (ed.), *Anglo-Norman Studies XXV. Proceedings from the Battle Conference, 2002* (Woodbridge, 2003), 47–64, at 50–1.
43 Chris Wickham, 'The Sense of the Past in Italian Communal Narratives,' in Paul Magdalino (ed.), *The Perception of the Past in Twelfth-Century Europe* (London, 1992), 173–89, at 174.
44 Ibid., 175.
45 Fletcher, *The Episcopate*, 27.
46 Samuel Astley Dunham, *History of Spain and Portugal, Vol. IV* (London, 1835), 170.
47 The veracity and unique perceptions of the author's descriptions of the border skirmishes in al-Andalus in 1133 are praised by Manuel Criado de Vale in *Historia de Hita y su Arcipreste: vida y muerte de una villa mozárabe* (Guadalajara, 1998), 61.
48 Lk. 1.2.
49 Acts 1.3.
50 *CAI*, 149. Peréz González considers that such statements, together with the biblical reminiscences that illuminate the narrative of the *CAI*, suggest that he was an eyewitness to the many events he describes; Peréz González, 'Influencias Clasicas y Biblicas,' 351.
51 *CAI*, 149.

52 Lk. 24.49.
53 Maya Sánchez, *CAI*, 150, n. 1 and in his scriptural index, 276.
54 Peréz González, 'Influencias Clasicas y Biblicas,' 351.
55 *CAI*, 150.
56 Ibid., 248.
57 *Poema*, 255.
58 See earlier in the text, n. 57.
59 Ibid.
60 *Poema*, 255.
61 Linehan, Review of *Chronica Hispana Saeculi XII*, 734. Salvador Martínez however, though not undermining Linehan's doubts about a single authorship, believes that it is the poem that represents the more conciliatory account: 'the coexistence for the benefit of Muslims and Christians, without annihilation of the former'; Salvador Martínez, *El PA*, 91.
62 *CAI*, 247.
63 This is a version of Eugene III's 1145 bull *Quantum praedecessores* that called for the Second Crusade (*PL*, Vol. 180, 1064–6) and was in part aimed at crusade and the reunion of churches. This is discussed by James Powell, 'Innocent III and Alexius III: A Crusader Plan That Failed,' in Marcus Bull and Norman Housley, *The Experience of Crusading, Book 1* (Cambridge, 2003), 96–102, at 97.
64 The pope's call for crusade purity which is supported by Bernard of Clairvaux is discussed by Purkis, *Crusading Spirituality*, 172–3. It seems certain too, that St Bernard actively promoted the Second Crusade: 'St Bernard not only preached the Second Crusade in the name of Eugenius III in 1145, but he was also closely related to the emergence of a new religious institute in the Church, that of the soldier-monk.' Jordan Aumann O. P., *Christian Spirituality in the Catholic Tradition* (London, 1985), 113.
65 *CAI*, 247.
66 *Poema*, 256. Although references to *maiores* and *minores* are indications of rank, in this context they almost certainly refer to age. This is certainly the sense in which the terms are used in the Spanish translation ('ruegan a los mayores e incitan a los jóvenes para que vengan todos') by Sanchez Belda, *Chronica Adefonsi Imperatoris*, 189.
67 *Poema*, 256.
68 Ibid.
69 The papal bull issued by Pope Eugenius III in 1145 at the beginning of the Second Crusade. The following is an extract of a translation provided by Purkis: 'Those who resolve to begin such a holy work ought to take no interest in multi-coloured clothes or minivers or golden or silver arms.' From Purkis, *Crusading Spirituality*, 174.
70 Commenting on Caffaro's secularism, Marvin B. Becker notes: 'Here, for the first time, was disclosed a communal sensibility linking the honor and fortune of a mercantile order with civic well-being.' Marvin B. Becker, 'Individualism in the Early Italian Renaissance,' in James Banker and Carol Lansing (eds), *Florentine Essays: Selected Writings of Marvin B. Becker* (Ann Arbor, MI, 2002), 258–84, at 269.
71 Purkis, *Crusading Spirituality*, 173.
72 Ibid., 165, 176.
73 *CAI*, 195.
74 Ibid.
75 Serafín Bodelón, *Literatura Latina de la Edad Media en España* (Madrid, 1989), 107.

76 Some of this section and from the section in Chapter 1 on exegesis and Beatus of Liébana appears in the following publication: Alun Williams, 'Advancing Dogs and Rushing Lions: Animals and the Imagery of Conflict in the *Poem of Almeria*,' in Antonella Liuzzo Scorpo (ed.), *A Plural Peninsula: Studies in Honour of Professor Simon Barton* (Leiden, forthcoming). I am grateful to Brill Publishers (Leiden) for agreeing to my use of this material.

77 Peter K. Klein, 'Introduction: The Apocalypse in Medieval Art,' in Susan Boynton and Diane J. Reilly (eds), *The Practice of the Bible in the Middle Ages: Production, Reception & Performance in Western Christianity* (New York, 2011), 188.

78 For a discussion of other possible authorial sources, see Ubieto Arteta, 'Sugerencias,' 320.

79 Alexandra Cuffel, *Gendering Disgust in Medieval Religious Polemic* (Notre Dame, IN, 2007), 199.

80 Tova Forti, *Animal Imagery in the Book of Proverbs* (Leiden, 2008), especially 52–3, 57–67.

81 David A. Wacks, *Framing Iberia: Māqamāt and Frametale Narratives in Medieval Spain* (Leiden, 2007), 123.

82 Simona Cohen believes that this imagery is linked to medieval guilt culture and its gloomy view of the human condition: 'animal images, in general, and those on water receptacles, in particular, were essential in conveying this perception.' Simona Cohen, *Animals as Disguised Symbols in Renaissance Art* (Leiden, 2008), 202.

83 For example, the writings of Paul Alvarus.

84 The book of Proverbs is a particularly rich source: 'Proverbs mentions many members of the animal kingdom. These include birds (sparrow, eagle/vulture, brook-raven), insects (ant, locust), reptiles (serpent/viper), wild animals (bear, lion, pig, dog, deer, rock-cony), domesticated animals (ox, goat, donkey, horse) and animals whose identification is problematic.' Forti, *Animal Imagery in the Book of Proverbs*, 11.

85 J. Kenneth Kuntz, 'Growling Dogs and Thirsty Deer: Uses of Animal Imagery in Psalmic Rhetoric,' in Robert L. Foster and David M. Howard (eds), *My Words Are Lovely: Studies in the Rhetoric of the Psalms* (New York, 2008), 46–62, at 55.

86 *Poema*, 256.

87 'Why art thou cast down, O my soul? and why art thou disquieted within me? hope thou in God; for I shall yet praise him, who is the health of my countenance, and my God' (Ps. 42.11).

88 Ps. 42.10.

89 Mk 7.27: 'But (Jesus) said unto her, Let the children first be filled: for it is not meet to take the children's bread and to cast it unto the dogs.'

90 Mk 7.28: 'And she answered and said unto him, Yes, Lord: yet the dogs under the table eat of the children's crumbs.' It is interesting how the woman responds with the term catelli (literally 'small dogs' or 'puppies') which has the effect of turning a slur into a term of endearment.

91 John Block Friedman, *The Monstrous Races in Medieval Art and Thought* (New York, 1981), 67.

92 D. H. Strickland, *Saracens, Demons and Jews: Making Monsters in Medieval Art* (Princeton, NJ, 2003), explores the range of deployment of this term and suggests that it may have been used descriptively as much as being a deliberate insult (159–60).

93 'irrational Christians, sons of dogs' (*CAI*, 228, 229). This took place, according to the author at a place known as Almodóvar de Tendas (*Almodouar de Tendas*), some 130 km NNW of Jaén, though the exact site or date of the conflict is uncertain.

94 *Poema*, 256.
95 This is suggested in certain Arabic sources. A variant twelfth-century hadith states: 'Angels Do Not Enter a House in which There Is a Dog or an Idol,' in Muhammad Ali Maulana, *A Manual of Hadith: The Traditions of the Prophet Muhammad* (London: Curzon Press, 2nd edn, 1978), 367, n. 2.
96 'The polemical weapons that Christianity had aimed against Judaism were now (i.e. from the Muslim invasion of Iberia) put into action to combat Islam. In view of the overwhelming negative view of dogs in Judaism and Islam, it is hardly surprising that Christians utilized them metaphorically to belittle both faiths.' Alberto Ferreiro, 'Simon Magus, Dogs, and Simon Peter', in Alberto Ferreiro (ed.), *The Devil, Heresy and Witchcraft in the Middle Ages: Essays in Honor of Jeffrey B. Russell* (Leiden, 1998), 45–91 at 64.
97 Believed to have been written before 850 and described by K. B. Wolf as 'a short and singularly unsympathetic life of Muhammad.' K. B. Wolf, 'Christian Views of Islam in Early Medieval Spain,' J. V. Tolan (ed.), *Medieval Christian Perceptions of Islam* (London, 1996), 85–108 at 93.
98 Gil, Juan Fernández (ed.), Alvarus, Epistulae, VI.9.10-11, *Corpus Scriptorum Muzarabicorum* 1 (Madrid, 1973), 201.
99 *Liber Apologeticus Martyrum* 16.53-4, 57-8, *CSM* I 2, 485–6.
100 *Talis* really means 'of such a sort,' and, often, according to context, 'so exceptional' and sometimes 'so bad' (i.e. not just 'so great'); so a plausible translation would be 'that such a great and exceptional prophet should.' *Tantus ac talis* would therefore suggest an ironic application.
101 Pilar Riesco Chueca (ed.), *Passio Argenteae et comitum*, in *Pasionario hispánico*, no. 19 (1995), 253–66, at 260.
102 Ann Christys, 'Cordoba in the Vita Vel Passio Argenteae,' in Frans Theuws, Mayke De Jong and Carine van Rhiju (eds), *Topographies of Power in the Early Middle Ages* (Leiden, 2001), 119–36, at 126.
103 *Poema*, 257.
104 Ibid., 258.
105 Ibid.
106 This is a reference to the Asturian contingent and its constant piety ('Irruit interea non ultimos impiger Astur'), but it may also allude to San Salvador of Oviedo whose aid the Asturians seek; ibid., 259.
107 Gen. 6-9. For a discussion of the resemblance of Ovid's account of the flood and the biblical narrative, see Caroline Jameson, 'Ovid in the Sixteenth Century,' in. J. W. Binns (ed.), *Ovid* (Abingdon, 1973), 210–24 at 210 *ff*.
108 *Poema*, 257.
109 Ibid.
110 Wacks cites works such as *Cantar de Mio Cid*, *Poema de Fernán González*, *Libro de Alexandre* and *Calila* (translated from Arabic into Castilian in the mid-twelfth century) as well as the use of the constellation Leo in *Judizios de las estrellas*, so the complex literary imagination associated with the lion (and possibly other animals too) may have been a source with which the author of the *CAI* had some familiarity; Wacks, *Framing Iberia*, 121.
111 Isa. 53.6, Jer. 11.19.
112 1 Kgs 22.17. See also Num. 27.17: 'sheep which have no shepherd.'
113 *Poema*, 257.

114 Ovid, *Metamorphoses*, Book 1, II. 304–5 in R. J. Tarrant (ed.), *Ovid's Metamorphoses* (Oxford Classical Texts, 2004). There are also echoes of the flood described in Gen. 7 and 8.
115 In addition to the comparisons with pursuing wolves and rushing lions, there are references to the activity of other creatures (*PA*, 257 and 263).
116 Martín de Riquer, *Manual de Heráldica Española* (Barcelona, 1942), 29.
117 *Poema*, 258: *Sunt in uexillis et in armis imperatoris Illius signa, tutantia cuncta maligna.*
118 James Todesca, 'The Crown Reviewed: The Administration of Coinage in León-Castile, c. 1085–1200,' in James Todesca (ed.), *The Emergence of Leó-Castile, c. 1065–1500: Essays Presented to J. F. O'Callaghan* (London, 2015).
119 *Poema*, 257.
120 Ibid., 258.
121 Barton and Fletcher, *El Cid*, 252.
122 Gen. 49.9.
123 Num. 24.9.
124 *Poema*, 260.
125 Ibid., 258.
126 Mic. 5.8.
127 2 Sam. 17.36.
128 Jer. 12.8.
129 *Poema*, 259.
130 Amos 3.8.
131 Rev. 5.5.
132 Isa. 11 contains prophecies which describe the Messiah as 'a rod from the stem of Jesse' and 'a root of Jesse' (*radix Iesse*) (vv. 1 and 10), Jesse being the father of David.
133 *Poema*, 258.
134 Ibid.
135 Ibid.
136 Giles Constable, *Crusaders and Crusading in theTwelfth Century* (Farnham and Burlington VT, 2008), 245; Barton and Fletcher, *El Cid*, 253 n. 16.
137 *CAI*, 149–50.
138 Lk 24.49.
139 One of those charged with spiritual guidance was Bishop Arnaldo himself, who may have been the author of the *CAI*; *Poema*, 267.
140 *CAI*, 149.
141 Barton and Fletcher, *El Cid*, 151.
142 *CAI*, 197.
143 *Poema*, 258.
144 *CAI*, 151, 152, 154, 156, 158, 173 and 204.
145 *Poema*, 265.
146 *Wis.* 12.22.
147 *Poema*, 265.
148 Though there are occasions in the main chronicle when the themes like rejoicing, judgement and revenge converge (e.g. each one … with great gladness and in the triumph of conquest, praising and praising God, who had bestowed to the king and those (with him) vindication and vengeance); *CAI*, 169.
149 Alfonso is seen as the equal of the Frankish king with whom appropriate comparison is made: 'Hic Adefonsus erat, nomen tenet imperatoris, facta sequens Caroli, cui

competit equiparari.' Their equality in arms and strength (*armorum ui*) as well as their comparable fame in war (*Gloria bellorum gestorum par fuit horum.*) ensured the veracity of such a comparison, though Charlemagne receives no further mention (*PA*, 255).

150 McCluskey, 'Malleable Accounts,' 218.
151 Joseph F. O'Callaghan, *A History of Medieval Spain* (New York, 1975), 232. Lineage is not explicitly referred to, though the phrase *Mente fuere pares* (*Poema*, 255) suggests an equality that seems to complement other traits and which were common to both men.
152 *Poema*, 266.
153 Saif al Dawla, heir to the Hūddid dynasty in Zaragoza which was displaced by Almoravids in 1110. The circumstances of his exile from Zaragoza are discussed by Richard Messier in *The Almoravids and the Meaning of Jihad* (Santa Barbara, CA: Praeger, 2010), 157.
154 *CAI*, 162. The use of the adjective *quidam*, with its overtones of anonymity and secondary significance, may suggest Zafadola's true position, notwithstanding his lineage, *vis-à-vis* the emperor.
155 *CAI*, 164.
156 Ibid.
157 Ibid., 163.
158 Barton, 'Islam and the West', 170–1.
159 Brian Catlos, *The Victors and the Vanquished: Christians and Muslims in Catalonia and Aragon, 1050–1300* (Cambridge: Cambridge University Press, 2004), 75.
160 Israel Burshatin, 'The Docile Image: The Moor as a Figure of Force, Subservience, and Nobility in the Poema de Mio Cid,' in *Kentucky Romance Quarterly*, Vol. 31 (1984), 269–80, at 272.
161 For discussion of a range of terms applied to Muslims in the *HS*, see Fletcher, 'A Twelfth-Century View,' 159.
162 For example, Lucas de Túy uses the term in *Chronicon Mundi*, though Olivia Remie Constable suggests that this was derived from a more widespread application in earlier texts, Olivia Remie Constable, 'Perceptions of the Umayyads in Christian Spanish Chronicles,' in Antoine Borrut and Paul M. Cobb (eds), *Umayyad Legacies: Medieval Memories from Syria to Spain* (Leiden, 2010), 105–30, at 119.
163 Gen. 21.13.
164 *CAI*, 189.
165 Jer 1.1-3.
166 Colin Smith, 'The Geography and History of Iberia in the *Liber Sancti Jacobi*,' in Maryjane Dunn and Linda Kay Davidson (eds), *The Pilgrimage to Compostela in the Middle Ages* (London, 1996), 23–42, at 39, n. 12.
167 'Concerning Moorish ethnology, it is interesting to point out that a Spanish synonym for Almoravid is *Moabita*, which again draws our attention to the Biblical people … We might also recall another synonym for Almoravid: Murabit or Marabout which phonetically corresponds to Moabite/Moabitarum.' From José V. Pimenta-Bey, 'Moorish Spain: Academic Source and Foundation for the Rise and Success of Western European Universities in the Middle Ages,' in Ivan Van Sermita (ed.), *Golden Age of the Moor Vol. 11* (Piscataway, NJ, 1991), 182–247, at 204.
168 Ann Christys, 'The History of Ibn Habib and Ethnogenesis in Al-Andalus,' in Richard Corradini, Max Diesenberger and Helmut Reimitz (eds), *The Construction of*

Communities in the Early Middle Ages: Texts, Resources and Artefacts (Leiden, 2003), 323–48, at 324.
169 Gen. 9.30-38.
170 *CAI*, 169.
171 See, for example, *CAI* 206 when the so-called King of Seville (*rex Sibiliae*) collected an army of Moabites, Haragenes and Arabs, following the destruction of the land around Seville by Count Rodrigo González's troops in 1132.
172 *CAI*, 188.
173 *CAI*, 162. The term *omne semen* is an example of familiar biblical language for which there are memorable OT precedents: 2 Kgs 17.20: 'And the Lord rejected all the seed of Israel'; Ps. 22.23: 'Ye that fear the Lord, praise him; all ye the seed of Jacob, glorify him'; Jer. 2.21: 'Yet I had planted thee a noble vine, wholly a right seed.'
174 *Poema*, 258.
175 Alfonso *el Batallador*, in accordance with the wishes of Urraca's father Alfonso VI of León-Castile, had married the queen following the death of her first husband (and father of Alfonso VII), Count Raymond of Burgundy (d. 1107). The restoration of many of these towns was followed by the so-called *Paces de Támara* (Peace of Támara) signed between the two Alfonsos in 1127. This is referred to in the *CAI* (154) as well as in texts from the thirteenth and fourteenth centuries, the *De Rebus Hispaniae* and in the *Chronicle of San Juan de la Peña*; all three are considered 'tendentious sources' by Clay Stalls who argues that this event and the circumstances preceding it have not been given adequate scholarly attention; Clay Stalls, *Possessing the Land: Aragon's Expansion into Islam's Ebro Frontier under Alfonso the Battler, 1104–1134* (Leiden, 1995), 53, n. 152.
176 *CAI*, 152–3.
177 Ibid., 150.
178 See earlier in the text, 166.
179 The date of this conflict is not known, though William Purkis refers to the event as 'one encounter with the Muslims in 1132' (Purkis, *Crusading Spirituality*, 176).
180 *CAI*, 205.
181 Ibid., 207.
182 Erin Kathleen Rowe, *Saint and Nation: Santiago, Teresa of Ávila and Plural Identities in Early Modern Spain* (Philadelphia, PA, 2011), 27.
183 Alan Thacker, '*Loca Sanctorum*: The Significance of Place in the Study of Saints,' in Alan Thacker and Richard Sharpe (eds), *Local Saints and Local Churches in the Early Medieval West* (Oxford, 2002), 1–46, at 2, 8 and 13.
184 Peter Brown, *The Cult of the Saints, Its Rise and Function in Latin Christianity* (Chicago, IL, 1981), 108.
185 See Patrick J. Geary, *Furta Sacra: Thefts of Relics in the Central Middle Ages* (Princeton, NJ, 1990), 28.
186 Benedicta Ward, *Miracles and the Medieval Mind: Theory, Record, and Event, 1000–1215* (Philadelphia, PA, 1987), 116.
187 Ibid.
188 Gen. 50.17 ('forgive (or *forget*) … the trespass of thy brethren').
189 Ps. 103.2.
190 Kevin G. Grove, *Augustine on Memory* (Oxford, 2021), 4.
191 Lk. 23.34.
192 *CAI*, 228, 229.
193 *CAI*, 227.

194 Rowe, *Saint and Nation*, 28.
195 The saint's apparition before the legendary battle is referred to by both Lucas de Túy (Lucae Tudensis, *Chronicon Mundi* (Corpus Christianorum, *Continuatio Mediaeualis* LXXIV) (Turnhout, 2003), 303 and Rodrigo de Toledo (Roderigo Jiménez de Rada, *Historia de rebus Hispanie sive Historia Gothica*, ed J. Fernández Valverde, CCCM LXII (Turnhout, 1987), 133.
196 *CAI*, 227.
197 *Poema*, 257.
198 It is so translated by Simon Barton (*El Cid*, 251) and William Purkis (*Crusading Spirituality*, 176). Luis Sánchez Belda (190) translates *dulcedine* more literally as *dulzura* rather than *benedición*.
199 Ps. 3.8.
200 Ps. 7.12,13 (Douay-Rheims).
201 *Poema*, 257.
202 According to Edward Mullins, the impact of the image of *Santiago Matamoros* 'immeasurably boosted the impact of the St James legend on Medieval and Renaissance Europe. It made him a tangible living hero, and ... offered proof of his active surveillance of the lives and fortunes of ordinary Christians.' From Edward Mullins, *The Pilgrimage to Santiago* (Oxford: Interlink, 2001), 14. Colin Smith cites a comparable image of St James, referred to in the *Estoria de España* and involving Don Alfonso of Aragón in 1231, who appears on a white horse and carrying a white banner, in a battle between Christians and Muslims and who is witnessed by both armies; Colin Smith, *Christians and Moors in Spain, Vol. II: 1195–1614* (Warminster: Aris and Phillips, 1989), 34, 35. Furthermore, there is an appearance of St James referred to in the *HS*, when he intercedes before the Battle of Coimbra (1064); here he is referred to as 'James, the knight of Christ' (*Iacobus Christi miles*), though he seems not to have been in martial guise (*HS*, 191).
203 Eph. 6.11, 12.
204 *CAI*, 149.
205 Muño Alfonso had reportedly killed his daughter for an act of infidelity and, although he was to grieve for his sin, showed no forgiveness for his daughter. In this he is compared with Jesus who forgave his enemies and urged that forgiveness be shown to the woman taken in adultery (see Jn 8.7); *CAI*, 237.
206 Ibid., 237: But Muño Alfonso mourned for this transgression for the remainder of his life, and he wanted to travel to Jerusalem on a pilgrimage.
207 Ibid.
208 Purkis, *Crusading Spirituality*, 165.
209 The quality of the influence is in doubt; Purkis draws attention to a forged letter from within the *LSJ*, the *Pseudo-Calixtus*, likely to have been written after 1124, the year of the pope's death (Purkis, *Crusading Spirituality*, 141 *ff*). See also Purkis's comments on the possibility of the *Historia Turpini* (found within the *LSJ*) providing a contemporary model on which the author of the *CAI* could draw: 'the *Historia* ought to be regarded as a kind of foundation legend for Iberian crusading that drew on the traditions of Carolingian myth and the growing popularity of pilgrimage to Compostela' (Purkis, 'Eleventh- and Twelfth-Century Perspectives,' 65. The idea is supported by Smith, 'Iberia in the *Liber Sancti Jacobi*,' 30 and 39, n. 12.
210 In *Regesta Pontificum Romanorum*, Calixtus II edited by U. Robert (Paris, 1891) II, 266–7, translation in L. and J. Riley Smith, *The Crusades. Idea and Reality, 1095–1274* (London, 1981), 73, 74.

211 Barton, *Aristocracy*, 155.
212 *CAI*, 237.
213 Judg. 16.
214 *CAI*, 172, 209.
215 Ibid., 172.
216 Mt. 21.33, Mk 12.1 and Lk. 15.13.
217 Mk 13.34.
218 Lk. 19.12.
219 *CAI*, 209.
220 Ibid., 172.
221 Barton, 'From Tyrants to Soldiers,' 35.
222 Dian Fox, *Kings in Calderón: A Study in Characterization and Political Theory* (London, 1986), 23.
223 *CAI*, 209.
224 For discussion of this, see Barton and Fletcher, *El Cid*, 217, n. 75.
225 *CAI*, 209.
226 Ibid.
227 Deut. 12.6.
228 Neh. 10.35; 12.43.
229 Ezek. 44.28; 48.14.
230 Deut. 26.8-10.
231 Rom. 8.23; 16.5; 1 Cor. 15.20; Rev. 14.4.
232 *Tob.* 1.6.
233 *CAI*, 209.
234 Ibid.
235 M.-D. Chenu argues that it was in the twelfth century that powerful Hebraic conceptions were felt throughout society and that the role of the bishop was more closely identified with moral leadership than with his work as teacher or prophet. This being so, the emphatic message of Christian sense of grievance and the need for revenge may be more easily understood; M.-D. Chenu, 'The Old Testament in Twelfth-Century Theology,' in *Nature, Man, and Society in the Twelfth Century* (Chicago, IL, 1968) 146–61, at 155–6.
236 Ps. 52.1. The Douay-Rheims version translates *in malitia* as 'in malice.'
237 Ps. 52.7.
238 Ps. 44.3.
239 Exod. 15.1, 2.
240 Amos 6.14. See also Job 8.14.
241 *Poema*, 257.
242 Mt. 2.6.
243 Lk. 2.11.
244 Gen. 19.24, 25.
245 Jon. 1.2.
246 Jon. 3.4
247 Especially Rev. 3.12 and 21.2, 4.
248 Barton, *Aristocracy*, 156.
249 Geoffrey West, 'History as Celebration: Castilian and Hispano-Latin Epics and Histories, 1080–1210 AD,' (PhD thesis, London University, 1975), 318–19.
250 *Poema*, 256, 258, 263, 267.
251 Pérez González, 'Influences Clasicas,' 351.

252 Barton and Fletcher, *El Cid*, 151.
253 The styles used by medieval authors to communicate effectively is discussed by Ernst Robert Curtius, *European Literature and the Latin Middle Ages*, trans. Willard R. Trask (Princeton, NJ, 1983), 149.
254 Purkis, *Crusading Spirituality*, 165.

Chapter 4

1 Possible influence on the *Poema de Mio Cid* is already noted; in the same work, Smith refers to the 'nobly heroic air of the *Chronica Adefonsi Imperatoris* and its integral, *Poema de Almería*' and suggests that the influence may have had wider circulation and possibly beyond Iberia. Smith, *Making of the Poema*, 127.
2 Wood argues that Isidore was well placed to elucidate on a vision of history since he had access to a great range of classical and patristic material and that much of this material still survives; Jamie Wood, *The Politics of Identity in Visigothic Spain: Religion and Power in the Histories of Isidore of Seville* (Leiden, 2012), 65*ff.*
3 Baloup, 'Reconquête et croisade,' 458.
4 Charles Wendell David (trans.), *The Conquest of Lisbon/De expugnatione Lyxbonensi* (New York, 2001).
5 Susanna A. Throop, 'Rules and Ritual on the Second Crusade Campaign to Lisbon, 1147,' in Miri I. Rubin (ed.), *Medieval Christianity in Practice* (Princeton, NJ, 2009), 86–94, at 88.
6 Fox, *Kings in Calderón*, 23.
7 Andrew Jotischky, *Crusades and the Crusader States* (London, 2017), 190.
8 For a brief discussion, see Jonathan Phillips, *The Second Crusade, Extending the Frontiers of Christendom* (New Haven, 2007), 136 and 310, n. 1. The authorship proposed by David, *The Conquest of Lisbon* 44, that is, that of Osbert, clerk of Bawdsey, is thought by modern scholars to have been superseded. Elisabeth Van Houts states unequivocally: 'The text was written in Portugal in the winter of 1147–48 by the priest Raol and addressed to Osbert of Bawdsey'; Elisabeth M. C. Van Houts, *The Normans in Europe* (Manchester, 2000), 272.
9 Purkis, *Crusading Spirituality*, 182.
10 Constable, *Crusades and Crusading*, 306.
11 *DEL*, 50–69.
12 Rogers, *Latin Siege Warfare*, 154.
13 Two speeches of importance are those of Bishop Peter of Oporto, one from the author himself and a dialogue centring chiefly on arguments for conflict proposed by Hervey of Glanvill. There is a further dialogue between John of Braga and a Muslim cleric; *De expugnatione*, 68–85.
14 The success of Ramon Berenguer in Tortosa in 1148 was achieved with Genoese support. To this we may add his victory at Lérida the following year. Phillips notes that the Genoese had commercial as well as religious motives for assisting in the victory at Tortosa: Jonathan Phillips, *The Crusades 1095–1197* (Harlow, 2002), 70.
15 F. Donald Logan, *A History of the Church in the Middle Ages* (London, 2002), 269.
16 *De expugnatione*, 70.
17 Ibid.

18 Ibid. This is lifted from Ps. 33.12, translated as follows: 'Blessed is the nation whose God is the Lord and the people whom he hath chosen for his inheritance.'
19 This antiphon (*Asperges me, Domine, hyssopo et mundabor*), was frequently used when a church was reconsecrated. For a brief discussion of Raol's liturgical content see Susanna A. Throop, 'Rules and Ritual on the Second Crusade Campaign to Lisbon, 1147,' in Miri I. Rubin (ed.), *Medieval Christianity in Practice* (Princeton, NJ, 2009), 90.
20 *De expugnatione*, 174.
21 Ibid., 99–113.
22 Ibid., 115.
23 Ibid., 114 (*federe societatis humane*).
24 Ibid.
25 Ibid., 116.
26 Though possibly Osbert of Bawdsey, believed by David to have been the author of *De expugnatione*.
27 *De expugnatione*, 149; compare with prophecies concerning the humiliation of Christ (Isa. 53.5; Mic. 7.4) as well as the synoptic references (Mt. 26.67; 27.29, 30; Mk 14.65; 15.17-19; Lk. 22.64).
28 'I press towards the mark for the prize of the high calling of God in Christ Jesus.'
29 *De expugnatione*, 152.
30 Maurilio Pérez González, *Crónica del Emperador Alfonso VII* (León, 1997), 18.
31 Maya Sánchez, *CAI*, 271–7. These refer only to the *CAI* Books 1 and 2; references in the *Poema* are not separately catalogued.
32 González, *Crónica del Emperador*, 19.
33 *De expugnatione*, 180.
34 Isa. 30.28, 29; compare 'And the bridle of error that was in the jaws of the people. You shall have a song as in the night of the sanctified solemnity' (Douay-Rheims) with ('And the bridle of error that was in the jaws of the people became a solemn song that was kept').
35 'Who changed the truth of God into a lie, and worshipped and served the creature more than the Creator, who is blessed for ever. Amen.'
36 *De expugnatione*, 182. The phrase *colla mentis* refers to spiritual or intellectual necks and is so translated by David, and is probably close in meaning to *uigo servitutis*/ 'yoke of bondage' in Gal. 5.1.
37 *Poema*, 265.
38 Mt. 20.22.
39 'This image of a cup filled with the bitter wine of suffering is taken from the Old Testament (e.g. Isa. 51.17, 22; Jer. 25.15; Lam. 4.21)'; Thomas G. Long, *Matthew* (Louisville KT, 1997), 229.
40 *CAI*, 198.
41 Ibid., 198–9.
42 Judg. 11.36 (Douay-Rheims).
43 Barton, *Aristocracy*, 175.
44 *De expugnatione*, 182.
45 *CAI*, 206.
46 Deut. 31.3.
47 Num. 31.9 (Moses subsequently imposed restrictions upon those who were permitted to remain alive).

48 'Events on the peninsula's east coast were of the utmost importance ... by the mid-1140s, Christians from all over western Europe perceived crusades in Iberia as being not only meritorious undertakings themselves, but also attractive in spite of the fact that the expeditions were no longer overtly propagated as being directly towards the Holy Sepulchre.' Purkis, *Crusading Spirituality*, 177.
49 The difficulties with the remoteness of the surviving manuscripts from the events described as well as an acknowledgement of the debate over authorship is summarized in Peter Linehan's review of *Chronica Hispana Saeculi*: 'The question of authorship, which has occasioned various bizarre theories, remains unsettled. (The editor's description of the strangest of these, concerning Pierre de Poitiers, as 'la hipótesis más brillante', must surely be tongue-in-cheek'), at 732.
50 *CAI* 216, *Poema*, 251, 252.
51 *HS*, 190–3.
52 *CAI*, 172, 209, 236–7.
53 In her discussion of the Feast of St Denis's dedication (1144), Ann Meyer notes: 'The ancient biblical idea of a temple as the resting place, throne, or palace of God serves as the conceptual basis for the use in the liturgy of specific psalms that extol Jerusalem,' in Ann R. Meyer, *Medieval Allegory and the Building of the New Jerusalem* (Woodbridge, 2003), 83.
54 Abigail Wheatley, *The Idea of the Castle in Medieval England* (York, 2004), 65.
55 Baloup, 'Reconquête et croisade', 465.
56 The potential loss of Iberian knights to the eastern crusade had been recognized by Pope Urban II in 1098 and this fear was repeated by prelates into the twelfth century even though there was a gradual merging of western and eastern crusading ideology; Phillips, *Second Crusade*, 247–8.
57 Catherine Clarke, *Literary Landscape and the Idea of England, 700–1400* (Cambridge, 2006), 90.
58 Ibid., 93: 'The extensive celebration of London as the place of Becket's birth represents a calculated attempt to wrest some of the saint's spiritual prestige back from Canterbury, the site of his martyrdom.'
59 Ezek. 38.12.
60 Adriaan H. Bredero, *Christendom and Christianity in the Middle Ages: The Relations between Religion, Church, and Society* (Grand Rapids, MI, 1994), 96.
61 Moshe Schein, *Gateway to the Heavenly City and the Catholic West* (Aldershot, 2005), 142.
62 *PL* 151; Norman Housley, *Contesting the Crusades* (Oxford, 2006), 102.
63 Dee Dyas, 'Medieval Patterns of Pilgrimage: A Mirror for Today?' in Craig G. Bartholomew and Fred Hughes (eds), *Explorations in a Christian Theology of Pilgrimage* (Aldershot, 2004), 92–109, at 94.
64 A striking example is found in Gal. 4.26: 'But which is above is free, which is the mother of us all.'
65 Lam. 1.17. This image is found elsewhere in the OT: in Ezek. 7.20-22 where the pollution seems specifically associated with the temple at Jerusalem rather than the city itself. There are oblique references in the passage from Ezekiel that continue to suggest the use of female imagery which is particularly apparent in the Masoretic text (the authoritative Hebrew text of the Jewish Bible) in which, according to David Halperin, the allusions are particularly striking; David Joel Halperin, *Seeing Ezekiel: Text and Psychology* (Philadelphia PA, 1993), 151–4.
66 Ezra 1.2, 3.

67 Mt. 5.14.
68 Ps. 122.6, 7.
69 Gal. 4.26-27.
70 Isa. 3.8.
71 Isa. 2.2: 'And it shall come to pass in the last days, that the mountain of the Lord's house shall be established in the top of the mountains, and shall be exalted above the hills; and all nations shall flow into it.'
72 Isa. 33.20 (Douay-Rheims).
73 Heb. 12.22.
74 Rev. 3.12.
75 Whether Toledo III in 589 or (as D. Rodrigo suggests) the anointing of King Wamba in 672 marks the establishment of Toledo as the urban hub of Catholic Spain is discussed by Linehan, *History and the Historians*, 387. However, Rodrigo's claim that Wamba was anointed in Toledo is not corroborated elsewhere (not, for example, by Archbishop Julian of Toledo nor by the Mozarabic Chronicler).
76 The successful siege of Toledo in 1085 is attributed to the direct intervention of Isidore in *Liber de miraculis*. Speaking through the archbishop of León, D. Cibrián, we are told: 'How by certain revelations and a warning given to the bishop of León who was devoted to the saint, that Isidore enabled King Alfonso to be victorious in Toledo.' From Lucas de Túy, *Milagros de San Isidoro*, translated into Spanish by Juan de Robles, 1525 (University of León, 1992).
77 *Poema*, 256. This is also suggested in Book 2, 59 (222) when the proclamation is made of Alfonso (Long live the emperor of León and Toledo!).
78 Ibid., 255.
79 Links between major medieval centres were common throughout Western Christendom; Catherine Clarke makes comparisons between London, Glastonbury, Troy and Jerusalem (Clarke, *Literary Landscape*, 94).
80 Linehan, *History and the Historians*, 12.
81 'Alī Bin Yusuf (1084–1143), King of Morocco (r. 1106–43) who was able to expand his empire into Iberia from 1110 onwards. His early gains were mostly reversed; Zaragoza was captured by Alfonso I of Aragón (*el Batallador*, r. 1104–34) in 1118 and Portuguese forces defeated 'Alī at the Battle of Ourique on St James' Day, 1139. Although the precise location of Ourique is uncertain, the victory of Afonso Henriques' (Afonso I, king of Portugal, d. 1185) Christian forces over the Almoravids enabled him to pursue a stable peace settlement that meant effective suzerainty of most of Portugal.
82 *CAI*, 199.
83 Ibid.
84 Jer. 19.7.
85 Prov. 29.8.
86 *CAI*, 199.
87 Jer. 18.15.
88 Dan. 10.13, 21.
89 *CAI*, 198.
90 Neh. 1–3.
91 Enrique Flórez, M. Risco, Manuel Risco, Angél González Palencia, *España Sagrada*, 51 vols (Madrid, 1747–1879), Vol. 1, 388.
92 *CAI*, 211.
93 Ibid., 223. This is a direct quotation from Mt. 23.39. See also Lk. 19.38, Ps. 117.26.

94 Mt. 21.9; Mk 11.10; Lk. 19.38.
95 Mt. 23.39; Lk. 13.35.
96 *CAI*, 180.
97 Dan. 3.7: 'the sound of cornet, flute, harp, sackbut, psaltery (see also 3.7, 10, 15). Here again, we encounter the way in which the author of the *CAI* uses the example of idolatry (in this case, the worship of Nebuchadnezzar's golden calf) to provide the literary backdrop to Christian celebration. Evil, it would seem, had been purged and instruments could perform their proper and edifying use. Or the author may have been alluding to 2 Chron. 21.27, 28.
98 *CAI*, 223.
99 Ibid., 230.
100 Ibid., 239.
101 Ibid.
102 2 Chron. 21.27, 28.
103 *CAI*, 237.
104 Ibid., 272.
105 2 Sam. 1.24.
106 Björn Weiler cites an incident recorded in the *Annals of Dunstable* which describe the extreme grief of Henry III of England over the death of Richard Marshal following injuries sustained at the Battle of the Curragh in 1234. Here a direct comparison is made with David's grief following the death of Jonathan and Saul; Björn Weiler, *Kingship, Rebellion and Political Culture: England and Germany, c. 1215–c. 1250* (Basingstoke, 2007), 84.
107 *Poema*, 257 and 258.
108 *CAI*, 181–4.
109 Stalls, *Possessing the Land*, 83.
110 Hugh Kennedy, *Muslim Spain and Portugal: A Political History of al-Andalus* (London, 1996), 153.
111 Demetrio Mansilla, *La documentacion pontificia hasta Inocencio III (965–1216)* (Rome, 1955), 43–5. Yet, however unwillingly, Toledo's ecclesiastical pre-eminence was established: 'On 15 October 1088, Urban II confirmed Toledo's status as the *Iglesia Primada de España*'; Lynette M. F. Bosch, *Art, Liturgy and Legend in Renaissance Toledo: The Mendoza and Iglesia* (University Park, PA, 2000), 31.
112 Bernard of Sédirac (d. 1125) was a French Cluniac who became Abbot of Sahagún in 1080, archbishop of Toledo in 1086 and Primate of Iberia in 1088.
113 Linehan, *History and the Historians*, 209.
114 O'Callaghan, *Medieval Spain*, 207.
115 Even this does not demonstrate that Alfonso VI had wholly transferred the seat of his authority to Toledo: 'Alfonso VI … did not make Toledo his capital, in the sense in which London, for example, was already effectively the capital of William I's England.' Linehan, *History and the Historians*, 233.
116 Emma Falque Rey (ed.), introduction, *Historia Roderici vel gesta Roderici Campidocti*, in *Chronica Hispana saeculi XII*, Part I, CCCM 71 (Turnhout, 1990), 3–98, at 48.
117 Jesús D Rodríguez-Velasco, *Order and Chivalry: Knighthood and Citizenship in Late Medieval Castile*, translated by Eunice Rodríguez Ferguson (Philadelphia, PA, 2010), 24.
118 The papacy had been able to impose the Roman rite on the church at Toledo, superseding the Visigothic or Mozarabic rite. The title, according to James Muldoon,

went some way to distance the monarchy from the pope's influence. James Muldoon, *Empire and Order: The Concept of Empire 800–1800* (Basingstoke, 1999), 56.
119 Julián Marías, *Understanding Spain* (Ann Arbor, MI, 1990), 136.
120 *CAI*, 182.
121 José A. Fernández Flórez (ed.), *Colección Diplomática del Monasterio de Sahagún (857–1300) IV (1110–1199)* (León: Centro de Estudios e Investigación 'San Isidoro': Archivo Historico Diocesano, 1991), 157.
122 *CAI*, 196–7, 223–4, 230.
123 *CAI*, 191–3 and *Poema*, 257–8.
124 The term 'Maccabees' is used to cover the two deuterocanonical books contained in the OT and not to other books that date from the third century BC of the same name and which are irrelevant to this study.
125 The differences in narrative of the two books are discussed by Jonathan A. Goldstein, *I Maccabees* (New York, 1976), 21: 'In contrast to the highly emotional narrative in Second Maccabees, the author of 1 Macc. presents a relatively sober narrative after the pattern of the historical books of the Hebrew Bible, especially the books of Samuel.'
126 See n. 41.
127 The historical background and circumstances of the revolt of the Maccabees against the Seleucid king, Antiochus Epiphanes (r. 175–164 BC) is described in 1 Macc. 1.
128 It is this proselytizing assertiveness which made them models for pre-Crusade literature too. Jonathan Phillips cites several examples, including the way William of Poitiers describes the Norman invasion of England (Phillips, *Second Crusade*, 56).
129 Janet L. Nelson, 'Carolingian Royal Funerals,' in Frans Thews and Janet L. Nelson (eds), *Rituals of Power from Late Antiquity to the Early Middle Ages* (Leiden, 2000), 131–84, at 164.
130 Reference is made to elements of the *Gesta Herwardi*, a Latin history of the life of Hereward the Wake, that draw on 'the phraseology of a biblical source (1 and 2 Macc.)' by Paul Dalton, 'The Outlaw Hereward "the Wake": His Companions and Enemies,' in Paul Dalton and John C. Appleby (eds), *Outlaws in Medieval and Early Modern England: Crime, Government and Society, c. 1066–1600* (Farnham: Ashgate, 2009), 7–36, at 12.
131 Thirteenth-century references will be considered, especially as they occur in *The Latin Chronicle of the Kings of Castile*, in the following two chapters.
132 Nicholas Morton, in his 2012 paper, 'The Defence of the Holy Land and the Memory of the Maccabees,' refers to the relative scarcity of references to the Maccabees in Iberian sources. (Taylor and Francis online: https://doi.org/10.1016/j.jmedh ist.2010.06.002), 275–93. In this respect, the allusions within *CAI* would seem to be a striking exception.
133 Phillips, *Second Crusade*, 56.
134 David Thomas and Alex Mallett, *Christian-Muslim Relations: A Bibliographical History Vol. 3 (1050–1200)* (Leiden, 2011), 612.
135 Ibid.
136 1 Macc. 3.6.
137 *CAI*, 183.
138 Ibid.
139 Ibid.
140 *CAI*, 162.
141 1 Macc. 4.24.

142 *CAI*, 158, 210, 225 and 229.
143 Reilly, *Alfonso VII*, 27.
144 Ibid.
145 Bernard McGinn, 'John's Apocalypse and the Apocalyptic Mentality,' in Richard K. Emmerson and Bernard McGinn (eds), *The Apocalypse in the Middle Ages* (New York, 1992), 3–19, at 16.
146 Identified as *Petrus* in *CAI* 1, 17, identified as Bishop Sancho de Larrosa (Barton and Fletcher, *El Cid*, 170, n. 51).
147 *CAI*, 157.
148 1 Macc. 3.18-19: 'It is an easy matter for many to be shut up in the hands of a few: and there is no difference in the sight of the God of heaven to deliver with a great multitude, or with a small company: For the success of war is not in the multitude of the army, but strength cometh from heaven' (Douay-Rheims).
149 1 Macc. 3.23.
150 Ariol Garcés is recorded as having held the tenancy at Castrojeriz from *c.* 1124 (perhaps from as early as 1116) until 1131 and of Corella (between Logroño and Zaragoza) until 1135: Antonio Ubieto Arteta, *Los Tenetes en Aragón y Navarra en el Siglos XI y XII* (Valencia, 1973), 190; A. Ubieto Arteta, *Creación y desarrollo de la corona de Aragón* (Valencia, 1987), 87. Castrojeriz is a small municipality on the *Camino de Santiago*, approximately 50 km west of Burgos.
151 1 Macc. 13.50.
152 *CAI*, 162 (he entreated the king to be favourable to him and to his men).
153 1Macc. 13.46.
154 *CAI*, 162.
155 The word is so translated in the AV and Douay-Rheims versions respectively.
156 1 Macc. 13.50: 'and when he had put them out from thence, he cleansed the tower from pollutions.'
157 *CAI*, 1.
158 Ibid., 162–3.
159 1 Macc. 1.11.
160 Ibid., 12.
161 Ibid., 13.
162 See also discussion of *sermo simplex* in Chapter 3.
163 *CAI*, 163.
164 Ibid.
165 1 Macc. 1.13 (Douay-Rheims).
166 Ibid., 1.6.
167 Ibid., 6.8.
168 *CAI*, 177.
169 It is so used in the *CAI*, Book 1, 58 (177). The two references in 1 Macc. (1.6 and 6.8) use *decidit in lectum*; the distinction between *cadere* (to fall) and *decider* (to fall) may be considered slight.
170 *CAI*, 175.
171 The career of Avengania (Ibn Ghānīya), whose Muslim forces defeated Alfonso I at Fraga (about 25 km south-west of Lérida), is noted by Hugh Kennedy; Kennedy, *Muslim Spain and Portugal*, 186–7, 189–92, 203–4.
172 Reilly, *Alfonso VII*, 267.
173 *CAI*, 170–1.
174 2 Macc. 9.5.

175 For example, 1 Sam. 16.7: 'for the Lord seeth not as man seeth; for man looketh on the outward appearance, but the Lord looketh on the heart.'
176 See also 2 Macc. 12.22 and 15.2.
177 Castilian count who fathered two illegitimate children by Queen Urraca and opponent of Alfonso VII. His defeat at Palencia in 1130 led to the confiscation of his fiefdoms and exile where he was briefly in the service of Alfonso I of Aragon. He died the following year in a jousting tournament with Count Alfonso Jordan of Toulouse outside the city of Bayonne.
178 Barton, *Aristocracy*, 115.
179 Christopher Brooke, *Europe in the Central Middle Ages 962–1154* (Abingdon, 2000), 208.
180 *CAI*, 171.
181 2 Macc. 9.5. This is one of two descriptions of the death of Antiochus and is considered to be a later, and perhaps less useful, account of the struggle than that in 1 Macc. 6.
182 2 Macc. 9.28.
183 Ibid., 13.
184 *CAI*, 196.
185 Ibid. The adjective *robustorum* suggests more than physical strength and can also imply maturity in judgement and bravery. These young men would be wise and of sound judgement despite their youth.
186 1 Macc. 6.51.
187 *CAI*, 200. See also 2 Sam. 14.1.
188 Ibid., 200–1.
189 Jamil M. Abu-Nasr, *A History of the Maghrib in the Islamic Period* (Cambridge, 1987), 86. Tāshufīn's brief period in power ended abruptly in 1145 when he was killed defending the city of Oran.
190 Mattathias (d. 165 BC) was the father of those who were eventually to lead the revolt of the Maccabees. The story of his story of faith-inspired defiance and eventual death is told in 1 Macc. 2.
191 1 Macc. 2.69. Compare with *CAI*, 200–1.
192 See also the response of Tāshufīn to the Almohad threat and particularly to the loss of Oran in Algeria in 1145 (*CAI*, 245).
193 *CAI*, 198.
194 Ibid., 154.
195 Antonio Maya Sánchez (*CAI*, 154, n. 10) lists the following: Num. 20.17, 22.26; Deut. 5.32, 17.11, 28.14; Josh. 1.7; 1 Sam. 6.12; 2 Sam. 2.19; 2 Kgs 22.2; 2 Chron. 34.2; Prov. 4.27; Isa. 9.20, 30: 21. It also has echoes of NT passages; John the Baptist urges his hearers to 'Prepare ye the way of the Lord, make his paths straight'/ (Mk 1.3) and this sense of personal focus is found in Phil. 3.14 where Paul sets himself the task of the single-minded journey: 'I press toward the mark for the prize.'
196 1 Macc. 13.17.
197 *CAI*, 155.
198 1 Macc. 13.16.
199 Ibid., 13.23. Tryphon seems to have been a title bestowed originally on the general Diodotus and the names in other sources seem to be interchangeable: ' "Tryphon" was originally more an epithet ("Magnificent," "Luxurious") than a name … Diodotus used the name Tryphon at least from the time in 168 Sel. Mac. [Macedonian Seleucid Era] (145/4 B.C.E.) when the Greek letters *TRY* appear on the

coins of Antiochus VI, surely as an abbreviation of the boy king's guardian.' From Goldstein, *I Maccabees*, 436, n. 39.
200 *CAI*, 155.
201 Patrizo Rigobon, 'Francisco María Tubino: Between Federalism and Iberianism', in Joan Ramón (ed.), *Iberian Modalities: A Relational Approach to the Study of Culture in the Iberian Peninsula* (Liverpool, 2013), 99–108, at 103.
202 *CAI*, 155.
203 Ibid., 154.
204 Ibid., 161–2.
205 Isabel Las Heras, 'Temas y figuras bíblicas en el discurso político de *Chronica Adefonsi Imperatoris*,' in N. Guglielmi and A. Rucquoi (eds), *El Discurso político en la Edad Media*, 122 (Buenos Aires, 1995), 117–40 at 124. And this is supported by Dunbabin who notes that Judas Maccabeus had joined Charlemagne or King Arthur 'within the panoply of new secular heroes'; Jean Dunbabin, 'The Maccabees as Exemplars in the Tenth and Eleventh Centuries,' in Katherine Walsh and Diana Wood (eds), *The Bible in the Medieval World: Essays in Memory of Beryl Smalley* (Oxford, 1985), 40.
206 Ibid., 159. From 1129, Ariol Garcés, a powerful Aragonese knight, is cited as Ejea's lord; Stalls, *Possessing the Land*, 133, n. 48. Pedro Díaz led the revolt in 1130 against Alfonso VII.
207 Ibid., 163.
208 1 Sam. 26.15: 'And David said to Abner, Art not thou a valiant man? And who is like to thee in Israel?'
209 Mt. 26.36-44; Mk 14.32-40; Lk. 22.39-46.
210 1 Sam. 26.3.
211 There is also evidence that those referred to by Goldstein as 'Antiochus' agents' were also involved in the further deception of trying to convince the Jews that a cult identifying the God of the Hebrews with the planet Jupiter, the so-called Queen of Heaven with Venus and a young god with Mercury or Saturn was the bona fide religion of Israel (Goldstein, *I Maccabees*, 157). This is an interpretation of 1 Macc. 3.48, but there is no evidence that the author of the *CAI* tried to use this account to shed light on the reign of Alfonso VII.
212 Goldstein, *I Maccabees*, 11.
213 1 Macc. 1.30.
214 Ibid., 1.31, 32.
215 *CAI*, 179.
216 Antonio Maya Sánchez (*CAI*, 179, n. 64) identifies three unequivocal gospel references (Mk 12.30; Mt. 22.37; Lk. 1027), and to these we may add examples such as Gen. 6.5 and Jer. 17.9. In Jeremiah, the reference is especially pertinent since the actions of the heart are linked directly to the notion of deceit: 'The heart is deceitful above all things, and dreadfully wicked: who can know it?'
217 *CAI*, 179.
218 Dunbabin, 'The Maccabees as Exemplars,' 32.
219 *Poema*, 256.
220 Ibid., 255.
221 *CAI*, 180.
222 *CAI*, 212.
223 Ibid.
224 Count Rodrigo Martínez.

225 *CAI*, 213.
226 1 Sam. 15.4.
227 1 Sam. 15.9.
228 *CAI*, 204.
229 A wider use of the way biblical and classical tropes were part of the literary armoury of the medieval writer is discussed by George A. Kennedy; George A. Kennedy, *Classical Rhetoric and Its Christian and Secular Tradition from Ancient to Modern Times* (Chapel Hill, NC, 1999), 220.
230 1Kgs 11.31.
231 Reilly, *Queen Urraca*, 294.
232 Barton, *Aristocracy*, 129.
233 Count Ramón and Ramiro's daughter, Petronilla, were not married (because of Petronilla's juvenile status) until 1150.
234 Especially fickle was the relationship between Navarre and Aragon-Barcelona, described by Reilly as 'quicksilver. No sooner was a peace patched up than one or the other party found itself unable to resist a momentary opportunity and the entire process had to begin again' (Reilly, *Alfonso VII*, 86).
235 This phrase is used by the author (*CAI*, 159) and in 1 Sam. 17.10 and is translated in the AV as 'fight together'; the Douay-Rheims gives 'let him fight with me hand to hand'.
236 Barton and Fletcher, *El Cid*, 172, n. 62.
237 *CAI*, 159.
238 2 Sam. 17.10.
239 Barton, 'Islam and the West,' 156.
240 Ubieto Arteta, 'Sugerencias,' 322.
241 See Denise K. Filios, 'Legend of the Fall: Conde Julián in Medieval Arabic and Hispano-Latin Historiography,' in Ivy A. Corfis (ed.), *Al-Andalus, Sepharad and Medieval Iberia* (Leiden, 2009), 219–34, at 230. In addition, these later chroniclers appropriated each other's work; this is especially the case with Rodrigo Jiménez de Rada, who in *DRH* made extensive use of the *CM* and was also aware of the narrative of Juan of Osma. See Bernard F. Reilly, 'Rodrigo Gimenez de Rada's Portrait of Alfonso VI of Leon-Castile in the *De Rebus Hispaniae*: Historical Methodology in the Thirteenth Century,' in Instituto d'España (ed.), *Estudios en homenaje a don Claudio Sanchez Albornoz en sus 90 años*, Vol. 3 (Buenos Aires, 1985), 90. The *CLRC*, like the *CAI*, also seems to be an independent piece of work without obvious traces of other Iberian influence; Bernard Reilly, 'The *Chronica Latina Regum Castellae*: Historical Composition at the Court of Fernando III of Castile, 1217–1252,' *Viator*, Vol. 41, No. 1 (2010), 145.
242 See later in the text for comparison with a single passage from Pelayo's *Chronicon*. There are also occasional brief borrowings from Sampiro, especially in Book 2, chapters 71–2 (*CAI*, 183–4).
243 Although Kaplan seeks to establish a link between the *Poema*, the *Poema del mio Cid* and Alfonso X's *Estoria*. This is with regard to the parallels with Álvar Fáñez (d. 1114), a military leader and nobleman who fought under Alfonso VI. These details are referred to in the *Poema* (263) and the *Estoria*; Kaplan, 'Friend "of" Foe', 153. See also Richard Fletcher, *The Quest for El Cid* (Oxford, 1989), 189. Such a reference may suggest the author's familiarity with the text of *Carmen Campidoctoris*, an anonymous late-eleventh-century poem recalling the deeds of El Cid Campeador. The text was held in the monastery of Santa María de Ripoll until the seventeenth

century; this strengthens the view that part of the education of the author of the *CAI* was at Ripoll. Barton and Fletcher, *El Cid*, 161.
244 Catlos refers to the *CAI* being 'so heavily laden with Biblical *topoi* and political propaganda' that the text needs to be read with extreme caution (Catlos, *Victors*, 22, n. 3). Propaganda appears to be pointless unless aimed at influencing a body of opinion and would suggest that the author had indeed a target audience.
245 *CAI*, 149.
246 The use of the term *lingua nostra* (our language) is a rare use of the possessive pronoun in the first-person plural (*CAI*, 198).
247 Barton, 'Islam and the West', 155.
248 *CAI*, 149.
249 Ibid., 248.
250 Ibid.
251 McCluskey, 'Malleable Accounts', 218.
252 Karl Reichl, 'Plotting the Map of Medieval Oral Literature', in Karl Reichl (ed.), *Medieval Oral Literature* (Göttingen, 2012), 3–70, at 18.
253 Fernández Conde draws attention to just one passage (*CAI*, 198-9) dealing with vengeance wrought against the Muslims, that may be compared with a similar account in Pelayo's *Chronicon* (79); Javier Fernández Conde, 'La obra del obispo ovetense D. Pelayo en la historiografía Española', *Boletín del Instituto de Estudios Asturianos* 25 (1971), 249-91 at 251–2. It is even possible, according to Ubieto Arteta, that an earlier set of annals may have informed some of the author's work; Ubieto Arteta, 'Sugerencias', 319.
254 *CAI*, 149: The suggestion that the author is presenting a narrative that is informed by his contacts with others is also made at the beginning of Book 2 (let us come to discuss the wars); Ibid., 195. This does not relate to the question of authorship, only to those to whom he is indebted.
255 There are suggestions that the author of the *CAI* relied on Mozarab refugees from North Africa for much of his knowledge of events in al-Andalus and the Maghreb; Barton, 'Islam and the West', 161.
256 McCluskey, 'Malleable Accounts', 219.
257 Barton and Fletcher, *El Cid*, 149.
258 Eyal Poleg, '"A Ladder Set Up on Earth": The Bible in Medieval Sermons', in Susan Boynton and Diane J. Reilly (eds), *The Practice of the Bible in the Middle Ages: Production, Reception & Performance in Western Christianity* (New York, 2011), 220.
259 O'Callaghan, *History of Medieval Spain*, 314; Barton, *Aristocracy*, 5.
260 Barton, *Aristocracy*, 5.
261 *Poema*, 255.
262 Ibid.
263 Ibid. [*linguam prebeque loquacem*].
264 Ibid.
265 *CAI*, 204.
266 Alfonso's military strategy against the Almoravids is discussed by Manuel Rojas Gabriel, 'Alfonso VII in the Face of the Reformulation of Power in al-Andalus, 1145–57: An Essay in Strategic Logic', *Journal of Military History*, Vol. 15 (2019), 117–47.
267 Ibid., 122.
268 Almería did not return to Christian control until 1489.

269 There are nine surviving manuscripts, all of which are copies made in the sixteenth, seventeenth and eighteenth centuries. These are described and discussed by Juan Gil in his introduction to the *CAI* (115–19). They are apparently derived from a glossed archetype held at the cathedral library at Toledo, but which is now lost. This is thought to have belonged to the fourteenth or fifteenth century, so even this was distant from the original compilation; Barton and Fletcher, *El Cid*, 149.

270 In addition, the term *posterorum per scripturam* (to posterity in written composition) suggests that just such a copy had been available or was part of the author's original purpose (*CAI*, 149).

271 Teófilo F. Ruiz, *A King Travels: Festive Traditions in Late Medieval and Early Modern Spain* (Princeton, NJ, 2012), 94.

272 Gerald of Wales, whose *Topography of Ireland* was read to audiences in Oxford on three successive days in *c.* 1188 was probably an exception; in general, manuscripts seem to have been copied and then circulated. See M. T. Clanchy, *From Memory to Written Record* (London, 1979), 272.

273 Fox, *Kings in Calderon*, 24.

274 Ubieta Arteta suggests that the author of the *CAI* made use of a set of annals in Book 1; Ubieto Arteta, 'Surgerencias', 319–20.

275 *Poema*, 267.

Chapter 5

1 For discussion of authorship, see later in the text.

2 Exceptions include the *Crónica Najerense* (Latin = *Chronica Naierensis*), a late-twelfth-century compilation of earlier histories, notably Pelayo's *Chronicon* which we considered in Chapter 2. It was probably a composition emanating from the Benedictine monastery of Santa María la Real in Nájera and it includes some epic fragments. This was probably a source for Lucas de Túy, Rodrigo Jiménez de Rada as well as for Alfonso X's late-thirteenth-century *Estoria*. The other near contemporary text with the *CAI*, the *Historia Roderici*, may also have been composed at Nájera, perhaps by a native of the Rioja (Barton and Fletcher, *El Cid*, 92). This is considered by scholars to be a historically reliable text; for a recent study that considers the text from ideological and chivalric perspectives, see Francisco Bautista, 'Memoria y modelo: una lectura de la *Historia* Roderici', *Journal of Medieval Iberian Studies*, Vol. 2, No. 1 (January 2010), 1–30.

3 The *CLRC* does not contain a specific dedication and its content and scope distinguish it from the much mightier tomes of Rodrigo and Lucas.

4 Peter Linehan, '*Columpna firmissima*: D. Gil Torres, the Cardinal of Zamora', in Simon Barton and Peter Linehan (eds), *Cross, Crescent and Conversion: Studies on Medieval Spain and Christendom in Memory of Richard Fletcher* (Leiden, 2008), 241–62, at 245.

5 Brian A. Catlos, *Kingdoms of Faith: A New History of Islamic Spain* (London, 2018), 284.

6 Ibid.

7 Linehan notes a statement from Bishop Sicard of Cremona (1155–1215) that European Christian civilization has been saved by the event. In *Monumenta Germaniae Historica*; reference by Linehan, *History and Historians*, 295, n. 106.

8. Theresa M. Vann, 'Twelfth-Century Castile and Its Frontier Strategies', in Donald J. Kagay and L. J. Andrew Villalon (eds), *The Circle of War in the Middle Ages: Essays on Medieval Military and Naval History* (Woodbridge, 1999), 21-32, at 29.
9. Julio González, *El reino de Castilla en la época de Alfonso VIII* (Madrid, 1960), 41. Berenguela briefly succeeded her brother Enrique in 1217 before renouncing the throne in favour of her son Fernando.
10. Linehan, *History and the Historians*, 295.
11. Charles Julian Bishko, 'The Spanish and Portuguese Reconquest, 1095-1492', in Kenneth M. Setton (ed.), *A History of the Crusades Vol. III, the Fourteenth and Fifteenth Centuries* (Madison, WI, 1975), 396-456, at 424.
12. Jotischky, *Crusades*, 207.
13. Linehan, *History and the Historians*, 295.
14. O'Callaghan, *Medieval Spain*, 248, 249.
15. Nikolas Jaspert, *The Crusades*, translated by Phyllis G. Jestice (Abingdon, 2006), 121.
16. In addition to the death of Alfonso VIII and the short reign of Enrique I, the period was plagued by flood, famine and civil war. See Derek Lomax, *The Reconquest of Spain* (London, 1978), 131.
17. Peter Linehan, 'Castile, Portugal and Navarre', in David Abulafia (ed.), *The Cambridge Medieval History V, c. 1198-c. 1300* (Cambridge, 1999), 668-702.
18. The third and shortest of our chronicles to be considered, the *Latin Chronicle of the Kings of Castile*, was possibly begun in the mid-1220s. In the introduction to his 2002 translation, O'Callaghan argues that there is evidence from within the chronicle that it was a work in progress before the death of Alfonso IX in 1230; *LCKC*, xxix.
19. Linehan, *History and the Historians*, 402. See also Teófilo F. Ruiz, *From Heaven to Earth, the Reordering of Castilian Society 1150-1350* (Princeton, NJ, 2004), 8.
20. *CLRC*, 89.
21. Janna Bianchini, *The Queen's Hand: Power and Authority in the Reign of Berenguela of Castile* (Philadelphia, PA, 2012), 14.
22. José María Villanueva Lázaro, *La Cuidad de León: De Romana a Románica* (Madrid, 1982), 243. See also Emma Falque Rey, 'Galicia and the Galicians in the Latin Chronicles of the Twelfth and Thirteenth Centuries', in James D'Emilio (ed. and trans.), *Culture and Society in Medieval Galicia* (Leiden, 2015), 400-28, at 417.
23. Ward cites the research of Enrique Jerez Cabrero who argues that the *CM* was completed on two redactions, the first in 1236-7 and the second in 1238; Enrique Jerez Cabrero, 'El Chronicon Mundi de Lucas de Tuy (c. 1238): Técnicas compositivas y motivaciones ideológicas' (PhD thesis, Universidad Autónoma de Madrid, 2006), 353-5, cited by Ward, *History and Chronicles*, 23.
24. Bianchini, *The Queen's Hand*, 16.
25. Much of Lucas's coverage of historical events is considered disproportionate; Aengus Ward notes the 'excessively lengthy' narrative of the reign of Wamba (672-80), but suggests that this might reflect the material available to the chronicler, rather than any requirement to draw attention to the events of Wamba's reign: Ward, *History and Chronicles*, 27.
26. Georges Martin, 'Fondations monastiques et territorialite. Comment Rodrigue de Tolède a inventé la Castille', in Patrick Henriet (ed.), *A la recherché de légitimités chrétiennes, Représentations de l'espace et du temps dans l'Espagne médiévale, IXe-XIIIe siècle* (Lyon, 2003), 243-62, at 244.
27. It was Julian who wrote *Historia Wambae Regis*, which Lucas seems to have used so extensively.

28 Ana Rodríguez López, 'Narratives of Expansion, Last Wills, Poor Expectations and the Conquest of Seville, 1248,' in John Hudson and Sally Crumplin (eds), *The Making of Europe: Essays in Honour of Robert Bartlett* (Leiden, 2016), 123–43, at 126.
29 It is worth noting that much of the ground covered in the *CM* which Rodrigo does not address is to be found in his other works such as *Historia Romanorum* and *Ostrogothorum Historia*; Brian Powell, *Epic and Chronicle: The Poema de Mio Cid and the Crónica de Veinte Reyes* (London, 1983), 31.
30 Linehan, *History and the Historians*, 317. Linehan's view of *DRH* as 'a rather narrow-minded work' (ibid.) is in contrast with his judgement on Alfonso X's *Estoria*, rather than with the writing of his contemporaries or predecessors.
31 *DRH*, 47–9.
32 Ward, *History and Chronicles*, 29. Ward also notes that Rodrigo generally avoids the use of direct speech, a device favoured by Lucas de Túy who follows the example of Julian of Toledo in *Wambae regis*; ibid., 181.
33 Ibid., 352.
34 The title *Primera Crónica General* is preferred by Ramón Menéndez Pidal in his 1906 edition, a work which is described by Fraker as 'a curious production' (Charles F. Fraker, 'Alfonso X, el sabio, King of Castile and León, Historical Works', *Medieval Iberia an Encyclopedia*, E. Michael Gerli (ed.) (London, 2003), 65–7, at 67) since it includes not only the *Estoria* but further material, not all of which is incorporated in other Latin chronicles.
35 Powell, *Epic and Chronicle*, 28.
36 Used when referring to Latin text and in general references to the text. The primary Latin text used is *Chronica Latina Regum Castellae*, edited by Luis Charlo Brea. Other editions used are *Crónica Latina de los Reyes de Castilla*, edited and introduced by M. Desamparados Cabanes Pecourt (Valencia, 1964) and *Crónica Latina de los Reyes de Castilla*. Introduction, textual criticism, translation into Spanish, notes and indices Luis Charlo Brea (Cadiz, 1984).
37 This abbreviation is used when referring to O'Callaghan's translation.
38 Juan appears in the third person in the chronicle (in the *CLRC*, 117, where he is referred to as *cancellarius*/chancellor and *Osomensis episcopus*/the bishop of Osma).
39 Although there is consensus around the figure of Juan of Osma, which is acknowledged by O'Callaghan, LCKC, xxx and xxxi, the initial claim for Juan's authorship was made by Derek Lomax, 'The Authorship of the *Chronique Latin des rois de Castille*,' *Bulletin of Hispanic Studies* 40 (1963), 205–11, at 205. See also Julio González, 'La Crónica latina de los Reyes de Castilla,' *Homenaje a don Agustín Millares Carlo* (2 Vols. Palma, 1975), 2: 55–70.
40 Inés Fernández-Ordóñez, 'La composición por etapas de la *Chronica latina regum Castellae* (1223–1237) de Juan de Soria,' *E-Spania: Revue électronique d'études hispaniques médiévales*, 2 (2006), 1-30
41 Colin C. Smith, 'The Vernacular,' in David Abulafia (ed.), *Cambridge Medieval History V, c. 1198–c. 1300* (Cambridge, 1999), 71–83, at 81.
42 Luis Charlo Brea, '¿Un segundo autor para la última parte de la *Crónica latina de los Reyes de Castilla*?' *Actas I Congreso Nacional de Latín Medieval* (León, 1995), 251–6. Charlo Brea refers to what he calls indications (*indicios*) that there may have been a further hand in Juan's chronicle: this is based on textual comparison as well as changes in pace, register and use of references.

43 Francisco Javier Hernández, 'La corte de Fernando III y la casa real de Francia: Documentación, crónicas y monumentos,' *Actas del VIII Congreso de Estudios Medievales: Fernando III y su tiempo* (Ávila, 2003), 104–55, at 111.
44 Peter Linehan, 'Juan de Soria: The Chancellor as Chronicler,' *e-Spania* [En ligne], 21 décembre 2006, mis en ligne le 16 août 2010, 1–12, at 3. URL: http://e-spania.revues.org/276.
45 González, *El reino de Castilla*, 9.
46 O'Callaghan, *LCKC*, xxx–xxxvii.
47 *CLRC*, 76.
48 O'Callaghan considers that Juan may have been charged with the writing of the chronicle by Alfonso VIII or by 'the titular royal chancellor, Martín de Pisuerga, archbishop of Toledo, for whom he had words of high praise' (*LCKC*, xxxvi).
49 *CLRC*, 95. The Third and Fourth Crusades are chronicled on 70–2 and the campaign of Emperor Frederick II on 101 and his struggles in Apulia on 59–60.
50 Bernard F. Reilly, 'Bishop Lucas of Túy and the Latin Chronicle Tradition in Iberia,' *The Catholic Historical Review*, Vol. 93, No. 4 (October 2007), 767–88, at 768.
51 Ibid.
52 Alan Deyermond believes that it was Rodrigo's ideology that triumphed in the court of Fernando III and that this writing 'rejected … the official outlook of the court.' Alan Deyermond, 'The Death and Rebirth of Visigothic Spain in the *Estoria de España*,' *Revista de Canadiense de Estudio Hispánicos*, Vol. 9, No. iii (Spring 1985; *Homenaje a Alfonso X, el Sabio* (1284–1984)), 345–67, at 347.
53 Bernard Reilly refers to the practice of medieval chroniclers to use or borrow the content of earlier texts but concedes that there is no evidence of Juan having done so; Reilly, '*Chronica Latina Regum Castellae*': 140–54, at 145.
54 Ruiz, *From Heaven to Earth*, 34.
55 Deyermond comments on the 'striking similarity' between the fall of Arthur's Britain as described by Geoffrey of Monmouth in *Historia regum Britanniae* and the fall of Visigothic Spain narrated by Rodrigo and Alfonso X: Deyermond, 'Death and Rebirth,' 355.
56 Américo Castro, Willard F. King and Selma Margaretten, *The Spaniards: An Introduction to Their History* (Berkeley, CA, 1971), 13. The citation from *DRH* is the title of chapter 12 (from Book 3), Roderici Ximenii de Rada, *Historia de Rebus Hispaniae Sive Historia Gothica* (CCCM 72) (Turnholt, 1987), 106. The substantive usually spelt *excidii* (nominative case) is so given in the *DEH*. The citation from *CM* is taken from Book 4, 8 (228).
57 The first count of Castile is Fernán González (r. c. 930–970). He is succeeded by García González (r. 970–995), Sancho García (r. 995–1017) and García Sánchez (r. 1017–29) who was the last independent count of Castile. He was succeeded by Fernando I who was king of León-Castile between 1035 and 1065.
58 *CLRC*, 36 (The Lord inspired him with beneficial advice to besiege Toledo).
59 O'Callaghan, *LCKC*, xxxix.
60 References to the power and disposition of God are made four times in the paragraph devoted to the activities of Alfonso VI in Toledo; *CLRC*, 36.
61 Acknowledging similarities, Maya Sánchez also concedes that no firm link has been established (*CAI*, 115).
62 Biblical influence on the artistic representations within the cloister of the monastery of San Juan de la Peña, in the region of Huesca, built *circa* 1190 is considered by Pamela Patton, especially in relation to interpretations of the Temple of Solomon,

together with representations of sacred events; Patton, *Pictorial Narrative*, 65–6. Further biblical sources of inspiration in monumental architecture as well as art (what is referred to as 'a fashionable concern with Jerusalem') is discussed by David Simon, 'Late Romanesque Art in Spain,' in Jerrilynn D. Dodds, Bernard F. Reilly and John Williams (eds), *The Art of Medieval Spain, A.D. 500–1200* (New York, 1994), 199–329, at 226–7.
63 See n. 28.
64 Toledo is, perhaps, the most singular example. Its importance as a politically important city with an ancient spiritual authority is discussed by Charles Lowell Tieszen, *Christian Identity amid Islam in Medieval Spain: Studies on the Children of Abraham* (Leiden, 2013), 148.
65 John Tolan, *Saracens: Islam in the Medieval European Imagination* (New York, 2002), 175.
66 Ibid., 182.
67 O'Callaghan, *Medieval Spain*, 86.
68 Linehan, *History and the Historians*, 357. See also Miriam Shadis, *Berenguela of Castile (1180-1246) and Political Women in the High Middle Ages* (New York, 2009), 9–10. Shadis also refers to the control of the royal chancery which suggests rivalry between Rodrigo and Juan.
69 Tolan, *Saracens*, 181. Linehan discusses Rodrigo's abiding and profound interest in the historic, ecclesiastical and military significance of Isidore's see, the city and bishopric of Seville; Peter Linehan, *Past and Present in Medieval Spain* (Farnham, 1992), 149.
70 *Najerense*, 3.
71 *CM*, 168.
72 Ibid.
73 O'Callaghan, *LCKC*, xix.
74 José Carlos Martín, *Braulio de Zaragoza: Renotatio librorum domini Isodori* (San Millán de la Cogolla, 2002), 5–7.
75 Mt. 2.12.
76 Ibid.
77 Bernard F. Reilly, *The Medieval Spains* (Cambridge, 1993), 156.
78 Ward, *History and Chronicles*, 127.
79 Manuel C. Díaz y Díaz, 'Isidoro en la edad media hispana,' in *Isidoriana* (León, 1961), 345–87; reprinted in Díaz y Díaz, *De Isidoro al Siglo XI. Ocho estudios sobre la vida literaria peninsular* (Barcelona, 1976), 141–201, at 197.
80 Aengus Ward, 'Review: Ksenia Bonch Reeves, Visions of Unity after the Visigoths. Early Latin Chronicles and the Mediterranean World,' in Erik Cooper and Sjoerd Levelt (eds), *The Medieval Chronicle 12* (Leiden, 2019), 223–6, at 225.
81 *CM*, 3.
82 Ecclus 19.2: 'Wine and women will make men of understanding to fall away.' This is quoted verbatim by Lucas (*CM*, 3).
83 *CM*, 3.
84 Ibid., 6.
85 The early sources that portray the life and martyrdom of St Hermenegild are discussed in Amy Fuller, *Between Two Worlds: The autos sacramentales of Sor Juana Inés de la Cruz* (Cambridge, 2015), 117.
86 According to tradition, Marcellus was a soldier who fought with great bravery in North Africa in 297–298 and was martyred because he refused to offer sacrifices to pagan gods.

87 *CM*, 6.
88 *gloriosus* and *doctore Yspaniarum* (ibid., 7 and 9).
89 J. N. Hillgarth, 'Spanish Historiography and Iberian Reality,' *History and Theory*, Vol. 24, No. 1 (February 1985), 23–43, at 28.
90 Isidore of Seville. *De Ecclesiasticis Officiis*, ed. and trans. Thomas L. Knoebel (Mahwah, NJ, 2008), 4.
91 *DRH*, 6.
92 Germán Bleiberg, Maureen Ihrie and Janet Pérez (eds), *Dictionary of the Literature of the Iberian Peninsula A-K* (Westport, 1993), 463. *Toledano* is a noun frequently used to refer to Rodrigo.
93 See also a comparison of the theories of the Six Ages of the World as proposed by Augustine of Hippo and Isidore: Wood, *Politics of Identity*, 121–7.
94 Paul Merritt Bassett, 'The Use of History in the *Chronicon* of Isidore of Seville,' in Alessandro Scafi (ed.), *Mapping Paradise: A History of Heaven on Earth* (Chicago, IL, 2006), 278–92, at 280.
95 Gen. 15.7: 'I am the Lord that brought thee out of Ur of the Chaldees.' Quoted in *CM*, 25.
96 Gen. 12.1.
97 *CM*, 27.
98 Barton draws attention to the family of Count Martín Flaínez (d. 1108), whose family was part of the Leonese-Castilian aristocracy under Alfonso VI and whose fortunes waned during the twelfth century; Barton, *Aristocracy*, 37–8.
99 *CM*, 72.
100 John H. Walton, Victor H. Matthews and Mark W. Chavalas, *The IVP Bible Background Commentary, Old Testament* (Madison, WI, 1997), 748.
101 The conflict was also more complex and it was not until the accession of the boy-pharaoh Ptolemy V (r. 204–181 BC) that Antiochus was able to press home his advantage, having reached an understanding (though not necessarily a formal treaty) with Philip V of Macedon (r. 221–179 BC). For further discussion see John T. Fitzgerald, 'Gadara: Philodemus' Native City,' in John T. Fitzgerald, Dirk Obbink and Glenn S. Holland (eds), *Philodemus and the New Testament World* (Leiden, 2004), 343–99, at 353, n. 42.
102 *CM*, 72. This is not an exact quotation from Is. which, in the Vulgate, reads: *'erit altare Domini in medio terrae Aegypti et titulus iuxta terminum eius Domini'* (Isa. 19.19), but the message is the same.
103 Acts 1.7. The translation is that from the Douay-Rheims version; the AV translates *momenta* as 'seasons.'
104 Mt. 24.36. The conflation of the two verses with Lucas's linking phrase is *CM*, 122.
105 Ecclus 7.40 (Douay-Rheims).
106 *CM*, 345, 346.
107 Ibid., 124.
108 Ibid., 123.
109 Phil. 1.18
110 *CM*, 160.
111 Rev. 2.6 and 15.
112 *CM*, 169.
113 For a discussion of their origins and the possible etymological derivation, see Irene Belyeu, *Revelation in Context* (Nashville, TN, 2006), 185, 186.
114 *CM*, 169; compare with Rev. 12.4.

115 The passages all reflect a righteous anger felt by God's people (Jer. 5.26-27; Prov. 18.3; Mt. 24.12; cf. *CM*, 210, 21). Such statements are also made in the context of anger directed towards the Jews.
116 *CM*, 210. Hosea's prophecy reads: 'Their princes shall fall by the sword for the rage of their tongue: this shall be their derision in the land of Egypt.' Lucas's substitution of *recia* (trap/net/snare) gives the passage a more sinister aspect; it will also be noted that the power and wrath of God are more directly appealed to.
117 Fletcher, 'A Twelfth-Century View', 150. Fletcher also refers to the fact that the author of the *HS* conspicuously raised the status of León from its description in *Translatio Sancti Isidori*.
118 *CM* IV, 289-93.
119 Charles F. Fraker, *The Scope of History: Studies in the Historiography of Alfonso el Sabio* (Ann Arbor, MI, 1996), 57.
120 This is a reference to the legendary victory in 722 of the Asturian prince Pelagius over the Muslims despite overwhelming odds. Covadonga, the scene of the famous victory deep in the Asturian mountains, about forty miles east of Oviedo.
121 *CM*, 227.
122 Tolan, *Saracens*, 182.
123 Simon Barton, 'The Roots of the National Question in Spain', in Mikuláš Teich and Roy Porter (eds), *The National Question in Europe in Historical Context* (Cambridge, 1993), 106-28, at 113.
124 Ibid.
125 Lucy Pick, *Conflict and Coexistence: Archbishop Rodrigo and the Muslims and Jews of Muslim Spain* (Ann Arbor, MI, 2004), 73.
126 O'Callaghan, *A History of Medieval Spain*, 515.
127 Linehan, *History and the Historians*, 354.
128 John Edwards, *The Spain of the Catholic Monarchs, 1474-1520* (Oxford, 2000), 41.
129 Lynn H. Nelson (trans.), *The Chronicle of San Juan de la Peña, a Fourteenth-Century Official History* (Pennsylvania, PA, 2002), 107, n. 1.
130 *DRH*, 317, 318.
131 *CM*, 345, 346. This does not include the reference to Ecclus 3.7 (122), noted earlier.
132 Nicholas Morton, 'Walls of Defence for the House of Israel: Ezek. 13:5 and the Crusading Movement', in Elizabeth Lapina and Nicholas Morton (eds), *The Use of the Bible in Crusader Sources* (Leiden, 2017), 403-20, at 416.
133 Job 5.18; Lam. 1.12; Jer. 31.15; Lam. 4.5; Isa. 13.15-16; Jer. 9.1; Isa. 13.19; Mk 13.2. References are in the order in which they appear in *DRH*.
134 Oppa (fl. after 712) was the bishop of Seville who took the part of the Muslims at Covadonga.
135 Douay-Rheims.
136 See *DRH*, 117.
137 Ibid.
138 Ibid., 108.
139 Isa. 13.15-19.
140 *DRH*, 266.
141 Rom. 8.35: 'Who shall separate us from the love of Christ? Shall tribulation, or distress, or persecution, or famine, or nakedness, or peril, or sword?'
142 Roth, *Jews, Visigoths and Muslims*, 49.

143 Jerrilynn D. Dodds, María Rosa Menocal and Abigail Krasner Balbale, *The Arts of Intimacy: Christians, Jews, and Muslims in the Making of Castilian Culture* (New Haven CT, 2008), 178.
144 Gifford Davis, 'The Development of a National Theme in Medieval Castilian Literature,' *Hispanic Review*, Vol. 3, No. 2 (1935), 153.
145 Hillgarth, 'Spanish Historiography,' 26.
146 Pablo Díaz, 'Visigothic Political Institutions,' in Peter Heather (ed.), *The Visigoths from the Migration Period to the Seventh Century: An Ethnographic Perspective* (Woodbridge, 1999), 321–72, at 342.
147 Theresa M. Vann, 'Reconstructing a "Society Engaged for War,"' in Donald J. Kagay and L. J. Andrew Villalon (eds), *Crusaders, Conditierri and Cannon: Warfare in Societies around the Mediterranean* (Leiden, 2003), 389–416, at 407.
148 Raphael Loewe, 'The Medieval History of the Latin Vulgate,' in G. W. H. Lampe (ed.), *The Cambridge History of the Bible, Vol. 2: The West from the Fathers to the Reformation* (Cambridge, 1969), 102–54, at 124. Loewe suggests that Isidore's approach may, in part, be due to discrepancies in the biblical text used in Spain and that outside Iberia.
149 H. Daniel-Rops (trans. Audrey Butler), *The Church in the Dark Ages* (London, 2001), 204.
150 Wood, *Politics of Identity*, 62.
151 Linehan, *History and the Historians*, 297–8.
152 *DRH*, 276.
153 *CLRC*, 61–2.
154 The provenance of the authorship is discussed in the preface to *Auto de los Reyes Magos*, edited with notes and indices by Sebastião Pestana (Lisbon, 1965) 8, 9. No specific author is suggested by Pestana, nor is it established whether he is of Gascon or Castilian origin.
155 Pick, *Conflict and Coexistence*, 194–5.
156 The Epiphany is the setting but without the Magi arriving at the manger. See Alan Deyermond, '"¿Rei otro sobre mí?": The Exile of the True King in Thirteenth-Century Castilian Literature,' in Rhian Davies and Annie Brooksbank Jones (eds), *The Place of Argument: Essays in Honour of Nicholas G Round* (Woodbridge, 2007), 3–16, at 8.
157 Ibid., 8–10.
158 Chris Lowney, *A Vanished World: Muslims, Christians, and Jews in Medieval Spain* (Oxford, 2005), 26, 27. See also Katherine Elliot van Liere, 'Renaissance Chronicles and the Apostolic Origins of Spanish Christianity,' in Katherine van Liere, Simon Ditchfield and Howard Louthan (eds), *Sacred History: Uses of the Christian Past in the Renaissance World* (Oxford, 2012), 121–44, at 127.
159 Justin K. Stearns, *Infectious Ideas: Contagion in Premodern Islamic and Christian Thought in the Western Mediterranean* (Baltimore, MD, 2011), 50, 51.
160 Andrew H. Merrills, *History and Geography in Late Antiquity* (Cambridge, 2005), 177.
161 Ibid., 227.
162 Tolan, *Saracens*, 174–82.
163 Davis, 'Development of a National Theme,' 53.
164 *DRH*, 106.
165 Ezek. 22.27; Zeph. 3.3.
166 *DRH*, 40–2.

167 Ibid., 74.
168 *CM*, 19.
169 *DRH*, 10; *CM*, 20.
170 The distinctiveness of a proto-language and its subsequent diversity among the sons of Noah is beyond the scope of this study, but is discussed by Hugh S. Pyper, *The Unchained Bible: Cultural Appropriations of Biblical Texts* (London, 2012), 106–7.
171 Ward, *History and Chronicles*, 29.
172 Linehan, *History and the Historians*, 398.
173 Ibid.
174 P. D. King, *Law and Society in the Visigothic Kingdom* (Cambridge, 1972), 50.
175 José María Monsalvo Antón, 'Construyendo discursos medievales sobre urbano: episodios de la ciudad de León bajo la monarquía asturiana ségun la cronista Cristiana,' in Gregorio del ser Quijano and Iñaki Martín Viso (eds), *Espacios de Poder y Formas Sociales en la Edad Media* (Salamanca, 2007), 220–41, at 231.
176 At the beginning of his *Historia,* Isidore declares: 'Of all the lands that exist between the west and India, you, holy and ever happy and mother of princes and people, O Spain, are the most beautiful.'
177 *CM*, 3.
178 Ibid., 5. Paul, in Rom. 15.24 refers to an intention to visit Spain: 'Whensoever I take my journey into Spain, I will come to you: for I trust to see you in my journey, and to be brought on my way thitherward by you, if first I be somewhat filled with your company.'
179 Davis, 'Development of a National Theme,' 150.
180 *CM*, 346 (Rom. 15.23-24; 1 Cor. 10.13; Gal. 4.4; Phil. 1.18).
181 The link is explored by John van Engen, 'Sacred Sanctions for Lordship,' Thomas N. Bisson (ed.), *Cultures of Power: Lordship, Status and Process in Twelfth-Century Europe* (Philadelphia, PA, 1995), 203–30, at 211: 'Power experienced in everyday reality and sanctioned by God himself (Rom. 13) was the presumed reality ... At the fourth Council of Toledo (633), plainly inspired if not drafted by Bishop Isidore (d. 633), the King was addressed for the first time as *minister Dei* and reminded that he was to answer to God for the people entrusted to his care.'

Chapter 6

1 See Powell, 'Historiography: Annals and Latin Chronicles,' 395. Rodrigo was also involved in promoting the see of Toledo against other prominent centres such as Seville and Santiago; Simon R. Doubleday, *The Lara Family: Crown and Nobility in Medieval Spain* (Cambridge, MA, 2003), 53. See also Linehan, *History and the Historians*, 357.
2 Richard Fletcher notes discreet as well as overt classical and biblical references in the *HS*; Fletcher, 'A Twelfth-Century View,' 153.
3 O'Callaghan, *Medieval Spain*, 314.
4 Barton and Fletcher, *El Cid*, 9.
5 Roth, *Jews, Visigoths and Muslims*, 51.
6 Jerrilyn D. Dodds, 'Islam, Christianity and the Problem of Religious Art,' in Jerrilyn D. Dodds, Bernard F. Reilly and John W. Williams (eds), *The Art of Medieval Spain, A. D. 500-1200* (New York, 1994), 26–37, at 27.

7   R. J. González-Casanovas, 'Cultural Discourse in Hispanic Historiography on the Reconquest and Conquest: Historicist Hermeneutics from Alfonso X to Las Casas,' in George F. Mclean, Antonio Gallo and Robert Magliola (eds), *Hermeneutics and Interculturation* (Washington, DC, 2003), 163–82, at 171.
8   Tom Nickson, *Toledo Cathedral: Building Histories in Medieval Castile* (University Park, PA, 2015), 53.
9   Jaume Aurell, *Medieval Self-Coronations: The History and Symbolism of a Ritual* (Cambridge, 2020), 232.
10 J. N. Hillgarth, *The Visigoths in History and Legend* (Toronto, 2009), 105.
11 Linda Martz, writing primarily about Toledo from the fifteenth century onwards, notes that following Alfonso's conquest of the city, it became a centre of learning, commerce and political intrigue. Linda Martz, *A Network of Converso Families in Early Modern Toledo: Assimilating a Minority* (Ann Arbor, MI, 2003), 1.
12 Bosch, *Art, Liturgy and Legend*, 31.
13 The impressive roll call includes Adelard of Bath and Gerard of Cremona; E. Glenn Hinson, *The Church Triumphant. A History of Christianity up to 1300* (Macon, GA, 1995), 381. See also Arnold Pacey and Francesca Bray, *Technology in World Civilization: A Thousand Year Memory* (Cambridge, MA, 2021), 51.
14 Hinson, *Church Triumphant*, p, 381.
15 References to Alfonso are mostly in chapter two (*CLRC*, 35–7). The death of Alfonso is also briefly mentioned in chapter three (*CLRC*, 37).
16 As we noted in Chapter 2, both Pelayo and the author of the *HS* deal with the reign of Alfonso VI (the *HS* does so in just seven paragraphs) and there are further references in the *Historia Compostelana* and *Crónica Najerense*, though the latter draws heavily on Pelayo's account.
17 *Chronicon*, 84–6. Although Pelayo's account eulogizes Alfonso's life, it is a relatively short encomium and one that is remarkable as much for its record of signs and wonders, including a portentous miracle accompanying his death, as with specific events of his reign.
18 Barton, *Aristocracy*, 12–20.
19 *CLRC*, 36.
20 Ibid.
21 Ibid. In what Ivy Corfis refers to as 'the complexity of cultural contact,' it should be noted that Jews too were among those who fought alongside Alfonso VI and may also have welcomed his conquest of Toledo; see the introduction by Ivy Corfis to *Al-Andalus, Sepharad and Medieval Iberia: Cultural Conflict and Diffusion* (Leiden, 2009), v.
22 The Amoravids and their Berber allies led by their emir Yūsuf ibn Tashufin (d. 1106) defeated the army of Alfonso VI at Sagrajas, near Badajoz, which seems to have resulted in considerable Castilian losses and further incursions into the south of the peninsula: William Farina, *St James the Greater in History, Art and Culture* (Jefferson, NC, 2018), 51. Although Sagrajas was a profound shock, Richard Fletcher warns against exaggerating its overall impact: Richard Fletcher, *Saint James's Catapult: The Life and Times of Diego Gelmírez of Santiago de Compostela* (Oxford, 1984), 118.
23 Corfis, *Al-Andalus*, v.
24 Fernández-Ordóñez, 'La composición,' 16.
25 *CLRC*, 36. Cambanes Pecourt adds *Deus* (16).
26 Gen. 2.7. The Douay-Rheims similarly translates *inspiravit*.
27 *CLRC*, 36.

28 Ecclus 21, especially verse 8.
29 An analytic comparison of references to Alfonso VI in *CM* and *DRH* is made by Reilly in 'Rodrigo Gimenez de Rada's Portrait,' 89.
30 Ibid., 92.
31 O'Callaghan, *LCKC*, xxii.
32 Reilly, 'Rodrigo Gimenez de Rada's Portrait,' 87.
33 For a discussion of the stated intentions of the author of the *HS*, see Chapter 2 of this volume.
34 Fernández-Ordóñez, 'La composición,' 21.
35 *CLRC*, 36.
36 Ibid.
37 Ibid.
38 Peter Linehan makes a similar observation about Rodrigo's claim about the way Muslims had interceded on the part of those who had suffered most grievously at the hands of Alfonso rather than retaliating to the military occupation: Linehan, *History and the Historians*, 221.
39 Pick, *Conflict and Coexistence*, 63.
40 *DRH*, 111.
41 Pick, *Conflict and Coexistence*, 64. Pick discusses the way in which cartularies prepared during the period of Rodrigo's tenure as well as a slightly earlier one would deal with the city's rights, property and constitution.
42 McCluskey, 'Malleable Accounts,' 216.
43 Linehan, *History and the Historians*, 223–4.
44 Chapter 1, p. 93.
45 Margarita López Gómez, 'The Mozarabs: Worthy Bearers of Islamic Culture,' in Salma Khadra Jayyusi (ed.), *The Legacy of Muslim Spain* (Leiden, 1992),174.
46 Hitchcock, *Mozarabs*, 126.
47 Linehan describes the circumstances on 18 December 1086 in which Alfonso VI appears to honour the Mozarabs by restoring the primatial see of Toledo on the feast day of the Annunciation in the Mozarabic calendar; but he had also, in his deed of endowment, defamed their past and imperilled their future; Linehan, *History and the Historians*, 216.
48 Dodds, Menocal and Balbale, *Arts of Intimacy*, 184: 'Rodrigo understood that there was no way to make an end run to reconquest, around Toledo's plurality.'
49 Linehan, *History and the Historians*, 224.
50 Theresa Earenfight, *Queenship and Political Power in Medieval and Early Modern Spain: Women and Gender in the Modern World* (Aldershot, 2005), 27.
51 2 Chron. 36.12; see also 2 Kgs 17.2, Jer. 52.2.
52 *CLRC*, 37; Gen. 6.6.
53 O'Callaghan, *LCKC*, 8, n. 1.
54 Gen. 6.5.
55 *CLRC*, 37. This is further suggested by a reference to Count Gómez (*comitte Gomicio*): 'who was far too intimate with the queen, over and above that which was fitting.'
56 David G. Pattison, 'The Role of Women in Some Medieval Spanish Epic and Chronicle Texts,' in Rhian Davies and Annie Brooksbank Jones (eds), *The Place of Argument: Essays in Honour of Nicholas G. Round* (Woodbridge, 2007), 17–30, at 25.
57 Therese Martin, *Queen as King: Politics and Architectural Propaganda in Twelfth-Century Spain* (Leiden, 2006), 7, 8.

58 See *Index Locorvm Sacrae Sciptvrae* in Charlo Brea's *CCCM* edition, 213–18.
59 This does not merely include references to the books of Dan. (nine references) and Rev. (six); in addition, the following biblical passages from within the text of the *CLRC* are reminiscent of apocalyptic language: Gen. 6.6 (used six times), Ecclus 10.4, Hab. 2.20, Jer. 31.15, Lam. 1.12, 12.11, Job 3.4 and 6, 9.13-15, 1 Macc. 7.17 and Wis. 17.5.
60 Juan's description of the advance of the Christian army at the Battle of Las Navas, 'They bore down on the enemy ready to die or conquer' (*CLRC*, 61) is also reminiscent of an early reference in Bernard of Clairvaux's 'For if the blessed die in the Lord, how much more blest are those who die for the Lord' (*PL* 182, Vol. 182, Col. 922). Bernard's exhortation is also dependent on Rev. 14.13: 'Blessed are the dead which die in the Lord.' See also O'Callaghan, *LCKC*, 49 n. 2.
61 Charles F. Fraker, 'The Latin Chronicle of the Kings of Castile,' in Anne Mette Hansen (ed.), *Variants 4* (2005) *The Book as Artefact Text and Border* (Amsterdam, 2005), 326–36, at 327.
62 O'Callaghan, *LCKC*, xxxvi.
63 *CLRC*, 37.
64 Ibid., 38.
65 See Isa. 13.5, 6; Hos. 4.16.
66 2 Chron. 21.7.
67 *CLRC*, 39.
68 Amnon Linder, *Raising Arms: Liturgy in the Struggle to Liberate Jerusalem in the Late Middle Ages* (Turnhout, 2003), 177.
69 Constantine Georgiou, 'Propagating the Hospitallers' *Passagum* Crusade Preaching the Liturgy in 1308–1309,' in Emanuel Buttigrieg and Simon Phillips (eds), *Islands and Military Orders, c. 1291–c.1798* (London), 53–64, at 61.
70 O'Callaghan, *LCKC*, 11, n. 1.
71 For example, Ps. 47.2: 'For the Lord most high is terrible; he is a great King over all the earth.' O'Callaghan also cites a reminiscence with Ecclus 10.4.
72 The *Poema de Fernán González*, a Castilian epic poem written in Old Castilian around 1255 by a monk from the Monastery of San Pedro de Arlanza, near Burgos.
73 Alan Deyermond, 'Uses of the Bible in the *Poema de Fernan Gonzalez*,' in David Hook and Barry Taylor (eds), *Cultures in Contact in Medieval Spain: Historical and Literary Essays Presented to L. P. Harvey* (King's College London, Medieval Studies 3) (London, 1990), 47–60, at 49.
74 It would also be worth referring to the *peccatis exigentibus*, linking military setbacks to the sins of the crusaders. The term had a long and much promoted history that was used by popes from Urban II and it seized the imagination throughout the crusading period; Jonathan Riley-Smith, *The First Crusade and the Idea of Crusading* (London, 1993), 133.
75 Philip B. Baldwin, *Pope Gregory X and the Crusades* (Woodbridge, 2014), 53.
76 Ibid., 59.
77 Reference to Chapter 2 in this volume.
78 *CLRC*, 41.
79 Ibid.
80 Hos. 10.9: The whole of Hosea's prophecy is a lament for Israel's decline, with the last chapter looking to the restoration of the kingdom.
81 See 1 Kgs 12–15; 2 Chron. 10–13.

82 *CLRC*, 41. The count's career and his ability to influence events (initially in Portugal, 1121–8) are outlined by Barton, *Aristocracy* (Appendix 1, 241–2).
83 Evelyn S. Procter, *Curia and Cortes in León and Castile 1072–1295* (Cambridge, 1980), 20.
84 1 Kgs 12.8: 'But he forsook the counsel of the old men, which they had given him, and consulted with the young men that were grown up with him, and which stood before him.'
85 And there may have been equally resonant contemporary parallels, the succession following the death in 1189 of Henry II of England. Since Enrique's lands at that time extended as far south as the Pyrenees, this would not have provided a remote association; Fernando Luis Corral, 'Alfonso VIII of Castile's Judicial Process at the Court of Henry II of England: An Effective and Valid Arbitration?' *Nottingham Medieval Studies*, Vol. 50 (2006), 22–42, at 22–4.
86 *Poema*, 257. Here he is praised for his kingly qualities (*Gloria regali fulget simul et comitali*).
87 Mk 3.24; see also Mt. 12.25, Dan. 2.41. A further injunction to the counsel a king might be expected to receive is found in Ps. 2.10: 'Be wise now therefore, O ye kings; be instructed, ye judges of the earth.'
88 *CLRC*, 39.
89 Ibid., 44–5.
90 Joseph J. Duggan, *The 'Cantar de Mio Cid': Poetic Creation in Its Economic and Social Contexts* (Cambridge, 1989), 70.
91 *CLRC*, 45.
92 Ibid.
93 Though there may be a reluctant admission of the king's bravery bordering on the foolhardy following the defeat at Alarcos: 'His men, in truth, understanding the danger that the danger that threatened all Spain, led him, reluctantly and resisting, away from the battle' (Ibid., 27). O'Callaghan seems to support this ambiguous verdict, suggesting the risks that Alfonso was prepared to take: 'Alfonso VIII chanced the future of his kingdom on a pitched battle at Alarcos on 19 July 1195' (O'Callaghan, *Reconquest and Crusade*, 142).
94 Ibid., 22–4.
95 Mt. 16.27; 25.31.
96 *CLRC*, 117.
97 See Chapter 4, 219. For Alfonso VII's triumphant return to Toledo, see *CAI*, 211.
98 *CLRC*, 64. Parallels with this psalm are encountered elsewhere to celebrate Christian victories over the infidel in medieval Europe. One such example is the celebrated victory of Simon de Montfort over the Albigensians in 1213 and his return in triumph to Paris three years later.
99 Mt. 23.39; Lk. 19.38.
100 Bosch, *Art, Liturgy and Legend*, 23, 24.
101 See *CLRC*, 68: 'Therefore as gladness turns to gloom and, in turn, how happiness succeeds misery.'
102 Ibid.
103 Josh. 23.14.
104 Mt. 26.41 ('the flesh is weak') and Isa. 53. The suggestion of Isa. 53 is especially interesting since it is regarded as a prophecy concerning Christ's passion. The link established between Alfonso VIII and the last week of Jesus' life would have an increased resonance.

105 See O'Callaghan, *LCKC*, 35 n. 10.
106 *CLRC*, 52.
107 Deut. 33.29.
108 Jean-Christophe Attias and Esther Benbana (trans. Susan Emanuel), *Israel the Impossible Land* (Stanford, CA, 2003), 83.
109 'Lacking a real capital until the sixteenth century, the peripatetic Castilian kings were crowned, became kings, and were buried in Oviedo, León, Santiago, Sahagún, Nájera, Burgos, Valladolid, Segovia, Toledo, Seville, and Granada. Their choices of burial places and sites for their enthronement show an obvious association with the Reconquest and the moving frontier.' Teófilo F. Ruiz, 'Unsacred Monarchy: The Kings of Castile in the Late Middle Ages,' in Sean Wilentz (ed.), *Rites of Power: Symbolism, Ritual and Politics since the Middle Ages* (Philadelphia, PA, 1985), 109–44, at 126.
110 Although the title is used to describe individuals who occur briefly in the chronicle, Álvaro Pérez, the son of Pedro Fernández who is referred to six times in the chronicle, is so described on a single occasion (*CLRC*, 90), as is a Moor of Córdoba, Ibn Harach, *Avenharach* (*CLRC*, 92).
111 Ibid., 78. There is a suggestion by Miriam Shadis that Juan's presentation of Berenguela at the point of her abdication is unsubtle and possibly one dimensional: 'Other evidence … suggests we should seek … a more nuanced understanding of Berenguela's actions,' Shadis, *Berenguela of Castile*, 91.
112 Jennifer C. Ward, *Women in Medieval Europe 1200–1500* (Harlow, 2002), 128.
113 H. Salvador Martínez, *Alfonso X, the Learned: A Biography*, translated by Odile Cisneros (Leiden, 2010), 31.
114 *CLRC*, 86.
115 *DRH*, p. 300. Rodrigo also uses the term *ut lac mellifluum* (like milk and flowing honey) and is clearly derived from Exod. 33.3: 'et intres in terram fluentem lacte et melle'/ 'Unto a land flowing with milk and honey.' This is part of the eulogy composed to celebrate the motherhood and piety of Berenguela and may be a further example of how a link with the Virgin Mary can be made.
116 Though there is an echo in Ps. 45.9: 'filiae regum in honore tuo stetit coniux in dextera tua in diademate aureo'/ 'Kings' daughters were among thy honourable women: upon thy right hand did stand the queen in gold of Ophir.'
117 *CLRC*, 85. The author, in his introduction to the speech so describes Berenguela: *nobilissima genitrice sua*. (most celebrated mother).
118 Lk. 1.42: 'benedicta tu inter mulieres et benedictus fructus ventris tui'/ 'Blessed art thou among women and blessed is the fruit of thy womb.'
119 This is not the only view of her influence and relationship with her son; Linehan describes her as 'possessive' and she is depicted as an overbearing and domineering mother; Peter Linehan, 'Juan de Soria: the Chancellor as Chronicler,' *e-Spania* [En ligne], 21 décembre 2006, mis en ligne le 16 août 2010, 6.
120 *CLRC*, 86.
121 Shadis, *Berenguela of Castile*, 123.
122 *CM*, 340.
123 *CLRC*, 86.
124 Ibid., 73.
125 Reilly, 'Historical Composition,' 143.
126 *CLRC*, 99.
127 Ibid.
128 Ibid., 106.

129 France, *The Crusades and the Expansion of Catholic Christendom*, 163. This argument seems to have been made originally by Simon Barton in 'A Forgotten Crusade: Alfonso VII and the Campaign for Jaén (1148),' *Historical Research*, Vol. 73, No. 182 (2000), 312–20.
130 *CLRC*, 100.
131 Ibid., 41.
132 Luis Moreno, 'Federalization in Multinational Spain,' in Michael Burgess and John Pinder (eds), *Multinational Federations* (Abingdon: Routledge, 2007), 86–107, at 90.
133 Procter, *Curia and Cortes*, 103.
134 Peter Linehan, *The Spanish Church and the Papacy in the Thirteenth Century* (Cambridge, 1971), 105.
135 *CLRC*, 85.
136 Ibid., 85, n. 43
137 O'Callaghan, *LCKC*, 88.
138 *CLRC*, 86.
139 O'Callaghan, *Reconquest and Crusade*, 84.
140 *CLRC*, 91 and 111.
141 Mt. 3.16.
142 *CLRC*, 85.
143 Ibid., 86.
144 Mt. 11.29.
145 Phil. 2.3: 'but in lowliness of mind let each esteem other better than themselves.'
146 Acts 2.3.
147 There are dozens of occasions when the image of fire is used in the Bible and was used in many different ways. And it was an important aspect to the spiritual armoury of God himself. He is shown in various forms of fire on many different occasions. Some of the earliest OT manifestations of this include the making of the Covenant with Abraham (Gen. 15.17), the burning bush (Exod. 3.2-4), pillar of fire (Exod. 13.21), on Sinai (Exod. 19.18), in the flame on the altar (Judg. 13.20) and God answering by fire (1 Kgs 18.24, 38).
148 *CLRC*, 89.
149 Ibid., 87: 'The King of Baeza at that time linked himself with our king.'
150 Ibid., 105.
151 Ibid., 110, 111.
152 1 Kgs 1.43, 47.
153 Jer. 38.9.
154 *CLRC*, 87.
155 Ibid., 117.
156 Mt. 25.31; see also Rev. 21.5: 'And he that sat upon the throne said, Behold, I make all things new.'
157 Antonio Alvarez-Ossorio, 'The Ceremonial of Majesty and Aristocratic Protest: The Royal Chapel at the Court of Charles II,' in Juan José Carreras and Bernardo García García (eds), trans. by Tess Knighton, *The Royal Chapel in the Time of the Habsburgs: Music and Ceremony in Early Modern Europe* (Woodbridge, 2005), 246–99, at 290.
158 Joseph F. O'Callaghan, *Alfonso X and the Cantigas de Santa Maria: A Poetic Biography* (Leiden, 1998), 55. O'Callaghan also draws on Ortiz de Zúñiga, *Anales* and Ricardo del Arco y Garay, *Sepulcros*, to cite reports of the frenzy that erupted

amongst a crowd during the examination of the king's body in 1668, three years prior to his beatification.

159 Fernando had laid the foundations of a system of royal patronage that controlled the appointments of major church officials and matters relating to the handling of church finances, according to terms agreed by the see of Rome. See Linehan, *Spanish Church*, 330.

160 Peter Linehan, *Spain, 1157–1300, A Partible Inheritance* (Oxford, 2008), 60, 61. *Tercias* were part of the tithe (or *diezmo*) designed for the construction of churches but were also used in more military endeavours, such as the Siege of Seville in 1247–8: O'Callaghan, *Reconquest and Crusade*, 161.

161 *CM*, 341.

162 Ibid.

163 *DRH*, 298.

164 *CLRC*, 65.

165 Ibid., 94.

166 Dodds, 'Religious Art', 27.

167 *CAI*, 204.

168 2 Chron. 34.8. The reign of King Josiah (r. 641–609 BC) who sought to rule in Jerusalem after the manner of King David and whose reign encompassed the rebuilding of the temple is an interesting OT parallel to the period following Fernando's capture of Córdoba.

169 *CLRC*, 47.

170 Charlo Brea, *Crónica Latina*, 15, n. 8. Charlo Brea's translation into Spanish, *arco de maldad* (bow of evil) is more emphatic and is perhaps closer to the AV which translates the psalmist's phrase *arcus inutilis* as 'deceitful bow'.

171 Jn 13.27; Lk. 22.3.

172 *CLRC*, 79.

173 Prov. 15.33.

174 Prov. 8.13: 'The fear of the Lord is to hate evil: pride, and arrogancy, and the evil way'; also 16.5: 'Every one that is proud in heart is an abomination to the Lord: though hand join in hand, he shall not be unpunished.'

175 See Est. 3.5, 6. Haman has been appointed as the king's grand vizier whose sin of pride brings about his downfall and death.

176 1 Tim. 6.4.

177 *CM*, 323. This observation is supported by Manuel Núñez Rodríguez ((There is) an aspect that fits the description of Alfonso IX by Lucas de Túy in *Chronicon Mundi* who balances the virtues of strength and mercy in the catholic faith), Manuel Núñez Rodríguez, *Muerte Coronada: El mito de los reyes en la Catedral compostelana* (Santiago de Compostela, 1999), 23.

178 *CM*, 333.

179 1 Tim. 6.12.

180 *CM*, 326.

181 'Hoc tempore ampliata est fides catholica in Yspania, et licet multi regnum Legionese bellis impeterent' (ibid.)

182 *CLRC*, 40.

183 Ibid., 39.

184 O'Callaghan, *LCKC*, xxv, xxvi.

185 *CLRC*, 80.

186 Isa. 38.6. See also 2 Kgs 20.6.

187 *CLRC*, 84.
188 Joseph F. O'Callaghan, 'The Beginnings of the Cortes in León-Castile,' *American Historical Review*, Vol. 74, No. 5 (June, 1969), 1503-37, at 1526.
189 *DRH*, 290-1.
190 Joel 3.1, 2; Isa. 1.26; Jer. 30.18.
191 Jerrilyn D. Dodds, *Architecture and Ideology in Early Medieval Spain* (University Park, PA, 1990), 140.
192 Saint Augustine, *City of God*, trans. Henry Bettenson (London, 2003), xliv.
193 See Michael Fieldrowicz, 'General Introduction,' in *Explorations of the Psalms 1-32* (Part 3, Vol. 15), translated by Maria Boulding OSB and edited by John E. Rotelle (New York, 2000), 13-66, at 49.
194 'Ask about the Council of Toledo when it was ruled by our king and yours, the glorious Sisebut. Isidore, archbishop of Seville, is a witness to these matters,' *DEL*, 118.
195 Damian J. Smith, *Crusade, Heresy and Inquisition in the Lands of the Crown of Aragon (c. 1167-1276)* (Leiden, 2010), 133.
196 *CLRC*, 86. The first part of this statement has an echo of Exod. 32.26: 'and [Moses] said, Who is on the Lord's side? let him come unto me.'
197 Dodds, 'Religious Art,' 27.
198 Ibid.
199 Diana Beuster, 'The Speech of Pope Urban II 1095 at Clermont in the Versions of *Gesta Francorum* and *Baldric of Dol*,' in *Readings in Medieval Latin* (Bloomington, IN, 2007), 2-14, at 4.
200 Jim Bradbury, *The Medieval Siege* (Woodbridge, 1992), 104.
201 Purkis, *Crusading Spirituality*, 121.
202 Nora Berend, 'The Expansion of Latin Christendom,' in Daniel Power (ed.), *The Central Middle Ages, 950-1320* (Oxford, 2006), 178-208, at 195.
203 Barton, 'Islam and the West,' 173.
204 Tolan, *Saracens*, especially 180-6.
205 *CLRC*, 89.
206 *CM*, 336.
207 Lev. 25.45.
208 Josh. 10.28: see also Deut. 20.6.
209 *HS*, 190.
210 An example is the treatment of the Moors following the fall of Úbeda in 1233 (*CLRC*, 106).
211 1 Chron. 34.2-5.
212 Roth, *Jews, Visigoths and Muslims*, 49, 50.
213 *CLRC*, 39, 40.
214 Ibid.
215 O'Callaghan, *Reconquest and Crusade*, 16.
216 *CLRC*, 41 and 45.
217 Ibid., 73.
218 In his description of the surrender of Córdoba, the author of *CLRC* implies that the Muslims under Ibn Hûd and Abû-l-Hasan, though wretched and lacking consolation, were enabled to leave the city because of the truce that was reached with Fernando (*CLRC*, 116).
219 *CM*, 127.

220 Ibid., 166.
221 Roth, *Jews, Visigoths*, 49.
222 For a discussion of the etymology and original application of these terms, see Ann Christys, 'Hispania after 711,' in H.-W. Goetz, J. Jarnut and W. Pohl (eds), *Regna and Gentes: The Relationship between Late Antique and Early Medieval Peoples and Kingdoms in the Transformation of the Roman World* (Leiden, 2003), 219–41, at 232.
223 *CLRC*, 100.
224 *CLRC*, 97.
225 Ibid., 92.
226 Ibid., 93. There are parallels in the *CAI* with Zafadola, discussed in Chapter 4 of this volume. See Barton, 'Islam and the West,' 175, and the person of Avengalvón in described by Burshatin in 'The Docile Image,' as 'a reassuring and picturesque figure' whose servility enables the Cid even more easily to emerge as a dominant, charismatic warrior (273–4).
227 Ibid., 112.
228 O'Callaghan, *LCKC*, 134, n. 2.
229 *CLRC*, 112.
230 Ibid., 111.
231 *CAI*, 213.
232 Christian pragmatism, as we have noted even within the trenchantly polemic *CAI*, finds a voice: 'Christians – both in León and elsewhere in the peninsula – had always been remarkably pragmatic in their dealings with the Muslim south.' Barton, 'Islam and the West,' 174.
233 *CAI*, 213.
234 Fletcher, *Quest*, 152.
235 Linehan, *History and the Historians*, 317.
236 Though Córdoba had been captured by Alfonso VII in 1146–8, after which it surrendered to the Almohads.
237 *CLRC*, 116.
238 Ibid.
239 Peter of les Vaux-de-Cernay, *The History of the Albigensian Crusade*, trans. W. A. Sibly and M. D. Sibly (Woodbridge, 1998), 84. There is a further possible parallel with El Cid in Murviedro and Valencia: 'The Campeador and his men rejoiced to see his standard flying from the highest point of the citadel,' in Ian Michael (ed.), Rita Hamilton and Janet Perry (trans.), *The Poem of the Cid, A Bilingual Edition with Parallel Text* (London, 1984), 86, 87.
240 Josh. 2.1: 'And Joshua the son of Nun sent out of Shittim two men to spy secretly, saying, Go view the land, even Jericho. And they went, and came into an harlot's house, named Rahab, and lodged there.'
241 *CLRC*, 110.
242 *CLRC*, 111.
243 Josh. 2.24.
244 *CLRC*, p. 111.
245 O'Callaghan, *LCKC*, 132.
246 He had received envoys (*nuncios*) from those who had entered Córdoba at Benavente, approximately halfway between León and Zamora (*CLRC*, 110).
247 Hillgarth, *Visigoths*, 111.
248 Reilly, 'Lucas of Túy,' 769.

249 We have already noted the author's reference to Baghdad (*CLRC*, 13); other examples include Marrakech (14) and Poitiers (51). All three cities are described as 'famous' (various declensions of *famosa*), though the adjective might also imply notoriety.
250 Though the author's treatment of the long reign of Alfonso VII is dealt with in just three chapters (*CLRC*, 39–41). Perhaps the loss of Almería followed by the division of Alfonso VII's kingdom, in themselves potential events for biblical comparison, may nevertheless have been seen as uncongenial subjects for documentation.
251 There is a very brief reference to the last king of the Goths: 'after the time of Rodrigo, king of the Goths'; *CLRC*, 116.
252 An extended version of the themes in this section can be found in my article, 'Images of Biblical Conflict in Castile, *c.* 1150–*c.* 1240; A Comparison of the *Chronica Adefonsi Imperatoris* and the *Chronica Latina Regum Castellae*,' *Al-Masāq*, published by Taylor and Francis on behalf of the Society for the Medieval Mediterranean, on 13 March 2015 (Vol. 27, No. 1, 77–92), available at: https://doi.org/10.1080/09503110.2015.1002236.
253 It is thus edited by Antonio Maya Sánchez who, in editing just the prose sections, aims to present to philologists and historians, a text of the greatest value and reliability; *CAI*, 112.
254 In his declaration of war against the Muslims, Fernando III (*CLRC*, 86) seeks the blessing of God in his venture ('in order that it may please you [i.e. his mother] that I declare war against the Moors').
255 *CAI*, 149.
256 Ubieto Arteta notes that the author is also sparing of praise to those outside the emperor's royal circle; Ubieto Arteta, 'Sugerencias,' 320.
257 *CLRC*, 42.
258 Reilly, '*CLRC*,' 140.
259 Compare, for example, two descriptions of Alfonso and Fernando: 'the glorious king of Castile ordered all his men' and 'the king … humbly and devotedly and as an obedient son'; *CLRC*, 45 and 84.
260 Powell, *Epic and Chronicle*, 28.
261 The successes of Alfonso VI were described by Malcolm Barber as a 'false dawn for the Christians' since Granada had been conquered by the Almohads in 1154 and Almería was to fall around the time of Alfonso's death (1157). Malcolm Barber, *Two Cities: Medieval Europe, 1050–1320* (London, 1992), 324.
262 Linehan, *Spain*, 10.
263 Though certain events, such as the conversion of the Muslim governor of Valencia, Zayd Abû Zayd, to Christianity in 1228/9 may have been recorded according to information received by the author by the papal legate, Halgrin; see María Desamparados Cabanes Pecourt (ed.), *Crónica latina de los reyes de Castilla* (Valencia, 1964), 92, 97, 98.
264 Reilly, '*CLRC*,' 145.
265 *CAI*, 221–2.
266 *CAI*, 149.
267 Ibid., 149–50. This has references to Ps. 74.12 and Lk. 24: 49, and the prologue has other biblical echoes (Lk. 1.1-3).
268 *CAI*, 154. Compare with Gen. 39.21: 'But the Lord was with Joseph.'

269 *CAI*, 155.
270 1 Macc. 13.7.
271 *PA*, 255.
272 *CLRC*, 86.
273 Ibid.

BIBLIOGRAPHY

Primary works and translations

Augustine, *City of God*, trans. Henry Bettenson (London, 2003).
Augustine, *De Doctrina Christiana*, 2. 16, *PL* 34, Migne, I.-P. (ed.), *Patrologiae cursus completus. Series Latina*, 217 vols (Paris, 1844–64), 47–9.
Augustine, *Augustine of Hippo: Homilies on the Gospel of John 1–40*, trans. Edmund Hill and ed. Allan D. Fitzgerald (New York, 2009).
Augustine, *The Fathers of the Church: St Augustine Tractates on the Gospel of John*, trans. John W. Rettig (Washington, DC, 1988).
Barton, Simon, and Richard Fletcher (eds and trans.), *The World of El Cid: Chronicles of the Spanish Reconquest* (Manchester, 2000).
Bede, *On Ezra and Nehemiah*, trans. Scott DeGregorio (Translated Texts for Historians, 47) (Liverpool, 2006).
Bernard of Clairvaux, *Bernard of Clairvaux: The Life and Death of Saint Malachy the Irishman*, trans. Robert T. Meyer (Kalamazoo, MI, 1978).
Bernard of Clairvaux, *S. Bernardi Opera Vol. 3, Tractatus et Opuscula*, ed. Jacques Leclercq and H. M. Rochais (Rome, 1963).
Charlo Brea, Luis (ed.), *Chronica Latina Regum Castellae*, CCCM 73 (Turnhout, 1997).
Charlo Brea, Luis (ed. and trans.), *Crónica latina de los reyes de Castilla* (Cádiz, 1984).
David, Charles Wendell (trans.), *The Conquest of Lisbon – De expugnatione Lyxbonensi* (New York, 2001).
Desamparados Cabanes, María Pecourt (ed.), *Crónica latina de los reyes de Castilla* (Valencia, 1964).
Estévez Sola, Juan A. (ed.), *Chronica Naierensis*, Juan A. Estévez Sola, CCCM 71A (Turnhout, 1995).
Falque Rey, Emma (ed.), *Historia Compostelana* CCCM 70 (Turnhout, 1988)
Falque Rey, Emma (ed.), 'Historia Roderici vel gesta Roderici Campidocti,' in *Chronica Hispana saeculi XII*, Part I, CCCM 71 (Turnhout, 1990), 3–98.
Flórez, Enrique (ed.), 'Anales toledanos I,' in *España Sagrada Theatro Geographico-Historico de la Eglesia de España*, Tomo xxiii (Madrid, 1767).
Gerald of Wales, *Expugnatio Hibernica*, ed. and trans. A. B. Scott and F. X. Martin (Dublin, 1978).
Gil, Juan Fernández (ed.), Alvarus, *Epistulae*, VI.9.10-11, *Corpus Scriptorum Muzarabicorum* 1 (Madrid, 1973).
Gil, Juan Fernández (ed.), 'Prefatio de Almaria,' in *Chronica Hispana saeculi XII*, Part I, CCCM 71 (Turnhout, 1990), 249–67.
Isidore of Seville. *De Ecclesiasticis Officiis*, ed. and trans. Thomas L. Knoebel (Mahwah, NJ, 2008).
Jerome, *Apology against Rufinus* (*PL*, Vol. 23, 16).
Jerome, *Fathers of the Church: St Jerome, Commentary on Galatians*, trans. Andrew Cain (Washington, DC, 2010).

Jerome, *Fathers of the Church: St Jerome, Commentary on Matthew*, trans. Thomas P. Scheck (Washington, DC, 2008).
López Pereira, Eduard (ed.), *Crónica mozárabe de 754 edición citica y traducción* (Zaragoza, 1980).
Lucas of Túy, *Chronicon Mundi*, ed. Emma Falque Rey, CCCM 74 (Turnhout, 2003).
Lucas of Túy, *Milagros de San Isidro*, translation into Spanish by Juan de Robles, 1525 (León, 1992).
Maya Sánchez (ed.), 'Chronica Adefonsi Imperatoris,' in *Chronica Hispana saeculi XII*, Part 1, CCCM 71 (Turnhout, 1990), 109–248.
Michael, Ian (ed.), Rita Hamilton and Janet Perry (trans.), *The Poem of the Cid, A Bilingual Edition with Parallel Text* (London, 1984).
Migne, I.-P. (ed.), *Patrologiae cursus completus. Series Latina*, 217 vols (Paris, 1844–64).
Nelson, Lynn H. (trans.), *The Chronicle of San Juan de la Peña: A Fourteenth-Century Official History* (Philadelphia, PA, 2002).
O'Callaghan, Joseph F. (ed. and trans.), *The Latin Chronicle of the Kings of Castile* (Tempe, AZ, 2002).
Orderic Vitalis, *The Ecclesiastical History, Vol. 2, Books 3 and 4*, ed. and trans. Marjorie Chibnall (Oxford, 1969).
Ovid, *Metamorphoses*, ed. R. J. Tarrant (Oxford: Oxford Classical Texts, Oxford University Press, 2004).
Pelayo of Oviedo, *Crónica del obispo Don Pelayo*, ed. Benito Sánchez Alonso (Madrid, 1924).
Pérez González, Maurilio (ed. and trans. into Spanish) *Crónica del Emperador Alfonso VII* (León, 1997).
Pérez de Urbel, Fray Justo (ed.), *Sampiro su crónica y la monarquia leonesa en el siglo X*, ed. Fray Justo Pérez de Urbel (Madrid, 1952).
Pérez de Urbel, Dom Justo and Atilano González Ruiz-Zorrilla (eds), *Historia Silense* (Madrid, 1959).
Pestana, Sebastião (ed.), *Auto de los Reyes Magos* (Lisbon, 1965).
Peter of les Vaux-de-Cernay, *The History of the Albigensian Crusade*, trans. W. A. Sibly and M. D. Sibly (Woodbridge, 1998).
Riesco Chueca, Pilar (ed.), 'Passio Argenteae et comitum,' in *Pasionario hispánico*, no. 19 (Seville, 1995), 253–66.
Riley-Smith, Louise, and Jonathan Riley-Smith (eds), *The Crusades. Idea and Reality, Documents of Medieval History, 1095–1274* (London, 1981).
Rodrigo Jiménez de Rada, *Historia de rebus Hispanie sive Historia Gothica*, ed. J. Fernández Valverde, CCCM 72 (Turnhout, 1987).
Sánchez Belda, Luis (ed.), *Chronica Adefonsi Imperatoris* (Madrid, 1950).
Smith, Colin (ed. and trans.), *Christians and Moors in Spain, Vol. 2: 1195–1614* (Warminster, 1989).
Ubieto Arteta, Antonio (ed.), *Crónicas anónimas de Sahagún* (Zaragoza, 1987).
Walsh, P. G. (ed. and trans.), *Love Lyrics from the Carmina Burana* (Chapel Hill, NC, 1993).
William of Malmesbury, *Gesta Regum Anglorum, The History of the English Kings Vol. 1*, ed. and trans. R. A. B. Mynors, R. M. Thomson and Michael Winterbottom (Oxford, 1998).

Secondary sources

Abu-Nasr, Jamil M., *A History of the Maghrib in the Islamic Period* (Cambridge, 1987).
Ailes, Marianne J., 'The Admirable Enemy? Saladin and Saphadin in Ambroise's *Estoire de la guerre sainte*,' in Norman Housley (ed.), *Knighthoods of Christ, Essays on the History of the Crusades and the Knights Templar, Presented to Malcolm Barber* (Aldershot, 2007), 51–64.
Alexander, David C., *Augustine's Early Theology of the Church: Emergence and Implications, 386–391* (New York, 2008).
Allen Smith, Katherine, *War and the Making of Medieval Monastic Culture* (Woodbridge, 2011).
Allies, Neil, 'The Monastic Rules of Visigothic Iberia: A Study of Their Text and Language' (Unpublished PhD thesis, University of Birmingham, 2009).
Allman, Dwight D., 'Sin and the Construction of Carolingian Kingship,' in Richard Newhauser (ed.), *The Seven Deadly Sins: From Communities to Individuals* (Leiden, 2007).
Alonso Álvarez, Raquel, 'El obispo Pelayo de Oviedo (1101–1153): Historiador y promotor de códices illuminados,' in Roberto J. López and Miguel Taín Guzmán (eds), *El legado de las catedrales* (Santiago de Compostela, 2010), 331–50.
Álvarez-Ossorio, Antonio, 'The Ceremonial of Majesty and Aristocratic Protest: The Royal Chapel at the Court of Charles II,' in Juan José Carreras and Bernardo García García (eds), translated by Tess Knighton, *The Royal Chapel in the Time of the Habsburgs: Music and Ceremony in Early Modern Europe* (Woodbridge, 2005), 246–99.
Ashe, Laura, *Fiction and History in England, 1066–1200* (Cambridge, 2007).
Astell, Ann W., *The Song of Songs in the Middle Ages* (New York, 1995).
Attias, Jean-Christophe, and Esther Benbana (trans. Susan Emanuel), *Israel the Impossible Land* (Stanford, CA, 2003).
Aumann, Jordan, O. P., *Christian Spirituality in the Catholic Tradition* (London, 1985).
Aurell, Jaume, *Medieval Self-Coronations: The History and Symbolism of a Ritual* (Cambridge, 2020).
Bailey, Matthew, *The Poetics of Speech in the Medieval Spanish Epic* (Toronto, 2010).
Balás, David L., and D. Jeffrey Bingham, 'Patristic Exegesis of the Books of the Bible,' in Charles Kannengiesser (ed.), *Handbook of Patristic Exegesis Vol. Two: The Bible in Ancient Christianity* (Leiden, 2006), 271–373.
Baldwin, Philip B., *Pope Gregory X and the Crusades* (Woodbridge, 2014).
Baloup, Daniel, 'Reconquête et croisade dans la *Chronica Adefonsi Imperatoris* (ca. 1150),' in Georges Martin and Jean Rondil (eds), *Cahiers de linguistique et de civilisation hispaniques médiévales* (Lyon, 2002), 453–80.
Bamford, Heather, *Cultures of the Fragment: Uses of the Iberian Manuscript 1100–1600* (Toronto, 2018).
Bango Torviso, Isidro, 'Historia del Arte Cristiano en España,' in Ricardo Garcia-Villoslada (ed.), *Historia de la Iglesia en España* (Madrid, 1982), 497–572.
Barber, Malcolm, *Two Cities: Medieval Europe, 1050–1320* (London, 1992).
Bartlett, Robert, *England under the Norman and Angevin Kings, 1075–1225* (Oxford, 2000).
Barton, Simon, *The Aristocracy in Twelfth-Century León and Castile* (Cambridge, 1997).
Barton, Simon, 'A Forgotten Crusade: Alfonso VII and the Campaign for Jaén (1148),' *Historical Research*, Vol. 73, No. 182 (2000), 312–20.

Barton, Simon, 'Islam and the West: A View from Twelfth-Century León,' in Simon Barton and Peter Linehan (eds), *Cross, Crescent and Conversion, Studies on Medieval Spain and Christendom in Memory of Richard Fletcher* (Leiden, 2008), 153–74.
Barton, Simon, 'Marriage across Frontiers: Sexual Mixing, Power and Identity in Medieval Iberia,' *Journal of Medieval Iberian Studies*, Vol. 3, No. 1 (March 2011), 1–25.
Barton, Simon, *Conquerors, Brides, and Concubines: Interfaith Relations and Social Power in Medieval Iberia* (Philadelphia, PA, 2015).
Barton, Simon, 'The Roots of the National Question in Spain,' in Mikuláš Teich and Roy Porter (eds), *The National Question in Europe in Historical Context* (Cambridge, 1993), 106–28.
Barton, Simon, 'From Tyrants to Soldiers of Christ: The Nobility of Twelfth-Century León-Castile and the Struggle against Islam,' *Nottingham Medieval Studies*, Vol. 44 (2006), 28–48.
Bassett, Paul Merritt, 'The Use of History in the *Chronicon* of Isidore of Seville,' in Alessandro Scafi (ed.), *Mapping Paradise: A History of Heaven on Earth* (Chicago, IL, 2006), 278–92.
Bautista, Francisco, 'Memoria y modelo: una lectura de la *Historia Roderici*,' *Journal of Medieval Iberian Studies*, Vol. 2, No. 1 (January 2010), 1–30.
Becker, Marvin B., 'Individualism in the Early Italian Renaissance,' in James Banker and Carol Lansing (eds), *Florentine Essays: Selected Writings of Marvin B. Becker* (Ann Arbor, MI, 2002), 258–84.
Belyeu, Irene, *Revelation in Context: A Literary and Historical Commentary on the Book of Revelation with Supporting Referents and Notes* (Nashville, TN; 2nd edition, 2006).
Berend, Nora, 'The Expansion of Latin Christendom,' in Daniel Power (ed.), *The Central Middle Ages, 950–1320* (Oxford, 2006), 178–208.
Beuster, Diana, 'The Speech of Pope Urban II 1095 at Clermont in the Versions of *Gesta Francorum* and *Baldric of Dol*' (scholarly paper), in *Readings in Medieval Latin* (Bloomington, IN, 2007), 2–14.
Bianchini, Janna, *The Queen's Hand: Power and Authority in the Reign of Berenguela of Castile* (Philadelphia, PA, 2012).
Birdshall, J. N., 'The New Testament Text,' in P. R. Ackroyd and C. F. Evans (eds), *The Cambridge History of the Bible Vol. 1: From the Beginnings to Jerome* (Cambridge, 1970), 308–77.
Bischoff, Bernard (trans. Michael Gorman), *The Manuscripts and Libraries in the Age of Charlemagne* (Cambridge, 2007).
Bishko, C. J., 'The Spanish and Portuguese Reconquest, 1095–1492,' in K. M. Setton and H. W. Hazard (eds) *A History of the Crusades*, Vol. III (Madison, 1975), 396–456.
Bishko, C. J., 'The Liturgical Context of Fernando I's Last Days according to the So-Called «Historia Silense»,' in *HS*, XVII–XVIII (1964-5), 47–59, reprinted in C. J. Bishko (ed.), *Spanish and Portuguese Monastic History 600–1300* (London, 1984).
Bishko, C. J., 'The Pactual Tradition in Hispanic Monasticism,' in C. J. Bishko (ed.), *Spanish and Portuguese Monastic History, 600–1300* (London, 1984), 1–43.
Bisson, Thomas N., *The Crisis of the Twelfth Century: Power, Lordship, and the Origins of European Government* (Princeton, NJ, 2009).
Bleiberg, Germán, Maureen Ihrie and Janet Pérez (eds), *Dictionary of the Literature of the Iberian Peninsula A-K* (Westport, CT, 1993).
Bodelón, Serafín, *Literatura Latina de la Edad Media en España* (Madrid, 1989).
Bolton Holloway, Julia, Joan Bechtold and Constance S. Wright, *Equally in God's Image: Women in the Middle Ages* (New York, 1990).

Bosch, Lynette M. F., *Art, Liturgy and Legend in Renaissance Toledo: The Mendoza and Iglesia* (University Park, PA, 2000).
Boyer, Louis, *The Christian Mystery: From Pagan Myth to Christian Mysticism*, trans. Illtyd Trethowan (London, 2004).
Boynton, Susan, 'Performative Exegesis in the Fleury *Interfectio puerorum*', *Viator: Medieval and Renaissance Studies* 29 (1998), 39–64.
Boynton, Susan, *Shaping a Monastic Identity: Liturgy and History at the Imperial Abbey of Farfa 1000–1125* (New York, 2006).
Boynton, Susan, 'The Bible and the Liturgy,' in Susan Boynton and Diane J. Reilly (eds), *The Practice of the Bible in the Middle Ages: Production, Reception & Performance in Western Christianity* (New York, 2011), 10–33.
Boynton, Susan, 'Restoration or Invention? Archbishop Cisneros and the Mozarabic Rite in Toledo,' *Yale Journal of Music & Religion*, Vol. 1, No. 1 (2015), 5–30.
Bradbury, Jim, *The Medieval Siege* (Woodbridge, 1992).
Bradshaw, Paul, and Maxwell E. Johnson, *The Eucharistic Liturgies: Their Evolution and Interpretation* (Collegeville, MN, 2012).
Bredero, Adriaan H., *Christendom and Christianity in the Middle Ages: The Relations between Religion, Church, and Society* (Grand Rapids, MI, 1994).
Brooke, Christopher, *Europe in the Central Middle Ages 962–1154* (Abingdon, 2000).
Broun, Dauvit, 'The Absence of Regnal Years from the Dating Clause of Charters of the Kings of Scots, 1195–1222,' in John Gillingham (ed.), *Anglo-Norman Studies XXV. Proceedings from the Battle Conference, 2002* (Woodbridge, 2003), 47–64.
Brown, Dennis, 'Jerome,' in P. F. Esler (ed.), *The Early Christian World Vols 1 – 2* (London, 2000), 1151–74.
Brown, Giles, 'Introduction: The Carolingian Renaissance,' in Rosamond McKitterick (ed.), *Carolingian Culture: Emulation and Innovation* (Cambridge, 1994), 1–53.
Brown, Peter, *The Cult of the Saints, Its Rise and Function in Latin Christianity* (Chicago, IL, 1981).
Brown, R. Allen, *The Normans and the Norman Conquest* (Woodbridge, 1969).
Bull, Marcus, *Knightly Piety and the Lay Response to the First Crusade: The Limousin and Gascony, c 970–c11304* (Oxford, 1993).
Bullough, Donald A., *The Age of Charlemagne* (London, 1980).
Buringh, Eltio, *Medieval Manuscript Production in the Latin West: Exploration with a Global Database* (Leiden, 2011).
Burman, Thomas E., *Religious Polemic and the Intellectual History of the Mozarabs, c. 1050–1200* (Leiden, 1994).
Burns, Christy L., *Gestural Politics: Stereotype and Parody in Joyce* (New York, 2000).
Burshatin, Israel, 'The Docile Image: The Moor as a Figure of Force, Subservience, and Nobility in the *Poema de Mio Cid*,' *Kentucky Romance Quarterly*, No. 31 (1984), 269–80.
Byassee, Jason, *Praise Seeking Understanding: Reading the Psalms with Augustine* (Grand Rapids, MI, 2007).
Cain, Andrew, and Joseph Lössl (eds), *Jerome of Stridon: His Life, Writings and Legacy* (Farnham, 2006).
Campbell, James, *Essays in Anglo-Saxon History* (London, 1986).
Camps, J. (ed.), *Cataluña en la Época Carolingia: Arte y Cultura antes del Románico* (Barcelona, 1999).
Canal Sánchez-Pagín, J. M., '¿Crónica silense o Crónica domnis sanctis?' *Cuadernos de Historia de España*, Vol. 63-4 (1980), 94–103.

Canal Sánchez-Pagín, J. M., 'Elías, canónigo rotense, posible autor de la *Chronica Adefonsi Imperatoris*,' *Anuario de Estudios Medievales*, Vol. 30, No. 2 (2000), 735-55.
Carlos Martín, José, *Braulio de Zaragoza: Renotatio librorum domini Isodori* (San Millán de la Cogolla, 2002).
Carr, Karen Eva, *Vandals to Visigoths: Rural Settlement Patterns in Early Medieval Spain* (Ann Arbor, MI, 2002).
Carracedo Fraga, José, 'Isidore of Seville as a Grammarian' (trans. Geraldine Barandiarán-Muñoz), in Andrew Fear and Jamie Wood (eds), *A Companion to Isidore of Seville* (Leiden, 2019), 222-44.
Carruthers, Mary, *The Book of Memory: A Study of Memory in Medieval Culture* (Cambridge, 2008).
Castro, Américo, *The Spaniards, An Introduction to Their History*, trans. Willard F. King and Selma Margaretten (Berkeley, CA, 1971).
Catlos, Brian A., *The Victors and the Vanquished: Christians and Muslims in Catalonia and Aragon, 1050-1300* (Cambridge, 2004).
Catlos, Brian A., *Kingdoms of Faith: A New Islamic History of Islamic Spain* (London, 2018).
Cavadini, John C., *The Last Christology of the West, Adoptionism in Spain and Gaul, 785-820* (Pittsburgh, PA, 1993).
Charlo Brea, Luis, '¿Un segundo autor para la última parte de la *Crónica latina de los Reyes de Castilla*?' in Maurilio Pérez González (ed.), *Actas I Congreso Nacional de Latín Medieval* (León, 1995), 251-6.
Chase, Colin (ed.), *Two Alcuin Letter-Books* (Toronto, 1975).
Chazan, Robert, '*Adversus Iudaeos* in the Carolingian Empire,' in Ora Limor and Guy G. Stroumsa (eds), *Contra Iudaeos: Ancient and Medieval Polemics between Christians and Jews* (Tübingen, 1996), 119-42.
Chenu, Marie-Dominique, 'The Masters of Theological "Science,"' in Jerome Taylor and Lester K. Little (trans.), *Nature, Man, and Society in the Twelfth Century, Essays on New Theological Perspectives in the Latin West* (London, 1968), 270-308.
Chenu, Marie-Dominique, 'The Old Testament in Twelfth-Century Theology,' *Nature, Man, and Society in the Twelfth Century, Essays on New Theological Perspectives in the Latin West*, trans. Jerome Taylor and Lester K. Little (London, 1968), 146-61.
Christys, Ann, 'Cordoba in the *Vita Vel Passio Argenteae*,' in Frans Theuws, Mayke De Jong and Carine van Rhijn (eds), *Topographies of Power in the Early Middle Ages* (Leiden, 2001), 119-36.
Christys, Ann, 'Hispania after 711,' in H.-W. Goetz, J. Jarnut and W. Pohl (eds), *Regna and Gentes: The Relationship between Late Antique and Early Medieval Peoples and Kingdoms in the Transformation of the Roman World* (Leiden, 2003).
Christys, Ann, 'The *History* of Ibn Habib and Ethnogenesis in Al-Andalus,' in Richard Corradini, Max Diesenberger and Helmut Reimitz (eds), *The Construction of Communities in the Early Middle Ages: Texts, Resources, Artefacts* (Leiden, 2003), 323-48.
Clanchy, M. T., *From Memory to Written Record* (London, 1979).
Clarke, Catherine A. M., *Literary Landscape and the Idea of England, 700-1400* (Cambridge, 2006).
Cochelin, Isabelle, 'When Monks Were the Book: The Bible and Monasticism (6th-11th Centuries),' in Susan Boynton and Diane J. Reilly (eds), *The Practice of the Bible in the Middle Ages: Production, Reception & Performance in Western Christianity* (New York, 2011), 61-83.

Coffey, Heather M., 'Contesting the Eschaton in Medieval Iberia: The Polemical Intersection of Beatus of Liébana's Commentary on the Apocalypse and the Prophet's Miʿrājnāma,' in Christiane Gruber and Frederick Colby (eds), *The Prophet's Ascension: Cross-Cultural Encounters with the Islamic Miʿrāj Tales* (Bloomington, IN, 2010).
Cohen, Simona, *Animals as Disguised Symbols in Renaissance Art* (Leiden, 2008).
Coleman, Janet, *Ancient and Medieval Memories: Studies in the Reconstruction of the Past* (Cambridge, 1992).
Colish, Marcia L., *Peter Lombard Vol. 1* (Leiden, 1993).
Colish, Marcia L., *Studies in Scholasticism* (Aldershot, 2006).
Collins, Ann, *Teacher in Faith and Virtue: Lanfranc of Bec's Commentary on Saint Paul* (Leiden, 2007).
Collins, Roger, 'Literacy in Early Medieval Spain,' in Rosamond McKitterick (ed.), *The Uses of Literacy in Early Medieval Europe* (Cambridge, 1990), 109–33.
Collins, Roger, *Early Medieval Spain, Unity in Diversity, 400–1100* (London, 1995).
Collins, Roger, 'Continuity and Loss in Medieval Spanish Culture: The Evidence of MS Silos, Archivo Monástico 4,' in Roger Collins and Anthony Goodman (eds), *Medieval Spain: Culture, Conflict and Coexistence* (Basingstoke, 2002), 1–22.
Collins, Roger, *Caliphs and Kings: Spain, 796–1031* (Chichester, 2012).
Collins, Samuel W., *The Carolingian Debate over Sacred Space* (New York, 2012).
Constable, Giles, *Crusades and Crusading in the Twelfth Century* (Farnham, 2008).
Constable, Olivia Remie, 'Perceptions of the Umayyads in Christian Spanish Chronicles,' in Antoine Borrut and Paul M. Cobb (eds), *Umayyad Legacies: Medieval Memories from Syria to Spain* (Leiden, 2010), 105–30.
Contreni, John C., 'Carolingian Church,' in Robert Benedetto (ed.), *The New Westminster Dictionary of Church History Vol. 1: The Early, Medieval, and Reformation Eras* (Louisville, KT, 2008).
Copeland, Rita, 'The Curricular Classics of the Middle Ages,' in Rita Copeland (ed.), *The Oxford History of the Classical Reception of English Literature, Vol. 1 (800–1558)* (Oxford, 2016), 21–34.
Corfis, Ivy, *Al-Andalus, Sepharad and Medieval Iberia: Cultural Conflict and Diffusion* (Leiden, 2009).
Coulstock, Patricia H., *The Collegiate Church of Wimborne Minster* (Woodbridge, 1993).
Cowell, Andrew, *The Medieval Warrior Aristocracy: Gifts, Violence, Performance and the Sacred* (Cambridge, 2007).
Crouzel, Henri, 'NT Exegesis,' in Karl Rahner (ed.), *Encyclopedia of Theology: A Concise Sacramentum Mundi* (New York, 1975), 124–33.
Cuffel, Alexandra, *Gendering Disgust in Medieval Religious Polemic* (Notre Dame, IN, 2007).
Curtius, Ernst Robert, *European Literature and the Latin Middle Ages* (Princeton, NJ, 1990).
Dahan, Gilbert, 'Genres, Forms and Various Methods in Christian Exegesis in the Middle Ages,' in Magne Sæbø (ed.), *The Hebrew Bible Old Testament: The History of Its Interpretation 1/2: The Middle Ages* (Göttingen, 2000), 196–235.
Dalton, Paul, 'The Outlaw Hereward "the Wake": His Companions and Enemies,' in Paul Dalton and John C. Appleby (eds), *Outlaws in Medieval and Early Modern England: Crime, Government and Society, c. 1066–1600* (Farnham, 2009), 7–36.
Daniel-Rops, Henri, *The Church in the Dark Ages*, trans. Audrey Butler (London, 2001).
Darby, Peter, *Bede and the End of Time* (Farnham, 2012).

Davies, G. Scott, 'Early Medieval Ethics,' in Lawrence C. Becker and Charlotte B. Becker (eds), *A History of Western Ethics* (Oxford, 2003), 43–52.
Davies, R. R., *Domination and Conquest: The Experience of Ireland, Scotland and Wales 1100–1300* (Cambridge, 1990).
Davis, Gifford, 'The Development of a National Theme in Medieval Castilian Literature,' *Hispanic Review*, Vol. 3, No. 2 (1935), 149–61.
Davis, Jennifer R., *Charlemagne's Practice of Empire* (Cambridge, 2015).
De Epalza, Mikel, 'Mozarabs: An Emblematic Christian Minority in Islamic al- Andalus,' in Salma Khadra Jayyusi (ed.), *The Legacy of Muslim Spain* (Leiden, 1992), 149–70.
Deiss, Lucien, *Springtime of the Liturgy* (St Paul, MN, 1967).
De Lubac, Henri, *Medieval Exegesis Vol. 2: The Four Senses of Scripture*, trans. E. M. Macierowski (Grand Rapids, MI, 2000).
De Sota, Francisco, *Chronica de los Príncipes de Asturias y Cantabria* (Madrid, 1681).
De Vale, Manuel Criado, *Historia de Hita y su Arcipreste: vida y muerte de una villa mozárabe* (Guadalajara, 1998).
Deyermond, Alan D., 'The Death and Rebirth of Visigothic Spain in the *Estoria de España*,' *Revista de Canadiense de Estudio Hispánicos*, Vol. 9, No. 3 (1985): *Homenaje a Alfonso X, el Sabio* (1284–1984), 345–67.
Deyermond, Alan D., 'Uses of the Bible in the Poema de Fernan Gonzalez,' in David Hook and Barry Taylor (eds), *Cultures in Contact in Medieval Spain: Historical and Literary Essays Presented to L. P. Harvey* (London, 1990), 47–60.
Deyermond, Alan D., '"¿Rei otro sobre mí?": The Exile of the True King in Thirteenth-Century Castilian Literature,' in Rhian Davies and Anny Brooksbank Jones (eds), *The Place of Argument: Essays in Honour of Nicholas G. Round* (Woodbridge, 2007), 3–16.
De Jong, Myake, 'The Emperor Lothar and His *Bibliotheca Historiarum*,' in R. I. A. Nip, H. van Dijk, E. M. C. van Houts, C. H. J. M. Kneepkens and G. A. A. Kortekaas (eds), *Media Latinitas, a Collection of Essays to Mark the Occasion of the Retirement of L.J. Engels* (Turnhout, 1996), 229–35.
De Jong, Myake, 'Exegesis for an Empress,' in E. Cohen and M. B. de Jong (eds), *Medieval Transformations: Texts, Power, and Gifts in Context* (Leiden, 2001), 69–100.
De Riquer, Martín, *Manual de Heráldica Española* (Barcelona, 1942).
Díaz, Pablo, 'Visigothic Political Institutions,' in Peter Heather (ed.), *The Visigoths from the Migration Period to the Seventh Century: An Ethnographic Perspective* (Woodbridge, 1999), 321–72.
Díaz y Díaz, Manuel C., 'La circulation des manuscrits dans la Péninsule Ibérique du VIIIe au XIe siècle,' *Cahiers de civilisation médiévale*, Vol. 12 (1969), 219–41.
Díaz y Díaz, Manuel C., 'Isidoro en la edad media hispana,' in *Isidoriana* (León, 1961), 345–87; reproduced in Díaz y Díaz, *De Isidoro al Siglo XI. Ocho estudios sobre la vida literaria peninsular* (Barcelona, 1976), 141–201.
Di Sciacca, Claudia, *Finding the Right Words: Isidore's* Synomyna *in Anglo-Saxon England* (Toronto, 2008).
Dodds, Jerrilyn D., *Architecture and Ideology in Early Medieval Spain* (University Park, PA, 1990).
Dodds, Jerrilyn D., 'Islam, Christianity and the Problem of Religious Art,' in Jerrilyn D. Dodds, Bernard F. Reilly and John W. Williams (eds), *The Art of Medieval Spain, A. D. 500–1200* (New York, 1994), 26–37.
Dodds, Jerrilynn D., María Rosa Menocal and Abigail Krasner Balbale, *The Arts of Intimacy: Christians, Jews, and Muslims in the Making of Castilian Culture* (New Haven, CT, 2008).

Dolan, Terence, 'Writing in Ireland,' in David Wallace (ed.), *The Cambridge History of Medieval English Literature* (Cambridge, 1999).
Doubleday, Simon R., *The Lara Family: Crown and Nobility in Medieval Spain* (Cambridge, MA, 2001).
Drews, Wolfram, *The Unknown Neighbour. The Jew in the Thought of Isidore of Seville* (Leiden, 2006).
Duff, E. Gordon, *Early Printed Books* (Cambridge, 1893).
Duggan, Joseph J., *The 'Cantar de Mio Cid': Poetic Creation in Its Economic and Social Contexts* (Cambridge, 1989).
Dunham, Samuel Astley, *History of Spain and Portugal, Vol. 4* (London, 1835).
Dunbabin, Jean, 'The Maccabees as Exemplars in the Tenth and Eleventh Centuries,' in Katherine Walsh and Diana Wood (eds), *The Bible in the Medieval World: Essays in Memory of Beryl Smalley* (Oxford, 1985), 31–41.
Durham Reynolds, Leighton, *Texts and Transmission: A Survey of the Latin Classics* (Oxford, 1983).
Dyas, Dee, 'Medieval Patterns of Pilgrimage: A Mirror for Today?' in Craig G. Bartholomew and Fred Hughes (eds), *Explorations in a Christian Theology of Pilgrimage* (Aldershot, 2004), 92–109.
Earenfight, Theresa, *Queenship and Political Power in Medieval and Early Modern Spain: Women and Gender in the Modern World* (Aldershot, 2005).
Ecker, Heather, 'How to Administer a Conquered City in al-Andalus: Mosques, Parish Churches and Parishes,' in Cynthia Robinson and Leyla Rouhi (eds), *Under the Influence: Questioning the Comparative in Medieval Castile* (Leiden, 2005), 45–66.
Edwards, John: *The Spain of the Catholic Monarchs, 1474–1520* (Oxford, 2000).
Emmerson, Richard K., 'Medieval Illustrated Apocalyptic Manuscripts,' in Michael A. Ryan (ed.), *A Companion to the Premodern Apocalypse* (Leiden, 2015), 21–66.
Escalona, Julio, Isabel Velázquez Soriano and Paloma Juárez Benítez, 'Identification of the Sole Extant Original Charter Issued by Fernán González, Count of Castile (923–970),' *Journal of Iberian Studies*, Vol. 4, No. 2 (September 2012), 259–88.
Evans, G. R., *Philosophy and Theology in the Middle Ages* (London, 1993).
Evans, G. R. *The Thought of Gregory the Great* (Cambridge, 1986).
Evans, Michael R., *The Death of Kings: Royal Deaths in Medieval England* (London, 2007).
Falque Rey, Emma, 'Galicia and the Galicians in the Latin Chronicles of the Twelfth and Thirteenth Centuries,' in James D'Emilio (ed. and trans.), *Culture and Society in Medieval Galicia* (Leiden, 2015), 400–28.
Farina, William, *St James the Greater in History, Art and Culture* (Jefferson, NC, 2018).
Farrell, Joseph P., *God, History and Dialectic: The Theological Foundations of the Two Europes and Their Cultural Consequences* (Chanute, KS, 1997).
Fernández-Conde, Javier, and Antonio Linage, *El Libro de los Testamentos de la catedral de Oviedo* (Rome, 1971).
Fernández-Conde, Javier, and Antonio Linage, 'La Renovación Religiosa,' in Ricardo Garcia-Villoslada (ed.), *Historia de la Iglesia en España* (Madrid, 1982), 339–401.
Fernández Flórez, José A. (ed.), *Colección diplomática del monasterio de Sahagún (857–1300)*, IV (11001199) (León: Centro de Estudios e Investigación 'San Isidoro': Archivo Historico Diocesano, 1991).
Fernández Marcos, Natalio, *Scribes and Translators: Septuagint and Old Latin in the Books of Kings* (Leiden, 1994).
Fernández-Ordóñez, Inés, 'El Cluniacense Pedro de Poitiers y la *Chronica Adefonsi Imperatoris* y *Poema de Almería*,' *BRAH*, Vol. 122 (1963), 154–93.

Fernández-Ordóñez, Inés, 'La técnica historiográfica del Toledano. Procedimientos de organización del relato,' *Cahiers de linguistique et de civilisation hispaniques médiévales*, No. 26 (2003): 187–221.

Fernández-Ordóñez, Inés, 'La composición por etapas de la *Chronica latina regum Castellae* (1223–1237) de Juan de Soria,' *E-Spania: Revue électronique d'études hispaniques médiévales*, Vol. 2 (2006), 1–30.

Ferreiro, Albert, 'Simon Magus, Dogs, and Simon Peter,' in Albert Ferreiro (ed.), *The Devil, Heresy and Witchcraft in the Middle Ages: Essays in Honor of Jeffrey B. Russell* (Leiden, 1998), 45–91.

Fieldrowicz, Michael, 'General Introduction,' in *Explorations of the Psalms 1–32* (Part 3, Vol. 15) trans. Maria Boulding O. S. B. and edited by John E. Rotelle (New York, 2000), 13–66.

Filios, Denise K., 'Legend of the Fall: Conde Julián in Medieval Arabic and Hispano-Latin Historiography,' in Ivy A. Corfis, *Al-Andalus, Sepharad and Medieval Iberia* (Leiden, 2009), 219–34.

Fitzgerald John T., 'Gadara: Philodemus' Native City,' in John T. Fitzgerald, Dirk Obbink and Glenn S. Holland (eds), *Philodemus and the New Testament World* (Leiden, 2004), 343–99.

Firey, Abigail, 'The Letter of the Law: Carolingian Exegetes and the Old Testament,' in J. D. McAuliffe, B. D. Walsh and J. W. Goering (eds), *With Reverence for the Word: Medieval Scriptural Exegesis in Judaism, Christianity, and Islam* (Oxford, 2010), 204–24.

Fletcher, Richard, *The Episcopate in the Kingdom of León in the Twelfth Century* (Oxford, 1978).

Fletcher, Richard, *The Quest for El Cid* (Oxford, 1989).

Fletcher, Richard, 'Reconquest and Crusade in Spain, c. 1050–1150,' in Thomas F. Madden (ed.), *The Crusades: Essential Readings* (Oxford, 2002), 51–68.

Fletcher, Richard, *Saint James's Catapult: The Life and Times of Diego Gelmírez of Santiago de Compostela* (Oxford, 1984).

Fletcher, Richard, 'A Twelfth-Century View of the Spanish Past,' in J. R. Maddicott and D. M. Palliser (eds), *The Medieval State, Essays Presented to James Campbell* (London, 2000), 147–62.

Flores, Ángel (ed.), *An Anthology of Medieval Lyrics* (New York, 1962).

Flórez, Erique, and Manuel Risco, *España Sagrada*, 51 vols, vol. 1 (Madrid, 1747–1879).

Forti, Tova L., *Animal Imagery in the Book of Proverbs* (Leiden, 2008).

Fox, Dian, *Kings in Calderón: A Study in Characterization and Political Theory* (London, 1986).

Fraker, Charles F., *The Scope of History: Studies in the Historiography of Alfonso el Sabio* (Ann Arbor, MI, 1996).

Fraker, Charles F., 'The Latin Chronicle of the Kings of Castile. Translated with an Introduction and Notes by Joseph F. O'Callaghan,' in Anne Mette Hansen (ed.), *Variants 4 (2005) The Book as Artefact Text and Border* (Amsterdam, 2005), 326–36.

France, John, *The Crusades and the Expansion of Catholic Christendom 1000–1714* (Abingdon, 2005).

Francomano, Emily C., 'Castilian Vernacular Bibles in Iberia, c. 1250–1500,' in Susan Boynton and Diane J. Reilly (eds), *The Practice of the Bible in the Middle Ages: Production, Reception and Performance in Western Christianity* (New York, 2011), 315–37.

Friedman, John Block, *The Monstrous Races in Medieval Art and Thought* (Cambridge, MA, 1981).

Fulk, R. D., and Christopher M. Cain, *A History of Old English Literature* (Oxford, 2003).
Fuller, Amy, *Between Two Worlds: The autos sacramentales of Sor Juana Inés de la Cruz* (Cambridge, 2015).
Fulton, Henry, 'Troy Story: The Medieval Welsh *Ystorya Dared* and *Brut* Tradition of British History,' in Juliana Dresvina and Nicholas Sparks (eds), *The Medieval Chronicle VII* (Amsterdam, 2011), 137–50.
García Moreno, Luís A., 'Spanish Gothic Consciousness among the Mozarabs in al-Andalus (VIII–X Centuries),' in Alberto Ferreiro (ed.), *The Visigoths: Studies in Culture and Society* (Leiden, 1999), 303–23.
Gargano, Innocenzo, 'San Gregorio Magno esegeta della Bibbia,' *Liber Annus* Vol. 54 (2004), 261–94.
Garrison, Mary, 'Alcuin, *Carmen ix* and Hrabanus, *Ad Bonosum*: A Teacher and His Pupil Write Consolation,' in John Marenbon (ed.), *Poetry and Philosophy in the Middle Ages: A Festschrift for Peter Dronke* (Leiden, 2000), 63–78.
Garrison, Mary, 'The Bible and Alcuin's Interpretation of Current Events,' *Peritia Journal of the Medieval Academy of Ireland*, Vol. 16 (2002), 68–84.
Garrison, Mary, 'The Emergence of Carolingian Latin Literature and the Court of Charlemagne (780–814),' in Rosamond McKitterick (ed.), *Carolingian Culture: Emulation and Innovation* (Cambridge, 1994), 111–40.
Garrison, Mary, 'Letters to a King and Biblical Exempla: The Examples of Cathuulf and Clemens Peregrinus,' *Early Medieval Europe*, Vol. 7, No. 3 (1998), 305–28.
Geary, Patrick, *Furta Sacra: Thefts of Relics in the Central Middle Ages* (Princeton, NJ, 1990).
Georgiou, Constantine, 'Propagating the Hospitallers' *Passagum* Crusade Preaching the Liturgy in 1308–1309,' in Emanuel Buttigrieg and Simon Phillips (eds), *Islands and Military Orders, c. 1291–c. 1798* (London, 2016), 53–64.
Gibson, Margaret T., *The Bible in the Latin West* (Notre Dame, IN, 1993).
Gibson, Margaret T., *Lanfranc of Bec* (Oxford, 1978).
Gilbert, Maurice J. S. J., 'Introduction to Kearns' Dissertation,' in Pancratius C. Beentjes (ed.), *Conleth Kearns, The Expanded Text of Ecclesiasticus: Its Teaching on the Future Life as a Clue to Its Origin* (Berlin, 2011), 9–21.
Gillingham, John, *The English in the Twelfth Century: Imperialism, National Identity and Political Values* (Woodbridge, 2000).
Gillingham, Susan, *Psalms through the Centuries, Vol. 1* (Oxford, 2008).
Glick, Thomas F., *Islamic and Christian Spain in the Early Middle Ages* (Leiden, 2005).
Glick, Thomas, Steven Livesey and Faith Wallis (eds), *Medieval Science, Technology, and Medicine: An Encyclopedia* (New York, 2015).
Glunz, H. H., *A History of the Vulgate in England from Alcuin to Roger Bacon: Being an Enquiry into the Text of Some English Manuscripts of the Vulgate Gospels* (Cambridge, 1933).
Goering, Joseph W., 'An Introduction to Medieval Christian Biblical Interpretation,' in J. D. McAuliffe, B. D. Walsh and J. W. Goering (eds), *With Reverence for the Word: Medieval Scriptural Exegesis in Judaism, Christianity, and Islam* (Oxford, 2010), 197–203.
Goffart, Walter, 'Bede's *uera lex historiae* Explained,' *Anglo-Saxon England*, Vol. 34 (2005), 111–16.
Goldstein, Jonathan A., *I Maccabees: A New Translation with Introduction and Commentary* (New York, 1976).

González, Julio, *El reino de Castilla en la época de Alfonso VIII* (Madrid: Escuela de Estudios Medievales, 3 Vols, 1960).
González, Julio, 'La Crónica latina de los Reyes de Castilla', *Homenaje a don Agustín Millares Carlo* (2 Vols, Palma, 1975), Vol. 2, 55–70.
González-Casanovas, R. J., 'Cultural Discourse in Hispanic Historiography on the Reconquest and Conquest: Historicist Hermeneutics from Alfonso X to Las Casas,' in George F Mclean, Antonio Gallo and Robert Magliola (eds), *Hermeneutics and Interculturation* (Washington, DC, 2003), 163–82.
Gonzálvez, Ramón, 'The Persistence of the Mozarabic Liturgy in Toledo after A.D. 1080,' in Bernard F. Reilly (ed.), *Santiago, Saint-Denis, and Saint Peter: The Reception of the Roman Liturgy in León-Castile in 1080* (New York, 1985), 157–86.
Graff, Harvey J., *The Legacy of Literacy: Continuities and Contradictions in Western Culture and Society* (Chicago, IL, 1991).
Grant, Robert M., and David Tracy, *A Short History of the Interpretation of the Bible* (London, 1984).
Graves, Michael, 'The "Pagan" Background of Patristic Exegetical Methods,' in Mark Husband and Jeffrey P. Greenman (eds), *Ancient Faith for the Church's Future* (Downers Grove, IL, 2008), 93–109.
Grove, Kevin G., *Augustine on Memory* (Oxford, 2021).
Gyug, Richard, 'Early Medieval Bibles, Biblical Books, and the Monastic Liturgy in the Beneventan Region,' in Susan Boynton and Diane J. Reilly (eds), *The Practice of the Bible in the Middle Ages: Production, Reception & Performance in Western Christianity* (New York, 2011), 34–60.
Hall, Alaric, 'Interlinguistoc Communication in Bede's Hist*oria ecclesiastica gentis Anglorum*,' in Alaric Hall, Olga Timofeeva, Agnes Kiricsi and Bethany Fox (eds), *Interfaces between Language and Culture in Medieval England: A Festschrift for Matti Kilpiö* (Leiden, 2010), 37–80.
Halperin, David J., *Seeing Ezekiel: Text and Psychology* (Philadelphia, PA, 1993).
Hanson, R. P. C., 'Biblical Exegesis in the Early Church,' in P. R. Ackroyd and C. F. Evans (eds), *The Cambridge Bible Vol. 1: From the Beginnings to Jerome* (Cambridge, 1970), 412–53.
Hanson, R. P. C., *Allegory and Event: A Study of the Sources and Significance of Origen's Interpretation of Scripture* (Louisville, KT, 2002).
Harmless, William S. J., *Augustine in His Own Words* (Washington, DC, 2010).
Harris, Anne F., 'The Iconography of Narrative,' in Colum Hourihane (ed.), *The Routledge Guide to Medieval Iconography* (Abingdon, 2017), 282–94.
Harris, Jennifer A., 'The Bible and the Meaning of History in the Middle Ages,' in Susan Boynton and Diane J. Reilly (eds), *The Practice of the Bible in the Middle Ages: Production, Reception & Performance in Western Christianity* (New York, 2011), 84–104.
Harris, M. Roy, 'Translations of John XII and XIII–XVIII from a Fourteenth-Century Franciscan Codex (Assisi, Chiesa Nuova MS. 9),' *Transactions of the American Philosophical Society*, Vol. 75, No. 4 (1985), 1–149.
Hazbun, Geraldine, *Narratives of the Islamic Conquest of Medieval Spain* (New York, 2015).
Henriet, Patrick, '*Historia Silense*: "The History of Silos,"' in David Thomas and Alex Mallett (eds), *Works on Christian-Muslim Relations: A Bibliographical History, Vol. 3 (1050–1200)* (Leiden, 2009), 370–4.

Hernández, Francisco-Javier, 'La corte de Fernando III y la casa real de Francia: Documentación, crónicas y monumentos,' *Actas del VIII Congreso de Estudios Medievales: Fernando III y su tiempo*, Edition 9 (2003), 104–55.
Herrin, Judith, *The Formation of Christendom* (Princeton, NJ, 1987).
Hilhorst, A., 'Biblical Scholarship in the Early Church,' in J. den Boeft and M. L. van Pollvan de Lisdonk (eds), *The Impact of Scripture on Early Christianity* (Leiden, 1999), 1–19.
Hillgarth, J. N., 'Spanish Historiography and Iberian Reality,' *History and Theory*, Vol. 24, No. 1 (February 1985), 23–43.
Hillgarth, J. N., *The Visigoths in History and Legend* (Toronto, 2009).
Hinson, E. Glenn, *The Church Triumphant: A History of Christianity up to 1300* (Macon, GA, 1995).
Hitchcock, Richard, *Mozarabs in Medieval and Early Modern Spain: Identities and Influences* (Aldershot, 2008).
Holder, Arthur G., 'Bede and the New Testament', in Scott DeGregorio (ed.), *The Cambridge Companion to Bede* (Cambridge, 2010), 142–55.
Holmes, Urban T., *A History of Christian Spirituality: An Analytical Introduction* (Harrisburg, PA, 2002).
Housley, Norman, *Contesting the Crusades* (Oxford, 2006).
Hughes, Kevin L., *Constructing Antichrist: Paul, Biblical Doctrine, and the Development of Doctrine in the Early Middle Ages* (Washington, DC, 2005).
Hunter Blair, Peter, *The World of Bede* (Cambridge, 1990).
Irvine, Martin, *The Making of Textual Culture: 'Grammatica' and Literary Theory, 350–1100* (Cambridge, 1994).
Iogna-Prat, Dominique, *Order and Exclusion: Cluny and Christendom Face Heresy, Judaism and Islam (1000–1150)*, trans. Graham Robert Edwards (New York, 2002).
Jameson, Caroline, 'Ovid in the Sixteenth Century,' in. J. W. Binns (ed.), *Ovid* (Abingdon, 1973), 210–24.
Jaspert, Nikolas, *The Crusades*, trans. Phyllis G. Jestice (Abingdon, 2006).
Johnson, Luke Timothy, and William S. Kurz S. J., *The Future of Catholic Biblical Scholarship: A Constructive Conversation* (Cambridge, 2002).
Jotischky, Andrew, *Crusades and the Crusader States* (London: Routledge, 2017).
Jurgens, William A., *The Faith of the Early Church Fathers, Vol. 3* (Collegeville, MN, 1979).
Kahn, Walter, *Romanesque Bible Illumination* (New York, 1982).
Kaplan, Gregory B., 'Friend "of" Foe: The Divided Loyalty of Álvar Fáñez in the *Poema de Mio Cid*,' in Cynthia Robinson and Leya Rouhi (eds), *Under the Influence: Questioning the Comparative in Medieval Castile* (Leiden, 2005), 153–72.
Kaske, R. E., Arthur Groos and Michael W. Twowey, *Medieval Christian Literary Imagery: A Guide to Interpretation* (Toronto, 1988).
Kauntze, Mark, *Authority and Imitation: A Study of the Cosmographia of Bernard Silvestris* (Leiden, 2014).
Kauffman, Claus Michael, *Biblical Imagery in Medieval England, 700–1500* (Turnhout, 2003).
Kelly, Joseph F.,Kelly, Joseph F., 'Carolingian Era, Late,' in Allan Fitzgerald and John Cavadini (eds), *Augustine through the Age: An Encyclopedia* (Cambridge, 1999), 129–32.
Kelly, Joseph F., 'Bede's Use of Augustine for His *Commentarium in principium Genesis*,' in Frederick van Fleteren and Joseph C. Schnaubelt OSM (eds), *Augustine: Biblical Exegete* (New York, 2001), 189–96.

Kelly, Michael J., *Isidore of Seville and the Liber Ludiciorum: The Struggle for the Past in the Visigothic Kingdom* (Leiden, 2021).
Kennedy, George A., *Classical Rhetoric and Its Christian and Secular Tradition from Ancient to Modern Times* (Chapel Hill, NC, 1999).
Kennedy, Hugh, *Muslim Spain and Portugal: A Political History of al-Andalus* (London, 1996).
Kessler, Stephan C., S. J., 'Gregory the Great: A Figure of Tradition and Transition in Church Exegesis,' in Magne Sæbø (ed.), Hebrew Bible Old Testament: The History of Interpretation (Göttingen, 2000), 135–47.
Kessler, Stephan C., S. J., 'Gregory the Great,' in Charles Kannengiesser, *Handbook of Patristic Exegesis Vol. Two: The Bible in Ancient Christianity* (Leiden, 2006), 1336–68.
Kienzle, Beverley Mayne, *Cistercians, Heresy and Crusade in Occitania, 1145–1229* (Woodbridge, 2001).
King, P. D., *Law and Society in the Visigothic Kingdom* (Cambridge, 1972).
Klein, Peter K., 'Introduction: The Apocalypse in Medieval Art,' in Susan Boynton and Diane J. Reilly (eds), *The Practice of the Bible in the Middle Ages: Production, Reception & Performance in Western Christianity* (New York, 2011), 159–99.
Kleiner, Fred S., *Gardner's Art through the Ages: The Western Perspective*, Vol. 1, 13th edn (Boston, MA, 2009).
Kleist, Aaron J., *Striving with Grace: View of Free Will in Anglo-Saxon England* (Toronto, 2008).
Kogman-Appel, Katrin, *Jewish Book Art between Islam and Christianity: The Decoration of Hebrew Bibles in Medieval Spain* (Leiden, 2004).
Kosto, Adam J., *Making Agreements in Medieval Catalonia: Power, Order, and the Written Word 1000–1200* (Cambridge, 2004).
Kuntz, J. Kenneth, 'Growling Dogs and Thirsty Deer: Uses of Animal Imagery in Psalmic Rhetoric,' in Robert L. Foster and David M. Howard (eds), *My Words Are Lovely: Studies in the Rhetoric of the Psalms* (New York, 2008), 46–62.
Las Heras, Isabel, 'Temas y figuras bíblicas en el discurso político de *Chronica Adefonsi Imperatoris*,' in N. Guglielmi and A. Rucquoi (eds), *El Discurso político en la Edad Media* (Buenos Aires, 1995), 117–40.
Lawrence-Mathers, Anne, *Medieval Meteorology: Forecasting the Weather from Aristotle to the Almanac* (Cambridge, 2020).
Leclercq, Dom Jean, 'The Exposition and Exegesis of Scripture: From Gregory the Great to St Bernard,' in G. W. H. Lampe (ed.), *The Cambridge History of the Bible, Vol. 2: The West from the Fathers to the Reformation* (Cambridge, 1969), 183–97.
Leclercq, Dom Jean, *The Love of Learning and the Desire for God: A Study of Monastic Culture* (New York, 1974).
Leonardi, Claudio, 'Aspects of Old Testament Interpretation in the Church from the Seventh to the Tenth Centuries,' in Magne Sæbø (ed.), *Hebrew Bible Old Testament: The History of Interpretation* (Göttingen, 2000), 135–47.
Levy, I. C., *The Bible in Medieval Tradition: The Letter to the Galatians* (Cambridge, 2011).
Levy, I. C., 'Commentaries on the Pauline Epistles in the Carolingian Era,' Steven R. Cartwright (ed.), *A Companion to St Paul in the Middle Ages* (Leiden, 2013), 145–74.
Linage Conde, Antonio, *Los origenes del monacato benedictino en la Peninsula Ibérica Vol. 3* (León, 1973).
Linder, Amnon, *Raising Arms: Liturgy in the Struggle to Liberate Jerusalem in the Late Middle Ages* (Turnhout, 2003).

Lindsay, W. M., *Notae Latinae: An Account of Abbreviation in Latin Manuscripts of the Early Minuscule Period (c. 700–850)* (Cambridge, 1915).
Linehan, Peter, *Past and Present in Medieval Spain* (Farnham, 1992).
Linehan, Peter, *The Spanish Church and the Papacy in the Thirteenth Century* (Cambridge, 1971).
Linehan, Peter, 'Religion, Nationalism and National Identity in Medieval Spain and Portugal,' in Stuart Mews (ed.), *Religion and National Identity, Papers Read at the Nineteenth Summer Meeting and the Twentieth Winter Meeting of the Ecclesiastical History Society* (Oxford, 1982), 161–99.
Linehan, Peter, 'Review of *Chronica Hispana Saeculi XII. Part I*,' *Journal of Theological Studies*, Vol. 43 (1992), 731–7.
Linehan, Peter, *History and the Historians of Medieval Spain* (Oxford, 1993).
Linehan, Peter, *The Ladies of Zamora* (Manchester, 1997).
Linehan, Peter, 'Castile, Portugal and Navarre,' in David Abulafia (ed.), *The Cambridge Medieval History V, c.1198–c.1300* (Cambridge, 1999), 668–702.
Linehan, Peter, '*Columpna firmissima*: D. Gil Torres, the Cardinal of Zamora,' in Simon Barton and Peter Linehan (eds), *Cross, Crescent and Conversion: Studies on Medieval Spain and Christendom in Memory of Richard Fletcher* (Leiden, 2008), 241–62.
Linehan, Peter, *Spain, 1157–1300. A Partible Inheritance* (Oxford, 2008).
Linehan, Peter, 'Juan de Soria: The Chancellor as Chronicler,' *e-Spania* [En ligne], 21 décembre 2006, mis en ligne le 16 août 2010, 1–12
Loewe, E. A., 'The *Codex Cavensis*: New Light on Its Later History,' in Robert P. Casey, Silva Lake and Agnes K. Lake (eds), *Quantulacumque: Studies Presented to Kirsopp Lake, 1937* (London, 1937), 325–31.
Loewe, Raphael, 'The Medieval History of the Latin Vulgate,' in G. W. H. Lampe (ed.), *The Cambridge History of the Bible, Vol. 2: The West from the Fathers to the Reformation* (Cambridge, 1969), 102–54.
Logan, F. Donald, *A History of the Church in the Middle Ages* (London, 2002).
Lomax, Derek W., 'The Authorship of the *Chronique Latine des rois de Castile*,' *Bulletin of Hispanic Studies*, Vol. 40 (1963), 205–11.
Lomax, Derek W., *The Reconquest of Spain* (London, 1978).
López Gómez, Margarita, 'The Mozarabs: Worthy Bearers of Islamic Culture,' in Salma Khadra Jayyusi (ed.), *The Legacy of Muslim Spain* (Leiden, 1992), 171–5.
Louth, Andrew, *The Church in History Vol. Three: Greek East and Latin West, the Church AD 681–1071* (New York, 2007).
Lowe, E. A. (ed.), *Codices Latini Antiquiores, Part XI* (Oxford, 1966).
Lowney, Chris, *A Vanished World: Muslims, Christians, and Jews in Medieval Spain* (Oxford, 2005).
Luis Corral, Fernando, 'Alfonso VIII of Castile's Judicial Process at the Court of Henry II of England: An Effective and Valid Arbitration?' *Nottingham Medieval Studies*, Vol. 50 (2006), 22–42.
McClure, Judith, 'Bede's Old Testament Kings,' in Patrick Wormald, Donald Bullough and Roger Collins (eds), *Ideal and Reality in Frankish and Anglo-Saxon Society: Studies Presented to J. M. Wallace-Hadrill* (Oxford, 1983), 76–98.
McCluskey, Raymond, 'Malleable Accounts: Views of the Past in Twelfth-Century Iberia,' in Paul Magdalino (ed.), *The Perception of the Past in Twelfth-Century Europe* (London, 1992), 211–25.

McGinn, Bernard, 'John's Apocalypse and the Apocalyptic Mentality,' in Richard K. Emmerson and Bernard McGinn (eds), *The Apocalypse in the Middle Ages* (New York, 1992), 3-19.
McGowan, Andrew B., 'God in Early Latin Theology: Tertullian and the Trinity,' in Andrew B. McGowan, Brian E. Daley S. J. and Timothy J. Gaden (eds), *God in Early Christian Thought: Essays in Memory of Lloyd G. Patterson* (Leiden, 2009), 61-82.
McKitterick, Rosamond, *History and Memory in the Carolingian World* (Cambridge, 2004).
McKitterick, Rosamond, 'The Carolingian Renaissance of Culture and Learning,' in Joanna Story (ed.), *Charlemagne, Empire and Society* (Manchester, 2005), 151-66.
MacLean, Simon, *Kingship and Politics in the Late Ninth Century: Charles the Fat and the End of the Carolingian Empire* (Cambridge, 2003).
McLynn, Neil B., *Ambrose of Milan* (Berkeley, CA, 1994).
McWilliam, Joanne E., 'The Context of Spanish Adoptionism: A Review,' in Michael Gervers and Ramzi Gibran Bikhazi, *Conversion and Continuity: Indigenous Christian Communities in Islamic Lands Eighth to Eighteenth Centuries* (Toronto, 1990), 75-88.
Maloy, Rebecca, *Inside the Offertory: Chronology and Transmission* (Oxford, 2010).
Mansilla, Demetrio, 'Dos Códices Visigóticos de la Catedral de Burgos,' *Hispania Sacra* 2 (Madrid, 1949), 381-418.
Mansilla, Demetrio, *Catálogo de los Códices de la Catedral de Burgos* (Madrid, 1952).
Mansilla, Demetrio, *La documentación pontificia hasta Inocencio III (965-1216)* (Rome, 1955).
Mansilla, Demetrio, 'La supuesta metrópoli de Oviedo,' *Hispania Sacra*, 8 (Madrid, 1955), 259-74.
Marsden, Richard, *The Text of the Old Testament in Anglo-Saxon England* (Cambridge, 1995).
Marías, Julián, *Understanding Spain* (Ann Arbor, MI, 1990).
Martens, Peter W., *Origen and Scripture: The Contours of an Exegetical Life* (Oxford, 2012).
Martin, Dale B., *Pedagogy of the Bible: An Analysis and Proposal* (Louisville, KT, 2008).
Martin, Georges, 'Fondations monastiques et territorialité. Comment Rodrigue de Tolède a inventé la Castille,' in Patrick Henriet (ed.), *A la recherché de légitimités chrétiennes, Représentations de l'espace et du temps dans l'Espagne médiévale, IXe- XIIIe siècle* (Lyon, 2003), 243-62.
Martin, Therese, *Queen as King: Politics and Architectural Propaganda in Twelfth-Century Spain* (Leiden, 2006).
Martínez, H. Salvador, *Alfonso X, the Learned: A Biography*, trans. Odile Cisneros (Leiden, 2010).
Martínez, Marcos G., 'Regesta de Don Pelayo, Obispo de Oviedo,' *Boletín del Instituto de Estudios Asturianos*, Vol. 18 (1964), 211-28.
Martz, Linda, *A Network of Converso Families in Early Modern Toledo: Assimilating a Minority* (Ann Arbor, MI, 2003).
Matilla Tascón, Antonio, *Guía-Inventario de los Archivos de Zamora y su Provincia* (Madrid, 1964).
Matter, E. Ann, *The Voice of My Beloved: The Song of Songs in Medieval Christianity* (Pennsylvania, PA, 1990).
Matter, E. Ann, 'The Apocalypse in Early Medieval Exegesis,' in Richard K. Emmerson and Bernard McGinn (eds), *The Apocalypse in the Middle Ages* (New York, 1992), 38-50.
Maulana, Muhammad Ali, *A Manual of Hadith: The Traditions of the Prophet Muhammad* (London, 1978).

Mayhew, Nicholas J., 'Scotland: Economy and Society,' in John Bintliff (ed.), *A Companion to Archaeology* (Oxford, 2003), 107–24.
Menéndez Pidal, Ramón, *The Cid and His Spain*, trans. Harold Sunderland (Ann Arbor, MI, 1934).
Mentré, Mireille, *El Estilo Mozárabe: La Pintura Cristiana Hispánica en Torno al Año Mil* (Madrid, 1994).
Merrills, Andrew H., *History and Geography in Late Antiquity* (Cambridge, 2005).
Messier, Ronald A., *The Almoravids and the Meaning of Jihad* (Santa Barbara, CA, 2010).
Metzger, Bruce M., *The Text of the New Testament: Its Transmission, Corruption, and Restoration* (Oxford, 1968).
Metzger, Bruce M., *The Early Versions of the New Testament* (Oxford, 1977).
Meyer, Ann R. *Medieval Allegory and the Building of the New Jerusalem* (Woodbridge, 2003).
Minnis, Alastair, *Medieval Theory of Authorship: Scholastic Literary Attitudes in the Later Middle Ages* (Philadelphia, PA, 1988).
Monsalvo Antón, José María, 'Construyendo discursos medievales sobre urbano: episodios de la ciudad de León bajo la monarquía asturiana ségun la cronista cristiana,' in Gregorio del ser Quijano and Iñaki Martín Viso (eds), *Espacios de Poder y Formas Sociales en la Edad Media* (Salamanca, 2007), 220–41.
Moore, Michael E., 'Royal and Episcopal Power in the Frankish Realms' (Unpublished PhD thesis, University of Michigan, 1993).
Morano Rodríguez, Ciriaca, *Glosas marginales de Vetus Latina en las Biblias Vulgatas españoles: 1–2 Samuel* (Madrid, 1989).
Moreno, Luis, 'Federalization in Multinational Spain,' in Michael Burgess and John Pinder (eds), *Multinational Federations* (Abingdon, 2007), 86–107.
Moreno Hernández, Antonio, *Las glosas marginales de Vetus Latina en las Biblias Vulgatas españoles: 1–2 Reyes* (Madrid, 1992).
Morton, Nicholas, 'The Defence of the Holy Land and the Memory of the Maccabees' (Taylor and Francis on-line: https://doi.org/10.1016/j.jmedhist.2010.06.002, 2012), 275–93.
Morton, Nicholas, 'Walls of Defence for the House of Israel: Ezek. 13:5 and the Crusading Movement,' in Elizabeth Lapina and Nicholas Morton (eds), *The Use of the Bible in Crusader Sources* (Leiden, 2017), 403–20.
Muldoon, James, *Empire and Order: The Concept of Empire 800–1800* (Basingstoke, 1999).
Mullins, Edwin, *The Pilgrimage to Santiago* (Oxford: Interlink, 2001).
Nees, Lawrence, 'Problems of Form and Function in Early Medieval Bibles from Northwest Europe,' in John Williams (ed.), *Imaging the Early Medieval Bible* (University Park, PA, 1999), 121–78.
Nelson, Janet L., 'Carolignian Royal Funerals,' in Frans Thews and Janet L. Nelson (eds), *Rituals of Power from Late Antiquity to the Early Middle Ages* (Leiden, 2000), 131–84.
Nepaulsingh, Colbert I., *Towards a History of Literary Composition in Medieval Spain* (Toronto, 1986).
Nickson, Tom, *Toledo Cathedral: Building Histories in Medieval Castile* (University Park, PA, 2015).
Nicolson, Marjorie Hope, *Mountain Gloom and Mountain Glory: The Development of Aesthetics of the Infinite* (Ithaca, NY, 1997).
Nuñez Rodríguez, Manuel, *Muerte Coronada: El mito de los reyes en la Catedral compostelana* (Santiago de Compostela, 1999).

Ovidio, Capitani, Ovidio, Giuseppe Galasso and Roberto Salvini, 'The Normans in Sicily and Southern Italy,' Lincei Lectures, 1974 (Oxford, 1977).
O'Callaghan, Joseph F., 'The Beginnings of the Cortes in León-Castile,' *American Historical Review*, Vol. 74, No. 5 (1969), 1503–37.
O'Callaghan, Joseph F., *A History of Medieval Spain* (New York, 1975).
O'Callaghan, Joseph F., *Alfonso X and the Cantigas de Santa Maria: A Poetic Biography* (Leiden, 1998).
O'Callaghan, Joseph F., *Reconquest and Crusade* (Philadelphia, PA, 2003).
Ó Corrain, Donnchádh, 'Irish Legends and Genealogy: Recurrent Aetiologies,' in Tore Nyberg (ed.), *History and the Heroic Tale: A Symposium* (Odense, 1985).
Ogden, Dunbar H., *The Staging of Drama in the Medieval Church* (Cranbury, NJ, 2002).
Pacey, Arnold, and Francesca Bray, *Technology in World Civilization: A Thousand Year Memory* (Cambridge, MA, 2021).
Pattison, David G., 'The Role of Women in Some Medieval Spanish Epic and Chronicle Texts,' in Rhian Davies and Annie Brooksbank Jones (eds), *The Place of Argument: Essays in Honour of Nicholas G Round* (Woodbridge: Boydell and Brewer, 2007), 17–30.
Patton, Pamela A., *Romanesque Cloister: Cloister Imagery and Religious Life in Medieval Spain* (New York, 2008).
Paxton, F. S., 'Curing Bodies – Curing Souls: Hrabanus Maurus, Medical Education, and the Clergy in Ninth-Century Francia,' *Journal of the History of Medicine*, Vol. 50 (1995), 230–52.
Payne, Stanley G., *Spanish Catholicism: An Overview* (Madison, WI, 1984).
Pendergast, John S., *Religion, Allegory and Literacy in Early Modern England, 1560–1640: The Control of the Word* (Aldershot, 2006).
Perarau, Josep, *Jornades internacionals d'estudi sobre el Bisbe Feliu d'Urgel. Crònica estudis* (Barcelona, 2000).
Pérez González, Maurilio, 'Influencias clásicas y bíblicas en la *Chronica Adefonsi Imperatoris*,' in Maulirio Pérez González (ed.), *I Congreso Nacional de Latín Medieval* (León, 1995), 349–55.
Pérez Llamazares, Julio, *Catálogo de los Códices y Documentos de la Real Colegiata de San Isidoro de León* (León, 1923).
Peters, F. E., *The Monotheists: Jews, Christians, and Muslims in Conflict and Competition Vol. 2, The Words and Will of God* (Princeton, NJ, 2003).
Phillips, Jonathan, *The Crusades 1095–1197* (Harlow, 2002).
Phillips, Jonathan, *The Second Crusade, Extending the Frontiers of Christendom* (New Haven, CT, 2007).
Pick, Lucy K., *Conflict and Coexistence, Archbishop Rodrigo de Toledo and the Muslims and Jews of Medieval Spain* (Kalamazoo, MI, 2004).
Pimenta-Bey, José V., 'Moorish Spain: Academic Source and Foundation for the Rise and Success of Western European Universities in the Middle Ages,' in Ivan Van Sermita (ed.), *Golden Age of the Moor Vol. 11* (Piscataway, NJ, 1991), 182–247.
Plötz, Robert, '*Pregrinato ad Lumina Sancti Jacobi*,' in John Williams and Alison Stones (eds), *The Codex Calixtus and the Shrine of St James* (Tübingen, 1992), 37–50.
Poleg, Eyal, '"A Ladder Set Up on Earth": The Bible in Medieval Sermons,' in Susan Boynton and Diane J. Reilly (eds), *The Practice of the Bible in the Middle Ages: Production, Reception & Performance in Western Christianity* (New York, 2011), 205–27.

Poole, Kevin R., 'Beatus of Liébana: Medieval Spain and the Othering of Islam,' in Karolyn Kinane and Michael A. Ryan (eds), *End of Days: Essays on the Apocalypse from Antiquity to Modernity* (Jefferson, NC, 2009).
Potter, Robert, *The Early English Morality Play: Origins, History, and Influence of a Dramatic Tradition* (London, 1975).
Powell, Brian, *Epic and Chronicle: The Poema de Mio Cid and the Crónica de Veinte Reyes* (London, 1983).
Powell, Brian, 'Historiography: Annals and Latin Chronicles up to *de Rebus Hispaniae*,' E. Michael Gerli (ed.), *Medieval Iberia: An Encyclopaedia* (New York, 2003), 393–5.
Powell, James, 'Innocent III and Alexius III: A Crusader Plan that Failed,' in Marcus Bull and Norman Housley, *The Experience of Crusading, Book 1* (Cambridge, 2003), 96–102.
Procter, Evelyn S., *Curia and Cortes in León and Castile 1072–1295* (Cambridge, 1980).
Purkis, William J., *Crusading Spirituality in the Holy Land and Iberia c.1095–c.1187* (Woodbridge, 2008).
Purkis, William J., 'Eleventh- and Twelfth-Century Perspectives on State Building in the Iberian Peninsula,' *Reading Medieval Studies*, Vol. 36 (2010), 57–75.
Pyper, Hugh S., *The Unchained Bible: Cultural Appropriations of Biblical Texts* (London, 2012).
Reichl, Karl, 'Plotting the Map of Medieval Oral Literature,' in Karl Reichl (ed.), *Medieval Oral Literature* (Göttingen, 2012), 3–70.
Reilly, Bernard F., *The Kingdom of León-Castilla under Queen Urraca, 1109–1126* (Princeton, NJ, 1982).
Reilly, Bernard F., 'Rodrigo Gimenez de Rada's Portrait of Alfonso VI of Leon-Castile in the *De Rebus Hispaniae*: Historical Methodology in the Thirteenth Century,' in Instituto d'España (ed.) *Estudios en homenaje a don Claudio Sanchez Albornoz en sus 90 años*, Vol. 3 (Buenos Aires, 1985), 87–97.
Reilly, Bernard F., *The Medieval Spains* (Cambridge, 1993).
Reilly, Bernard F., *The Kingdom of León-Castilla under King Alfonso VII, 1126–1157* (Philadelphia, PA, 1998).
Reilly, Bernard F., 'Bishop Lucas of Túy and the Latin Chronicle Tradition in Iberia,' *The Catholic Historical Review*, Vol. 93, No. 4 (2007), 767–88.
Reilly, Bernard F., 'The *Chronica Latina Regum Castellae*: Historical Composition at the Court of Fernando III of Castile, 1217–1252,' *Viator*, Vol. 41, No. 1 (2010), 140–54.
Reilly, Diana J., 'Lectern Bibles and Liturgical Reform,' in Susan Boynton and Diane J. Reilly (eds), *The Practice of the Bible in the Middle Ages: Production, Reception & Performance in Western Christianity* (New York, 2011), 105–25.
Reinhardt, Klaus, and Horacio Santiago-Otero, *Biblioteca Bíblia Ibérica Medieval* (Madrid, 1986).
Reinhardt, Klaus, and Ramón González, *Catálogo de Códices Biblicos de la Catedral de Toledo* (Madrid, 1990).
Reventlow, Henning Graf, *History of Biblical Interpretation, Vol. 2: From Late Antiquity to the End of the Middle Ages*, trans. James O. Duke (Atlanta, GA, 1994).
Rico, Christophe, 'New Testament Greek,' in David E. Aune (ed.), *The Blackwell Companion to the New Testament* (Malden, MA, 2010), 61–77.
Rigobon, Patrizo, 'Francisco María Tubino: Between Federalism and Iberianism,' Joan Ramón (ed.), *Iberian Modalities: A Relational Approach to the Study of Culture in the Iberian Peninsula* (Liverpool, 2013), 99–108.
Riley-Smith, Jonathan, *The First Crusade and the Idea of Crusading* (London, 1993).
Risco, Manuel, *Historia de Alfonso VII el Emperador* (León, 1792; facsímile).

Roberts, Bleddyn J., 'The Old Testament: Manuscripts, Text and Versions,' in G. W. H. Lampe (ed.), *The Cambridge History of the Bible, Vol. 2: The West from the Fathers to the Reformation* (Cambridge, 1969), 1–26.

Roberts, Kathleen Glenister, *Alterity and Narrative: Stories and the Negotiation of Western Identities* (New York, 2007).

Rodríguez López, Ana, 'Narratives of Expansion, Last Wills, Poor Expectations and the Conquest of Seville, 1248,' John Hudson and Sally Crumplin, *The Making of Europe: Essays in Honour of Robert Bartlett* (Leiden, 2016), 123–43.

Rodríguez-Velasco, Jesús D., *Order and Chivalry: Knighthood and Citizenship in Late Medieval Castile*, trans. Eunice Rodríguez Ferguson (Philadelphia, PA, 2010).

Roest, Bert, 'Mendicant School Exegesis,' in Susan Boynton and Diane J. Reilly (eds), *The Practice of the Bible in the Middle Ages: Production, Reception & Performance in Western Christianity* (New York, 2011), 179–204.

Rogers, Randall, *Latin Siege Warfare in the Twelfth Century* (Oxford, 1992).

Rojas Gabriel, Manuel, 'Alfonso VII in the Face of the Reformulation of Power in al-Andalus, 1145–57: An Essay in Strategic Logic,' *Journal of Military History*, Vol. 15 (2019), 117–47.

Roth, Norman, *Jews, Visigoths and Muslims in Medieval Spain, Cooperation and Conflict* (Leiden, 1994).

Rowe, Erin Kathleen, *Saint and Nation: Santiago, Teresa of Avila, and Plural Identities in Early Modern Spain* (Pittsburgh, PA, 2011).

Ruiz, Teófilo F., 'Unsacred Monarchy: The Kings of Castile in the Late Middle Ages,' in Sean Wilentz (ed.), *Rites of Power: Symbolism, Ritual and Politics Since the Middle Ages* (Philadelphia, PA, 1985), 109–44.

Ruiz, Teófilo F., *From Heaven to Earth, the Reordering of Castilian Society 1150–1350* (Princeton, NJ, 2004).

Ruiz, Teófilo F., *A King Travels: Festive Traditions in Late Medieval and Early Modern Spain* (Princeton, NJ, 2012).

Salvador Martínez, H., *El 'Poema de Almería' y la épica románica* (Madrid, 1975).

Satterlee, Craig Alan, *Ambrose of Milan's Method of Mystagogical Preaching* (Collegeville, MN, 2002).

Schein, Moshe, *Gateway to the Heavenly City and the Catholic West* (Aldershot, 2005).

Schildgen, Brenda Deen, *Power and Prejudice: The Reception of the Gospel of Mark* (Detroit, MI, 1999).

Shadis, Miriam, *Berenguela of Castile (1180–1246) and Political Women in the High Middle Ages* (Basingstoke, 2009).

Shah-Kazemi, Reza, 'From the Spirituality of *Jihād* to the Ideology of Jihadism,' in Joseph E. B. Lumbard (ed.), *Islam, Fundamentalism and the Betrayal of a Tradition, Revised and Expanded: Essays by Western Muslim Scholars* (Bloomington, IN, 2009), 119–48.

Shepherd, Geoffrey, 'English Versions of the Scriptures Before Wyclif,' in G. W. H. Lampe (ed.), *The Cambridge History of the Bible, Vol. 2: The West from the Fathers to the Reformation* (Cambridge, 1969), 362–87.

Sheppard, Alice, *Families of the King: Writing Identity in the Anglo-Saxon Chronicle* (Toronto, 2004).

Sholod, Barton, *Charlemagne in Spain: The Cultural Legacy of Roncesvalles* (Geneva, 1966).

Simon, David, 'Late Romanesque Art in Spain,' in Jerrilynn D. Dodds, Bernard F. Reilly and John Williams (eds), *The Art of Medieval Spain, A.D. 500–1200* (New York, 1994), 199–329.

Smalley, Beryl, 'The Exposition and Exegesis of Scripture: The Bible in the Medieval Schools,' in G. W. H. Lampe (ed.), *The Cambridge History of the Bible, Vol. 2: The West from the Fathers to the Reformation* (Cambridge, 1969), 197–220.
Smalley, Beryl, *The Study of the Bible in the Middle Ages* (Notre Dame, IN, 1978).
Smalley, Beryl, *The Gospels in the Schools c. 100–1280* (London, 1985).
Smith, Colin, *The Making of the Poema de Mio Cid* (Cambridge, 1983).
Smith, Colin, 'The Geography and History of Iberia in the *Liber Sancti Jacobi*,' in Maryjane Dunn and Linda Kay Davidson (eds), *The Pilgrimage to Compostela in the Middle Ages* (London, 1996), 23–42.
Smith, Colin, 'The Vernacular,' in David Abulafia (ed.), *The Cambridge Medieval History V, c.1198–c.1300* (Cambridge, 1999), 71–83.
Smith, Damian J., *Crusade, Heresy and Inquisition in the Lands of the Crown of Aragon (c. 1167–1276)* (Leiden, 2010).
Smith, Lesley, *The Glossa Ordinaria: The Making of a Medieval Bible Commentary* (Leiden, 2009).
Sønnesyn, Sigbjørn Olsen, *William of Malmesbury and the Ethics of History* (Woodbridge, 2012).
Sparks, H. F. D., 'Jerome as a Biblical Scholar,' in P. R. Ackroyd and C. F. Evans (eds), *The Cambridge History of the Bible Vol. 1: From the Beginnings to Jerome* (Cambridge, 1970), 510–41.
Spiegel, Gabrielle M., *The Past as Text: The Theory and Practice of Medieval Historiography* (Baltimore, MD, 1999).
Springer, Sister Maria Therese of the Cross, *Imagery and Works of Saint Ambrose* (Washington, DC, 1931).
Stalls, Clay, *Possessing the Land: Aragon's Expansion into Islam's Ebro Frontier under Alfonso the Battler, 1104–1134* (Leiden, 1995).
Stearns, Justin K., *Infectious Ideas: Contagion in Premodern Islamic and Christian Thought in the Western Mediterranean* (Baltimore, MD, 2011).
Stevenson, Kenneth, 'The Transfiguration Sermon of Peter the Venerable, Abbot of Cluny,' in Melanie Ross and Simon Jones (eds), *The Serious Business of Worship: Essays on Honour of Bryan D. Spinks* (London, 2010), 78–87.
Strickland, D. H., *Saracens, Demons and Jews: Making Monsters in Medieval Art* (Princeton, NJ, 2003).
Suárez Beltrán, Soledad, 'Los origenes y la expansión del culto a las reliquias de San Salvador de Oviedo,' in J. I. Ruíz de la Peña (ed.), *Las peregrinaciones a Santiago de Compostela y San Salvador de Oviedo en la Edad Media* (Oviedo, 1993), 37–55.
Sullivan, John, 'Reading Habits, Scripture and the University,' in David Lyle Jeffrey and C. Stephen Evans (eds), *The Bible and the University* (Milton Keynes, 2007), 216–32.
Swanson, R. N., *The Twelfth-Century Renaissance* (New York, 1999).
Sweeney, Marvin A., *I and II Kings: A Commentary* (Louisville, KT, 2007).
Taft, Robert, *The Liturgy of the Hours in the East and West: The Origins of the Divine Office and Its Meaning for Today* (Collegeville, MN, 1993).
Thacker, Alan, '*Loca Sanctorum*: The Significance of Place in the Study of Saints,' in Alan Thacker and Richard Sharpe (eds), *Local Saints and Local Churches in the Early Medieval West* (Oxford, 2002), 1–46.
Tobin, Stephen, *The Cistercians: Monks and Monasteries of Europe* (New York, 1996).
Thomas, David, and Alex Mallett (eds), *Christian-Muslim Relations: A Bibliographical History Vol. 3 (1050–1200)* (Leiden, 2011).
Thomson, Rodney M., *William of Malmesbury* (Woodbridge, 2003).

Throop, Susanna A., 'Rules and Ritual on the Second Crusade Campaign to Lisbon, 1147,' in Miri I. Rubin (ed.), *Medieval Christianity in Practice* (Princeton, NJ, 2009), 86–94.

Tieszen, Charles Lowell, *Christian Identity amid Islam in Medieval Spain: Studies on the Children of Abraham* (Leiden, 2013).

Todesca, James, 'The Crown Reviewed: The Administration of Coinage in León-Castile, c. 1085–1200 in James Todesca (ed.), *The Emergence of Leó-Castile, c. 1065–1500: Essays Presented to J. F. O'Callaghan* (London, 2015).

Tolan, John V., *Saracens: Islam in the Medieval European Imagination* (New York, 2002).

Trilling, Renée R., *The Aesthetics of Nostalgia: Historical Representations in Old English Verse* (Toronto, 2009).

Ubieto Arteta, Antonio, 'Sugerencias sobre la *Chronica Adefonsi Imperatoris*,' *Cuadernos de Historia de España*, Vol. 25, No. 6 (1957), 317–26.

Ubieto Arteta, Antonio, *Los Tenetes en Aragón y Navarra en el Siglos XI y XII* (Valencia, 1973).

Ubieto Arteta, Antonio, *Creación y desarrollo de la corona de Aragón* (Valencia, 1987).

Van Engen, John, 'Sacred Sanctions for Lordship,' in Thomas N. Bisson (ed.), *Cultures of Power: Lordship, Status and Process in Twelfth Century Europe* (Philadelphia, PA, 1995), 203–30.

Van Houts, Elisabeth M. C., *The Normans in Europe* (Manchester, 2000).

Van Liere, Frans, 'Biblical Exegesis through the Twelfth Century,' in Susan Boynton and Diane J. Reilly (eds), *The Practice of the Bible in the Middle Ages: Production, Reception & Performance in Western Christianity* (New York, 2011), 157–78.

Van Liere, Frans, 'The Literal Sense of the Books of Samuel and Kings: From Andrew of St Victor to Nicholas of Lyra,' in Philip D. W. Krey and Lesley Smith (eds), *Nicholas of Lyra: The Senses of Scripture* (Leiden, 2000), 59–82.

Van Liere, Katherine Elliot, 'Renaissance Chronicles and the Apostolic Origins of Spanish Christianity,' in Katherine van Liere, Simon Ditchfield and Howard Louthan (eds), *Sacred History: Uses of the Christian Past in the Renaissance World* (Oxford, 2012), 121–44.

Vann, Theresa M., 'Twelfth-Century Castile and Its Frontier Strategies,' Donald J. Kagay and L. J. Andrew Villalon (eds), *The Circle of War in the Middle Ages: Essays on Medieval Military and Naval History* (Woodbridge, 1999).

Vann, Theresa M., 'Reconstructing a "Society Engaged for War,"' in Donald J. Kagay and L. J. Andrew Villalon (eds), *Crusaders, Conditierri and Cannon: Warfare in Societies Around the Mediterranean* (Leiden, 2003), 389–416.

Van Oort, Johannes, *Jerusalem and Babylon: A Study into Augustine's* City of God *and the Sources of His Doctrine of the Two Cities* (Leiden, 1991).

Vásquez de Parga, Luis, *La División de Wamba* (Madrid, 1943).

Villanueva Lázaro, José María, *La Cuidad de León: De Romana a Románica* (Madrid, 1982).

Viñayo González, Antonio, Vicente García Lobo and Ana Suárez González, *Patrimonio cultural de San Isidoro de León* (León, 2001).

Wacks, David A., *Framing Iberia: Māqamāt and Frametale Narratives in Medieval Spain* (Leiden, 2007).

Walker, Rose, *Views of Transition: Liturgy and Illumination in Medieval Spain* (London, 1998).

Walsh, Richard G., *Mapping Myths of Biblical Interpretation: Playing the Texts 4* (Sheffield, 2001).

Walton, John H., Victor H. Matthews and Mark W. Chavalas (eds), *The I.V.P. Bible Background Commentary, Old Testament* (New York, 1997).
Ward, Aengus, *History and Chronicles in Late Medieval Iberia: Representations of Wamba in Late Medieval Narrative Histories* (Leiden, 2011).
Ward, Aengus, 'Review: Kservia Bonch Reeves, Visions of Unity after the Visigoths. Early Latin Chronicles and the Mediterranean World,' in Erik Cooper and Sjoerd Levelt (eds), *The Medieval Chronicle 12* (Leiden, 2019), 223–6.
Ward, Benedicta, *Miracles and the Medieval Mind: Theory, Record, and Event, 1000–1215* (Philadelphia, PA, 1987).
Ward, Benedicta, 'Bede, the Bible and the North,' in Philip McCosher (ed.), *What Is It That the Scripture Says? Essays in Biblical Interpretation, Translation and Reception in Honour of Henry Wansbrough OSB* (London, 2006), 156–65.
Ward, Jennifer C., *Women in Medieval Europe 1200–1500* (Harlow, 2002).
Weedman, Mark, *The Trinitarian Theology of Hilary of Poitiers* (Leiden, 2007).
Weiler, Björn, *Kingship, Rebellion and Political Culture: England and Germany, c.1215–c.1250* (Basingstoke, 2007).
Weiler, Björn, *Paths to Medieval Kingship in Medieval Latin Europe, c. 950–1200* (Cambridge, 2021).
Wenzel, Siegfried, *Latin Sermon Collections from Later Medieval England* (Cambridge, 2005).
Werckmeister, O. K., 'The Islamic Rider in the Beatus of Girona,' *Gesta*, Vol. 36, No. 2, *Visual Culture of Medieval Iberia* (1997), 101–6.
West, Geoffrey, 'History as Celebration: Castilian and Hispano-Latin Epics and Histories, 1080–1210 AD' (Unpublished Ph.D. thesis, London University (Queen Mary's), 1975).
Wheatley, Abigail, *The Idea of the Castle in Medieval England* (York, 2004).
White, Carolinne, *Early Christian Poets: The Early Church Fathers* (London, 2000).
Wickham, Chris, 'The Sense of the Past in Italian Communal Narratives,' in Paul Magdalino (ed.), *The Perception of the Past in Twelfth-Century Europe* (London, 1992), 173–89.
Wieland, Gernot R., '*Ge mid wige ge mid wisdome*: Alfred's Double-Edged Sword,' in A. E. Christa Canitz and Gernot R. Wieland (eds), *From Arabye to Engelond: Medieval Studies in Honour of Mahmoud Manzalaoui on his 75th Birthday* (Ottawa, 1999), 217–28.
Williams, Alun, 'Advancing Dogs and Rushing Lions: Animals and the Imagery of Conflict in the *Poem of Almeria*,' in Antonella Liuzzo Scorpo (ed.), *A Plural Peninsula: Studies in Honour of Professor Simon Barton* (Leiden, 2023), 378–99.
Williams, Alun, 'Images of Biblical Conflict in Castile, *c.* 1150–*c.* 1240; A Comparison of the *Chronica Adefonsi Imperatoris* and the *Chronica Latina Regum Castellae*,' *Al-Masāq*, Vol. 27, No. 1 (2015), 77–92.
Williams, John, 'The Bible in Spain,' in John Williams (ed.), *Imaging the Early Medieval Bible* (University Park, PA, 1999), 179–218.
Williams, John, *Early Spanish Manuscript Illumination* (New York, 1977).
Williams, John, 'León: The Iconography of a Capital,' in Thomas N. Bisson (ed.), *Cultures of Power: Lordship, Status and Process in Twelfth-Century Europe* (Philadelphia, PA, 1995), 231–58.
Williams, John, 'Purpose and Imagery in the Apocalypse Commentary of Beatus of Liébana,' in Richard K. Emmerson and Bernard McGinn (eds), *The Apocalypse in the Middle Ages* (New York, 1993), 217–33.

Wolf, K. B., 'Christian Views of Islam in Early Medieval Spain,' in J. V. Tolan (ed.), *Medieval Christian Perceptions of Islam* (London, 1996), 85–108.

Wood, Diana, 'Clement VI and the Political Use of the Bible,' in Katharine Walsh and Diana Wood (eds), *The Bible in the Medieval World: Essays in Memory of Beryl Smalley* (Oxford, 1985), 237–49.

Wood, Jamie, 'A Family Affair: Leander, Isidore and the Legacy of Gregory the Great in Spain,' in Andrew Fear and Jamie Wood (eds), *Isidore of Seville and His Reception in the Early Middle Ages: Transmitting and Transforming Knowledge* (Amsterdam, 2016), 33–56.

Wood, Jamie, *The Politics of Identity in Visigothic Spain: Religion and Power in the Histories of Isidore of Seville* (Leiden, 2012).

Wormald, Francis, 'Bible Illustration in Medieval Manuscripts,' in G. W. H. Lampe (ed.), *The Cambridge History of the Bible, Vol. 2: The West from the Fathers to the Reformation* (Cambridge, 1969), 309–37.

Wreglesworth, John, 'The Chronicle of Alfonso III and Its Significance for the Historiography of the Asturian Kingdom, 718–910 AD' (Unpublished D.Phil. thesis, University of Leeds, 1995).

Wreglesworth, John, 'Sallust, Solomon and the *Historia Silense*,' in David Hook (ed.), *From Orosius to Historia Silense, Four Essays on Late Antique and Early Medieval Historiography of the Iberian Peninsula* (Bristol, 2005), 97–129.

Young, Frances, *Biblical Exegesis and the Formation of Christian Culture* (Peabody, MA, 2002).

INDEX

Note: Page numbers with "n." refers text from notes.

Abd-al-Rahman III, caliph of Córdoba 211 n.75
Abelard of Bath, English philosopher 19
Abraham, OT patriarch 25, 56, 63–5, 90, 91, 139, 200 n.289, 252 n.147
Absolom, son of David 30
Abu Yusuf Ya'qub, Almohad caliph 77
Adam and OT typology 19, 56, 65, 185 n.44, 200 n.289
Adoptionism 39, 198, n.272, 199 n.273, 206 n.385
Afonso I, king of Portugal 91, 103, 230 n.81
Afonso II, king of Portugal 181 n.29
Agareni. see Hagarenes
Agobard of Lyon 39
Ailred of Rievaulx 29
al-Andalus 1, 3, 23, 28, 40, 88, 95, 101, 102, 108, 127, 129–31, 156, 171, 177, 198 n.264, 202 n.330, 208 n.9, 212 n.103, 219 n.47, 237 n.255
Alange, 166
Alarcos, battle 77, 130, 135, 154, 250 n.93
Albares, monastery 198 n.263
Albigensians 133, 163, 251 n.98
Alcuin of York 18, 26–8, 39, 41, 192 n.165, 193 n.176, 193 n.181, 194 n.203
Aldhelm, abbot of Malmesbury 187 n.79
Alexander II, pope 44
Alexander the Great 112, 116
Alfonso I, *el Batallador*, king of Aragón 90, 91, 113, 114, 116, 119–20, 123, 124, 151, 208 n.7, 215 n.175, 217 n.26, 231 n.81, 234 n.171, 234 n.177
Alfonso I, king of Asturias 56, 57
Alfonso III, king of León, Galicia and Asturias 36, 51–2, 56, 125, 207 n.2, 209 n.25
Alfonso V, king of León 52
Alfonso VI, king of León, Galicia and Castile 42, 53–7, 62–5, 67, 71, 74, 108, 109, 111, 133, 135, 147–51, 153, 154, 162, 167, 169, 171, 208 n.10, 208 n.19, 209 n.22, 210 n.50, 211 n.78, 214 n.144, 224 n.175, 232 n.115, 236 n.241, 237 n.243, 242 n.60, 243 n.98, 247 n.16, 248 n.21, 248 n.22, 248 n.29, 248 n.47, 255 n.236, 256 n.262
Alfonso VII, emperor-king of Leon-Castile 1, 3, 23, 52, 73–80, 85, 89–92, 98, 101, 103, 105, 108, 109, 111–24, 127, 148, 153–5, 167, 171, 172, 176, 224 n.175, 234 n.177, 235 n.206, 235 n.211, 251 n.97, 255 n.236, 256 n.250
Alfonso VIII, king of Castile 5, 77, 129, 130, 132, 143, 144, 154–6, 158, 171, 173, 239 n.16, 241 n.48, 250 n.85, 251 n.104
Alfonso IX king of León 154, 156, 161, 166, 239 n.18, 254 n.177
Alfonso X, *el sabio*, king of Castile, León and Galicia 132, 134, 135, 137, 148, 204 n.362, 237 n.243, 238 n.2, 240 n.30, 240 n.34, 241 n.55, 247 n.7
Alfonso Jordan, count of Toulouse 124, 234 n.177
Alicante 71
'Alī ibn Yūsuf, emir of the Almoravids 109, 118, 119, 230 n.81
al-Mansūr. *see* Almanzor
Almanzor, grand vizier 60, 61, 210 n.49, 212 n.103
Almería 1, 4, 74–7, 79, 80, 87, 89, 94, 102–6, 110, 113, 122, 125–7, 154, 171, 176, 179 n.2, 216 n.8, 216 n.11, 217 n.24, 218 n.39, 238 n.268, 256 n.250, 256 n.262
Almohads 63, 77, 108, 118, 119, 127, 129, 130, 158, 234 n.192, 255 n.236, 256 n.262

Almoravids 1, 87, 90, 92, 98, 105, 108, 109, 117, 118, 127, 150, 165, 176, 213 n.123, 223 n.153, 224 n.167, 230 n.81, 238 n.266
Alonso de Santa María de Cartagana, bishop of Burgos 141
Alvito, bishop of León 54
Ambrose of Milan 12–14, 39, 46, 185 n.49–51, 186 n.52
Andrew of St Victor, Augustinian canon 190 n.123
Andújar 105
Anglo-Normans 5, 28, 29, 32, 163, 194 n.209
Anglo-Saxons 15, 32, 186 n.64, 193 n.193, 195 n.223
Anonymous Chronicle of Sahagún 177
Anselm of Laon 19, 20, 189 n.117
Antiochus III, king of Syria 139
Antiochus IV Epiphanes, king of Seleucid empire 113, 114, 116–18, 121, 176, 232 n.127, 234 n.181, 243 n.101
Apringius of Beja, Church Father 199 n.279
Arianism 12, 13, 42, 56, 137, 143, 144
Ariol Garcés, knight of Aragón 115, 120, 233 n.150, 235 n.306
Arnaldo (Bishop of Astorga) 3, 45, 75–7, 79, 80, 113, 126, 127, 171, 204 n.364, 217 n.15, 217 n.16, 222 n.139
Asturian kingdom 57, 71, 162, 207 n.2, 208 n.19
Asturias 3, 34, 37, 39, 56, 61, 93, 117, 137, 176, 213 n.144
Athanasius, St 184 n.29
Augustine of Hippo 11–14, 16, 18, 30, 31, 39, 46–8, 93, 162, 182 n.12, 183 n.24, 186 n.52, 186 n.56, 190 n.123, 197 n.253, 198 n.273, 199 n.275, 199 n.279, 212 n.93
Avenceta, unidentified governor of Seville 83, 93
Ávila 92, 158
Æthelheard, archbishop of Canterbury 26, 27, 193 n.176
Æthelred, Northumbrian king 26, 27

Baal 78, 79, 165
Babylon 17, 109
Badajoz 96, 248 n.22
Baeza 131, 164, 252 n.149
Barcelona 113, 122, 124, 171, 198 n.273, 236 n.234
Basil the Great, St 184 n.29
Bayonne 124, 234 n.177
Beatus of Liébana 39, 40, 81, 199 n.274, 199 n.279, 199 n.280, 199 n.81, 200 n.288, 201 n.298, 206 n.385, 220 n.76
Bede 11, 14–18, 30, 46–8, 183 n.16, 183 n.17, 186 n.58, 187 n.79, 188 n.81, 188 n.84, 188 n.88, 189 n.118, 194 n.203, 196 n.233, 205 n.373
Belorado 92
Benedict Biscop, Abbot of Jarrow 183 n.16
Berbers 127, 129, 130, 166, 248 n.22
Berenguela, queen of Castile 4, 75, 130, 131, 152, 156, 157, 161, 171, 173, 217 n.22, 218 n.30, 239 n.9, 251 n.111, 251 n.115, 252 n.117
Bernard de Sédirac, metropolitan archbishop of Toledo 42, 111, 150–2, 231 n.112
Bernard of Clairvaux 32, 44, 80, 219 n.64, 249 n.60
Biblia Hispalense (see *Codex Toletanus*) 939
Bologna 20, 190 n.128
Braga 42, 43, 103
Braulios de Zaragoza 137
Burgos 4, 40, 42, 45, 46, 92, 113, 132, 133, 141, 148, 158, 159, 161–3, 169, 205 n.366, 206 n.389, 233 n.150, 249 n.72, 251 n.109
Burriana (Valencia) 158

Caffaro da Caschifellone di Rustico, Genoese writer 80, 179 n.2, 220 n.70
Calahorra 190 n.128
Calatrava 110, 142
Calixtus II, pope 95
Carrión 92, 133
Cassiodorus, Italian statesman 15, 182 n.8, 186 n.58, 196 n.242
Castrojeriz 92, 115, 120, 233 n.150
Cathar heresy. *see* Albigensians
Charlemagne 1, 18, 25–8, 41, 54, 59, 60, 78, 89, 217 n.14, 223 n.149, 235 n.205
Charles II 'the Bald,' Holy Roman Emperor 113

Children of Israel 25, 26, 57, 58, 96, 105–6, 110
Christians, Christianity *passim*
Cicero (Marcus Tullius Cicero) 13, 195 n.223
Cistercians 43, 44, 201 n.298, 204 n.353, 204 n.4
Clavijo 93, 94
Clemens, friend and pilgrim 25, 26
Clement VI, pope 24
Clement VIII, pope 138
Cluny, Cluniacs 20, 42–4, 75, 95, 111, 150, 151, 188 n.90, 231 n.112
Concubines, concubinage 63, 64
Codex Amiatinus 10, 182 n.7
Codex Cavensis. see La Cava Bible
Codex Goticus Legionensis. see León Bible
Codex Grandior 10, 182 n.8
Codex Toletanus 38
Coimbra 43, 54, 55, 58, 106, 225 n.202
Compludo, monastery 42
Constantine, Roman emperor 52
Córdoba 74, 93, 109, 117, 127, 131–3, 136, 142, 143, 154, 155, 159, 160, 163, 165–9, 171, 172, 177, 180 n.19, 204 n.359, 205 n.366, 211 n.75, 251 n.110, 253 n.168, 255 n.218, 255 n.236, 256 n.246
Córdoban martyrs 84, 94, 180 n.19
Coria 123, 160
Council of Burgos 42
Council of Rheims 76
Council of Toledo
   (635) 138
   (633) 246 n.181
Covadonga, battle 54, 141, 244 n.120, 245 n.134
Crónica Najerensis 69, 136, 215 n.187, 238 n.2
Crónicas anónimas de Sahagún. see Anonymous Chronicle of Sahagún
crusade and crusading 4, 25, 30, 73, 75, 76, 79, 80, 90, 95, 96, 101–3, 106, 107, 112–14, 133, 143, 153, 156, 159, 163, 164, 170, 180 n.21, 219 n.63–4, 225 n.209, 229 n.48, 229 n.56, 250 n.74
Cuenca 213 n.123

Damietta, battle 159
David, biblical king 18, 19, 27, 30, 56, 58, 59, 62–4, 67, 86, 103, 110, 120, 124, 153, 165
Deutz, monastery 189 n.118

Donatists 13
Don Elías, church canon 75
Douay-Rheims Bible, 116, 121, 197 n.249, 206 n.390, 211 n.48, 225 n.200, 227 n.236, 228 n.34, 229 n.42, 230 n.12, 234 n.148, 234 n.155, 234 n.165, 236 n.235, 244 n.103, 244 n.105, 245 n.135, 248 n.26
drama 1, 9, 22, 68, 73, 89, 106, 107, 112, 125–7, 155, 166, 172, 191 n.139
Duero, river and valley 61, 74, 90, 91

Ebro Valley 71, 77
ecclesiastical libraries 9, 10, 20, 33, 35, 42–5, 48, 53, 72, 81
   Burgos 45, 46, 205 n.360, 206 n.309
   León (Collegiate Church of San Isidore) 48
   San Millán de la Cogolla 40
   Toledo 46, 47, 127, 238 n.269
   Valeránica 40
Einhard, Frankish scholar 53, 59, 63
El Cid, *see* Rodrigo Díaz
Elipandus, metropolitan archbishop of Toledo 39
Enrique I, king of Castile 130, 142, 152, 158, 161, 171, 239 n.9, 239 n.16
Ephrem the Syrian 13
Escorial, monastic library 40, 200 n.295
Eugenius III, pope 76, 79
Eve, type of Mary 19
exegesis 10–33
   allegorical 2, 11–16, 21, 23–4, 47
   apocalyptic 39, 40, 48, 200 n.285
   biblical 16, 17, 22, 24, 25, 33, 40, 41, 144, 183 n.16, 184 n.28, 185 n.50, 186 n.58, 188 n.81, 199 n.277
   Carolingian 11, 18–20
   historical 12
   medieval 22
   moral 12, 17, 23
   mystical 21, 44
   patristic 12–14, 23, 182 n.12, 186 n.56
   performative 22

Felix, bishop of Urgell 39
Fernando I, count of Castile 51–5, 59, 62, 63, 140, 145, 165, 209 n.22, 210 n.50, 242 n.57

Fernando III, king of Leon-Castile 4, 5, 77, 129, 131, 133, 142, 152, 154, 157–69, 171, 173, 177, 237 n.241, 241 n.52, 256 n.254
Fernando IV, King of Castile 148
Fernán González, count of Castile 133, 136, 242 n.57
Florentius of Valeránica, monk 41, 48, 201 n.303, 206 n.392
forgiveness. *see* mercy
Francia 15, 26, 40–2, 78, 204 n.353
Franks 54, 60, 61
Frederick II, Holy Roman Emperor 133, 241 n.49
Fructuosus of Braga-Dumio, bishop and archbishop 42, 202 n.322, 202 n.323
Fruella I, Asturian king 56
Fruella II, Asturian king 58
Fulgentius, bishop of Ruspe 13, 39

García González, count of Castile 242 n.57
Garcia Ramirez IV, king of Navarre 121, 124
Gaufredus Malaterra, Benedictine monk 28, 30, 31, 194 n.215
Geoffrey Gaimar 29, 33
Gerald of Wales 28, 31–3, 195 n.223
Gerard of Corbie, Benedictine abbot 33
Gerard of Cremona, Italian polymath 247 n.13
Girona Manuscript 200 n.297
glosses 30, 37–9, 47
 glossae ordinariae 19, 20
 glossa interlinearis 19, 189 n.117
 magna glossatura 19
Godwin, Earl 29
Gonzalo de Berceo, Riojan priest 40
Gonzalo Peláez, count of Asturias 117, 123
Granada 117, 251 n.109, 256 n.262
Gregorian chant 69
Gregorian Reforms 44
Gregory I (the Great), pope 14–18, 31, 39, 53, 194 n.203, 211 n.89
Gregory II, pope 44
Gregory VII, pope 42
Guadalajara 105
Guadalquivir, river 122, 127, 167
Gyrth Godwinson 29

Hadrian I, pope 39
Hagar, maidservant to Abraham 63, 64, 66
Hagarenes 28, 90, 91, 110, 123, 194 n.202
hagiography and hagiographers 17, 21, 40, 53, 92, 209 n.25
Harold II, king of England 28, 29, 193 n.193
Henry II, king of England 32, 250 n.85
Henry of Huntingdon 29
Hereward the Wake 113, 232 n.130
Hervey de Glanvill, Anglo-Norman military leader 103
Hexapla 12, 183 n.23
Hilary of Poitiers, bishop 199 n.273
Hippolytus of Rome 12, 184 n.28
Historia Compostelana 51, 177, 207 n.6, 215 n.171, 215 n.178, 247 n.16
Historia Roderici 111, 177, 207 n.6, 238 n.2
Hystoria Albigensis, 168
holy cities 106–12
homily. *see* sermon
Hrabanus Maurus, abbot of Fulda 18, 46, 188 n.99, 189 n.102, 189 n.118, 193 n.181
Huesca 75, 242 n.62

Ibn Harach, Córdoban noble 166, 257 n.110
Ibn Hûd, Muslim leader 166, 25 n.218
ideology 33, 47, 52, 72–4, 80, 81, 88, 91, 95, 96, 101, 102, 104, 106–8, 112, 119, 126, 141, 146, 149, 163, 164, 175, 229 n.56, 241 n.52
Ildefonsus, archbishop of Toledo 16, 131
Innocent III, pope 219 n.63
Isaac, son to Abraham and Sarai 64, 139
Ishmael, son to Abraham and Hagar 63, 64, 90
Ishmaelites 86, 91, 166
Isidore, bishop of Seville 4, 5, 14–18, 30, 31, 36, 38, 39, 42, 45, 48, 52–55, 62, 63, 94, 101, 107, 108, 129, 131, 134–47, 161, 163, 166, 169–71, 176, 177, 181 n.30, 181 n.32, 183 n.16, 187 n.72, 187 n.79, 197 n.250, 198 n.273, 206 n.394, 207 n.399, 227 n.2, 230 n.76, 242 n.69, 243 n.93, 246 n.176, 254 n.194
Islam, *passim*

Jaén 76, 77, 131, 164, 171, 221 n.93
Jaime I, king of Aragón 158, 160
James of Compostela, St 55, 57, 59, 80, 89–95, 106, 146, 217 n.114, 225 n.202, 230 n.81
Jeremiah, prophet of the apocalypse 19, 26, 47, 57, 109, 159
Jerome 12–14, 17, 30, 31, 35–9, 46, 47, 183 n.20, 183 n.25, 185 n.39, 185 n.41, 185 n.42, 185 n.45, 185 n.47, 185 n.49, 188 n.81, 188 n.88, 196 n.239, 197 n.250, 200 n.285, 200 n.297
Jerusalem 17, 56, 57, 64, 80, 87, 95–7, 106–11, 113, 115, 121, 138, 153, 156, 162, 164, 168, 225 n.206, 229 n.53, 230 n.65, 231 n.79, 242 n.62, 253 n.168
Jesus, *passim*
Jews, Judaism 16, 17, 35, 40, 56, 68, 88, 91, 110–14, 116, 118, 140, 144, 148, 153, 156, 176, 183 n.25, 206 n.397, 221 n.96, 230, n.65, 235 n.211, 244 n.115, 248 n.21
Joan, countess of Ponthieu 142
John of Brienne, Fifth Crusade leader 159
John Cassian 12, 13
John Chrysostom, St 46, 184 n.29
Juan of Osma, bishop and chancellor 4, 45, 46, 129, 131, 132, 134, 135, 148–50, 152–4, 156, 158, 159, 160–3, 165, 166, 169–73, 176, 196 n.237, 204 n.363, 206 n.389, 236 n.241, 240 n.38, 241 n.39, 241 n.48, 241 n.53, 249 n.60
Judas Maccabeus 112, 114, 120, 140, 235 n.205
judgement 19, 27–9, 40, 54, 56, 57–7, 59, 60, 61, 63, 67, 68, 71, 72, 77, 85, 95, 97, 105, 113, 117–19, 122, 123, 129, 140, 142, 152, 161, 165, 166, 170, 172, 175, 209 n.42, 223 n.148, 234 n.185
Julian of Ceuta, legendary count 60
Julian of Toledo 131, 140, 230 n.75
Julius Caesar 30, 194 n.201
Justin of Caesarea, martyr 13, 183 n.25

kingship 16, 18, 19, 27, 55–9, 64, 67, 144, 156, 158, 171
knights and knighthood 25, 84, 86, 92, 97, 102, 107, 120, 159, 163, 167, 235 n.206

La Cava Bible *(Codex Cavensis)* 37
La Cava (Salerno), monastery 37, 38
Lamego 54, 165
Las Navas de Tolosa, battle 129, 130, 132, 143, 144, 151, 155, 249 n.60
Leander, bishop of Seville 48, 137, 202 n.322, 206 n.394
Leo the deacon 46
Leo I, pope 12
León, city and kingdom 3, 4, 9, 37, 38, 45, 48, 51–8, 61–73, 80, 84–92, 97, 106, 109–12, 114, 119–23, 126, 127, 129, 131–4, 136, 140, 145, 147, 148, 151, 154, 158, 160, 161, 163, 166, 176, 180 n.22, 198 n.263, 201 n.298, 204 n.359, 208 n.20, 208 n.22, 209 n.23, 211 n.75, 213 n.103, 214 n.144, 217 n.22, 230 n.76, 244 n.117, 255 n.232, 256 n.246
León Bible of 960 *(Codex Goticus Legionensis)* 41–2
León-Castile, united Hispanic kingdom 1–6, 9, 10, 16, 37, 43–5, 51, 52, 54, 63, 73, 74, 77, 80, 83, 92, 101, 102, 108, 120, 123, 129, 143, 149, 151, 153, 175–7, 201 n.300, 208 n.7, 224 n.175, 242 n.57
Leovigild, king 137
Lérida 77, 117, 228 n.14, 234 n.171
letters 25, 26, 28, 31, 47, 53, 158, 183 n.16, 186 n.58, 192 n.163, 194 n.203, 235 n.199
Levites 17
Liber de miraculis Sancti Isidori 48
Liber Sancti Jacobi 95, 223 n.166
Lindisfarne 26–8, 192 n.165
Lisbon 4, 71, 77, 101–6, 163, 176
liturgy 2, 5, 6, 10, 11, 20–3, 33–5, 42, 43, 45, 59, 67, 69, 107, 143, 153, 175, 190
Logroño 190 n.128, 233 n.150
Louis VIII, king of France 133
Lucas, bishop of Túy 4, 5, 38, 45, 48, 129, 131–46, 147–50, 152, 156, 157, 160, 161–6, 169, 171, 176, 177, 181 n.32, 207 n.389, 223 n.162, 225 n.195, 230 n.76, 238 n.2, 240 n.23, 240 n.25, 240 n.32, 254 n.177

Maccabees 28, 46, 91, 112–22, 138, 176, 232 n.124, 234 n.190, 234 n.127, 234 n.132
Madrid 38, 71
Magdalene, Mary 69, 71
Maghreb 118, 127, 196 n.243, 237 n.255
Mallorca 158
Martin at Tours, St 26
martyrs/martyrdom 13, 84, 91, 92, 113, 137, 138
Mary, St, Virgin 19, 46, 92, 93, 109, 144, 156–8, 203 n.337, 251 n.115
Mattathias Maccabeus 112, 118, 234 n.190
Melito of Sardis 183 n.25
mercy 57–9, 61, 66–8, 71, 92, 93, 106, 114, 115, 118–19, 142, 166, 170, 209 n.42, 215 n.165, 215 n.170, 225 n.205, 254 n.177
Mérida 131
Minerve 168
mission 3, 59, 75, 76, 79, 87, 94, 101–3, 107, 113, 147, 166, 170, 176
Moabites 28, 90, 91, 110, 122, 123, 165, 224 n.171
Molina de Aragón 115
monarchianism 182 n.14
monastic/monasticism 10–14, 18, 20–3, 28, 33, 37–45, 48, 52, 53, 67, 72, 77, 81, 120, 164, 191 n.142, 202 n.322
Montiel, battle 110
Montpelier, 113
Morocco 165
Moses, OT patriarch 19, 25, 93, 97, 200 n.289, 229 n.47
mosques 122, 143, 151, 167, 169, 172
Mozarabic Bible (León Bible of 920) 37, 38
Mozarabic rite/liturgy 38, 42, 43, 46, 59, 151, 200 n.288, 202 n.326, 202 n.329–30, 203 n.331–2, 232 n.118
Mozarabs 151, 167, 198 n.264, 208 n.9, 248 n.47
Mudéjars 167
Muhammad, the prophet 83, 84, 136, 137, 160, 163, 166
Muño Alfonso 93, 95, 99, 110, 225 n.205–6
Muslim, Muslims *passim*

Nájera 92, 205 n.375, 238 n.2, 251 n.109
Navarre 43, 46, 74, 80, 81, 89, 91, 120–2, 124, 130, 131, 236 n.234

Nineveh 97, 106, 161
Noah, OT patriarch 56, 64, 65, 140, 213 n.113, 246 n.170

Oppa, bishop of Seville 142, 245 n.134
Oran, city in North Africa 234 n.189, 234 n.192
Ordoño II, king of León 145
Ordoño III, king of León 211 n.75
Oreja 234 n.189, 234 n.192
Origen of Alexandria 12, 182 n.12
Osma 4, 43, 45, 46, 129, 132, 148
Ourique, battle 231 n.81, 231 n.81
Ovid 17, 31, 53, 85, 98, 222 n.114
Oviedo 34, 35, 65, 67–8, 71, 77, 118, 141

'Pagan' king of Toledo 69–71
Palencia 75, 113, 234 n177
Pamplona 61, 114, 115
pandects 10, 38
Paris 20, 190 n.128, 205 n.366, 251 n.98
Paul Alvar *(Paulus Alvarus)*, Mozarab scholar 84, 88, 184 n.31, 220 n.83, 221 n.98
Paul the Deacon 46
Pedro de Arlanza, monastery 249 n.72
Pedro de Lara, count of Castile 89, 124
Pedro Díaz del Valle 120, 123, 124, 236 n.206
Pedro IV, king of Aragón 141
Pelagius, Visigothic nobleman 141, 142, 244 n.120
Pelayo, bishop of Oviedo 3, 44, 51–3, 57, 65–71, 77, 83, 88, 89, 140, 148, 152, 213 n.144, 214 n.147–148, 214 n.151, 215 n.175, 215 n.178, 237 n.242, 237 n.253, 238 n.2, 247 n.16, 247 n.17, 247 n.147
Pentateuch 96
Peregrinus-Isidore text 197 n.250
pericopes 6, 20, 21, 48
Peter the Chanter (Petrus Cantor) 190 n.123
Peter Chysologus, St and bishop of Ravenna 12
Peter Comestor 47, 190 n.123
Peter Lombard 19, 48, 197 n.253
Peter de las Vaux-de-Cernay, Cistercian monk 168, 255 n.239

Peter of Oporto, bishop 103, 228 n.13
Peter of Poitiers, Cluniac theologian 47, 75, 188 n.90
Peter the Chanter (Petrus Cantor) 190 n.123
Peter the Venerable, abbey of Cluny 44, 47
Philip II Augustus 212 n.105
piety 21, 32, 55, 58, 63, 64, 73, 80, 87, 94, 97, 99, 103–6, 109 n.107, 113, 118, 119, 158–60, 176, 189 n.107, 221 n.106
Pippin, first king of Carolingian dynasty 18
Plato 13
prophecy 2, 14, 24, 26, 57, 97, 105, 109, 139, 159, 162, 244 n.116, 250 n.80
Pseudo-Calixtus 225 n.85
Ptolemy IV 139
Pyrenees 102, 250 n.85
Pythagoras 13

Ramiro I of Asturias, count 61, 93
Ramiro I, king of Aragón 63, 64
Ramiro II of Aragón 121, 124, 236 n.23
Ramiro II of León 58, 211 n.75
Ramiro III of León 60, 212 n.103
Ramiro Fróilaz, Leonese magnate 87, 89, 91
Ramón Berenguer IV, count of Barcelona 76, 77, 124, 217 n.16, 228 n.14
Raol, priest 3, 102, 103, 227 n.8, 228 n.19
Raymond de Sauvetât, abbot of Cluny 95
Raymond of Burgundy, count 224 n.175
Reccared I, Visigothic king 143
reconquest (*Reconquista*) 5, 73, 95, 111, 162, 164
Regula Benedicti 42
Rehoboam, biblical King of Israel 56, 63, 154
retribution. *see* judgement
Reccared, Visigothic king 56, 57, 60, 143, 211 n.78
Ripoll 40, 45, 237 n.243
Risco, Manuel 75
Robert Guiscard 30, 195 n.219
Robert of Normandy, duke 30
Rodrigo Díaz, *El Cid* 111, 207 n.6, 255 n.226, 255 n.239
Rodrigo González, count 95, 105, 224 n.171

Rodrigo Jimenez de Rada, archbishop of Toledo 4, 5, 45, 48, 75, 129, 131–8, 140–5, 147–52, 154–6, 158, 160–2, 165–7, 169, 171, 176, 177, 180 n.224, 181 n.32, 191 n.139, 196 n.237, 197 n.245, 206 n.389, 207 n.6, 215 n.171, 225 n.195, 230 n.75, 236 n.241, 238 n.2, 239 n.3, 240 n.29, 240 n.32, 241 n.52, 241 n.55, 242 n.68, 242 n.69
Rodrigo Martínez, count of León 122, 236 n.224
Rodrigo Sánchez de Arévalo, bishop of Oviedo 141
Roger de Hauteville 30

Sagrajas, battle 149–51, 167, 213 n.123, 248 n.22
Sahagún 42, 51–3, 75, 76, 150, 208 n.7, 209 n.22
Salamanca 71, 96–9, 106, 158
Sallust (Gaius Sallustius Crispus), Roman historian 31, 53, 57, 63
Sampiro, bishop of Astorga 51, 54, 131, 140, 145
Samson, OT judge 95, 185 n.44
Samuel, OT prophet 9, 123, 159
Sánchez-Pagín, José María Canal 53, 75
Sancho I, king of León 58, 61
Sancho II, king of Castile 111
Sancho III, king of Castile 77
Sancho III *Garcés el Mayor*, King of Navarre 63
Sancti Martini Legionesis opera 48
San Domingo de Silos, monastery 34, 201 n.298
San Isidoro de León, monastery 41, 131
San Juan de la Peña, monastery 201 n.300, 242 n.62
San Martín, canon of the Collegiate Church of Saint Isidore in León 48
San Millán de la Cogolla, monastery 40, 41
San Pedro de Arlanza, monastery 249 n.72
San Servando (Toledo), monastery 34, 45, 75, 126
Santa María de Ripoll, monastery 34, 237 n.243
Santa María la Real de Nájera, monastery 92, 205 n.375, 238 n.2, 251 n.109
Santiago de Compostella 55, 65, 207 n.6

Sarai, wife of Abraham 63, 90, 213 n.133
Saul, first king of Israel 67, 110, 120, 122, 123, 231 n.106
Sayf al-Dawla, amir of Rueda. *see* Zafadola
Second Crusade 103, 113, 153, 180 n.21, 219 n.63, 219 n, 64, 219 n.69, 227 n.5
Segovia 92, 251 n.109
Septuagint 183 n.20, 196 n.239
sermon 2, 10, 13–15, 20–2, 27, 31, 35, 40, 43, 45–8, 81, 103, 181 n.31, 183 n.16, 183 n.25, 184 n.28, 184 n.33, 191 n.139, 205 n.366
Seville 4, 38, 52, 74, 83, 91, 105, 108, 117, 163, 224 n.171, 243 n.69, 247 n.1, 252 n.109, 253 n.160
Sevillian Bible 37
Sicard of Cremona 21, 239 n.7
siege warfare 1, 105, 108, 113–15, 118, 124, 158, 179 n.2, 216 n.8, 216 n.11, 230 n.76, 242 n.58, 253 n.160
Silves, Portuguese city 109
Simon Maccabeus 115, 119–21, 172
Simon de Montfort 168, 251 n.98
Sisebut, king of the Visigoths 140, 163, 254 n.164
Sixto-Clementine Vulgate 11
Smaragdus of Saint Mihiel 41, 46, 205 n.366, 206 n.392
Solomon, Hebrew king 17–19, 56, 62, 63, 120, 153, 154, 188 n.90, 242 n.62

Tagus Valley 71, 74, 105, 109
taifa 108, 115, 150
Tamarón, battle 64
Tariq ibn Ziyad, Umayyad commander 61, 150
Tāshufīn, Almoravid emir 92, 109, 118, 234 n.189, 234 n.192
Tassilo of Bavaria 25
Teresa, daughter of Vermudo II 69–71
Tertullian of Carthage 11, 182 n.14
Theodulf of Orleans 41
Toledo 4, 17, 39, 42–8, 52, 62, 63, 70, 71, 75, 80, 89, 90, 95, 105, 108–12, 118, 126, 127, 129–38, 140, 142, 144, 145, 147–56, 161, 162, 167–9, 171, 191 n.139, 200 n.288, 202 n.329, 202 n.30, 203 n.335, 204 n.364, 205 n.380, 230 n.75, 230 n.6, 231 n.111, 232 n.118, 238 n.269, 242 n.64, 247 n.1, 247 n.11, 248 n.21, 248 n.47, 249 n.48, 251 n.97, 251 n.109
Tortosa 77, 228 n.14
Toulouse 190 n.128
Tours Bible 41
Troy 109
Trujillo 131
Tryphon 119–21, 172, 235 n.199
Tynconius, North African Donatist 199 n.279

Úbeda 131, 255 n.210
Uclés, battle 63, 213 n.123
Umayyad Caliphate of Córdoba 131
Upper Ebro Valley 71
Urban II, pope 107, 111, 148, 163, 229 n.56, 231 n.111, 250 n.74
Urraca, queen of Castile 63, 74, 92, 118, 151–3, 208 n.7, 208 n.20, 215 n.175, 234 n.177

Valencia 117, 196 n.237, 216 n.8, 255 n.239, 257 n.264
vengeance 53, 66–8, 82, 86, 89, 95, 102, 105, 106, 118, 122, 124, 152, 160, 165, 170, 176, 215 n.170, 223 n.148, 226 n.235, 237 n.253
Vermudo II, king of Galicia and León 57, 65–9, 209 n.42, 212 n.103, 214 n.154
Vermudo III, king of León 64
Vetus Latina 11, 12, 17, 35–7, 42, 182 n.8, 182 n.13, 188 n.84, 196 n.241, 197 n.246, 197 n.253, 198 n.258
Villafranca Montes de Oca 92
Virgil (Publius Vergilius Maro), Roman poet 17, 31, 53, 63,98
Viseu, 165
Visigothic miniscule 37, 38, 46
Visigothic monarchy 54, 56, 108, 141, 163, 171
Visigothic rite. *see* Mozarabic rite
Visigoths, *passim*
Vitalis, Orderic 29, 77, 193 n.194
Vulgate 2, 11, 17, 19, 21, 28, 31, 35–9, 42, 58, 81, 96, 170, 182 n.13, 196 n.241, 197 n.246, 197 n.250, 198 n.258, 206 n.390, 211 n.72, 211 n.90, 213 n.143, 214 n.160, 217 n.13, 244 n.102

Walafrid Strabo, 19
Wamba, king of the Visigoths 207 n.2, 230 n.75, 240 n.25
Wearmouth-Jarrow 11, 182 n.7
William Fitzstephen 107
William I, king of England, the Conqueror 30
William II, king of England 30
William of Malmesbury 2, 28–30, 32
William of Newburgh 32, 179 n.4
William of Poitiers 232 n.128
William VI, count of Montpelier 217 n.16

Witch of Endor 19
Wittiza, king of the Visigoths 52, 53, 57, 60

Yūsuf ibn Tashufin 248 n.22

Zafadola, king 90, 91, 115, 116, 121, 223 n.154, 255 n.226
Zamora 45, 256 n.246
Zaragoza 90, 110, 115, 121, 123, 137
Zayd Abû Zayd, Muslim governor of Valencia 257 n.264

www.ingramcontent.com/pod-product-compliance
Lightning Source LLC
Chambersburg PA
CBHW071807300426
44116CB00009B/1225